THE POLISH ROAD FROM SOCIALISM

THE POLISH ROAD FROM SOCIALISM

THE ECONOMICS, SOCIOLOGY, AND POLITICS OF TRANSITION

Edited by WALTER D. CONNOR and PIOTR PŁOSZAJSKI
with ALEX INKELES and WŁODZIMIERZ WESOŁOWSKI

M.E. Sharpe
Armonk, New York
London, England

Support for this book was provided to the International Research and Exchanges Board
(IREX) by the U.S. Department of State, which administers the Soviet and East European
Training Act of 1983 (Title VIII).

Library of Congress Cataloging-in-Publication Data

The Polish road from socialism: the economics, sociology, and politics of transition /
edited by Walter Connor, Piotr Płoszajski.
p.   cm.
Includes bibliographical references and index.
ISBN 0-87332-886-8
1. Poland—Social conditions—1980–
2. Poland—Politics and government—1989–
3. Socialism—Poland—History—20th century.
I. Connor, Walter D.
II. Płoszajski, Piotr.
HN538.5.P645   1992
306′.09438—dc20
91-27626
CIP

Printed in the United States of America

The paper used in this publication meets the minimum requirements of
American National Standard for Information Sciences—
Permanence of Paper for Printed Library Materials,
ANSI Z39.48–1984.

BB   10   9   8   7   6   5   4   3   2   1

IN MEMORIAM

Stefan Nowak
(1922–1989)
Magdalena Sokołowska
(1925–1989)

CONTENTS

PART 4: FROM ONE TRUTH TO MANY VOICES

PREFACE

This book, the collective product of American and Polish scholars, represents a good deal of cooperation, and the accumulation along the way of some debts to be acknowledged gratefully here.

Credit for the critical inspiration goes to Allen Kassof, director of the International Research & Exchanges Board (IREX), and the associate director, Vivian Abbott. Their joint conception, in the spring of 1989, of the need for a book that would provide perspective on the then accelerating forces of change in Poland's politics, economy, and society was "sold," without too much effort, to the editors at a meeting in Princeton. Shortly after that, Connor made a brief trip to Warsaw to consult with Płoszajski and others who joined the "Polish side" of the project – a trip that coincided with the final week run-up to the June 1989 elections to the Sejm and Senate and thus with the early phases of the transformations discussed in the pages to follow.

The institutional support both of IREX and of the Institute of Philosophy and Sociology of the Polish Academy of Sciences (IFiS PAN), under Płoszajski's directorship, was critical to the whole project. Planning for the initial conference in Poland was completed in January 1990 on another Connor visit to Warsaw that followed by a few days the massive price rises of that year's beginning: the "shock therapy" of Finance Minister Leszek Balcerowicz. On May 22–25, the Polish and American scholars assembled at the Academy of Sciences' Mądralin conference center outside Warsaw for the "phase one" conference. On October 21–24 the same people, papers refined and revised, assembled again, this time in Princeton at the Chauncey Conference Center of the Educational Testing Service. We thank the staffs of both Mądralin and the Chauncey Center for the provision of near-ideal conference venues. Also to be thanked is Marian Zelazny of the IREX staff, for the handling of organizational details, and with the help of Adrienne Poulton, for keeping the publication process on track.

Seeking advice and counsel of the ultimate organization of the present book after the Princeton conference, the editors "drafted' Alex Inkeles and Włodzimierz Wesołowski for this purpose, and gratefully acknowledge their valuable organization and editorial suggestions.

The editors would further like to thank several scholars who joined us at one or both conferences but who, for various reasons mainly involving the academic occupational disease of overcommitment, could not contribute papers to this volume: on the Polish side, Professor Janusz Łętowski, Wojciech Sokolewicz, Andrzej Straszak, and Stanisław Lis; on the American, Andrzej Korboński, Alex Inkeles, Ewa Morawska, Stanisław Pomorski, Kazmierz Poznanski, Sarah Terry, Jane Curry, and David Ost, and from the United Kingdom, Professor Jerzy Kolankiewicz.

What is offered here, then, is a product of Polish–American "collaboration": a collaboration, however, that has its roots not in recent political upheavals but in long-term scholarly and personal relations, much ramified, that stretch back for both communities of scholars to the post-1956 period and the end of Polish Stalinism. Through relatively "good" and "bad" times in Poland, that collaboration and those relationships have persisted, to the benefit of both sides. It is fitting, then, that this book is dedicated, on behalf of all its contributors, to two eminent scholars on the Polish side, both major contributors to such collaboration and both now sadly gone: it is our hope that it continues a tradition to which they gave so much.

About the Authors

Jack Bielasiak is Associate Professor of Political Science at Indiana University, and directs its Polish Studies Center. Among other works, he has co-edited and contributed to *Polish Politics: Edge of the Abyss* (1984.)

Wojciech Bieńkowski is a specialist in international trade and competitiveness at the Main School of Economics in Warsaw; in 1984–1985, he was a Senior Fulbright Fellow at the Russian Research Center, Harvard University.

Jan Bossak directs the World Economy Research Institute at the Main School of Economics, Warsaw, and is author among other works of *USA-EEC-Japan: Economic Rivalry and Cooperation* (1983).

Keith Crane is Senior Economist at PLANECON, an economic research firm specializing in socialist/postsocialist economies, and the author of many articles on the Polish and other East European economies.

Stanisław Gebethner is Professor of Political Science at Warsaw University, and an authority on constitutional law.

Krzysztof Jasiewicz directs election and voting behavior studies at the Polish Academy of Sciences' Institute of Political Studies; at the time of publication, he is Visiting Professor of Sociology at Washington and Lee University; he has authored many works on public opinion and political behavior and was a major contributor to the *Polacy '80 ('81, '84, '88)* book series.

Michael D. Kennedy is Assistant Professor of Sociology at the University of Michigan, Ann Arbor. He authored *Professionals, Power and Solidarity in Poland* (1991).

Piotr Łukasiewicz is a senior researcher at IFiS PAN. A specialist on the sociology of everyday life and attitudes, he is author of *Porządek społeczny w potocznych wyobrażeniach i przekazach* (The Social Order in Popular Images and Messages) 1991.

Mirosława Marody, of Warsaw University's Institute of Sociology, served as Visiting Professor at Rutgers University in 1990–91. Her works include the co-edited *Rzeczywistość polska i sposoby radzenia sobie z nią* (Polish Reality and Means of Coping With It), 1987.

David S. Mason is Associate Professor of Political Science at Butler University, and author among other works of *Public Opinion and Political Change in Poland, 1980–1982* (1985).

Edmund Mokrzycki is Professor of Sociology and department head at IFiS PAN. He is a specialist in theoretical sociology. Among his publications in English is *Philosophy of Science and Sociology,* Routledge and Kegan Paul, London (1983).

Jan Mujżel, a senior Polish economist, based in the Institute of Economics, Polish Academy of Sciences, was an advisor to the Prime Minister's office during the Mazowiecki premiership, and is the author of numerous books and articles on economic problems and reform.

Krzysztof Nowak works at the Institute of Sociology of Warsaw University, and has published voluminously in the area of public opinion.

Janusz Reykowski, one of Poland's senior psychologists, is Professor and Head of the Institute of Psychology of the Polish Academy of Sciences. He spent 1990–1991 as a Fellow at the Hoover Institution on War, Revolution and Peace. His works include *Logic of Fight: Psychological aspects of the sociopolitical conflict in Poland* (1984).

Andrzej Rychard is director of IFiS PAN, and was Visiting Professor at the University of Chicago and the Polish Studies Center at Indiana University in 1990–91. He is author of *Władza i interesy w gospodarce* (Power and Interests in the Economy), 1987.

Adam Sarapata, one of Poland's premier students of the sociology of work and industry, has divided his career over IFiS PAN, the Institute for the Organization of the Machine Industry, and currently, the Institute of Culture in Warsaw. He has been Visiting Professor at the Universities of Michigan, Virginia, and California (Berkeley). Among his recent works is *Portret biurokracji* (A Portrait of Bureaucracy), 1990.

Andrzej Siciński is Professor and department head at IFiS PAN, and a specialist on the sociology of culture, life styles, and civil society. Among his recent works are the edited volumes *Styl życia w miastach polskich: u progu kryzysu* (Life Styles in Polish Cities: On the Verge of Crisis), 1988; *Dom we współczesnej Polsce* (Home in Contemporary Poland), in press.

Ben Slay is Assistant Professor of Economics at Bates College, and an author of articles on East European foreign trade, with special emphasis on Poland and Hungary.

Edmund Wnuk-Lipiński directs the recently established Institute of Political Studies at the Polish Academy of Sciences; among his works in English, co-edited and authored with Tamas Kolosi, is *Equality and Inequality Under Socialism: Poland and Hungary Compared* (1983).

Editors

Walter D. Connor is Professor of Political Science, Sociology and International Relations at Boston University, and a Fellow of the Russian Research Center at Harvard University. Born in 1942, he received his PhD degree from Princeton University in 1969. He served on the faculty of the University of Michigan and the University of Virginia. He is the author, among other books, of *Socialism, Politics and Equality: Hierarchy and Change in Eastern Europe and the USSR* (1979); *Socialism's Dilemmas: State and Society in the Soviet Bloc* (1988); and *The Accidental Proletariat: Workers, Politics and Crisis in Gorbachev's Russia* (1991).

Piotr Płoszajski is Professor of Organizational Sociology and Management at the Polish Academy of Sciences, Warsaw. He studied at the University of Łódź, the Harvard Business School and the Sloan School of Management, MIT. In 1987–91 he was director of the Institute of Philosophy and Sociology of the Polish Academy of Sciences where he now heads the Department of Management Systems. He lectures on management of change, organization theory, and transformation processes at the University of Warsaw and several other European and U.S. universities. Among his latest books are: *Between Reflection and Action: The Dilemmas of Management Theory* (1985), *Knowledge for Change: Developing Practical Theory* (1990), *Philosophy of Social Choice* (1990), and *Polish Reforms: Entrepreneurship in the Making* (1991).

Włodzimierz Wesołowski, one of Poland's senior sociologists, is the author of the classic *Classes, Strata and Power* (in Polish, English, and other translations). He is Professor at IFiS PAN, and a foreign member of the National Academy of Sciences, U.S.A. He spent 1990–91 as Visiting Fellow of the Woodrow Wilson International Center for Scholars in Washington.

Alex Inkeles is Senior Fellow at the Hoover Institution on War, Revolution, and Peace, and Professor of Sociology Emeritus at Stanford University. He studies social and individual change in developing and developed countries, with special emphasis on Eastern Europe.

INTRODUCTION
Background to Crisis

Walter D. Connor
and
Piotr Płoszajski

With the election of Lech Wałęsa to Poland's presidency in 1990 – or, more properly, with the conclusion of an open election campaign that pitted the leader of the Solidarity of 1980–81 against Prime Minister Tadeusz Mazowiecki, himself chosen after the "electoral revolution" of June 1989 – Poland concluded another stage in the process of reclaiming a political heritage suppressed for nearly half a century.

That heritage was, in fact, somewhat ambiguous. The interwar Poland, restored to Europe's map after over a century's absence, in the wake of the collapse of the Russian, Austro-Hungarian, and German empires, while culturally "Western" had not managed to maintain electoral democracy past 1926 nor to effect any politics of compromise between an authoritarian nationalist right and a democratic left (to say nothing of a suppressed, Soviet backed communist movement). But it was "authentic," it was real; what Soviet occupation and domination from 1944 on brought was something very different, a denial of the national heritage. For many years, Poland was perhaps the unhappiest and, over the long run, the most difficult satellite for Stalin, Khrushchev, Brezhnev, and their successors. It adapted – more than some, whose vision is of Poland as a "hero nation," could recognize – to Sovietization but never made a lasting peace with the "revolution" that had come "from above – and abroad." No truly stable state/society balance was ever achieved, and the conflict between the two was to play out over the course of nearly half a century before its final resolution. The "peaceful crisis" of 1988–89, which began with the summer 1988 strikes of a newly resurgent Solidarity, passed through the government–Solidarity "roundtable" negotiations of early 1989, and ended in the "negotiated" scenario of parliamentary (Sejm and Senate) elections of June 1989 with a resounding defeat for the ruling Polish United Workers' Party (PZPR), was the last of crisis prone regime.

For the nonspecialist reader, and simply to recapitulate the main points of Polish development since 1944 in order to provide a context for the essays that follow, we offer in the remainder of this introduction a terribly simplified, but brief, summary of the history of what was, until yesterday, the Polish *People's* Republic but now again bears, in symbol and substance, the name – Polish Republic – it assumed after Poland's rebirth in the Treaty of Versailles.

*   *   *

Soviet type rule came to Poland in the wake of World War II – "from above and abroad" – as it did in the rest of Eastern Europe, save for Yugoslavia and Albania. The communists' forceful absorption of the socialists (to form the "united" PZPR) and the emasculation of two other "parties" (United Peasant, Democratic) to satellite status concentrated political power early on, just as nationalization and confiscation concentrated economic resources in the hands of a monocratic state.

The early phase of "people's democracy" – Soviet-approved "gradualism" on the socialist path – gave way, following Tito's defection from the Soviet camp in 1948 and the "Comintern crisis," to a new program to press on with large-scale industrialization, agricultural collectivization, and "Sovietization" in detail. Władysław Gomułka's government – heavily "home communist" – and Gomułka himself thus gave way by 1949 to a more "Muscovite" regime of hard-line doctrinaire Stalinists, who had largely spent the war years in Moscow and had few illusions about Soviet intent and demands.

The "Stalinist" phase (from 1949 on) saw maximal state pressure on society, but compared to the experience of other East European states at the same time, it was on the whole *less* violent. No "blood purge," no execution of the fallen Gomułkaites came – very different from the fates of Slánsky in Czechoslovakia and Rajk in Hungary. Collectivization of the farms moved forward but lagged well short of completion. Pressures on the Church were intense, but any notion of reducing it to the state of the Orthodox church in the USSR seems to have fallen before a realism about the strength of Catholicism as a cultural, spiritual, and social institution in a society now – unlike prewar Poland – ethnically almost homogeneously Polish.

However "moderated" the Stalinism, it still *was* Stalinism, worse than the pre 1949 period, confirming (or disconfirming) some of the projections of writers who had addressed earlier the "feel" of postwar Poland, the sense that the wartime Poland of German occupation, of the "underground state" and the Home Army, was giving way to what had been settled at Yalta – the handing over of Poland to a permanent victimization by communist Russia.

After Stalin's death in 1953, inertia carried the Stalinist programs forward a bit longer, but the leadership, under Bolesław Bierut, was confused, no longer confident, and now more open to pressures and factions within the PZPR and from society. From late 1954 on, it was a leadership gradually weakened – though one that learned seemingly little from the growing resistance. In 1955, the press and literary journals began to show signs of resistance, criticism, "truth telling" about the years just gone by.

The year 1956 would set the tone for the next fourteen years in Poland. Pressure had built up at home. In Moscow, Khrushchev's denunciation of Stalin's crimes at the Twentieth CPSU Congress in February brought further crisis to the parties elsewhere. Bierut sickened and died in Moscow in March, to be succeeded by the more compromise prone Edward Ochab. Social discontent was growing under economic pressure; June saw the Poznań workers' riot, with fifty dead. By the fall – with Gomułka readmitted to the PZPR and his forces gathering strength – the stage was set. The "Polish October" saw the retreat of the Stalinists and the reinstallation – against a backdrop of Soviet reluctance, but with the threat of an otherwise ungovernable Poland – of Gomułka as head of the PZPR. Ostensibly, Poland resumed its "own" road toward socialism. Concessions were made to the intelligentsia, to the Church, to agriculture: collectivization was now "voluntary" and hence rapidly reversed, leaving Poland with a small-scale private agriculture that would later nonetheless prove wasteful and inefficient. Workers' councils would play a large role in factory management. Polish society had projected many hopes on the returned Gomułka: after a "honeymoon" period, it would become clear that many were misplaced.

While the concessions to the Church and the farmers remained – and while Polish cultural and creative life would never again be subject to anything like the socialist realist cage around Soviet culture – the hopes of workers and intellectuals were dimmed by the late 1950s. Through the 1960s, life was "bearable," but economic problems, and the gap between expectations and performance, remained. Gomułka survived a complicated political challenge in 1968. Protests and strikes by Warsaw University students and professors were suppressed by the police; with the party, a "nationalist" reactionary wing labeled the students ungrateful children of Stalinist-period bureaucrats and played the card of anti-Semitism against a Gomułka accused of too much tolerance of Zionism and dual loyalties, of "Stalinist" (many of them Jewish) parents. Gomułka weathered the storm by presiding over the quasi forced emigration of most of Poland's remaining Jews; the challenge was blunted.

He did *not* survive December 1970. Growing economic problems and a growing burden on the state budget from the subsidies for basic foods that kept retail prices below procurement prices forced Gomułka's government to impose large price rises in December. The Baltic port cities exploded in strikes, lives were lost, and Gomułka gave place to Edward Gierek, the party leader from Katowice. In the 1968 crisis, the students and intelligentsia had found the workers, if anything, on the side of the police. In Gomułka's last hours, the workers were the active element, but they acted alone, the intelligentsia "sitting out" this conflict. Six years later, intimations of alliance between the two groups, absent in 1968 and 1970, would emerge.

Gierek gave up – after some pressure – on the price increases and aimed instead at large scale economic growth, technological upgrading, and consumerism. Poland "opened itself" to foreign credits and technology transfer and experienced significant growth in the first half of the 1970s. But this was at the cost of a rapidly mounting hard currency foreign debt, and Poland's economy would not, *could* not, bring into operation imported plants in time to produce the exports to pay those debts before they grew to crisis proportions. Economic imbalances and a still-growing subsidy burden then "forced" Gierek, in the summer of 1976, to decree price rises once again. In a reprise of 1970, workers struck and protested, and, facing crisis, Gierek's government rescinded the increases. But unlike 1970, the aftermath of the strikes saw prominent intellectuals rally to the workers' side and recognize as a political-moral issue of national significance the workers' economic grievances. The response found organizational expression in the intellectuals' foundation of the Committee for the Defense of Workers (KOR), which pressed for the release of jailed workers and the restoration of fired workers to their jobs. This self defined mandate was later expanded to include broader political reform and civil liberties objectives, expressed in a renaming of the organization as the "Committee for Social Self-Defense" (KSS "KOR").

The 1976–80 period saw the partial "mobilization" of various social groups, the rapid growth of an "underground" – but quite visible – press, and a further weakening of the state's grip on society. To oversimplify a complicated picture, it might be said that society's fear of what the state might do to it had diminished; so also had any hopes society might have entertained that this state, this leadership, could do much for it, even were it to try. A looming economic crisis had much to do with the latter development, while society had seen some hope, and thus been somewhat emboldened, by the election of the Cardinal Archbishop of Kraków to the papacy in 1978 as John Paul II. His 1979 visit to Poland, to unprecedented and well-organized rallies and pilgrimages, showed Polish society's organizational competence as well as its general mood. Poland had overborrowed, "overbuilt," and built the wrong things, in the wrong sectors. The borrowed money had financed the rising living standards of the first half of the decade, as well as misdirected development, but debt service ratios had mounted, and Poland was now a clear "credit risk." Import cutbacks and economic disorder were now felt in stagnating or declining living standards and shortages. GNP fell in 1978–79, and the stage was set for yet another crisis.

Prices, again, were the immediate precipitant. What was, in effect, an attempt to raise meat prices drastically by moving the supply from the price-subsidized state retail network to more expensive "commercial" stores set off, in July-August 1980, the growing strike wave whose epicenter was the Lenin shipyard in Gdańsk. Workers occupied the shipyards rather than going into the streets, invited advisors from the intelligentsia to join them, and waited for the government to negotiate on their demands. The government did: these are the "bare bones," the skeletal structure of the drama that saw the emergence of Lech Wałęsa, the founding of the "independent self-governing trade union" Solidarity.

We are well within the period covered most heavily by many of the contributors whose works follow in this book. Poland's "Solidarity" period began with Gierek's fall, to be replaced by Stanisław Kania as party leader, and saw the gradual emergence to broader responsibilities of Minister of Defense Wojciech Jaruzelski: in February 1981, he received the prime ministerial portfolio, while continuing as minister of defense. In October 1981, after that summer's inconclusive effort by the PZPR to reinvigorate itself via quasi open intraparty elections and the "extraordinary" Ninth Party Congress, he added to these jobs the PZPR first secretaryship.

The complicated politics of August 1980–December 1981 admit of no easy summary. What had started as a labor movement, an independent trade union, became also "Solidarity" as a political force, as an organizational expression of societal unity versus a regime Poland had not chosen. The economic situation worsened – something the regime blamed on the use of the strike weapon in various disputes. The government lost authority, lost any monopoly on communications, lost confidence, clearly, in its ability to generate any consensus under which it could "govern." Solidarity, on the other hand, experienced the emergence of some tactical divisions and never made a bid for power. There was intermittent dialogue between the government and Solidarity, but with little trust on either side. Soviet security concerns, meanwhile, in the declining years of the Brezhnev regime, mounted sharply: however Moscow viewed the Polish situation, it was obviously far from anything that might be characterized as the exercise of the "leading role" of the Polish party. History will judge how domestic, versus Soviet, concerns weighed in December. It does record that at midnight, December 12, 1981, Jaruzelski declared martial law ("state of war"). Solidarity leaders, including Wałęsa, were jailed or interned. The period of Solidarity "I" was over.

Martial law was repression, but not terror. It was a dashing of national hopes for many; a promise, perhaps, of bringing some "order" back to a deteriorating economic situation for some others. It did not really accomplish the latter, but it did break the price deadlock, and Poles began to feel the impact of price rises without any real improvement in other areas of economic performance. Pressures on academics, journalists, and elements of the independent intelligentsia were great. "Underground" elements of Solidarity continued to exist but in a context of continued disagreement about tactics and about the future of the organization. Society was divided and dispirited, largely immobilized, when, a year after its declaration, martial law was "suspended" in December 1982, then formally lifted in July 1983: an end made less significant by a new set of laws, a "legislative cage," that sought to constrain the social forces that had broken out in 1980. Wałęsa, released from internment in November 1982, was officially regarded as a "private citizen," a shipyard electrician once newsworthy, but in a different time. The Nobel Peace Prize committee thought otherwise and awarded him its laurels in October 1983.

Society remained divided, dispirited: economics made life harsh, people "adapted." The years 1983–88 were "lost" time, in some sense, with the economy burdened by a massive debt growing now not from new capital borrowings but from the accumulation and roll over of unpaid – and unpayable – interest. Jaruzelski's government asserted a commitment to "renewal" in the political and economic spheres, an attempt to advance those legitimate aspirations and interests that had emerged in 1980–81, but in no sense did the state/society gap close. The main guarantors of political stability were the government's presumed readiness to resort to force if needed, the demoralization that left society passive and somewhat divided in the reasons – political or economic – for which it found the regime wanting, and the USSR's interest in maintaining order in its largest satellite.

The third factor was altered when Gorbachev came to power in the USSR in 1985, although the significance of his succession would not emerge for some time. But as the rhetoric of *glasnost'* and *perestroika* gradually changed much of the texture of Soviet political and intellectual life, the rationale for the maintenance of the East European empire against the popular will of subject peoples also began to erode. The domestic regimes were left, ultimately, to their own resources, and Poland's was the first to prove that those resources would not suffice to maintain it.

A wave of strikes in the spring and summer of 1988 drew on a worsening economic situation and a growing sense of a government at bay, on the defensive. Solidarity had returned. At the end of a turbulent August, Wałęsa met with Interior Minister and Politburo member Czesław Kiszczak. The regime had "reached out," and while the next months showed a reluctance to recognize the resurgent Solidarity in legal terms, and indeed a confrontational spirit to a degree, time was running out on the regime. Solidarity and other "underground" opposition organizations had met and come to various political agreements in September. Prime Minister Messner's government resigned in the same month, to be headed by a new one under Mieczysław Rakowski. The signals of the fall and early winter were contradictory, but the sense was that change – major change involving the regime and the state – could not be long delayed. A Politburo reshuffle followed the governmental one, on December 21, to strengthen this impression.

The cautious dance of reluctant partners eventuated in the roundtable talks of early 1989; their results, the legal recognition of Solidarity and some other opposition groups (in April) and an agreement on new elections to the two houses of the national legislature on June 4. A complicated formula guaranteed 65 percent of the seats in the Sejm to the PZPR and the "Allied" United Peasant and Democratic parties but left the Senate elections completely open. Solidarity-backed candidates swept the Senate; elections "produced" the predetermined proportions in the Sejm. But, with the PZPR political collapse obvious, especially after second-round runoff elections, percentages meant little. Elements of the Peasant and Democratic parties "crossed the aisle" in the Sejm to join the Solidarity side, and the formation of a new government to reflect the political earthquake of the elections thus emerged as the critical political issue. In July, Jaruzelski won the election as president from the Sejm by one vote – evidence of Solidarity's political strength as well as its tactical observance of the "spirit" of the roundtable accords. But on the matter of a new government, Solidarity stood, given its clear victory, on the "all-or-nothing" principle: no "grand coalition" with what was left of the PZPR, now under Rakowski as first secretary.

Jaruzelski managed to win Sejm approval on August 2 of his choice of General and Interior Minister Czesław Kiszczak, who earlier in the year had opened official contact with Wałęsa, as prime minister. With Kiszczak's failure to form a government and negotiations between Wałęsa and Peasant and Democratic party leaders toward another sort of coalition proceeding, Kiszczak resigned the office on August 14. By the end of August, the Sejm had elected Tadeusz Mazowiecki, Catholic journalist and Solidarity-backed candidate, as prime minister. On September 12, a new Solidarity-led coalition government was chosen: political compromise and Jaruzelski's prerogatives as president left the interior and defense ministries in the hands of the PZPR – Kiszczak continuing in the first, General Florian Siwicki in the latter. But the long story of "People's Poland," of PZPR rule, was over. Solidarity, nine years after its foundation, would now face the problems, not only of an economy at the breaking point and of popular expectations that peaceful political revolution would bring all sorts of benefits swiftly, but of the transition from opposition to governance. A new, and contentious, Polish politics had been born – its agenda, complex and multifaceted, is the subject of the essays that follow.

Poland's economic problems are massive, and progress toward their solution on a number of fronts is a sine qua non to the health of the postcommunist system. Jan Mujżel addresses problems of economic reform and the privatization of the hypertrophic state-owned sector via the sell off of small enterprises, the establishment of new private-sector enterprises by Polish and foreign capital, and the harder task of the breakup and privatization of large state enterprises. He deals with hard issues: the time required to denationalize industrial giants, the lack of capital and "demand" for shares in such enterprises, the fears that yesterday's bureaucratic bosses will become new equity owners – "nomenklatura capitalists" – at bargain prices, and persistent worker desires for self-management and the political-social need to accommodate these in ways that do not run against the necessary logic of the market. Keith Crane deals with the matter of efficient allocation of capital under the old and new economics – an issue only to be judged finally by the results, after the fact – and the difficulties of shifting from the old system of "soft" budget constraints on managers to a new, harder context of investment decision. That investment capital, both from Polish and foreign sources, is relatively short at present complicates the economic move forward and places yet a greater premium on efficient allocation.

Despite significant recent (1991) debt relief, Poland still remains heavily indebted to Western governments and banks, technologically lagging in the competitive international economy into which it must fit itself. Benjamin Slay discusses some of the problems dating from the Gierek period of Poland's turning outward in the 1970s to the West for modernization-on-credit and the costly misallocation, in poorly chosen projects and overlarge scale, of borrowed funds that led to the crisis of the late 1970s. Mounting debt and creditor worries forced a 50 percent cut of (often needed) imports of equipment in 1979–82, as living standards fell sharply at home following a plummeting national income. The partial reforms launched after martial law was imposed did little to help foreign trade performance but did help discredit the general economic design and prepare for the economic moves that would in 1989 and after make for a more realistic approach to the world market.

Jan Bossak and Wojciech Bieńkowski direct their attention to the root incompatibility of the old political legal order of state ownership and central planning (though the latter began to fall apart in the 1980s) with anything but partial, and generally ineffective, "in system" reforms, and the moves toward economic transformation that came with the political revolution of 1989. They assess the difficulties of moving beyond the stabilizing, deflationary policies of the Balcerowicz Plan's "shock therapy," which commenced on January 1, 1990 – complicated by concerns about energy costs attendant on the Gulf crisis and falling Soviet deliveries of oil to Poland – and toward a future oriented strategy focused on growth, while keeping inflationary tendencies under control.

Freed from the dominance of the old regime – a dominance moderated somewhat throughout most of the communist period by various forms of group-specific and broad-based resistance – Polish society stands at the edge of a new era, with the possibility of pursuing unfulfilled aspirations but also burdened by the deeply ingrained continuities of forty-five years of partial adjustment to a distinct political-economic environment. Włodzimierz Wesołowski and Edmund Wnuk-Lipiński address issues of change in the bases of socioeconomic inequality, and the principles for legitimating that inequality. Society never fully accepted "functional" or "meritocratic" justifications under the communist regime, since both merit and function were related to the premises of that regime. Nor were the consequent inequalities easily squared with a broad, if sometimes vague, egalitarianism widespread in the societal consciousness. That egalitarianism, however moderated by acceptance of the transition to the market, will be tested by the emergence of property as a growing basis of inequality, and issues of "social justice" can be expected to occupy a prominent place in politics and policy problems.

Adam Sarapata traces public moods – satisfaction and dissatisfaction as citizens, workers, and consumers – in their relation to the pervasive bureaucratization of life under Polish economic and state administration. Data show an accelerating collapse of people's faith in government as a guarantor of the public interest in the 1980s, while the opinions of bureaucrats at the same time grew more defensive and reluctant to personalize fault in themselves. Broad hostility toward bureaucracy by a society seeing itself as "victimized" remains and puts a premium on new modes of administration – however difficult these may be to achieve.

Piotr Łukasiewicz and Andrzej Siciński concentrate on "everyday life" attitudes of the population, pointing out the persistence of orientations that tended to make claims on the communist state and generated dependency on it while "rejecting" it – attitudes that today tend to leave society still defining itself in opposition to the state, the "elite." These are manifested in apathy and a reluctance to participate, to assume active responsibility for furthering the democratic transition. Popular views that "nothing had changed" in late 1989 – early 1990 under the Mazowiecki government may have simply reflected a combination of old stereotypes and economic pressures. Still, the way forward to a "civil" society will be a hard one. Krzysztof Nowak explores the ambiguous linkage between "democratic" political values and promarket economic values in the period since the emergence of Solidarity in 1980, a main point being that pro-Solidarity workers, in 1980–81 or under martial law and its aftermath, had certain real interests in the preservation of the employment levels and securities of the old system, things that Solidarity did not explicitly attack. Through the mid 1980s, many more favored broad government responsibility for the economy than showed the convictions of "classical liberals." This mind set only eroded as the economic crisis became more evident in the period leading up to 1988–90. The 1990 reform, launched in a political "vacuum" wherein new owner groups were not organized and workers faced new, harsh adjustments, was thus facilitated less by deep promarket convictions than by a general confidence accorded to the new government and an economic situation catastrophic enough to prepare the majority of society for radical moves.

David Mason deals with a number of ambiguities in public opinion and difficulties in ascertaining clear trends and tendencies. "Generalized" support for the new government combines with public apathy as expressed in rather low election turnouts – not critical in a society like the United States, where this is accompanied by low expectations of government "outputs," much more serious when as in Poland, people do expect the state to guarantee many things. While in the latter half of the 1980s, public opinion began to move away from equality, and toward "freedom" as an ideal (and thus facilitated a recrudescence of support and approval of Solidarity, from an 11–13 percent low in 1984–85 to 25 percent in 1988 and 75 percent by March 1989), there are still rather high levels of support for limits on unequal outcomes, and a certain amount of confusion in images of what a new politics requires. Nearly equal (and large) numbers agreed, in 1988, that the nation "needed a strong leader" *and* "a choice between candidates of varying views": not totally irreconcilable aspirations, but hard to accommodate with democratic politics still in an early stage of re-invention.

The processes and structures of politics are influenced by, but in turn feed back into, the society. Poland, at present, presents many ambiguities in the emergence of the "new politics." Andrzej Rychard poses two alternative political dilemmas: an excess of potential political participants over the supply of facilitating institutional structures, or a structural "democratization" that has moved *ahead* of the social forces ready to offer it *active* support. He finds each an accurate reflection of distinct times: the first, of the period when society finally overwhelmed the old regime; the second, characteristic of the current, difficult phase in politics. The politics of 1989 was deeply rooted in *values*, that added up to a rejectionist view of the communist state, with less emphasis on what people were *for*; the difficulty now is in making a transition to a legitimate, competitive, politics of *interests* rather than values, where group divisions can be recognized and negotiated while maintaining a political/societal unity on the overarching level of values.

Krzysztof Jasiewicz concentrates his attention on various indicators of political diversity emerging from the "old" Solidarity in the period running up to the 1990 presidential elections. Reflected partly in the division, for campaign purposes, of the unified Solidarity of 1989-early 1990 into the "center-right" PC (Center Alliance) and the center-left ROAD (Civic Movement–Democratic Action), this diversity still spreads inconsistently, across continua of liberal versus populist, democratic versus authoritarian, "pan European" versus xenophobic opinion. Programmatic ideological differences between the two factions were less pronounced than a tendency, itself not totally consistent, for voters more angry and radical to vote for Wałęsa and the PC, those less so inclined, for Mazowiecki and ROAD. But all institutions enjoyed less public confidence by late 1990 than they had in late 1989 – the political "credit" available after June 1989 has largely been consumed.

Jack Bielasiak pursues the problem of moving from the Solidarity "heritage" of national consensus and unity, based in normative rejection of the old system, toward the legitimation of a heterogeneity of views expressing different interests, which were submerged in the old Solidarity. The difficulty is reflected in the reluctance of either PC or ROAD to present itself as a "party" and their common tendency to claim "true successorship" to the old Solidarity. Into this vacuum, where politics based on distinct interests remain unexpressed, has come a proliferation of small parties and movements, each still reluctant to offer itself as less than a purveyor of a general solution: a real party system can only emerge with difficulty as long as all groups act as "guardians of political philosophies" rather than "proponents of particular interests."

Janusz Reykowski links the individual to sociopolitical change via data from sociopsychological research. Public readiness for systemic change in the late 1980s drew not only on "democratic" orientations but also on those orientation syndromes labeled "social harmony" and "social rights." Rising levels of education, highly correlated with the "democratic" orientation, expanded the size of the group oriented toward political change, while the interest in change of those oriented toward "social rights" – typically less educated and lower in the occupational hierarchy – was heightened by the failure of the system to "deliver" according to their expectations in its economic performance. People of both orientations could be catalyzed into action by a "hope" that change might be possible (critical here was the Pope's 1979 visit) and a goal for change (which Solidarity emerged in 1980 to provide). Change was aided as well by the fact that, through the 1980s, the ruling PZPR was itself subject to internal politicking that ultimately, by the end of the decade, had isolated those irreconcilable to any change, helping lead to the Round Table of 1989 and the end of the old regime in a bloodless transition.

Stanisław Gebethner offers a review of, and speculations on, structural and legal changes in the wake of 1989 and the difficulties of fitting newly designed political structures to a "politics" that bears, simultaneously, marks of the old apathy opposition to the "state," and the democratic possibilities and risks of the present. Treading the line between power too concentrated and a state too "strong" on the one hand, and a constitutionalism that may leave the state structures too vulnerable to instability and manipulation on the other, is not an easy task; it is made more difficult by the continuing economic difficulties.

Mirosława Marody traces the path of rejection of the "old" political system and a (less clear) acceptance of the new in public attitudes, and the interaction of attitudes with actions over the course of the 1980s. The rise of the 1980–81 Solidarity, for all the national unity it evoked, coincided with a deepening economic crisis, which, ultimately, made martial law somewhat more acceptable. People sought to cope, in the period up to 1985, either by a return to traditional self-reliance in provisioning, or via exploiting ("parasitic innovation") economic possibilities in the increasingly anarchic economy: "making pickles," or "making money." Still, the radical rejection of socialism in principle came late: among youth in a 1987 survey, 58 percent still felt "building socialism" was worth some effort. With the 1989 collapse, however, people on the whole have cast themselves into a "collective lot" rather than showed any strong tendencies toward active political participation. Thus, public attitudes still focus on politics as a source of values and goods – on outputs – and the major concern is how these are distributed rather than how they are produced, and how citizens might become involved as actors, rather than audience, in that productive process.

By way of conclusion, two contributors offer broader perspectives on the heritage of political traditions and perceptions, current issues, and future contingencies. Edmund Mokrzycki explores the impact of the legacy of "real socialism" – the Sovietized order of 1945–89 – in the current conditions of the economy and society. As he puts it, despite overwhelming evidence of a popular rejection of "socialism" as a system, many groups and individuals will also tend to attempt "to live under socialism after it has been abolished."

Why? Because forty years of a nonmarket economy, of various principles of "privilege" determining the circulation of commodities, and of a regime determining the distribution of privilege have created a social structure in which real "group interests" of workers, farmers, white collar personnel, and professionals are linked to aspects of the old system. Each, un-selfconsciously, can as a group reject socialism and at the same time demand special attention to the interests it developed under the socialist order.

Behind what still remains of the notion of a diverse society unified by traditional Christian-Catholic ethics and a solid sense of the overall "national interest," in Mokrzycki's view, there is emerging the beginning of a "vehement struggle" over limited goods; systemic change is still in a very early, and uncertain, stage of legitimation.

Michael Kennedy invites, finally, attention to linkages between "normative foundations" and the research focuses and strategies of Polish sociology in one of its richest areas – that of inequality. (Polish sociology itself, at various points in the pre 1989 period, was not only politically sensitive but also, in its personnel, research enterprise, and findings, a political factor.) This further relates to a set of questions in the "state and society" area, distinguishing not only these two but "civil" from "political" society and from the public sphere – questions that invite inquiry into the multiple possibilities of various balances between an emergent polity and a society yet to be fully energized in a Poland seeking, in the post "Soviet bloc" period, a future not only within its territorial boundaries but in a world of which it is inextricably a part.

*   *   *

What the contributors, Polish and American, present in this book is neither a romantic version of the course of Polish politics nor a celebratory account of the recovery of national independence and freely chosen government. Rather, they offer a variety of hard minded analytic perspectives on what comes when the "party is over" – not just the end of the PZPR's dominance of polity and economy but the "party" marking its downfall and Poland's entry onto the uncertain road toward an internationally competitive market economy, a political democracy wherein parties represent, and legitimate, competing interests, and a "civil society" to support the democratic polity. The old long-running drama of "society versus state," of "Solidarity versus the communist regime," with its simple, clear dichotomies, is largely concluded, and with it, many sharp clarities are gone. Now the messy, but hopeful, "politics" – of economics, of group interests, of competing visions of a just society based on combinations of individual autonomy and social welfare – begins.

Part 1

From Command to Market

SOME PRACTICAL PROBLEMS OF PRIVATIZATION – THROUGH POLISH EYES

Jan Mujżel

A Linchpin of Economic Transformation

A fundamental restructuring of ownership relations is now recognized by all participants and observers backing Poland's economic transformation as one of its main, if not decisive, tasks. They are also in agreement that the essence of the restructuring is denationalization, and that a key element in denationalization is a significant growth of the share and importance of private owner-ship – that is, so-called privatization.

This emphatic rejection of "real socialist" values and systemic pillars stems from a set of arguments, the most important of which are as follows:

– Private property in connection with free access to all economic resources and fields of activity (free entry) makes an indispensable condition for the development of entrepreneurship and the spirit of innovation, and thus of technological and organizational progress;

– Free development and a considerable or prevailing share of private property in the economy are the basis of the competitive market and its coordinating mechanism. These depend, in particular, on the appearance of a capital market and, resulting therefrom, the effective allocation of economic resources;

– The managers of private enterprises are effectively encouraged, indeed forced, to behave according to the needs of economic efficiency, because they either own the enterprises or are under control of the owners;

– Private property is a natural basis of political democracy. It affords people independence and protection from the state;

– With the deepening collapse of the real socialist economies and recognition of the system's permanent inability to respect natural human rights and political freedom, the program of extensive privatization has received strong and growing support from basically all parts of Polish public opinion.

The Polish Reality

The first Polish Solidarity-led government, formed in September 1989, defined the essence of the intended property reform as an "introduction of the institutions of market economy, tested by the developed Western countries." "The chief anticipated forms of ownership include commercial companies, enterprises owned by their employees, and socialized enterprises." The restructuring of ownership would be characterized by broad privatization "as a means to improve economic and production efficiency and to absorb unemployment" which would inevitably result.

The official implementation documents and practical activities include three forms of privatization: large-scale, small-scale, and "founding" (the creation of new businesses). So far, none of these has developed satisfactorily. The small-scale and "founding" types of privatization, unhampered by the objective limitations on large-scale privatization, are scoring some good results, but in general much below expectations. In the sphere of large-scale privatizations, which are supposed to start intensively in 1991, the basic regulations worked out by the government and passed after some delay by the parliament are still the source of objections and controversies in various circles.

Real and considerable progress was thus achieved in 1990, mainly thanks to so-called small-scale privatization – central and local governments selling various property components and smaller, usually nonproductive, shops – and "founding" privatization – establishing new domestic and foreign firms. Neither of those forms covers the "core" of a socialized economy, i.e., large state-owned enterprises, whose importance is, however, enormous, because they exist primarily as the result of initiatives and risks taken by individuals, contribute to the appearance of differentiated and competitive market structures, and provide an important channel for the inflow of foreign capital and technology.

The government predicts that by the end of 1990, 200–300 small state-owned firms and about 70 percent of state-owned retail trade will be made private. According to forecasts of the Central Planning Board, privatization and the expansion of existing private firms will increase industrial production in the private sector by about 5 percent in 1990 (as compared with 1989), with an annual production decrease in the industry taken as a whole of about 24 percent.

The real results of privatization in the first six to nine months of 1990 were not entirely positive. Between January and September, 278,500 individual private businesses were established, but at the same time 192,200 were liquidated or suspended, amounting to a 13.7 percent net increase compared with the end of 1989. The number of individual private trade firms increased by an astounding 171.7 percent. On the other hand, the number of individual private production (handicraft) firms underwent a net decrease of 5.7 percent, while service decreased by 6.2 percent. In the middle of September 1990 there were 26,300 private commercial companies and 1,306 joint-venture companies, which amounted to a considerable growth of 120.2 and 199.5 percent, respectively, compared with the end of the year.

The value of sales in private industry with fixed prices increased in the first half of 1990 by about 2 percent as compared with the first half of 1989, while according to a similar calculation, a 6.6 percent decrease was noted in private construction and a 6 percent decrease in private transportation services. The percentage share of the private sector grew in all these areas: in industry from 7 percent in the first half of 1989 to 8.5 percent in the first half of 1990; in construction from 22.8 percent to 26 percent; and in transportation to 6 percent. Altogether, however, the dynamics of the nonagricultural private sector slowed in the first half of 1990. The overall number of people employed in this sector increased by about 15 percent in the second half of 1989 as compared with the previous half year and by about 3 percent in the first half of 1990. In addition to the restraining impact of recession, credit, tax, currency, and licensing barriers, though relaxed, were still present, as were social and political uncertainty. The rapid growth of market-oriented rents became a new barrier in many cases. It should be added that reprivatization, an especially complicated but very important problem, remained unsolved in most important areas.

Three processes for large-scale privatization of the main group of state-owned enterprises seem to be leading at the present initial stage: setting up a legal and organizational basis for the complete transformation of property; the beginning of these transformations; and the development of commercial companies according to the law passed by the previous, communist-dominated, parliament, including companies with the participation of socialized property usually referred to as "nomenclature."

The work on legislation dealing with large-scale privatization has been subject to criticism. Among the many reservations were objections to the length of preparatory discussions and formal procedures as well as to the lack of vigor in governmental initiatives and concepts. Regardless of the correctness of these objections, governmental and parliamentary discussions and efforts from October 1989 to mid-July 1990 were not futile. The new laws "On Privatization of State Enterprises" and "On the Formation of the Ministry of Property Transformations" passed by the parliament on July 13,

1990, are undoubtedly more mature and convincing than numerous sub-sequent projects, although they are not free of serious weaknesses. Weakness can presumably be considered a natural consequence both of the novelty of these particularly difficult acts and of their unavoidable political comp-romises:

– From the viewpoint of the principle of pluralism and of the integrity of the solutions, these acts can be perceived as lacking the overall ability to regulate property systems and especially employee private ownership. Mo-dern employee private ownership seems to be a promising option due both to its potential in raising the efficiency and quality of work conditions and to its popularity among influential employee representatives;

– The free distribution of state property, especially in the form of common privatizational coupons anticipated in the act, is potentially a real danger for state property itself, for public finances, for the course of privatization, as well as for the future ownership structure. This distribution would probably reduce national investment funds, whereas their maximal activation is a condition for recovering from the present catastrophic state of property both technically and structurally. One should consider increasing constraints and tensions in public finances not only because of the miserable state of basic social services but also because of the fact that state property is encumbered with a heavy foreign debt and obligations connected with past expropriation. The exact amount of these encumbrances is still not known. As for the coupons, their emission, distribution, and turnover is bound to bring the danger of methodological and technical traps and social conflicts, a danger that is difficult to evaluate considering the lack of experience. Coupons may undermine the purchase of shares according to market rules and in the end generate unwanted structures of a capital market and of ownership as a whole. Altogether, coupon distribution can make this enterprise totally pointless;

– The extensive power of governmental bureaucracy can interfere with the requirement of strong social control of privatization as a basic change in the overall system and in working conditions. This extensive administrative power appears in privatization modes provided by the new law, in the transformation of state enterprises into commercial companies, and in the liquidation of these enterprises not caused by their insolvency.

The government chose twelve big, highly profitable industrial enterprises as the first to be privatized. In September 1990, seven of these were transformed on the basis of the new law into treasury commercial companies owned by the state. The sale of their shares began in November of this year. In the end of October and the beginning of November, twelve more big enterprises were transformed into treasury commercial companies as a first step toward their privatization. Moreover, one medium-sized enterprise (the Meat Company in Inowrocław) was sold to its employees with the application of existing state credit. Thus, by the beginning of November, the radical property transformation according to the new regulations affected twenty mostly large state enterprises.

The Minister of Property Transformations, W. Kuczyński, predicts that as a result of all forms of privatization, it will be possible to reduce the state share in national property in 1991 by 15 percent and in the following year by an additional 20 percent. At that speed, the state would lose its leading position in the property structure of the economy in the third year of privatization. In the end of 1988, the share of the socialized sector in Polish fixed assets was equal to 77.7 percent, while in productive fixed assets, to 79.4 percent.

In the middle of 1990 there were 21,500 private commercial companies and 4,500 socialized commercial companies (with the prevailing share of socialized property), the latter founded mainly in 1988 and 1989 on the basis of legislation that preceded the political breakthrough in 1989. An important, though difficult to evaluate, part of both groups is made up of the so-called nomenclature companies, which are subject to general opposition and criticism. They intercept the property of the state sector in a nonequivalent way and are characterized by parasitic relations with its units. According to the estimates of the Highest Chamber of Control (NIK), such companies are cooperating closely with about three-fourths of the largest state enterprises. The dynamics of this pathological privatization was blocked to a certain degree in 1989-90, but the damage it caused can hardly be compensated for, despite the new parliamentary act "On the Return of Profits Made Unjustly at the Cost of the State Treasury."

Some Remarks and Comments on Polish Privatization

The focus here is on the controversial issues of large-scale privatization, i.e., those relating to large and medium-sized state enterprises within industry and related sectors. Unresolved problems also existed in the area of small-scale and "founding" privatization. The governmental projects of the second half of 1990, however, provide broader and more convincing perspectives for these two latter processes than in the case of large-scale privatization.

A requirement for the success of implementing the new privatization law is its deep "socialization." This term should be understood as the strong control and direct participation of organized society in the process of decision making. There are at least two arguments in its favor:

(a) the significance of the privatizational decisions that will be crucial to society and will last for years; and

(b) with the present state of knowledge, the criteria of effectiveness applied in making all or most of these decisions imply the extensive role that will be played by value judgments and ideological premises.

The practical consequences stemming from the new privatization law can be classified in the following way.

– The governmental authority to make decisions concerning privatization against the will of the employees should be as discrete and well justified as possible. Particularly in such cases as the refusal to transform an enterprise into a commercial company, the transformation of an enterprise into a commercial company, and the liquidation of an enterprise for reasons other than its inability to function efficiently or its insolvency. The socialization of decisions exercised in this way would be an important confirmation of the belief that employees are supposed to play an active and weighty role in the reshaping of ownership. It is worth stressing that it does not interfere with efficiency. Tough self-financing of the enterprises and control of the competitive market make the employees, more than any other group, interested in their plants' functioning within efficient property-relations and organizational forms. Failure in the accomplishment of this claim would cause conflicts, making the radical privatization unnecessarily difficult and in the broader perspective destabilizing the new system.

– The privatization carried out by governmental agencies should be under continuous and active parliamentary supervision. It is not only a question of giving "the basic direction to privatization" and determining the "destination of means thus gained" on which the July act elaborates explicitly. Thorough supervision seems necessary for the administration to make decisions like "a good householder," as it was accurately stated in the privatizational theses of the present Hungarian government. It includes, above all:

(a) optimum choice in the timing of privatization and the speed of its implementation from the point of view not of statistical effects but of the need for assertive systemic changes on the one hand and care for national assets on the other;

(b) the application of thought-over and professionally chosen forms of the sale of property;

(c) a solid evaluation of assets using methods compatible with market logic and enabling complete social control; and

(d) a concern that the property is conveyed to new owners who would really be capable of subordinating the behavior of the privatizated enterprises to long-term efficiency criteria.

One of the most difficult and controversial problems of large-scale privatization is ensuring demand for the privatizated state property. In dealing with this problem, one should concentrate primarily on the diversity of applied tools. Such an approach is the outcome of copious discussion on the subject, already existing projects, and first experiences. The policy of applying diverse tools gained a legislative foundation in Poland in the July privatization acts. The remainder of the discussion shall be confined to the tools that either appear underestimated or have caused doubts in plans of the Polish government and privatization practice.

Credits. Various forms of credit granted to firms, institutions, and individuals can and should become a leading tool. Accompanied by modern financing techniques on the one hand, and state involvement on the other, they create extremely broad opportunities. Credit for privatization can be unlimited, provided some requirements – primarily a certain participation of the buyer's liquid assets and firm guarantees – are met. Such credit does not present the threat of an excessive money supply if it is harmonized with the use of revenues from the sale of state assets. The active involvement of the treasury and central bank in credit action is of crucial importance when financial institutions are insufficiently developed and their market resources are limited. For example: the treasury can sell the indebted property for an accordingly lowered price, then the debt can be repaid from the profits made on the sale. Special credit systems can be made available to different groups of potential buyers, including all workers of the state and other sectors.

Asset appraisal evaluation. An appraisal evaluation of the privatized enterprise or part thereof is of crucial importance in determining the relations between demand and supply both in every individual case and on the macrolevel. The prospects for many enterprises in their present situation are hardly favorable and even hopeless. Their appraisal evaluation according to market logic must obviously be low, sometimes symbolic or even negative, irrespective of the book value, which may change the understanding of constraints of demand and ideas about overcoming them.

Tax reductions. These can and should have an important role in stimulating savings, investing, and especially the use of means collected for purchasing state property by different subjects. This tool has so far been underestimated in governmental projects. The only step in this direction is the promise to exempt bonuses and rewards from enterprises' profits from taxation starting in 1991 if half their value is paid to the employees in the form of privatized enterprise shares. Tax reductions could have broader application, starting with the personal income tax, but also perhaps institutional (corporate) income tax.

Free distribution. Reservations about free privatization coupons (vouchers) distributed among citizens have already been presented. Once the privatization acts are passed, after governmental declarations on the subject, the implementation of such coupons will become unavoidable. But their scope can reasonably be minimized. If the acceleration of privatization would, after all, require stimulating demand by more extensive free distribution, the idea of the free assignment of a certain part of shares and coupons to some public and social institutions – namely, state commercial banks (eventually later privatized) and other state enterprises (crossholding), social insurance funds and other funds if they are important and durable, and some educational and public service institutions (e.g., universities and foundations worth of support) – should receive definite support. A requirement for the assignment of free property shares to these institutions would have to be a corresponding reduction of their financing from the state budget. If applied on a reasonable scale, such an approach seems to be socially convincing, usually rationalizing the efficiency of the above-mentioned institutions and restraining the extent of budgetary redistribution; it could become an important factor both in capital market development and in price formation for shares of the privatized enterprises.

Leasing. This form would probably not have an important role in privatizing big enterprises. Despite its well-known weak points, it can nonetheless be a useful solution in certain circumstances because of its flexibility and ability to ease demand constraints for privatized property.

The interests and aspirations of employees are not sufficiently taken into account in the July privatization acts, as has already been pointed out. Legal provisions regarding this point consist in the following:

(a) the partial authority of employees and their councils to decide about the transformation of a state enterprise into a commercial company or its liquidation in order to implement privatization;

(b) the election of one-third of the supervisory board in the privatized company as long as over half of its shares belongs to the treasury;

(c) enabling employees to purchase preferentially (at a market price reduced by 50 percent) up to 20 percent of the privatized company shares, with a statutory limit of the total value of the preferences;

(d) providing the governmental supervisory organ consents, enabling an employee-owned company to lease and purchase the liquidated enterprise or part thereof, but only on the stipulation that the company has at its disposal a certain amount of capital.

The scope of governmental administrative power to make decisions concerning privatization is not the only problem that needs additional legal regulations in order to secure the position of employees. There are at least two other issues that may be considered important and require some legal modification.

First is the lack of favorable, not only legal, conditions for creating and developing a system of employee private property that is dependant on their will, financed mainly by the part of the company's profits and credits that is allocated for this purpose, and supported by a reasonable tax preference justified by equity accumulation. The most mature and best-verified form of this system are the well-known ESOPs (employee stock ownership plans), started in the mid-1950s in the United States. Since then, ESOPs have been developed dynamically in the United States and elsewhere, but this development – contrary to popular opinion – can hardly be associated with rescuing failing enterprises. One should not expect that companies with an employee stock ownership system will be more than an experimental form of privatization, at least in the near future, because of the difficult requirement of obligatory employee savings and the risk connected with their investing. This does not, however, diminish the economic and especially sociopolitical significance of this privatization option.

The other drawback is the lack of general regulations guaranteeing employees the possibility of having their own representation (minority, advisory, informational) in the governing bodies of the bigger enterprises, regardless of the form of their ownership and organization. The same is true of privatizated enterprises or those already operating as private. One of the basic forms of dealienating and activating the employees is through participation, the form accepted and exercised today in a growing number of developed market economies.

Privatization and Other Systemic Transformation Problems

It seems that on the basis of accumulated knowledge and experience, one may formulate some more general points concerning privatization and the interdependencies between privatization and other ownership and systemic changes in Central Europe, or at least in Poland. Some of those points are discussed below.

– *Reconstruction of ownership may not be a one-time act.* Owing to its special significance, restructuring property relations should without any doubt be implemented with maximum consistency and as soon as possible. However, it may not be a one-time act or a very rapid process. Ownership transformations always entail complicated social changes, entangled in conflicts of ideas and interests and progressing via various interactions and decisions. Currently, in Poland and presumably in other Central European economies, the complications are exceptionally vast since it is additionally necessary to solve numerous and difficult organizational, methodological, and financial problems and limitations, such as: distributing rights when transforming state ownership; a market-oriented valuation of state assets; and financing the purchase of state property and establishing new private businesses with little savings and nonexisting developed market financial institutions, including a capital market. A reconstruction of ownership will have to remain, as usual, a combination of new legislation, implementation of decisions made by the government, and spontaneous processes.

– It is realistic to assume that at least within the next several or a dozen years the *postcommunist economies will be characterized by a pluralistic ownership structure.* In other words, we shall have a so-called mixed economy. The reasons are as follows: a multisectoral economy at the starting point; the fact that there are a number of enterprises that cannot or should not be privatized; and the time required for privatization. Regardless which privatization variant is chosen, it must be a long-term process. This is the case even if we take a most radical variant into account, in which privatization is the reverse of nationalization, that is, it embraces at least all state enterprises that can be privatized and is executed according to an administrative procedure based on political decisions and a law expressing it. Prospects for a mixed economy become even more obvious if an alternative way is chosen in place of decreed privatization, namely, a predominantly spontaneous evolution, taking place to a great extent through initiatives from below and a selection carried out by market forces on efficiency criteria. It seems that the direction of such evolution should be regarded as open to some extent. A decisively growing share and role of various private enterprises, both domestic and foreign, would be comparatively certain. But on the other hand, will it lead to the elimination of all or almost all transformed nonprivate enterprises that can be privatized? I think that a clear answer to this question is not possible today.

– *The existence of state-owned firms, at least in a longer perspective, is presumably inevitable.* However, it is impossible to tolerate them as they are at present. Attempts at reforms in this sphere undertaken a few times have not produced results that would meet needs and expectations. State-owned enterprises at the beginning of the 1990s without any doubt differ greatly from their predecessors. Nevertheless, they are still unprepared to operate rationally and creatively in the emerging market economy. Summing up a long and comprehensive discussion on the subject, most probably the following are the tasks of an urgent reconstruction of existing state-owned enterprises: activating pluralistic forms and equally pluralistic ownership and organizational changes; commercializing all sides of the activity; and restructuring both the scope and organization of owner functions performed by state bodies. These tasks are supplemented by a postulate that the environment, which is understood primarily as the emergence of a competitive market as the main regulator of enterprise performance, will be changed.

– *The transformation of existing state-owned enterprises into commercial joint stock or limited-liability companies* is becoming the main line of their privatization or commercialization.

For at least three years, commercial companies have been making a stunning career in the Polish economy. The phenomenon of an "explosive" interest in joint-stock and limited-liability companies seems to manifest that, apart from unquestionable positive aspects, there are severe drawbacks or outright pathologies here. Companies of this type happen often to be so-called nomenclatura firms based on improperly acquired national property. They are frequently established to avoid tax payments and to grab profits by acting as middlemen in trading goods that are in short supply or as subcontractors of socialized firms. After the present deformations have been removed, commercial companies will presumably become a key factor in the restructuring of property relations. Premises for such a viewpoint are quite obvious. Joint-stock and limited-liability companies are the most flexible and efficient way for partial and complete privatization of state-owned enterprises, including with the participation of foreign capital. Questions of privatization aside, such companies are a tested form of facilitating capital formation and of continuous adaptations in organizational structure. They may also strengthen efficiency-oriented motivation with regard to both managers and worker collectives.

A specific type of commercial company is one with a built-in system of employee ownership. In its mature form, it has developed dynamically, becoming an international movement. The chief attraction of this form is that it combines the high economic and social position of labor with private ownership and a market economy in their modern and efficiency-generating organization into a harmonious unit. On the other hand, one can see in it a factor moderating sharp differences with respect to property and income undermining social stability. So it may happen that commercial companies with a system of employee ownership will become an interesting alternative way to restructure ownership as a nonconventional form of privatization.

– There is *insufficient reason,* be it theoretical or empirical, *to state that a broadly privatized economy is in conflict with industrial democracy and participative management.* On the contrary, much evidence confirms their ability to contribute to the performance of a market economy: first, because they can release significant economic energy; and second, because they fulfill directly the needs of contemporary man who increasingly wants to participate actively or even creatively in decision-making processes in his work place. Obviously, the specific scope and forms of employees' self-management and participation will have to conform to the efficiency logic of a predominantly private market economy. Without this adjustment, they would indeed lose the ability to survive and develop.

*   *   *

The experience of privatizing nationalized sectors and enterprises is abundant and instructive. Many countries in Western Europe, Latin America, and elsewhere have gone through such changes or are just going through them. Poland and other countries in Central and Eastern Europe, which managed to get rid of the discredited doctrine and practice of real socialism, will undoubtedly make use of the experience. However, the restructuring of the system of ownership facing us today is incomparable with respect to both its scale and its complexity. It requires many new answers and frequently, it seems, unconventional paths of development.

POLAND AND THE INTERNATIONAL ECONOMY IN THE 1980s
The Failure of Reforming Socialist Foreign Trade and Prospects for the Future

Ben Slay

If they have done nothing else, the 1980s have demonstrated the ineffectiveness of reforming socialism per se as a solution to Poland's economic problems. The failure of reforms introduced during the 1980s also paved the way for the transformation from socialism to capitalism currently being attempted by the Mazowiecki government. (Whether capitalism will prove to be more effective in dealing with these problems remains to be seen.) Nowhere was the failure of reform more important than in the area of foreign economic relations. Poland began the decade with an economic collapse largely caused by balance-of-payments tensions and the inability of the government and the Polish United Workers' Party (PUWP) to implement an effective adjustment program. Although improving foreign-trade performance was an important reform goal, especially during the 1986–89 "second stage" of reform, variations on the socialist theme were unable to prevent the near doubling of Poland's foreign debt during the 1980s. And despite the country's 1986 readmission to the International Monetary Fund and World Bank, Poland was only marginally closer to regaining its creditworthiness at the end of the decade than it had been at the start.

In addition to discussing the causes of Poland's foreign-trade problems, this essay examines the factors behind the failure of the 1980s' reforms to solve these problems, the legacies left by these reforms for the ensuing attempt at transforming socialism into capitalism, and their implications for the future of Poland's economic relations.

Foreign Trade: The Problems

Many of Poland's foreign-trade (and other economic) problems can be traced to the establishment of Soviet-type socialism in Poland during 1948-53. While a complete explanation of this economic system's characteristics would go beyond the bounds of this essay, its most important trade-discouraging features in the Polish case are perhaps the following.

– the nationalization of most enterprises and capital in industry and foreign trade;

– direct central planning, in which enterprise autonomy is curtailed and production and trading activities are oriented toward plan fulfillment, rather than toward wealth creation based upon market signals;

– the state monopoly on foreign trade, in which foreign-trade activities are controlled by the Foreign Trade Ministry and its agents, foreign trade organizations (FTOs);

– the inconvertibility of the zloty;

– autarchic external policies, meant to reduce the destabilizing impact of international commodity and capital flows upon the domestic economy as well as to take advantage of internal developmental possibilities;

– a reorientation in economic and political relations toward the Council for Mutual Economic Assistance (CMEA) and other socialist countries, at the expense of integration with the international economy.

The shortcomings of the Soviet foreign-trade model are well documented (Holzman), and the Polish case was no exception (Poznański). Reliance upon domestic and CMEA supplies of natural resources led to overdeveloping the country's extractive and metallurgical sectors and, ultimately, ecological devastation. The bureaucratic CMEA trading mechanism, combined with Poland's virtual isolation from the international economy, prevented the realization of gains from trade through specialization based upon comparative advantage. Isolation from Western technologies and products exacerbated Poland's economic backwardness and technology gap vis-à-vis the West, and contributed to popular and consumer dissatisfaction at home. Such tensions played an important role in the strikes and unrest of 1956, 1970–71, 1976, 1980–81, and 1988.

In light of these difficulties, the PUWP in 1971 decided to reduce Poland's isolation from the international economy. According to the PUWP's "New Economic Strategy," Western licenses, technology, investment, and consumer goods, purchased on credit, were to be the catalyst for improving living standards and economic growth. By modernizing the country's industrial and agricultural base and improving the supply of consumer goods and thus work incentives, these imports were to generate increases in Polish hard-currency exports and thus provide the foreign exchange to pay off the credits.

As implemented, this "import-led" growth strategy had two major defects (Siwiński in Marer and Siwiński, pp. 26–27). First, it was not accompanied by systemic reforms to increase the microeconomic efficiency of investment and foreign-trade decisions. Much of the imported technology and many investment goods were therefore misallocated and failed to generate the anticipated improvements in Poland's export capacity. Second, the strategy was applied on too large a scale relative to the Polish economy's ability to absorb this infusion of technology and investment goods. Gross investment increased by 30 percent during the 1970s and reached 38 percent of national income in 1975 (*ibid.*, p. 27). Ill-advised projects with long gestation periods and significant future hard-currency requirements (e.g., the *Huta Katowice* metallurgical complex) played an important role in this investment boom. The number of unfinished investments grew, so that the value of unfinished projects in 1981 was 4.4 times greater than the value of projects begun in that year *(ibid)*. In the end, this strategy of import-led growth generated significant increases in Poland's hard-currency import propensity without producing commensurate increases in the country's hard-currency export capacity. The rapid rise in Poland's external indebtedness, which reached $ 24.1 billion in 1980, was the predictable result.[1]

The consequences of external indebtedness for the Polish economy were extensive. Most immediate was the economic collapse of 1979–82, when national income declined by approximately 25 percent.[2] This collapse was triggered by a 50 percent reduction in the volume of hard-currency imports, upon which the Polish economy had become so dependent. Living standards took a sharp drop: per-capita consumption fell by 17 percent during 1981–82 and only just regained its 1980 level in 1988, the year in which Poland's postcollapse recovery reached its peak.[3] Reductions in the supply of consumer goods were accompanied by large increases in the population's money holdings, further stoking the inflationary fires and creating a large "inflationary overhang" of forced savings (Herer and Sadowski).[4] Shortage pressures necessitated the formal rationing of gasoline, meat, chocolate, and

[1] This figure, taken from the Central School of Planning and Statistics' World Economy Research Institute's 1988 report, entitled *Polish Economy in the External Environment in 1980s* (p. 76), includes both convertible and non-convertible-currency net debt.

[2] All data are expressed in constant prices and are taken from official Polish sources except where otherwise noted.

[3] These consumption statistics are derived from *dochód narodowy podzielony*, i.e., national income less net exports. This decline in consumption is even more striking in light of the policy of protecting consumption by reducing the share of output devoted to investment. While consumption reached its 1978 level in 1985, for example, investment in that year measured only 46.5 percent of its 1978 level.

[4] During 1979–81 (the three years immediately preceding the reform's introduction), national income fell in real terms by 2.3, 6, and 12 percent, respectively, while nominal incomes grew at yearly rates of 10.2, 12, and 30.3 percent, respectively. Retail prices increased yearly by 6.6, 8.9, and 21.2 percent, i.e., at about half the pace necessary to absorb the increases in nominal incomes given the downward trend in real output.

other foodstuffs. This was the backdrop against which occurred the strikes of 1980–81 and the appearance of the Solidarity trade union and then other opposition groups. Second, the external disequilibrium forced the Polish government in March 1981 to announce its inability to service the country's debt and to request debt rescheduling. Along with the political and economic instability of the 1980-81 period, the rescheduling request severely damaged Polish creditworthiness on international financial markets and marked the beginning of Poland's ten-year struggle to regain it (Marer and Siwiński). Third, and perhaps most important, Poland's debt burden effectively destroyed the option of continued isolation from the international economy. Sustained recovery from the economic crisis required much greater integration with the West. This, in turn, required far-reaching reform of the economic system.

Poland's Foreign Trade Reforms in the 1980s

The First Stage

Despite foreign trade's crucial importance to a successful economic reform and recovery from the economic crisis, the official reform drafted during 1980–81 (*Kierunki*) and implemented during 1981–82 (subsequently known as the "first stage" of reform) paid relatively little attention to foreign trade. While a thorough description of the first stage would exceed this essay's scope, its most important elements included:[5]

– the "3 Ss": enterprise self-reliance, self-financing, and self-management. The importance of this slogan lies in its emphasis (in principle) upon the abolition of mandatory enterprise plan targets and central input allocation; the use of financial instruments to influence enterprise behavior; partial decentralization of price and wage determination; and the introduction of workers' councils;

– reductions in the functions of the central administration through abolishing the traditional intermediate-layer organs and shrinking the staff and budget of the branch and functional ministries and offices;

– the application of greater discipline in monetary and credit policies in order to firm up enterprise budget constraints and make prices, wages, and other financial variables more meaningful.

In terms of foreign trade, the blueprint for the first stage of reform contained the following elements:[6]

---

[5] For information on the first (and second) stages of the Polish economic reforms, see Crane, Fallenbuchl, Gomułka and Rostowski, Jermakowicz and Krawczyk, Kemme, Marer and Siwiński, Mieszczańkowski, and Slay.

[6] For more on Poland's foreign-trade reforms, see Slay in Kemme.

– as a corollary to increased enterprise autonomy, firms were authorized to (request to) conduct foreign-trade activities independent of the Foreign Trade Ministry and its agents, the FTOs. This was intended to encourage competition among FTOs and to allow enterprises to interact directly with foreign firms, if they so desired;

– the close link between the ministry and the FTOs was to be broken, in order to encourage the FTOs to behave more like commercial organizations. The ministry was reduced in size and reorganized, in order to reduce its control over operational decisions made by FTOs and producing enterprises and to redirect its focus to macrotrade and industrial-policy issues;

– the majority of FTOs were transformed into joint-stock companies under the ownership of the FTOs' major domestic clients as well as of the ministry. This was intended better to integrate production and trade activities, particularly in terms of improving domestic firms' information about world markets, as well as to generate enterprise investments in export-oriented projects;

– direct-planning instruments in foreign-trade management were to be replaced by financial instruments. In particular, the different commercial and tourist exchange rates were to be replaced by a unified "submarginal" exchange rate, guaranteeing the profitability of at least 75 percent of Poland's exports. This would allow a closer linkage between domestic and world-market prices, especially for raw materials and primary products. Deviations in domestic prices by more than 5 percent from world-market prices were supposed to trigger compensating revaluations;

– joint ventures and other forms of interenterprise cooperation between Polish and foreign firms were to be encouraged. Cooperation agreements were sought with firms from Western and CMEA countries;

– exporting enterprises were permitted to retain a certain portion of their hard-currency export receipts in order to finance hard-currency imports;

– traditional central rationing of foreign exchange was to be supplemented by loans and auctions of convertible currencies conducted by the Foreign Trade Bank.

The final two reform steps were intended to create an internal market for convertible currencies (Rymarczyk). As a whole, these changes were to lead to zloty convertibility at some future, unspecified date. The more immediate concern was improving export performance, especially in the hard-currency area.

For a variety of reasons, the first stage of reform (1981–86) failed to achieve its goals, both in foreign trade and in the economy generally. The PUWP was on balance more interested in suppressing and then parrying the political challenge posed by Solidarity and the opposition than it was in conducting a major economic overhaul. Therefore, reforms perceived as excessively destabilizing politically or that threatened the position of the party and state bureaucracies were implemented incompletely or not at all. Reform of the central administration was halfhearted; the industrial ministries, intermediate-layer organs, and Planning Committee essentially retained their traditional size and functions (Piesiewicz). Although draconian price increases were executed, their reductions in purchasing power were offset by compensating wage increases for militant workers. Subsidies for the traditional heavy industrial and mining lobbies prevented any reorientation in investment and industrial policies; the completion of many ill-advised investment projects suspended during the late 1970s was attempted during this time. The expansionary monetary and credit policies required to finance this largest perpetuated enterprise soft budget constraints (Kornai), fueled shortage pressures, and reduced the efficacy of financial instruments as measures of enterprise success and as instruments of central control. In such an environment, the preservation and expansion of direct central controls over enterprise production and supply decisions were inevitable (Fallenbuchl).

These problems also appeared in the foreign-trade reform. The desire to loosen the Foreign Trade Ministry's structural controls over the FTOs and producing enterprises was not carried into practice. The core of the structural reform, transforming the FTOs into independent, commercial joint-stock companies had few positive effects and a number of undesirable side effects to boot. First, not all the FTOs were transformed into joint-stock companies. As of June 1986, in addition to thirty-eight joint stock FTOs, twelve traditional FTOs were still active, as were thirteen foreign-trade "associations" (which seemed to be relatives of the joint-stock FTO), two FTOs organized as cooperatives, as well as fifteen other intermediate-level trading organizations acting as intermediaries between foreign firms and the Polish enterprises that founded them. Second, the Foreign Trade Ministry by law was the majority shareholder in all the new joint-stock companies, which afforded the ministry almost as much leverage over the new FTOs as over the old. This leverage was used to prevent domestic firms from exercising their choice among "competing" FTOs intended by reform legislation (Rymarczyk).

Shortage conditions in the domestic economy played havoc with pricing and exchange-rate policies, worsening the zloty's overvaluation and exacerbating difficulties in linking domestic to world market prices. Although a unified exchange rate was formally introduced in 1982, the goal of submarginality was honored mostly in the breach. A study commissioned by Warsaw's Institute of Prices and Markets found that in 1984, around 40 percent of Poland's hard-currency exports were unprofitable at current exchange rates. If the profitability of coal exports was ignored (the official prices for coal were estimated to cover only about one third of the social costs of production) approximately 50 percent of hard-currency exports became unprofitable.

As a result, domestic prices played a catch-up game with world-market prices: successive devaluations would widen the gap between world-market and domestic prices, while the correction principle would be applied too gradually to make up the difference between devaluations. In the end, the hoped-for rationalizing effects of world-market prices upon the domestic price system failed to materialize, and shortages of imported raw materials, primary products, and other goods continued. These shortages provided a justification for the maintenance of traditional central rationing and subsidy programs administered by the Foreign Trade Ministry, the resurgent branch ministries, and their agents. Enterprise export incentives continued to be weak, since budget constraints remained soft and virtually everything produced by Polish firms could be sold at home.

The attempt at establishing the internal hard-currency market during the first stage of reform was similarly ineffective and essentially consisted of introducing foreign-exchange accounts for exporting enterprises. Hard-currency auctions administered by the Foreign Trade Bank played an insignificant role in allocating foreign exchange (less than 1 percent of the yearly stock of hard currency had been allocated through auctions during 1982–86 [Boffito in Marer and Siwiński; Tarnowski]). Enterprises with retention accounts were not permitted to participate in the auctions or to sell their export receipts to other firms, although they were allowed to use them as payment for services rendered. The percentage of hard-currency imports financed by these accounts did not rise above 30.2 percent (in 1985) of total hard-currency imports, and the percentage of export revenues retained by enterprises was held to a limit of 20 percent (Boffito in Marer and Siwiński; Mizsei; Rymarczyk; Slay in Marer and Siwiński). The percentage of export receipts retained by enterprises was generally determined according to sector- and enterprise-specific criteria; purchases made with these funds were often subjected to administrative controls and substantial delays.[7]

Although the Council of Ministers issued regulations in 1976 permitting investment in small-scale manufacturing by Poles living abroad, as of January 1, 1982, only 144 production licenses had actually been granted by the authorities. The 1979–82 economic collapse brought a change of attitude, and the Sejm liberalized the 1976 law during the summer of 1982. The spectre of empty shelves in Polish stores proved an alluring one to potential investors: 374 licenses were granted in 1982, and 190 more in 1983. By mid-1985, the figure stood at 736, not including the 436 applications for licenses that had been denied (Loch).

The Polish authorities were initially so desperate for increased consumer goods production that the *polonia* firms were given a three-year income-tax

---

[7] In early 1986, for example, exporters were experiencing delays of up to twelve months in obtaining permission to use their "own" export receipts.

holiday, although other tax liabilities remained in force. By 1984, these firms accounted for 9.8 percent of total output in small-scale manufacturing; in the minds of many Polish consumers, *"firmy polonijne"* had become synonymous with Western standards, better quality – and higher prices. As the economic recovery continued, however, the *polonia* firms activities encountered criticism from defenders of the primacy of state industry, and the firms' regulatory environment became more uncertain. In July 1983, three modifications in the 1982 regulations were introduced: (1) the income tax exemption was made conditional upon the reinvestment of one third of the profits in the firm; (2) the *polonia* enterprises were required to sell 50 percent of their export receipts to the state treasury (at the official exchange rate); and (3) the postexemption tax rate on gross income was increased by more than 50 percent. The minimum investment requirement was raised in January 1985 to $100,000 as well. As a result of the tax holiday's expiration in 1985 and the above-mentioned (and other) disincentives, the number of *polonia* firms decreased between mid-1985 and early 1986, while their share of total exports began to decline in 1984. It is interesting to note that the 1986 joint venture law prohibited large-scale ventures with *polonia* firms.

This is not the type of track record likely to inspire confidence in potential large-scale investors. As one observer noted about the *polonia* firms (Plesiński, 1987), "The economic benefits of their activities turned out to be incomparably smaller than the propaganda and psychological damage which has resulted from the policy instability they have faced."

The first stage of reform scarcely addressed CMEA trade. The Foreign Trade Ministry continued to issue import quotas and mandatory export targets both for traditional FTOs and the joint-stock FTOs, which were supposed to be free of direct ministerial supervision (Rymarczyk). While the FTOs were not, in most cases, supposed to issue production targets to enterprises in order to fulfill CMEA export obligations, little changed in this area. Although the reform did envision the introduction of competitive bidding procedures in import allocation, they were applied only in hard-currency import allocation, not for CMEA imports, and on an insignificant scale (Zarzycki). The sole innovation in CMEA foreign trade was the 1985 creation of enterprise *transferable ruble* retention accounts. Since, however, transferable rubles do not allow their possessor to make claims upon other CMEA countries' currencies or products, the significance of these accounts was necessarily limited.

Joint ventures with firms from other CMEA countries, primarily the USSR, Hungary, Czechoslovakia, and Bulgaria, were also attempted, especially during 1986–87. Because of their small numbers (approximately two dozen in 1987), and since these ventures were produced by the traditional CMEA mechanism, it is difficult to ascribe much significance to them (*Polish Economy in the External Environment in 1980's*, p. 64).

The Second Stage

Poland's 1986 (re)admission to the International Monetary Fund and the World Bank and the call for a "second stage" of economic reform at the PUWP's tenth congress in that year in effect constituted an admission that the reform's "first stage" had been found wanting, especially in terms of foreign trade. The second stage, as it took shape during 1986–89, attempted to correct the first stage's shortcomings. Its most important steps were the following:

– The Foreign Trade Ministry's structural control over trade was further loosened. FTO ownership regulations were again liberalized, so that the ministry's ownership share could fall below 51 percent (except for products of "central importance to the national economy"), and virtually all state enterprises became able to purchase shares in FTOs. As part of the October 1987 reform of the central administration, the ministry was again reorganized (becoming the "Ministry for International Economic Cooperation") and absorbed further cuts in budget and staffing (Szwarc). Other important institutional changes included the creation of the Export Development bank (1986) and the beginnings of the commercialization of the banking system (1988).

– A number of changes were introduced aimed at expanding the enterprise foreign-exchange retention system. Reducing the variability of different retention rates as well as granting exporting enterprises ownership rights to the funds in their accounts may have been the most beneficial changes; restrictions on interenterprise hard-currency transfers were also loosened. However, these changed were accompanied in 1987 by some steps backwards as well, including: (1) reducing the percentage of export revenues retained by 20 percent; (2) requiring enterprises to purchase the hard currency in "their" accounts (at the official exchange rate); and (3) requiring that these purchases take place within the first three months of the time of deposit (otherwise, the enterprise could lose the right of purchase).

– Pursuing a more "active" exchange-rate policy to tighten the link between domestic and world-market prices. The zloty was devalued against the dollar by approximately 40 percent in nominal terms (around 15 percent in real terms) during late 1986 and early 1987, allowing closer adherence to the submarginal exchange-rate policy since the second half of 1987. The year 1988 saw further liberalization of import and export prices, reductions in the number of centrally rationed imports, and the introduction of stronger tax and bonus incentives for exporting enterprises (*Program realizacyjny*).

– Legislation authorizing large-scale joint ventures between Polish and Western firms was enacted in 1986 and significantly liberalized in December 1988. In addition to relaxing the 1986 law's requirement that at least 50 percent of the capital invested in any joint project must be owned by the Polish government, simplifying the licensing and administration of joint ventures, and reducing the share of export revenues sold back to the Polish government, the 1988 legislation permitted all economic organizations, regardless of ownership, to engage in any legal business activity (Kowalska).

Did All This Make Any Difference?

The link between economic reform and changes in economic performance is quite murky; the impact of even well-designed and correctly implemented reforms can be obscured or negated by unfavorable developments in the economic environment or by side effects of policy decisions not directly related to reform. In any case, a thorough analysis of the degree to which reforms in the 1980s had an impact upon Polish foreign-trade performance would go beyond the scope of this essay.

Still, numerous factors point to an absence of improvement, indeed a deterioration, in Polish foreign-trade performance during the 1980s. In terms of statistics, Poland's share of world imports and exports declined (in nominal terms) during 1978–85 from 1.2 to 0.5 and 1.1 to 0.6 percent, respectively; the share of exports fell further, to 0.5 percent during 1985–87 (*Polish Economy in the External Environment in 1980's*, p. 45). Poland's per-capita trade turnover (the sum of per-capita exports and imports divided by two) fell from $508 in 1980 to $307 in 1986, the lowest among the seven European CMEA countries (*ibid.*, p. 46). Poland's net debts during 1981-88 increased from $24.2 to $37.5 billion, and from 2.9 to 6.3 billion transferable rubles. While certain improvements in foreign-trade performance do coincide with the introduction of reforms in 1981–82 (e.g., replacing the hard currency trade deficits of the 1970s with surpluses during 1982–88; partial recovery from the economic collapse of 1979–82 during 1982–88, etc.), other factors, such as favorable weather conditions, cyclical improvements in factory productivity, and the militarization of the extractive industries, were probably more important in explaining this turnaround (*Gospodarka w latach 1981–1985*).

In terms of behavior, the following information is noteworthy. As of June 1986, approximately 110 producing enterprises and cooperatives had received permission to conduct trading activities independent of the Foreign Trade Ministry; similar rights had been granted to 172 private individuals, many of whom were involved in the *polonia* firms. On paper, these were indeed favorable developments. In practice, however, matters looked a little different. In 1985, for example, only 67 of the 104 non FTO legal entities (mostly enterprises, cooperatives, and producer organizations created by enterprises and cooperatives) actually took advantage of their direct trading rights. For individuals, the figures were 46 out of 169. So despite Poland's desperate need for increased contacts with Western firms, know-how, and technology, the vast majority of Polish enterprises and individuals authorized to interact directly with Western firms in 1986 did not do so. It would be difficult to come by a better illustration of the failure of reform.

The reform's second stage did bring improvement in some areas. Between January 1988 and June 1989, for example, the number of large-scale joint ventures increased from 5 to 250 (Żukowska). According to official data, the number of agents permitted to interact directly with foreign firms increased from 349 in 1985 to 905 by the end of 1988. However, the extent to which these developments resulted in changes in foreign-trade behavior is difficult to verify, since information concerning the number of agents actually taking advantage of their direct trading rights in 1988 was not published. The fate of the enterprise currency-retention system under the second stage was likewise unclear. Although the number of enterprise accounts increased from 838 to 6,615 during 1985–88, the share of hard-currency imports purchased from these accounts declined during this time from 30.2 to 24.6 percent.[8] As with the reform's second stage in general, it seems that the positive effects of these changes in foreign trade were largely overwhelmed by the explosion of inflationary pressures and the collapse of the PUWP's political position during 1988–89.

It is always tempting to blame unfavorable developments upon external factors, such as terms-of-trade reversals and Western economic sanctions, beyond the control of reformers and policy makers. These arguments do not hold up under close inspection, however. While Poland's terms of trade declined during 1980–84, they improved during 1984–88, and the country's hard-currency terms of trade were more favorable in 1988 than they had been in 1980. And if the policy of economic sanctions against Poland pursued by the United States and Western Europe during much of the decade were beyond the control of the Polish government, the same can not be said of the act that precipitated the sanctions: the December 13, 1981, declaration of martial law. Indeed, the events of 1989–90 seem to indicate that political compromise and accommodation, both at home and abroad, are necessary preconditions for successful economic reform. Instead, the causes of the failure of reform during 1980–88 lie closer to home: expansionary monetary and credit policies, the continuation of soft enterprise budget constraints, and the unreformed CMEA trading mechanism, through which approximately half of Polish trade turnover occurred.

From Reform to Transformation: The Legacies

When the Mazowiecki government took power in August 1989, it inherited the flotsam and jetsam left after a decade of economic dislocation and reform of socialism in general, and socialist foreign trade in particular. On the minus

---

[8] This discrepancy can partially be explained by the fact that prior to 1987 retention accounts were shared by exporters, while changes introduced during the second stage made it easier for individual firms to have their own accounts.

side, the transformation faced a reform-weary public and a traumatized, suspicious economic administration. The economic growth that had resumed in 1982 was coming to an end, inflation had reached triple-digit levels, inflationary expectations were rampant, and the hard-currency trade surplus of 1982–88 was dissolving into deficit. The unprecedented nature of this new "transformation problem" brought with it a different set of vexing problems, including the absence of capital markets and unemployment programs. CMEA trade was in a flux, and the Soviet Union, Poland's largest trading partner, was itself in a recession. What would otherwise be bright prospects for improved trade relations with the West were dimmed by uncertainty surrounding German unification and European integration.

On the plus side, the reforms of the 1980s also left a number of positive legacies. First, not only did their inability to solve Poland's economic problems discredit socialism as a system: the reductions in economic security that came with the reforms (e.g., inflation) helped prepare Polish society for the downside of capitalism. Second, the Mazowiecki government enjoyed a degree of popular and working-class support unmatched in modern Polish history. This support made possible the construction of a social contract between the rulers and the ruled, a necessary precondition for the austerity measures introduced in January 1990. Although the reforms of the 1980s were unable to solve the country's problems by themselves, they did lay the necessary framework for the transformation by their progress in constructing market mechanisms in Poland. In terms of foreign trade, enterprises have experienced almost a decade of increased autonomy and responsibilities. Direct contacts between domestic firms and foreign suppliers and customers have been established, and production for export has become more important. FTOs have been partially freed of direct ministerial supervision and have begun to act in a more commercial fashion. The number of joint ventures has increased substantially since 1988. To the extent that shortage pressures and soft enterprise budget constraints had, by 1988, become the key obstacles to generating further changes in enterprise behavior, the austerity measures and financial discipline introduced in January 1990 should, hopefully, remove them and make possible behavioral changes that had not been possible before. And finally, the collapse of the PUWP and Soviet-type socialism in Poland was accompanied by the dissolution, or possibly transformation, of the Soviet bloc.

Perhaps the most important legacy of the reforms lies in the area of convertibility. By the time of the PUWP's collapse in the summer of 1989, the dollar's role in the Polish second economy (Wiśniewski) had increased to the extent that convertibility of the zloty had become a realistic possibility. Specifically, Polish goods and/or currency had become convertible into Western currencies in the following ways:

(a) household access to the "traditional" dollar economy, consisting of: (1) the PEWEX and Baltona hard-currency stores; (2) household dollar accounts held in Polish banks; and (3) *bony towarowe*, the semi-convertible notes issued by the Polish government and redeemable in the hard-currency stores, which could be purchased by Polish citizens, with zloty (Ledworowski and Wyźnikiewicz);

(b) household access to the "legalized" (previously black-market) dollar economy, consisting of free-market transactions in currencies, housing, automobiles, and consumer durables;

(c) exchange of convertible currencies at the official, "submarginal" exchange rate (e.g., the allocation of foreign exchange to enterprises for centrally determined imports);

(d) the system of enterprise currency-retention accounts, from which exporters can draw funds either to purchase hard-currency imports or to pay other firms for services rendered (*wsad dewizowy*);

(e) the hard-currency auctions conducted by the Foreign Trade Bank, in which permission to purchase convertible currencies (at the official exchange rate) is sold to enterprises.

In essence, these different activities revolve around two different exchange rates generated by two very different types of transactions: the official rate, reflecting the zloty cost of obtaining $0.75–$0.80 worth of export revenue; and the free-market rate, reflecting the shadow cost of a dollar to those unable to obtain it at the official exchange rate.[9] Convertibility was achieved by legalizing the black-market rate rather than trying to force the official rate upon the second economy. (This approach was, of course, aided by a billion $ currency-stabilization loan from the International Monetary Fund.) In any case, achieving convertibility would have been much more difficult, perhaps impossible, without the enterprise retention accounts and, to a lesser extent, the hard-currency auctions – both reform steps of the 1980s.

Of course, the success of this approach to convertibility remains an open question; much still depends upon the development of capital markets and the Polish financial system, monetary and fiscal policies, improvements in export performance, and further progress in restoring Poland's creditworthiness.

[9] Actually, *four* different sets of zloty-dollar exchange rates were in effect: (1) the official, unified, sub-marginal rate, applying to transactions described in (c) and (d) above; (2) the black-market rate (which generally exceeded the official rate by a factor of 3.5–4) applying to transactions described in (b) above; (3) the price for *bony towarowe* described in (a) above, which differed marginally from (and therefore functioned as a proxy for) the black-market rate; and (4) the rate generated by the hard-currency auctions (e), which fluctuated wildly and at times exceeded the black-market rate. Since only a small fraction of foreign exchange was allocated through the auctions, and since the price for *bony* was linked to the black-market rate, exchange rates essentially boiled down to the submarginal and black-market rates.

Prospects for the Future

While the significance of these changes within Poland should not be underestimated, the changes now occurring in Western Europe, the Germanys and the Soviet Union are potentially more important. The more rapidly Poland becomes a part of an integrated European economy, the larger the pay-offs to its internal reforms will be.

Prior to the collapse of the German Democratic Republic in late 1989, the prospects for a major infusion of West German capital and Poland's subsequent inclusion into a future common economic European house were not unpromising. Western Europe seemed to be heading inexorably toward an economic and political union in which the West German role would be important but not dominant. The integration of reformist East European states like Poland at some later date (à la the French "concentric circle" model) was clearly implied. Poland could have been a major benefactor of West German (and other international) capital, thanks to progress with reform and the country's geographic proximity to West Germany as well as to the potential riches of the Soviet market.

German unification changes all this. First, the unification process per se promises economic turbulence for Western Europe, as seen, for example, in the general European (and not only European) concern about the inflationary side effects of a one-to-one conversion of GDR ost marks into deutsche marks. This turbulence and the political stresses it generates are certain to slow the pace of integration and remove the benefits of Polish inclusion further into the future. Second, German unification is likely to redirect a significant share of West German (and other) capital away from Poland toward (what used to be) East Germany. And third, European integration, even if successful, will now produce a European Community dominated by Germany. Whatever its economic benefits, it is difficult to imagine Poles as happy residents in a common European house owned by Germans.

Equally important issues concern the future of *perestroika*, the Soviet Union (Poland's largest trading partner), and the CMEA (through which the majority of Polish trade continues to flow). One of the lessons of the 1980s is that, in the absence of reforming the CMEA trading mechanism, the impact of Polish foreign-trade reforms is likely to be minimal. On the other hand, a genuine marketization of CMEA trade based upon agreements concluded by profit-oriented enterprises facing world-market prices, hard budget constraints, and convertible currencies could yield major benefits to all member states. Although the CMEA can not supply Poland with capital and modern technology, CMEA trade in the long run could still provide important gains from trade, gains currently blocked by the bureaucratic nature of the CMEA mechanism. Moreover, Poland's convertible zloty and proximity to the vast Soviet market suggest that, even in the short run, Poland could play a profitable role as a transit point for Western exports and joint ventures destined for the USSR.

Much also depends upon the fate of *perestroika* within the USSR. While regression to a Brezhnevian or even neo-Stalinist Soviet government is not likely to recreate socialism in Poland, such a government could prevent CMEA reform and cause numerous problems for its East European neighbors. The more immediate difficulties, however, concern *perestroika's* failure as a reform program and the myriad of crises now engulfing the USSR. The worsening Soviet economic recession, which, according to some observers, began as far back as 1988 (Kontorovich), does not bode well for the USSR's smaller East European trading partners. Moreover, some of the ethnic instability emanating from the Soviet Union could spread to Poland (e.g., Ukrainian separatism).

The fates of *perestroika* and European integration are not unrelated. *Perestroika's* economic reforms are most likely to succeed if, in addition to reforming the Soviet economy and marketizing the CMEA, Soviet republics (or newly independent states) are able to achieve the same position vis-à-vis the USSR as the smaller Western European states would enjoy in a unified Europe: national autonomy combined with genuine political and economic integration into the larger community. It is in a Europe united from the Atlantic to the Urals that Polish foreign trade, and the Polish economy, have the best chances to prosper.

In any case, Poland's disappointing foreign-trade performance during the 1980s implies that considerable potential for improvement exists. Poland's seacoast, its skilled labor force and technical base, and its location in the center of Europe all comprise important potential gains through foreign trade for the Polish economy. Whether the transition to capitalism now being attempted will allow Poland to harvest this potential remains to be seen.

References

Baka, W., ed. 1982. *Polska reforma gospodarcza*. Warszawa: Państwowe Wydawnictwo Ekonomiczne.

Brumberg, A., ed. 1983. *Poland: Genesis of a Revolution*. New York: Vintage Books.

Burzyński, A. 1989. "Comments on Foreign Investment Law of 23rd of December, 1988." Manuscript, Warszawa.

Crane, K. 1986. "Foreign-Trade Decisionmaking under Balance of Payments Pressure: Poland versus Hungary." *East European Economies: Slow Growth in the 1980's*, vol. 3, US Congress Joint Economic Committee. Washington, DC: Government Printing Office, pp. 434–49.

Fallenbuchl, Z. 1986. "The Economic Crisis in Poland and Prospects for Recovery." In *East European Economies: Slow Growth in the 1980's*, vol. 3, US Congress Joint Economic Committee. Washington, DC: Government Printing Office, pp. 359–98.

—— 1984. "The Polish Economy Under Martial Law," *Soviet Studies*, October, pp. 513–27.

Gomułka, S., and J. Rostowski. 1984. "The Reformed Polish Economic System 1982–83." *Soviet Studies*, July, pp. 386–405.

Gospodarka w latach 1981–85. 1986. Warszawa: Konsultacyjna Rada Gospodarcza.

Herer, W., and W. Sadowski. 1981. "Nawis Inflacyjny," *Życie gospodarcze*, August 9.

Holzman, F. 1974. *Foreign Trade Under Central Planning*. Cambridge, MA: Harvard University Press.

Jermakowicz, W., and R. Krawczyk. 1985. *Reforma gospodarcza jako innowacja społeczna*. Warszawa: Młodzieżowa Agencja Wydawnicza.

Kemme, D., ed. 1990. *Poland: Transition to the Second Stage*. Minneapolis: University of Minnesota Press.

Kierunki reformy gospodarczej. 1981. Warszawa: Książka i Wiedza.

Kleer, J., and J. Poprzeczko. 1987. "Dobry towar za dobrą cenę," *Polityka*, January 24, p. 3.

Kontorovich, V. 1989. "Recession: The Painful Product of Soviet Reform," *The Wall Street Journal*, August 30, p. A10.

Kornai, J. 1980. *Economics of Shortage*. Amsterdam, New York, and Oxford: North Holland.

Kowalska, M. 1989. "Signum Temporis," *Życie gospodarcze*, January 1, p. 2.

Koźmiński, A. 1985. *Gospodarka na punkcie zwrotnym*. Warszawa: Państwowe Wydawnictwo Ekonomiczne.

Ledworowski, D., and B. Wyźnikiewicz. 1987. "Polskie eldolorado," *Polityka*, Export-Import Section, June 20, pp. 13, 15.

Lipiński, S. 1987. "Wycisnąć każdego dolara," *Życie gospodarcze*, September 6, pp. 1, 8.

—— 1986. "W dewizowym krzywym kole," *Życie gospodarcze*, April 6, pp. 1, 4.

Lipowski, A. 1988. *Mechanizm rynkowy w gospodarce polskiej*. Warszawa: Państwowe Wydawnictwo Naukowe.

Loch, J. 1986. "Tęsknota za konsekwencją," *Polityka*, June 14, p. 5.

Marer, P., and W. Siwiński, eds. 1987. *Creditworthiness and Reform in Poland: Western and Polish Perspectives*. Bloomington: Indiana University Press.

Mieszczańkowski, M. 1987. "Krótka historia reformy," *Życie gospodarcze*, May, 17, pp. 1, 4.

Mizsei, K., "A valutavisszatérités lengyel rendszer." Budapest: Institute for World Economics, 1986 [a].

Pełnomocnik rządu ds. reformy gospodarczej. 1985. *Raport o realizacji reformy gospodarczej w 1984 roku*. Warszawa: Rzeczpospolita, August.

Piesiewicz, Z. 1987. "Biurokracja nam rośnie," *Polityka*, January 10, p. 3

Plesiński, K. 1987. "I chciałabym i boję się," *Życie gospodarcze*, November 1, p. 7.

—— 1986. "0 spółkach z kapitałem zagranicznym," *Życie gospodarcze*, May 4, p. 2.

Plowiec, U. 1984. *The Functioning of Poland's Foreign Trade: Experience and Prospects*. Warszawa: Instytut Koniunktur i Cen.

Polish Economy in the External Environment in 1980's. 1988. Warszawa: SGPiS.

Poznański, K. 1986. "Economic Adjustment and Political Forces: Poland Since 1970." *International Organization*, Spring, pp. 455–87.

Program realizacyjny drugiego etapu reformy gospodarczej: Projekt. 1987. Warszawa: Rzeczpospolita, October.

Reforma gospodarcza: Zbiór ustaw i przepisów wykonawczych. 1983. Warszawa: Państwowe Wydawnictwo Ekonomiczne.

Rymarczyk, J. 1985. "Próba diagnozy," *Życie gospodarcze*, August 18, p. 8.

Slay, B. 1989. "Economic Reform in Poland and Hungary." Unpublished Ph.D. dissertation, Department of Economics, Indiana University, Bloomington, IN.

Szwarc, K. 1987. "Reforma centrum," *Życie gospodarcze*, October 25, p. 7.

Tarnowski, P. 1987. "Przetargi w 'Szwarcbanku'," *Polityka*, Export-Import Section, June 20, p. 15.

Wiśniewski, J. 1986. "The Economy and Its Shadow," *Eastern European Economics*, Summer, pp. 29–39.

"Z zagranicznym kapitałem." 1986. *Życie gospodarcze*, March 16, p. 11.

Zarzycki, Z. 1985. "Tanio kupiłaś." *Życie gospodarcze*, December 1, p. 12.

Żukowska, B. 1989. "Dobre koncepcje nie starzeją się," *Życie gospodarcze*, January 29, p. 7.

RESOURCE ALLOCATION: CAPITAL

Keith Crane

Because of the breadth of the topic of resource allocation the focus on the allocation of one particular resource, capital, has been chosen in part because two prime failures of the previous system were the inefficient use of existing capital stocks and the choice of investments. In addition, the creation of a system that will efficiently intermediate between savers and investors and create conditions for choosing the most efficient investments seems more daunting than allocating other resources. The Balcerowicz program has adopted a fairly straightforward solution for the allocation of consumer goods or intermediate products: markets. These have sprung up overnight. The institutional structure for the allocation of capital, on the other hand, continues to be in the formative stage.

This essay assesses how capital is allocated under the new economic system in Poland. The essay begins with an analysis of the inefficiencies of allocation of capital under the 1982–88 economic system. It then describes how capital is to be allocated and savings generated under the Balcerowicz program. It concludes with an assessment of the extent of changes to date in the system of capital allocation in Poland.

The Allocation of Capital Under the 1982-88 System

The Role of the Center

Under the economic system that emerged in Poland after martial law, only half the investments in the state and cooperative sector were financed through profits and amortization from enterprises.[1]

---

[1] In 1983, enterprises provided 48.6 percent of total investments in the state and cooperative sectors; in 1984, 51.6 percent; and in 1985, 52.4 percent (*Mały Rocznik Statystyczny*, 1987, p. 125).

The other half was provided by and determined by the central and local governments, social funds, and cooperative housing associations. The large role of the government in determining investment was due to the continuing belief by members of the Planning Commission and the central government that their preferences for investment should dominate.

Because monetary policy was accommodatory and prices controlled, many markets, including those for investment goods such as machinery and construction materials, failed to clear. Since markets were not allowed to function, some other method of allocating inputs had to be used. The Polish central authorities chose to allocate roughly half of fuels and important raw materials and an even higher percentage of imports through orders from the Planning Commission or branch ministries. Thus, even when a decision was made to start an investment project, the materials and means to construct the project were frequently not available.

Other formal and informal measures have been instrumental in allocating the remaining goods and services.[2] Producers of inputs such as steel products, cement, and other construction materials had to sell all or almost all of their output to central wholesalers. The wholesalers did not operate as profit-maximizing enterprises. They chose their customers on the basis of instructions from the Planning Commission, branch ministry requests, and orders from the Council of Ministers. Branch ministry requests in turn were decided on the basis of requests from associations and large enterprises.

Although the National Bank was given a more important role in assessing investment projects, the choice of important government-funded projects was still made by the Council of Ministers, for whom rate of return was only one criterion. At lower levels, the ability of a manager to obtain materials and construction workers depended heavily on his bureaucratic clout and relations with the contractor. Bargaining power and past patterns of resource allocation were therefore the primary means of deciding who gets what in this system.

The center also attempted better to ensure that its preferences, rather than the preferences of the branch ministries, were enforced, through the introduction of a system of "government orders" for products that the government decided were priority items. Enterprises bid for these orders, and if their bid was accepted, they were guaranteed the necessary inputs to manufacture the products.

To finance the preferences of the central authorities in investment, substantial taxes were imposed, many levied on the enterprise sector. Enterprises paid PFAZ (a tax on increases in the wage bill), profit taxes, and turnover tax. They also had to turn over a share of amortization, which was akin to a tax on capital.

[2] *Poland: Reform, Adjustment and Growth*, vols. 2–3 (Washington, DC: World Book, 1987), pp. 20–21.

These taxes took a very large share of enterprise resources. In 1985, PFAZ taxes in a sample of 2,211 Polish firms averaged 15.9 percent of the wage bill, and profit taxes took an average of 47 percent of profits (the median was 52.7 percent) and ranged from 5.1 to 70 percent of total profits. Turnover taxes averaged 4.8 percent of production sold.[3] In this same sample, enterprises paid from 7.2 to 78 percent of amortization to the national budget in 1985.[4] Thus, the government set highly variegated, seemingly arbitrary tax and amortization retention rates.

The Role of the Enterprise

Despite the dominant position of the center in determining investment projects, enterprise managers were also important actors. In many cases, they were the people who initiated projects and they ultimately determined the form and effectiveness of the actual investment. Thus, the incentive system and the responses by enterprise managers played a crucial role in determining the demand for and types of investment.

During the 1982–88 reform, the primary goal of enterprise managers was to stay in the good graces of their founding organization, usually the branch ministry, and, to a lesser extent, of the workers' councils. The branch ministries had several goals. The weights of these entries varied over time as policies and personnel changed. However, because of the government's emphasis on preserving labor peace, the ministry's primary goal often boiled down to keeping the work force content. For the enterprise manager, this meant increasing workers' wages. One of the easiest ways to increase wages was to increase after-tax, after-subsidy profits. Polish enterprises have not faced a "hard budget constraint" as defined by Kornai.[5] The government has been willing to bail out all large loss-making firms with subsidies or by forgiving loans. However, enterprises that continued to post losses found that life became difficult. A few enterprises went bankrupt, the first a small metal-working firm in Zabrze, and the number of firms in financial difficulties rose. Firms that fell into financial difficulties were overseen by an appointee of the National Bank and had to work out a program to restore themselves to financial health. In effect, the old manager found that his former power was curtailed or that he was out of a job. For these reasons, avoiding losses became an important objective for enterprise managers.

[3] U. Wojciechowska, G. Pasznik, and A. Szeworski, "Sytuacja ekonomiczna przedsiębiorstw przemysłowych w 1985 roku," *Raporty*. Warszawa: Instytut Gospodarki Narodowej, 1987, p. 16. These authors conduct an annual statistical analysis of over 2,000 (of a total of 5,496) Polish industrial enterprises based on data from the Polish Statistical Office. The firms in the sample produce most of Poland's industrial output.

[4] *Ibid.*, p. 23.

[5] J. Kornai, *The Economics of Shortage*. New York: North Holland, 1980.

Table 1

Relationship Between Profit Margins and Development Funds

	Loss-Making	0–5	5–15	15–30	>30
Profits as a Percentage of Total Sales					
Mean	−13.1	31.2	35.6	61.1	81.8
Median	−15.9	1.6	20.1	27.3	36.7
Number of Enterprises	15	333	971	631	261

Source: U. Wojciechowska, G. Pasznik and A. Szeworski, "Sytuacja ekonomiczna przedsiębiorstw przemysłowych w 1985 roku," *Raporty*, Warszawa: Instytut Gospodarki Narodowej, 1987, pp. 33, 37.

Profits were also pursued because they were an important source of investment funds. As shown in Table 1, profits have been positively correlated with the rate of increase in funds available for investment. Forty-one percent of the enterprises interviewed by Wojciechowska (1986) financed their investments from the development fund, which was derived from profits. The second most important source of funding was subsidies from the national or local governments (30 percent of the enterprises); bank credit was used by only 14.2 percent.

In the classic Soviet-type system, enterprise managers push for investments in new capacity because the larger the enterprise, the higher the manager's salary. Investments also tend to facilitate the fulfillment of plan targets because they can remove short-run bottlenecks.

The incentives for investment in the Polish reformed system are not all that different. Enterprise managers interviewed by Wojciechowska (1986) said they invested to increase production, improve the quality of products, develop exports, improve the technological level of production, conserve on labor, energy, and materials, and protect the environment. Ministerial and customer pressure to expand production provided another incentive to invest, as did the desire to remove bottlenecks. Both these motives made it possible to increase profits or expand production. The former enabled the enterprise manager to keep his own job and keep his workforce happy; the latter pleased the ministry.

Changes in Capital Efficiency and Investment Allocation

Despite this emphasis on investment, it was generally poorly used. The 1982–88 system failed to induce increases in capital productivity, nor did it redirect investment to more productive sectors.

Rocznik Statystyczny contains information on investment by industrial sector and on capital used in industry as a whole. These data, coupled with data on profitability provided in Wojciechowska et al. (1987), were used by this author to assess the effectiveness of the 1982 reform in improving Polish economic efficiency.

Factor productivity growth is compared for two periods: 1975–78, the years before the economic crisis, but also years when the government began to try to tighten its belt; and 1983–85, the first three years after the reform. Factor productivity growth is defined as the change in the ratio of net industrial output to two factors: the stock of fixed capital, and hours worked in industry.

Table 2 compares factor productivity growth for these two periods.

Despite the apparent superior performance in terms of capital productivity growth, the figures mask tremendous declines experienced in capital productivity. The ratio of net material product (NMP) produced by socialized industry to capital was 65 percent lower in 1985 than in 1975. On the other hand, the ratio of NMP produced in socialized industry to hours worked was 3 percent higher in 1985 than in 1979, showing an absolute rise in the productivity of labor. In sum, capital employed by socialized industry was used notably less efficiently in the 1982–88 period.

A second indicator of the poor utilization of capital in the 1980s is shown by changes in the allocation of investment. Wojciechowska et al. (1987) provides information on profits as a percentage of gross sales and on profits per worker. Although these categories are not equivalent to rates of return and are heavily influenced by capital labor ratios,[6] they provide a rough indication of relative profitability. Comparisons of sectors ranked by profitability with their shares in total employment and investment in socialized industry provide some indication of the success of the reform in reallocating resources toward more profitable sectors.

Table 2

Factor Productivity Growth in Polish Socialized Industry

Year	Output/Capital Ratio	Output/Labor Ratio
1975	.401	.343
1976	.401	.371
1977	.388	.397
1978	.364	.412
1979	.330	.407
1980	.303	.395
1981	.249	.367
1982	.232	.383
1983	.238	.384
1984	.242	.406
1985	.242	.422

[6] For example, the electricity-generating industry registers the highest profits per worker because it is very capital intensive.

1	2	3
Average Annual Rates of Increase		
1975-78	−2.42	4.62
1983-85	.64	3.22

Table 3 shows the average share by industrial sector of investment and employment in socialized industry for the 1975–78 and 1983–85 periods, gross profit margins, and profits per worker. The industries are arranged in descending order.

Table 3

Investment and Employment Shares and the Profitability of Socialized Industry

Industry	Gross Profit Margins	Profits Per Worker	Percent of Investment	Percent of Investment	Percent of Labor Force	Percent of Labor Force
	1985	1985	1975–78	1983–85	1975–78	1983–85
Light	33.5	248.8	5.1	5.2	17.7	15.2
Other	30.5	296.0	1.5	1.6	2.4	3.3
Power	27.3	3460.1	8.7	15.5	1.7	2.3
Machine Building	27.1	348.3	25.1	22.3	33.4	34.0
Chemicals	19.4	502.1	11.1	10.0	7.1	6.6
Construction Materials	17.4	203.7	10.9	7.4	12.1	10.6
Metallurgy	9.8	550.9	16.8	5.8	5.4	5.0
Coal	2.5	141.9	8.4	16.2	7.9	10.0
Food	−2.6	332.5	9.2	11.9	11.3	11.8

Table 3 shows that capital and labor flows have been the *reverse* of what one would expect based on profitability considerations. The coal and food industries have had the worst profitability performance, yet these two industries and electricity generation have registered the largest gains in the shares of investment. Both industries have also registered strong increases in their shares of employment at the expense of apparently more profitable industries. These figures may merely reflect the irrational Polish price system, in which goods facing high excess demand, such as meat and coal, have relatively lower fixed prices and therefore are not profitable. They also reflect industry-specific technologies, e.g., the relatively fixed capital labor ratios in electricity generation. Perhaps the low profitability of the sectors to which capital and labor are being reallocated also reflects the high costs of old production technologies; new investment may be more profitable. However, the figures indicate the very limited role of profits in determining the allocation of investments and labor. Prices failed to reflect relative scarcities and were not used to direct investment flows. One of the consequences of the slow recovery and the sharp decline in output between 1979 and 1982 has been much lower shares of utilized national income devoted to investment. This has led to complaints of decapitalization, i.e., the capital stock is wearing out and not being replaced. According to enterprise managers, this has reached substantial proportions (Table 4).

Table 4

Decapitalization in a Sample of Polish Industrial Enterprises

Industry	Percent of Total Capital Stock Fully Depreciated		
	1983	1984	1985
Metallurgy	60.2	62.3	64.8
Machine building	44.4	47.6	49.5
Chemicals	45.5	47.0	49.3
Textiles	64.4	64.5	65.7
Food Processing	43.0	44.1	42.7

Source: U. Wojciechowska and J. Lipiński, "Funkcjonowanie przedsiębiorstw w 1985 roku," *Raporty* Warszawa: Instytut Gospodarki Narodowej, 1986, p. 29.

Enterprise managers complained they lacked both financial and physical resources for investment. Although not as important a constraint on production in the mid-1980s as labor and input shortages, the quality and size of the capital stock was cited as a binding constraint on the volume and quality of production by 20 percent of a group of managers.[7] Moreover, because of the lack of development funds or limitations on importing machinery, enterprises were constrained to repair older machinery, even though the cost of the repairs was greater than the cost of replacing it with new machinery.

Capital Allocation Under the Balcerowicz Plan

It is still too early to evaluate whether the Balcerowicz Plan has improved capital productivity. Investment by its nature is a long term phenomenon; ten months is too short a time to evaluate the impact of the plan on the allocation of capital. It is possible, however, to assess the internal consistency of the

[7] U. Wojciechowska and J. Lipiński, "Funkcjonowanie Przedsiębiorstw w 1985 roku," *Raporty*. Warszawa: Instytut Gospodarki Narodowej, 1986, p. 10.

plan and identify potential problems and areas of promise. It is also possible to evaluate initial trends since the passage of the plan. This section is designed to achieve this end.

Efficient Use of the Existing Capital Stock

Economists traditionally consider the stock of capital, as opposed to labor, as fixed over the short run. Capital does not flow freely from one use to another, rather there is a lengthy process of adjustment whereby the capital stock in a declining industry depreciates and is not replaced; new flows are channeled into expanding industries.

The process of adjustment is proceeding with a vengeance in Poland today. Enterprise managers are faced with a whole new set of relative prices and demands and are being pushed to make profits or go out of business. Initially, most managers hoped the government would go back to operating as usual and postponed changes. Managers did raise prices under the expectation that inflation would continue at the rapid rates of 1989. As unsold products piled up in warehouses, however, managers began to face pressures to alter their ways. As in developing countries such as Mexico and Turkey that have engaged in restructuring by opening up their economies, managers have begun to search for markets abroad. Hard currency exports have risen 11 percent in the first six months of the year as managers have pushed Polish goods abroad. Managers also responded by furloughing workers and closing various production lines. To this point, most have been able to keep their factories from closing, although layoffs have increased. Unemployment was 820,000 in 1990, or 4.8 percent of the 1989 labor force. In March unemployment was only 200,000. It is continuing to grow. Enterprise managers are also beginning to make other attempts to cut costs, now that more of them are convinced the government will not bail them out. Factory managers have kept wages firmly under control. Although the cost of living increased by 70 percent in January and enterprises could have raised wages by 20 percent, wages only rose 1.3 percent because enterprises did not have the funds to provide more.[8]

As the tight monetary policy continues to bite, some enterprises will go bankrupt. Bankruptcies will serve to withdraw portions of the capital stock from the production process. Other enterprises will survive but will close unprofitable production lines. The closure of unprofitable production lines, often temporarily but in some cases permanently, accounted for much of the decline in output in the first three months of the year.

---

[8] J. Baczyński, "Dokąd prowadzą te schody?" *Polityka*, no. 7, February 17, 1990, p. 1.

The success of the reform will depend not on its efficiency in retiring outmoded or poorly utilized capital stock, although this Schumperterian destruction is also of importance for ecological as well as economic reasons, but by its efficiency in channelling investment to its most efficient uses. The very tight budget constraint imposed by the national government on enterprises should serve, if it holds, to make enterprises use their existing capital much more efficiently. To the extent continued survival depends on modernization which involves investment, the new system should also serve to improve the efficiency of investment. However, at this point there is little in the new system to lead to an optimal allocation of resources between investment and consumption or for enterprises to choose an optimal level of investment, i.e., one where the marginal revenue product of capital equals its cost.

The heart of the problem, as in so much of the process of creating a market economy, is the question of ownership. Despite efforts by the government to impose cash restraints on state-owned firms and tie managerial evaluations to profitability, interviews with enterprise managers published in the press portray great concern about survival, but not about maximizing profits.[9]

Changes in Ownership

The Polish authorities, like the Hungarians, have concluded that the only solution to this problem is to privatize most industrial enterprises. Thus, restructuring involves the diversion of investment not only from declining to expanding industries but also from the state to the private sector.

In a speech to the Sejm in April 1990, Deputy Prime Minister Leszek Balcerowicz emphasized that the next stage of the Polish reform package is restructuring, and restructuring implies privatization.[10] Balcerowicz argues that without privatization the reform will not succeed. Because private companies are run by those interested in cutting costs, improving product quality, and organizing work well, if strong competitive pressures exist, the private property leads to more efficient utilization of resources. If Poland is to successfully emerge from its current economic problems, it will need to use all its resources as efficiently as possible. Private ownership will also stimulate people to become active and dynamic and acts as a guarantee of personal freedoms. Balcerowicz concludes that there is no alternative. A market economy without extensive private ownership will be less dynamic and have higher unemployment than if the state sector remains dominant. The government has decided to follow the tried and true model of capitalist

---

[9] J. Olska, "Cywile zbiednieli," *Polityka*, 1990, no. 6.

[10] *Rzeczpospolita*, April 6, 1990, p. 4.

market economies; a third way is a costly experiment that other countries are welcome to try but is not for Poland. The Polish people are no longer willing to be economic guinea pigs.

Acting on these beliefs, the Polish government introduced a bill on privatization in the spring of 1990. The bill finally became law in July and called for the conversion of state-owned enterprises into joint stock companies, followed by their sale to domestic and foreign investors. The law was substantially modified in the Sejm. Workers' councils must vote in favor of the conversion of their enterprises into joint stock companies. Once transformed, they receive the right to purchase 20 percent of the companies' stock at reduced prices. In addition, the government is discussing issuing vouchers to the population, whereby they are granted shares in Polish enterprises.

The Polish government's plans for privatization provide for diverse forms of ownership. The draft law provides for employee stock ownership programs, partnerships, cooperatives, and single proprietors as well as joint stock companies and foreign ownership.

The government has broad support from the Polish electorate for privatization in principle. A recent opinion poll found two thirds of Poles support privatization. However, over half (55 percent) were against sales to foreign businessmen, Polish businessmen, or private shareholders.[11] The only form of privatization supported by over half the respondents was employee stock ownership. Thus, the way in which companies are to be privatized is almost as important as the transfer of ownership itself.

Because of concern about the manner of privatization, the government is advocating very public, open sales of companies. A preferred mechanism is the public sale of shares after conversion to joint-stock companies. Regulations also make it possible to sell individual parts of enterprises as well as entire companies in the event of bankruptcy. But in all cases privatization will be carried out openly. To assuage worker concerns, the draft law provides workers in state enterprises transformed into joint stock companies with the opportunity to purchase up to 20 percent of the stock on preferential terms. The government also intends to facilitate purchases of shares by small buyers. It also envisages possibilities for transferring enterprises to workers who wish to form their own company or cooperative.[12] Because of the number of firms that need to be privatized and the share of industrial assets in state-owned industries, the Polish government is skeptical about how much can be learned from the British or West German experiences. They believe they will need to develop a specifically Polish method of transferring ownership.

The government plan does not foreclose state ownership. State enterprises will play a continuing, if smaller, role, if they can survive and perform well in

---

[11] P. Pacewicz, "Prywatyzacja: tak, tak, nie, nie," *Gazeta Wyborcza*, April 20, 1990, p. 3.

[12] *Rzeczpospolita*, April 6, 1990, p. 4.

a competitive environment. The government is also encouraging municipalities to take over local companies, if they think they can operate them effectively.

The government argues that privatization has begun, especially within the framework of public land, building plots, apartments, buildings, and small commercial and processing facilities. However, it is currently too slow, which is why amendments to the Civil Code are needed. They will make it possible to speed up the process. Amendments to the Real Estate Tenancy Law to introduce market-oriented uses of commercial premises are especially important.

The Polish state sector currently consists of about 7,000 enterprises. Of these, the government believes 1,000 will remain in the hands of the state, leaving 6,000 to be privatized. During the privatization period, these firms will be transferred to the Ministry of Ownership Transformation. Because of the number of enterprises and the lack of financial markets, the transitional period will not be brief.

One of the concerns of the government is that enterprises would be disenfranchised of their rights to self-management and independent decision making during the transition period. This could lead to a dangerous concentration of power.

One of the key problems for an effective privatization program is the limited demand for financial assets. A number of commentators have noted that savings and cash balances are only a few trillion zlotys, equal to a tiny fraction of the book value of Polish state enterprises which has been estimated at 100 trillion zlotys.[13] To some degree this concern is overexaggerated. Because of very high rates of inflation and the inconvertibility of the zloty, Polish households have generally chosen to save in dollars rather than zlotys. Those that have saved in zlotys found most of their wealth disappeared through the inflation tax. Convertible currency assets are on the order of several billion dollars. Convertible currency deposits in state banks ran 3 billion in 1989. Households also saved through purchases of consumer durables and real estate. Thus, household assets consist of considerably more than zloty savings and cash balances.

This said, the current demand for financial assets is limited. Poland is just beginning to create a securities market. Very few firms have had a Western-style financial audit, so it is difficult for professional investors, let alone the average saver, to make intelligent choices about the prospects of various firms. Despite the wide array of methods the government is offering through which enterprises can be privatized, limited domestic demand for financial assets is likely to be a continuing problem. If this is the case, foreign investors will be able to purchase Polish assets relatively cheaply, which could create political problems.

[13] Z. Krajewska, "Harsh Blows," *Rzeczpospolita*, April 6, 1990, pp. 1, 2.

Privatization has engendered the most dissent from the government's total economic program in the Sejm. Ryszard Bugaj and Czesław Kowalski have criticized the government on the grounds that it has not informed the public that there will be winners and losers with privatization. They argue that the government needs to provide credits to accelerate privatization, but there is no commercial banking system to finance them. The dissenters argue only speculators and the former nomenklatura have the money to buy firms. Working class people will not have the opportunity to benefit from privatization. Some deputies have insisted Poles be given shares in state enterprises to generate support for privatization and assuage the pain of transition to a market system.

Investment and Savings

The discussion to this point has focused on improving the utilization of the existing capital stock through privatization and restructuring through closures. However, in the long run growth will only be possible if current levels of investment are maintained and are allocated more efficiently.

The problem of privatization is different from that of investment. Privatization is a process of exchanging assets: the government wants to exchange industrial and other assets of uncertain worth for financial assets such as dollars or zlotys. Because of limited supplies of financial assets, it may be more profitable to sell these corporations to foreign bidders. However, this problem focuses on an exchange of stocks; assets held by the enterprises and the household sector are more or less fixed at any particular point in time. The conundrum facing the government is how to create a system to exchange the two.

Investment is a problem of generating and allocating a flow. In the past, Poland invested a substantial share of output. Fixed capital investment equaled 21.6 percent of GDP in 1987. However, it is not clear whether this ratio will be maintained in the future. If it drops substantially, long term economic growth rates will suffer and the economy might even stagnate.

The reason for concern is that in the past, the government was responsible for most Polish savings. The government imposed high taxes on Polish enterprises and consumers, which were then channeled into investment. In the future, savings will have to be generated voluntarily from the household sector or from foreign investors. In very few countries has foreign capital played much of a role in terms of aggregate savings; its primary role has been the transfer of technologies and managerial skills through multinationals. Thus, Poland, like the rest of Eastern Europe, will in all likelihood have to rely on domestic savings for investments.

In the future, although the government may be a net saver, it does not want to be the primary source of investment funds. Traditionally the corporate sector absorbs savings. Consequently, investment levels in Poland will depend on how much of their income people are willing to save.

There is little information on the share of disposable income the household sector is likely to save. On the one hand, consumer expectations are high; as earnings rise, Polish citizens are likely to spend them so as to bring their levels of consumption closer to the European average. Moreover, during this period of adjustment, Poles are spending their savings in order to preserve former consumption levels in the face of declines in real incomes. On the other hand, the introduction of a market economy to Poland has increased uncertainty. In the face of uncertainty, people frequently tend to save more. The government has also helped generate high real interest rates so the rate of return on savings has increased. Thus, unfortunately, this very important question will remain unanswered for a year or two.

The Development of Financial Institutions

The efficient allocation of what savings there will be will depend on the development of a market-oriented financial system. Poland is in the throes of developing such a system. Although the outlines are becoming clearer, the details are still muddy.

Poland separated the money issue bank from the commercial banking system before the Balcerowicz program. It is currently difficult to ascertain how well the new commercial banks are operating. The breakup of the former system was primarily along regional lines, so most of the banks are close to monopolists in their home region, which has undoubtedly not contributed to competition in the financial sector. These banks also hold substantial debts by uncreditworthy state-owned enterprises, which affects their own creditworthiness. In the case of Hungary, these bad loans form such a large share of the banks' balance sheets that the solvency of the entire system has been threatened. This may be the case in Poland as well.

In addition to the large regional commercial banks, 1989 and 1990 has seen the proliferation of a set of new financial institutions. These provide the best promise that Poland will be able quickly to establish a modern financial sector. Some of these institutions, like the Export Development Fund, are operated by the state and are targeted toward particular sectors or purposes, in this case financing proexport investments. The entrepreneurial drive of some state managers or bureaucrats has led to the setup of other institutions. For example, the Postal Bank S.A. intends to establish a network of branches throughout Poland within three years, providing a broad range of financial services in zlotys and foreign currencies. Like post banks in other countries, it will use post offices. Some services will be performed by mail carriers. The postal administration will have controlling interest, but shares are also being sold to the general public.[14] Private banks are being established by the Association of Employee Self Management Functionaries (January 12, 1990) and by Solidarity. Private banks have proliferated during the year; even foreign banks have begun to be set up.

In addition to banks, the government is trying to set up other financial institutions. The Bureau of the Government Plenipotentiary for Ownership Transformation created in October 1989 is charged with preparing a stock and bond market as well as with the task of privatization. The Ownership Transformation Agency, formed from the staff of the bureau, is conducting research on the creation of stock and bond markets and a Securities Commission (state) and Stock Exchange (private).

Evaluation and Conclusions

The government's program for restructuring, in contrast to its program for stabilization, remains more on paper than in concrete. At this stage there is little empirical evidence concerning its results. One is therefore left only with theoretical analysis.

The government's program is well designed to improve the utilization of the existing capital stock. The government has introduced incentives and an environment that compels enterprises to cut costs and improve efficiency. Because of the past poor use of capital, improving capital utilization is a prime area where improvements can be expected. Improvements in capital productivity were one of the major successes of the Thatcher government. Despite the differences in economic systems, some of the same improvements should be seen in Poland for the same reasons they occurred in Britain.

The government is on more treacherous ground when it comes to improving the efficiency with which investments are allocated. Poland has a very rudimentary system of financial markets. Although private banks are being established, many of these have specific purposes and objectives that run counter to maximizing the efficiency with which investment is allocated. For the time being, Poland appears to be proceeding cautiously concerning the quickest way to improve the allocation of capital: invitations to foreign banks to set up subsidiaries in Poland. Popular opposition to foreign ownership of Polish firms may also slow the restructuring and privatization processes.

The big unanswered question for Poland is the likely levels of aggregate savings and investment in the coming years. Here government policy

[14] "A Bank at the Post Office," *Rzeczpospolita*, January 8, 1990, p. 2.

provides few clear signals. As noted above, in light of the expectations of Polish consumers, households are unlikely to save a high share of income. Current government tax policy neither penalizes nor reinforces this proclivity. On the one hand, a large share of tax revenues are derived from consumption taxes. On the other, the government taxes away a large share of enterprise profits (and potential savings). Thus we end on a frustratingly inconclusive note: long term growth in Poland will depend on domestic savings, yet it is too soon to know how current economic policies will affect these rates.

ADJUSTMENT AND COMPETITIVENESS

Jan Bossak
Wojciech Bieńkowski

Systemic Changes: Reforms Versus Transformation

This essay deals in broad terms with adjustment and international competitiveness in formerly socialist countries. In particular, it seeks to show how
the two are interrelated. An adjustment process is understood here not only
as a mere response of an economy to its changing economic environment but
as a process of fundamental political and economic transformation.

There is no way to implement an economic program of adjustment that
can bring us to an efficient and competitive economy unless it is coupled with
political transformation. This hypothesis is supported by the experience of
Central Eastern European countries. All their attempts at reforming their
economies until 1989 resulted in retreat and failure. The main reason for
those failures was a lack of corresponding changes in ideological principles
and the political system.

The Roundtable Agreement reached in Poland between the then-ruling party
(Polish United Workers' Party – PUWP) and the Solidarity opposition, the
election victory of Solidarity, and the formation of the first noncommunist
government in Eastern Europe made it possible to give up reforming the socialist
system and experimenting with a "third way" between state socialism and
capitalism. It enabled the start of a process of transforming a socialist system to
a parliamentary democracy and a state socialist economy to a market one.

Lifting political constraints to economic reforms helped shift the basic
question of adjustment facing Central Eastern European countries from
what to reform to how to build a system that would provide both democracy
and economic efficiency.

Besides the importance of the relationship between social values (ideology) and the political and economic system, it is important to see the difference between reforming the existing system and making the transition to a new one.

Graph 1
Systemic Changes: Reforms Versus Transformation and the Relationship Between the System of Values (Ideology) and the Political and Economic System

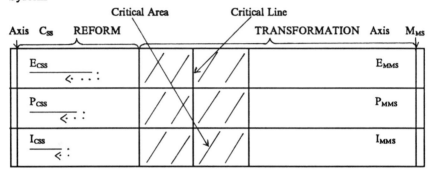

Where:
- Axis C_{SS} stands for a Central Socialist System in its most rigid (extreme), Stalinist, form; axis M_{MS} stands for a Market Multiparty System, reflecting an ideal "free market" and "Greek democracy" version;

and
- E_{CSS} stands for the Economic Sphere, reflecting a state-owned and centrally controlled economy;
- P_{CSS} refers to an authoritarian, one-party system, and
- I_{CSS} refers to the set of values in which a citizen is a subject with little or no political and/or economic freedom to choose or possess;
- I_{MMS}, P_{MMS}, and E_{MMS} refer, respectively, to the set of values in which a citizen, not a state, is an object; in which there is a parliamentary, multiparty system; in which private ownership in the economy prevails, labor and capital markets freely operate, and the economy is open.

Moving from Axis C_{SS} toward Axis M_{MS} means *reform* or *transformation*, respectively. Vectors symbolize the direction of changes, and their length symbolizes the historical intensity of changes in particular elements (spheres) of the system. Vectors drawn in dotted lines in a reverse direction illustrate the retreat from reforms. *Transformation differs from reform.* A *reform* means changes in the system that modify it but do not change its core elements and its nature. *Transformation* means such a degree of changes in the system that brings about a change in its core elements and nature. The moment of transition from reforms to transformation (moving from the left to the right) is depicted by a *"critical area"* sphere, which refers to three layers (economic, political, and ideological).

Adjustment and Competitiveness in the Context of the Economic Program

There is no relevant theory of making the transformation from socialism and a state economy to democracy and a market economy or practice. However, it is widely accepted that a radical economic adjustment program has to be preceded by democratic transformations. An economic adjustment is difficult because it leads to a decline in real incomes and a new pattern of distribution of national income. The costs of the process are high and painful. Therefore, any adjustment has to gain popular social support or consent. This cannot be achieved without democratization of the political system. Political freedom and economic freedom go hand in hand. Freedom of choice is necessary to gain support or consent and to mobilize the resources of social energy and invention. The opening up of new political and economic prospects and chances for individual and collective political and economic activity helps to mitigate painful adjustment costs.

The economic system of a country is closely tied to a whole set of sociopolitical and legal institutions, which form a so-called superstructure. The superstructure determines the character of ownership of means of production and therefore the economic order and its functioning. The stability and smooth functioning of social, political, and economic systems depend on their compatibility. Changing one element of the whole system sets an adjustment process in motion.

It is not surprising that transformation in the superstructure determines to a large degree the scope of economic reforms. Until 1989, so-called economic reforms in Poland and Hungary could not cross the boundary determined by the political and legal order based on state ownership and central management. Economic reforms without simultaneous political reforms were partial and disappointing despite the progress achieved in introducing elements of the market and progressive decentralization.

Over the past several decades, the Polish economy has become inefficient and rigid. In an attempt to achieve a prescribed pattern of production, various direct and indirect controls were introduced. The system was designed to promote, support, and protect selected producers in the belief that this could lead to a dynamic economy. The entire economy and society were mobilized to achieve this aim. At the same time, the authorities protected labor and heavily subsidized consumption and social welfare because of ideological commitment. Distorted factor markets, monopoly and overprotection, and the lack of an autoregulatory mechanism built into the economic system led to declining efficiency and rigidities despite efforts undertaken by central authorities.

In Poland during the eighties, the role of central planning gradually diminished. Branch ministries, which used to control enterprises, were abolished in 1988, and central annual plans used to specify detailed output objectives and large centrally managed investment programs were abandoned. In 1989 a Law on Enterprises provided the basis for the unrestricted development of the private sector.

However, only when a Solidarity-led government came to power in September 1989 was the road opened to fundamental transformations of the economic system.

Despite previous reforms, the socialized-sector enterprises accounted for over 90 percent of value added in the industrial sector. The deficit of the public sector has had a highly negative impact on the overall economic balance. Therefore, cutting subsidies, restoring budgetary balance, and strengthening the financial discipline of public enterprises were essential for the stabilization program. Moreover, the question of demonopolizing the economy, introducing competition, and increasing efficiency could not be tackled without reforming the socialized sector operating under state ownership.

However, the immediate objective of the new government was to fight hyperinflation and only then to build a new economic system. This program is based on the explicit assumption that efficiency cannot be restored without demonopolization, privatization, competition, and capital and labor markets. As property relations form the basis for an economic system and determine the way it operates, transforming the ownership structure has become a crucial element of the new economic system.

It is essential to point out that at the beginning of this transition stage, the balance of power in the parliament and the position of the Solidarity-led government seemed to be basically sound. Poland traditionally had been pulled by political tensions. The current Polish situation differs from that of the other East European countries in that it is based on the mass Solidarity movement with a more than ten-year tradition and on its own institutions.

Until the middle of 1990, political stability was additionally strengthened by disbanding the PUWP coalition government and by a spirit of national consensus. At this stage of transforming the economic system, political stability and popular support were a valuable asset.

The governmental economic program agreed with calls by the International Monetary Fund and the World Bank for stabilizing the economy and transforming the economic system. At the first stage of the reform, stabilization was the top priority, but from the middle of 1990, the key elements of the program have been systematic reforms, demonopolization, privatization, factor markets, competition, and the development of small and medium-sized enterprises.

The Balcerowicz-IMF program of stabilization and systemic reforms led to a dramatic, almost 30 percent decline in real incomes in the first ten months of its implementation. A deflationary policy resulted in recession and growing unemployment. The drop in production and sales was reaching 30 percent, and unemployment climbed from zero to one million.

This determined effort to carry out the program of economic stabilization and the relatively broad social support it gained made it possible to receive a promise of considerable economic and financial support from abroad. Foreign – namely, Western – support in response to the efforts undertaken by Polish society is politically motivated and as such should be regarded as an investment in peace and a future European political and economic infrastructure.

It is a cause for concern, however, that a short-term adjustment program dominated by anti-inflationary considerations seems to be overshadowing or postponing the undertaking of some institutional (i.e., modern banking in the institutional and functional sense) and structural, growth-oriented adjustment programs because:

– temporary stabilization benefits are achieved at the expense of high present and future costs;

– excessive secondary costs lead to the erosion of popular support for the government.

Short-term adjustment helps to bring down inflation and improve trade and current balances. This is a result of absorption and switching effects. However, trade and current improvements should not be regarded as evidence of increasing international competitive capacity.

International competitive capacity is generally determined by relative changes in the mobilization of economic resources, changes in efficiency, technology and market innovation, and financial credibility. Without an increase in the relative rate of savings, time of work, utilization of productive capacities, economic efficiency, technological progress, and market innovation accompanied by financial balance, there is no real progress in international competitive capacity.

International competitive capacity also depends on the possibility of restricting the growth of demand and changing the structure of expenditures and relative prices. However, when absorption of demand by a deflationary policy leads to recession and a decline in employment and economic efficiency, what results cannot be termed increased competitive capacity, even when it produces an export surplus by a forced switch of supply to export and a reduction of imports.

Although in the first ten months of 1990 trade and Poland's current account improved remarkably (giving a $4 billion trade surplus) as a result of absorption and switching, this fact cannot be regarded as evidence of improved international capacity to compete, since it has been accompanied by a decline in national income produced. A sharp decline of national income produced clearly indicates that the stabilization program implemented with great determination by the Mazowiecki government is costly and that the adjustment policy and adjustment mechanisms are still inefficient.

One cannot expect that economic instruments typical for market economies will produce the same results when they are used by formerly socialist countries that entered the path of making the political and economic transition to democratic societies and market economies. Comprehensive and radical measures are needed to fight hyperinflation. However, it is not enough to apply deflationary, monetary, and fiscal instruments to achieve durable stabilization without the prior introduction of a modern monetary banking system and capital markets. It seems that after depressing demand by stringent, restrictive policies, it is time to switch more vigorously to systemic reforms not only as a means to enhance the mobility and elasticity of the economy but also as the main absorbers of demand (for example, through a sellout of state enterprises).

However, the Polish Memorandum of Development Policy addressed to the IMF and the World Bank (September 1990) categorically rejected the relaxation of fiscal and monetary rigor. It pointed to the disruptive effects of increased oil prices, tumbling energy supplies from the Soviet Union, and the quicker-than-expected transition to hard-currency trade and world market prices with the Soviet Union and other Central European countries. In 1991 Poland will have to face a loss of at least $1.5 billion on the transition to trade with the Soviet Union based on the dollar and world market prices. Moreover, the Soviets announced that due to their domestic difficulties, they will substantially reduce their purchases in Poland.

The direct and indirect losses to Poland's economy caused by the Gulf conflict are very high. The amount to be lost due to Iraq's invasion of Kuwait has been estimated by the Polish Central Planning Board at $2.5 billion.

It is the coincidence of the new rise in the price of oil and the transition to hard-currency settlements with the Soviets and formerly socialist countries that causes real problems in Central European capitals. The inflationary effect of the inevitable transition will be dramatic irrespective of whether or not crude oil prices slide back to a precrisis level. Both crises create supply bottlenecks, and they both inflate local prices. They present the most serious external challenge to the fragile democracies and the promarket economic transition in Central Europe.

Despite broad social and political pressure and criticism of restrictive macroeconomic policies that led to a substantial drop in real per capita incomes, deep recession, and high unemployment, it is the Gulf conflict and the new terms of trade with the Soviets and other formerly socialist countries that forced the government to strengthen its restrictive character. At the beginning of October 1990, the National Bank of Poland raised the discount rate from 34 percent to 43 percent, and on October 10, 1990, it raised it further, to 54 percent. These restrictive monetary measures were aimed at suppressing inflationary tendencies, which reappeared in September–October. Moreover, they were intended to help build up international currency reserves to cushion the external shock resulting from the Gulf crisis and the new terms of trade with formerly socialist countries. Higher international reserves are needed to maintain a credible monetary policy and credit worthiness and to help finance an eventual Brady Plan type of operation.

The higher-than-expected economic and social cost of the stabilization program and slower progress in adjustment resulted in growing social tensions and pressure to accelerate the process of real, positive adjustment. This, coupled with highly unfavorable external developments, resulted in a heated political debate on the role of the state (the government, the president, parliament, political parties, etc.) and on ways and means of attaining political and economic objectives. L. Wałęsa's failure to force T. Mazowiecki's government to relax macroeconomic restrictive policies, accelerate systemic reforms, and start a more active industrial policy resulted in opening the debate on the presidency and the decision by W. Jaruzelski, acting president, to step down and open the road to new democratic elections. It became evident from the presidential campaign that no matter who wins, it is necessary to strengthen the role of the state in the adjustment process. A macroeconomic policy without adequate systemic reforms and policies supporting the rational reallocation of resources seems to be incompatible with the character of the transformation from a state to a market economy. Systemic reform and a structural industrial policy should be looked upon not as a danger to stability but as a means to moving from a forced stability accompanied by a recession to a financially sound growth oriented adjustment. Such a policy would help to increase credit worthiness and attract direct foreign capital investments.

Conclusions

For the transition of a society to democracy and a market orientation to be successful, this transition must be accompanied by a broad internationalization, an opening to the world. Formerly socialist countries must make every effort to move through the transition stage not only in the systemic area but also in a real one to join the family of democratic and developed market economies.

It must be stressed that systemic reforms in political and economic systems have to precede structural transformations leading to regaining international competitiveness. Only when Poland and other Eastern European countries regain their international competitive capacity can one say that they have accomplished their strategic objective and left a critical area.

Sound finances, systemic transformation, and a structural policy are the necessary elements of an open and growth-oriented adjustment strategy.

An economy that is competitive is one that is constantly adjusting to the changing economic environment (domestic and international) in which it operates and that has the ability to secure long-term positive factorial terms of trade. In other words, a competitive and open economy is not necessarily an economy with a balanced current account but rather a growth-oriented economy that participates in the international division of labor and gains from it.

Increased domestic savings should be used at least partly for the growth of domestic investments. The interest burden of Poland's foreign debt relative to GDP reached 6 percent in 1990, i.e., 15 percent of government expenditures. Thanks to the rescheduling accord signed in February 1990 with the Paris Club, actual interest payments are insignificant, but the debt keeps growing at an accelerating rate.

In 1991 and thereafter, privatization of state-owned enterprises could finance the development of small and medium sized private enterprises and help to relax the monetary policy necessary to stimulate investments and structural adjustment. However, the foreign-debt overhang is a direct threat to democratic and market-oriented transformations taking place in Poland. If Poland is to service the debt by using the proceeds from selling out state-owned enterprises, there will be little room for economic growth and social and political stabilization. Therefore, substantial debt relief for commercial and official debts is indispensable to give adjustment efforts in Poland a chance to succeed in building a competitive economy.

Part 2

From Constraint to Choice

TRANSFORMATION OF SOCIAL ORDER AND LEGITIMIZATION OF INEQUALITIES

Włodzimierz Wesołowski
Edmund Wnuk-Lipiński

In 1989 Poland entered a postcommunist period, the main aspects of which were the reemergence of Solidarity on the public scene, the gradual decay of the Communist party, the formation of a noncommunist government, and the introduction of market rules in a hitherto planned, state-owned, and state-administered economy.

In systemic terms, these changes indicate the beginning of the transition from totalitarianism to democracy and a market-oriented, capitalist economy.

These changes affect the social structure of Polish society and its pattern of inequalities. The shape of the social structure (and the inequality pattern) is secondary vis-à-vis the nature of social order, and particularly, the nature of market relations. The decline of the monocentric order, which was implemented in Poland after World War II, has also introduced new principles of structuring and offered a new normative basis for legitimation of inequalities.

Historical Background

Major transformations of social structure, which took place in the late forties and early fifties, were officially seen as the implementation of measures aimed at narrowing the differences between classes formed under postfeudal, early capitalism.

Prewar Poland had a traditional social structure, typical of that in all East European countries. It was composed of the gentry, bourgeoisie, middle class, peasantry, and working class. Thus, eliminating some segments of that structure, narrowing the economic and cultural gap between others, and first and foremost, creating a new structure was seen as a desired goal, aimed – in the long run – at creating a "modern," "socialist," and "just" social order.

The predominant mood was that land reform and the elimination of the gentry class was an act of "historical justice" for the peasantry. By contrast, the nationalization of industry was legitimized by the expectation that the exploitation of the working class would end. The communist authorities adopted deliberate measures to diminish economic and cultural differences among those segments of the class structure that were left intact but were conceived as material for further transformations.

The "old" social structure was very often described as obsolete, unfit for the demands of a modern economy, and unjustified in the light of communist ideology. The new type of structure foreseen for the coming and feasible stage of an industrialized socialist society was a version of meritocratic stratification. Such was the vision of many socialist theorists, including Karl Marx.

According to the socialist version of meritocracy, there should be an unequal distribution of income under socialism, because the differentiation of work performance remained; some people are more skilled and productive than others. Leaving aside a detailed interpretation of this approach, we may say that it acknowledges an income stratification. Underlying the cause of that stratification was a division of labor as manifested in various occupations with different degrees of "complexity" and skills (hence, education as well). There was an implicit assumption that this pattern of inequalities would be accepted by the population as "fair" and "just."

At the very outset of our analysis, however, we must say that this model did not materialize. Although in general terms of correlations between occupational groups and, say, average income or level of cultural participation, it was easy to discern its presence (particularly in the sixties and early seventies), a closer analysis showed a deep differentiation within each occupational stratum. Moreover, there were occupational groups with relatively few skills that earned a great deal more than those more skilled than they. Sociological studies revealed that in the seventies the level of education had gradually been losing its influence on the level of income. Branches of industry exerted much greater influence on the level of income than any other factor. Besides, there were other forces at work, not only the theoretical principle of socialist meritocracy, which led to an unclear wage structure that could be questioned even on the ground of official ideology. All this led to a growing dissatisfaction among the people, with the exception perhaps of coal miners, who enjoyed specially privileged salaries and various fringe benefits.

It is, of course, doubtful whether a close approximation of a "meritoc-ratic" model of remuneration for work is ever achievable, since departures from that model, which constantly undermine its operational significance, are common. Let us consider a few examples to make the picture more clear.

One such example was the economic pressure of the labor market: a constant demand for coal miners caused equally constant increases in their wages to make this kind of work more attractive.

However, the most damaging factor for the execution of the meritocratic principle was political. The consistent construction of the totalitarian state was responsible for many "deviations" in the stratification process. (Totali-tarianism is understood here as the rule of an uncontrolled elite, supported by a mass political party, and executed by bureaucratic institutions that pervade public life.) This peculiar social order introduced a new dimension into the social structure, namely, political affiliation.

In essence it represented a way of remunerating people for their work: partly for their occupational performance and partly for party activity. There was a steady increase in the number of bureaucratic positions at various levels, which could be achieved through the political acceptance of the Communist party. In time these positions developed into a separate stratum of middle-rank bureaucrats with relatively modest incomes but with power over ordinary citizens, broader access to scarce goods, and – above all – control of access to these goods. The stratum, known under the name "nomenklatura," intermingled with the political elite (which depended on its direct political support) and experienced a constant numerical growth. Such was the trend over the last four decades, during which corruption grew.

The power dimension pervaded the whole system of inequalities, modified the operation of other stratifying factors, and became more and more socially apparent. In consequence, there was a major shift in the social perception of stratification. For more and more people, stratification and the system of inequalities were above all a politically based social arrangement, and as such they were rejected as unjust and illegitimate. The nationwide strikes in 1980–81 which gave birth to the Solidarity movement may be seen as a threshold in popular thinking. Since then this kind of perception became widespread. The imposition of martial law in December 1981 gave rise to a new, dichotomous vision: communist power on the one hand, and that of society on the other.

The dramatic events of 1989, the resurrection of Solidarity, the victory of the opposition, and the dismantling of the totalitarian regime represent a new threshold. The economic, political, and societal orders enter the stage of profound, systemic transformation. This means that the new model of stratification has already started its formative process. Private property is now a powerful force of stratification, as are meritocratic principles. Democratic trends are reducing the role of political factors. Polish society is now undergoing profound changes in its social structure, but the outcome is not yet clear. One may expect that there will be a reemergence and numerical growth of a middle class, the formation of the stratum of managers and the stratum of professional politicians, etc.

Structural Inequalities and Their Evaluations

Polish society is a highly unstable and intricate mixture of institutions, groups, principles of action, and social norms of everyday striving. One can hardly call it a "societal system." Hence, it is difficult to describe the structured inequalities of such a society, its system of stratification or class structure, or its perception by people in terms of value judgment. It seems to us that, at best, some people are able to express their moral judgments of present inequalities in a very fragmented way (voicing, for example, their condemnation of the former nomenklatura's attempts to take over some portion of the national wealth in order to play the role of the new capitalist). People are unable to evaluate the system of inequalities comprising all elements of the social structure, because they are unable to imagine such an all-encompassing reality. For where there is no consistent social order, there cannot be a common value judgment about a system of inequalities.

In the last four decades of the communist experiment, few features of Polish society completely vanished, and even fewer were firmly established by the new social order. The social structure was not an exception from this general tendency. This is why the present social structure is a precarious mixture of coexisting elements of various "models" of class structure and of inequalities. In fact, we can distinguish precommunist, communist, and postcommunist elements of structural inequalities. Some of them are legitimized by one segment of society, others by another segment.

Precommunist patterns do not necessarily refer to the kinds of inequalities that are disappearing. In the sphere of precommunist patterns of inequalities, one finds not only the types of inequalities that fade away in a monocentric order but also those that have a universal nature and appear in all known social systems today. The latter are simply the types of inequalities that had existed in Polish society before it was reorganized along principles of the monocentric order.

Precommunist elements of the social structure included the "peasantry" (individual farmers) and, to a lesser degree, the working class. Small communities, of which these classes are composed, either in villages or in factories, display increasing understanding of group interests and a certain class-based cultural heritage. Emerging political parties and trade unions, as well as market mechanisms, will likely stimulate this process. Another example of a more universal pattern of inequalities is the division between rich and poor. Income inequalities were present before the institution of the communist order, during its reign, and they will persist in the postcommunist period. The universal character of this kind of inequality perhaps explains why it is so often a part of common perceptions of the social structure (Janicka, 1987): it is socially the most visible.

Because communist patterns of inequalities are unique, the question arises whether they are a by-product, as it were, of the functioning of the monocentric order, or whether they are a necessary condition for its stability.

An example of an inequality unique to communism might be the mechanism of the so-called nomenklatura, which penetrates more strongly in mechanisms of promotion, the higher and more strategic the positions involved. Many sociological studies have shown that Communist party members had higher incomes on average than the rest of the Polish population, even when factors such as education, sex, or managerial position were kept constant (Wnuk-Lipiński, 1989).

Another example is the inequality in the civil status of citizens. In the monocentric system, only supporters of the Communist party had the right to express their opinions and to defend their political and economic interests, etc. Supporters of alternative economic and political interests and of an alternative system of values had fewer (if any) basic civil liberties (Koralewicz and Wnuk-Lipiński, 1987).

Postcommunist inequalities are likely to return at least in part to the precommunist inequalities, for the main determinants in both cases are market mechanisms and property rights in economic relations. But there are new types of inequalities that are unique to the postcommunist period (at least in Poland). Along with the restoration of the market economy, there is the inevitable privatization of the means of production formerly controlled by the power structures. There are many examples of transfers of former political and administrative control over the means of production into legal property rights. Many members of the nomenklatura are now using their former political and administrative influence to gain privileged positions in the process of restoring a market economy. This fact has prompted popular criticism.

Inequalities in the Standard of Living

The material well-being of an individual or a group is the most important aspect of both market and nonmarket inequalities. There are two research orientations that address this dimension of inequalities. One of them is focused on the measurement of absolute deprivation, while the other deals with relative deprivation (Zwicky, 1984). Put simply, absolute deprivation is the study of the accumulation of various objectively measurable manifestations of material wants based on certain normatively established thresholds of poverty and the categorization of persons (or households) characterized by these accumulated wants (Beskid, 1987).

In the eighties, the dynamics of absolute deprivation in incomes was considerable (see Table 1).

Table 1

Poverty and Wealth Measured by the Level of Income per Capita According to Socio-Occupational Group (in percent) for 1982 and 1988.

Socio-occupational groups	Year	Income	
		low[1]	high[2]
Professionals	1982	0.6	21.6
	1988	10.7	27.7
Intermediate nonmanual	1982	4.3	8.5
	1988	15.1	18.7
Skilled workers	1982	9.0	8.1
	1988	23.5	10.1
Unskilled workers	1982	9.6	6.3
	1988	31.7	2.9
Private farmers	1982	12.8	15.3
	1988	40.2	11.7
Owners outside agriculture	1982	1.6	31.1
	1988	10.1	30.4

1. low income = less than 50 percent of an average income per capita in a household;
2. high income = more than 150 percent of an average income per capita in a household;
Source: E. Wnuk-Lipiński, 1989.

The data show that with regard to absolute deprivation, there are clear inequalities among various socio-occupational groups. However, the most important conclusion that we can draw from this comparison is that in the decade of the eighties, those in the lowest income group increased. This process embraced all categories of society, though to a different degree. The strongest signs of this tendency appeared among peasants and unskilled workers. The least affected were the professionals, intermediate nonmanuals (which consist mostly of the administrative apparatus), and private owners outside agriculture.

Relative Deprivation and Legitimation of Inequalities

If we look at social inequalities from the perspective of social legitimation, however, the measurement of absolute deprivation is not sufficient. For the main source of legitimation of certain patterns of inequalities is the distribution in various social categories of the feeling that the norms of social justice have not been violated (Moore, 1978).

Every pattern of inequalities can be socially legitimized under one set of conditions, and this social legitimation may be withdrawn under another set of conditions. In the eyes of society, a legitimized pattern of inequalities is "just," because at its base lies some principle or set of principles that are accepted not only by those whom this principle favors, but by those whom it does not. A nonlegitimized pattern of inequalities in the social perception is an "unjust" system, for the principle on which such a system grows is not accepted socially, at least by those who find themselves in a deprived situation on account of this system.

One can assume that the sources of deprivation are those social inequalities that have not acquired social legitimation. Crucial to the appearance of the feeling of deprivation, however, is the existence of certain socially accepted principles that constitute axiological criteria for the evaluation of the perceived patterns of inequality and one's place in them.

It seems that one can distinguish among at least four kinds of normative orders to which legitimation for certain patterns of inequalities can be referred: egalitarian, meritocratic, functional, and cultural. Egalitarian principles as a rule delegitimize social inequalities; other principles have high legitimizing potential, but under specific circumstances that potentially can be negated. We venture to argue that the negation occurred in Poland in relation to two principles: meritocratic and functional.

Norms of the egalitarian type appeal to the principle of equality of conditions ("an equal share to everybody"). Norms of this type are very often accepted by three categories of people. First, by those who would be relatively worse off if other principles were applied (e.g., meritocratic ones), and second, those who believe in the desirability of an alternative order. To the second category belong those persons who believe in the equality of conditions as a desirable and feasible state of affairs. Third, this principle is also often used by those who feel that they have little influence over the course of events, and in this context, appealing to the principle of egalitarianism might be treated as an emanation of what M. Marody called "learned helplessness" (Marody, 1987). This type of a purely existential basis for questioning inequalities exists in all three stages of Polish society: precommunist, communist, and postcommunist. The problem, however, remains of how often it is combined with other ways of delegitimating social inequalities.

It seems that in modern times, authoritarian political systems tend to use egalitarian phraseology in undermining the power of traditional influential classes and in mobilizing support for a new political order. Modern totalitarian ideology appeals for economic justice and tends to blame the "rich" for the misfortunes of the poor. Totalitarian rulers themselves, however, place much value on equality, which they officially condemn but which they use instrumentally as a device to uphold their revolutionary image. The population, half-indoctrinated and disillusioned, has developed very unstable convictions about what kind and span of inequality it favors and what kind and span it disfavors.

This instability, coupled with the augmenting condemnation of the communist regime as a sociopolitical system, contributes to the growing neutralization of the equality principle in people's thinking about social systems.

A series of empirical studies conducted in Poland indicate that egalitarian principles were especially prevalent in the fifties and sixties and, paradoxically it might seem, in 1980. One can observe a consistent decline of support for egalitarian ideology in Poland at the beginning of the eighties (Kolarska, 1986, p. 619), but in 1988 there were signs that the downward tendency had been halted (Kolarska, 1989). The psychological instability discovered in research may prompt us to hypothesize that the egalitarian norm may be used by some kind of populist movement in the future and can be merged with a rightist political orientation.

Norms of the meritocratic type refer to the principle of equal chances in filling occupational positions and receiving the remuneration commensurate with competence and responsibility attached to the given occupation. Norms of this type serve to legitimize inequalities that are the result of the unequal input of individuals and the rewards obtained proportional to them (Parkin, 1971, p. 13). On the basis of principles of this type, unequal social positions and the privileges connected with them are not questioned, but the rules of attaining these positions and the criteria for remuneration are.

In modern societies there is a strong tendency to accept meritocratic principles and see occupational stratification based on the level of education and level of expertise as legitimate. The corollary must be the open system of selection to occupational positions as well as the relative openness of the educational system.

As we have already mentioned, the system that was called "real socialism" claimed to satisfy meritocratic criteria to a high degree. However, in reality this was not the case. It is true that compared to the traditional type of class structure in Poland, the quasi-meritocratic inequalities that had been emerging together with modern industry and commerce resembled meritocracy. However, distortions were so great that people stopped accepting it. Actually, two main distortions ruined the possibility of meritocratic stratification. The first one was related to the selection process, and the second one to the remuneration system. In the selection process to higher positions of competence and responsibility (e.g., managerial posts), political affiliations counted more than expertise. As one study on career patterns to higher governmental positions and commanding posts in industry showed, these positions were given to members of the Communist party and not to the most able people. In the selection process, the level of formal education was taken into account only formally, and it was easy for a member of the party to complete the required level of education once he was already assigned to a higher post (Wasilewski, 1989).

The distortion of the remuneration system occurred through a systematic decline of the correlation between the level of education and the level of pay. The relative decline of salaries for professionals such as medical doctors, teachers, and architects was in proportion to the relative increase in the wages of unskilled workers. This was the trend throughout the sixties and seventies. At the end of the seventies and in the eighties, many unskilled and uneducated people received higher wages than educated people.

This trend was coupled with another one: very high remunerations for people at political and managerial posts, and additional "rewards" in the form of bonuses, such as bonuses for rare commodities unavailable for ordinary people.

The first distortion, i.e., the growing dissociation between educational levels and pay, caused a negative approach to education among young people. In consequence, the aspirations to mobility have been declining rapidly. The second distortion undermined the meritocratic perception of would-be reality. Allocation of higher posts exclusively to party members eliminated almost completely the belief that something resembling meritocracy may emerge in a system of "real socialism." This contributed to the overall lack of legitimacy of the system as such (Wesołowski and Mach, 1986).

Norms of a functional nature legitimize inequality patterns that directly contribute to the perceived "good functioning" and stabilization of a particular social order. So, here the matter would concern norms that appeal to the principle: "To each according to his/her functional usefulness to the system." The degree of social acceptance of these norms is closely linked to the acceptance of more basic principles legitimizing the system as a whole and not only to a specific pattern of inequalities. If the system itself is short of social legitimation, then consequently all inequalities that could be legitimized in terms of functional necessity must be short of social legitimation, too.

The acceptance of the functional criterion by the Polish population never occurred, although it was claimed to have been by the authorities. Some possibilities for such an acceptance emerged in the early seventies, but they were short-lived.

In that period, Poland received substantial Western credits for the modernization and reconstruction of industry. Along with new, modern investments, the role of engineers and technicians become more important and more socially visible. The representatives of this stratum were presented in official propaganda as harbingers of civilization's progress. The common perception of their role coincided with the official one. Engineers had been rewarded for their role by relatively high salaries. During this period, there was a chance for engineers to be universally perceived as a functionally important stratum with a historic mission of introducing a new type of rationality and better conditions in everybody's life.

However, the attempt to make engineers heroes of modernity and the party nomenklatura agents of modernization as well as Gierek's whole project of building a modernized economy failed, and consequently, the specific claim of making the emerging inequalities socially acceptable expired, too.

In the eighties, the universal disapproval of the system as such was linked with the rejection of any functional justification of inequalities existing within the system. Moreover, the domination of the ruled-ruling cleavage in the popular thinking was coupled with the perception of material privileges enjoyed by the ruling stratum. This caused an open condemnation of the existing division, which was perceived as combining two main dimensions: power and material privileges. In short, in the decade of the eighties, when the collapse of the communist social order became increasingly apparent, the chances for legitimation of inequalities on the basis of functional principles disappeared. Both at the beginning of the eighties and in 1988, the power structures were perceived as the main source of privileges that were not socially acceptable. In 1988 (Wnuk-Lipiński, 1989), this source of undeserved privileges was often indicated in the answers to open questions of our questionnaire. Nearly half of all respondents (or 73 percent of the designations among those who perceived the existence of undeserved privileges in Polish society) indicated power as a source of undeserved privileges. The market mechanism, or more precisely, its degenerated version in the centrally planned economy, was perceived much more rarely as a factor generating undeserved privileges. In sum, 12 percent of all respondents (18 percent of the respondents perceiving the existence of undeserved privileges) made some use of this criterion, naming the privileged groups as "speculators" or "owners in the private sector."

Of what do the nonlegitimized privileges consist? Most often they were defined by the respondents as informal or official (but beyond public control) access to goods, chiefly material (30 percent of the respondents); more rarely they mentioned high income or earnings (15 percent), a comfortable, easy life (10 percent), being exempt from law (3 percent), an easy job (2 percent), and other things.

In the social consciousness, access to such goods was most often associated with position in the power structure. Such a mechanism of distribution, however, did not have social consent.

To generalize our argument, we may say that two factors in combination contributed to the delegitimation of inequalities in the functional perspective; first, the perceived inefficiency of the global system and its high "irrationality," and second, the visibly undeserved privileges of those who ran the system.

There are, finally, norms of a cultural nature that may legitimize certain inequalities. Some patterns of inequalities are not regarded as "unjust" because they have always existed or are a part of some culturally important legacy. Questioning these norms (more precisely, the inequalities these norms legitimize) is at the same time at least a partial questioning of tradition. An example of inequalities that until recently have been legitimized by tradition are inequalities between men and women, which today are being ever more often questioned on the basis of egalitarian principles.

Both meritocratic and functional principles of the justification of social inequalities failed to produce legitimation of those inequalities in Poland where the role of cultural principles seems to operate differently. It is evident to every visitor of Poland that the cultural elite enjoys high prestige. Many sociological studies have documented a high evaluation of education, in spite of the steady deterioration of practical significance for the standard of living and occupational promotion.

Cultural stratification – composed of layers of education, stratified participation in cultural life, and an unequal role in developing and disseminating cultural goods – seems to carry a positive evaluation. It is not only widely approved but also believed to be somehow needed by the society. We do not know exactly whether it is linked to something that may be called functional usefulness of the cultural elite for society as a whole or rather to the historical context of Poland, and especially the particular role of the cultural elite in preserving Polish culture during the more than one hundred years in which the Polish state ceased to exist.

Whatever the causes, one can show that stratification by education differentiates participation in cultural life. Moreover, differences of this kind are not perceived – in popular thinking – as illegitimate, nor are they expected to be delegitimized by future societal development.

The popular high evaluation of the intelligentsia's professions is revealed in a series of studies on occupational prestige. All occupations that require university degrees received very high ranking. Moreover, the same professions were ranked lower on the income scale, which reflected the deteriorating economic status of professors, doctors, lawyers, and teachers.

Summary

It is easy to show that the normative foundations of the legitimation of inequalities discussed here are mutually contradictory. This leads to a situation in which the pattern of inequalities legitimized by one of these principles may be questioned on the basis of a principle in contradiction with it.

On the other hand, in a totalitarian social order, this contradiction may easily be used by a central power to neutralize the social and political strength of the segments of society that pose a threat to the absolute power of the center.

This is why the problem of legitimation of social inequalities seems to be significant not only for analytical purposes but also because of very practical reasons. Those who are able to add significant meaning to one kind of inequality and take away the meaning of other kinds of inequalities are in possession of a very powerful tool, for having such a tool provides the opportunity to neutralize one conflict and stimulate another. This tool is particularly dangerous in a totalitarian social order, where public opinion and democratic procedures of conflict resolution have ceased to function.

One can state in summary that while in a market economy the main factor generating specific inequalities is property and position in the market, in a communist social order such a main factor is power and position in the power structure. The main reason for this is that in the part of the economy that has been nationalized (which determines the shape of the entire economy), market laws have been suspended on behalf of the mechanism of central planning and centralized distribution of resources and goods (together with rare – in the market sense – consumer goods). This pattern of social inequalities was legitimized by the principle "To each according to his/her functional usefulness to the system." However, this kind of legitimation failed to be efficient, for the system itself suffered from continuous shortage of legitimation.

Particular factors generating inequalities always operate in a concrete social order. For example, certain factors will have a stronger influence in a market economy, while others, in a centrally planned one, and still others will have equal influence in both systems. So if one puts forward the thesis that in a market economy the factor generating specific inequalities seems to be property, and in a communist social order, power, this does not mean that these are the only factors establishing social inequalities.

We know that division of labor, which exists in both types of social orders, generates differentiations and inequalities. We also know that power plays a considerable role in generating inequalities in market systems, just as private ownership does in a centrally planned economy (especially in its Polish version). Finally, relative knowledge and occupational skills are another factor generating inequalities in both systems.

Hence, one can state that patterns of inequalities are the result of at least the following factors: the form of ownership of the means of production, the system of wielding power, the degree of complication of the division of labor, and the level of acquired knowledge and occupational qualifications.

The experience of the past decades supports the thesis that inequalities of an extrasystemic nature gained wider social legitimation than inequalities specific to the communist social order, which brought, as an effect an accumulation of conflict in the eighties along the social system/deprived social strata axis.

References

Beskid, L., Bokor, A., and Kolosi, T. 1987. "Deprivation of Living Conditions in Poland and Hungary," *Sisyphus. Sociological Studies*, vol 4.

Janicka, K. 1987. "Różnice społeczne w potocznym odczuciu." In *Nierówności i upośledzenia w świadomości społecznej*, E. Wnuk-Lipiński, ed. Warszawa: IFiS PAN.

Kolarska-Bobińska, L. 1986. "Pożądany ład społeczny i polityczny w gospodarce." In *Polacy'84. Dynamika konfliktu i konsensusu*. Warszawa: Uniwersytet Warszawski.

Kolarska-Bobińska, L. 1989. "Poczucie niesprawiedliwości, konfliktu i preferowany ład w gospodarce." In *Polacy'88. Dynamika konfliktu a szanse reform*. Warszawa: Uniwersytet Warszawski.

Koralewicz, J., and E. Wnuk-Lipiński. 1987. "Wizje społeczeństwa, zróżnicowań, nierówności w świadomości zbiorowej." *Studia Socjologiczne*, no. 1.

Marody, M. 1987. "Antynomie podświadomości zbiorowej." In *VII Ogólnopolski Zjazd Socjologiczny. Materiały*, E. Wnuk-Lipiński, ed. Warszawa: Polskie Towarzystwo Socjologiczne.

Moore, B., Jr. 1978. *Injustice: The Social Bases of Obedience and Revolt*. London: The Macmillan Press Ltd.

Narojek, W. 1985. "Pluralizm polityczny i planowanie, albo: Perspektywy pluralizmu w upaństwowionym społeczeństwie." Warszawa: IFiS PAN (mimeographed).

Parkin, F. 1971. *Class Inequality and Political Order*. New York and Washington.

Wasilewski, J. 1990. *Procesy rekrutacji do regionalnej elity władzy*. Wrocław: Ossolineum.

Wesołowski, W., and B. Mach. 1986. "Unfulfilled Systemic Functions of Social Mobility; Part I and Part II." In *International Sociology*, vol. 1, no. 1, and vol. 1, no. 2.

Wnuk-Lipiński, E. 1989. "Nierówności, deprywacje i przywileje jako podłoże konfliktu społecznego." In *Polacy'88. Dynamika konfliktu a szanse reform*. Warszawa: Uniwersytet Warszawski.

Zwicky, H. 1984. "Income Inequality and Violent Conflict." Sociological Institute, University of Zurich (mimeographed).

SOCIETY AND BUREAUCRACY

Adam Sarapata

Many individuals, groups, and entire societies depend on bureaucracy in varying degrees in various countries. The influence of bureaucracy is determined by the sphere that is subject to its control and the degree to which it is society oriented, i.e., how far its activity is in agreement with efficiency and the needs and interests of society.

In Poland, the relationship between society and bureaucracy consists mainly in the fact that the sphere controlled by bureaucracy is immense, it is often called totalitarian, while its orientation toward society is small and its efficiency is poor.

Here the term *bureaucracy* is used in both senses. In the first, it means the state and economic administration and the ways in which it controls society. In the second, it means pathological phenomena in public administration and the dysfunctions of that organization. The term is used both as a description and as a critical public appraisal.

One has to stress the essentially unique status and role of public administration in socialist countries. In a socialist country, where everything, or at least a great deal, is nationalized or socialized in some form or other, where the private ownership of means of production and other means is marginal or insignificant, and where at the same time there are notorious shortages of commodities, from bread and butter to apartments, public administration as the principal executor of the plans and programs of the Communist party performs above all a regulatory function – it is the omnipotent distributor of shortages. The relationship between citizens and public administration are focused not around technical matters, such as buying postage stamps and paying telephone bills or taxes, but around such vital issues as the supply of food, clothing, and industrial goods; the state of the infrastructure in one's place of residence; the state of buildings and public transportation; the granting by the administrative authorities of permits to buy an apartment, build a house, buy a plot of land, and have a telephone installed (waiting time over ten years); the allotment of an apartment (waiting time in most towns over fifteen years); permits to buy a few bags of cement, several square meters of plate sheet metal or some planks; the purchase of a tractor, in the case of farmers; admission to a hospital; admission of one's child to a kindergarten; and the granting of a passport for travel abroad.

The rise of Solidarity in August 1980, the most vigorous rebellion against the socialist order in the entire bloc, was thwarted by the imposition of martial law. The subsequent years started a period in Poland in which the authorities tried to demonstrate that the socialist system was reformable and that society accepted it in its real form. This essay tries to answer the question of how the social rebellion against the communist system accumulated in Poland. It is in particular concerned with the development of the relationship between society and the bureaucracy and with the formation of the attitudes of Polish society toward the omnipotence of socialist administration in 1983–88, that is, the period of the last endeavor by the Polish United Workers' Party to save communism in Poland.

The Condition of Polish Society

The condition of a given society can be analyzed and described, roughly speaking, in two ways: by using objective measures, such as the indicators of the state of public health and health care, consumption, housing conditions, the educational system, social integration, organizational activeness, political activeness, etc.; and by using subjective measures, which include questions about how people feel, about their satisfaction and happiness, the levels of optimism, alienation, and anomie. The results of studies pertaining to the subjective sphere, to how Polish people felt in the years 1983–87, shall be presented in a close connection with the functioning state administration and industrial management.

Let us start with the results of a representative study conducted in 1983.[1]

Over two-thirds of the respondents in 1983 stated that their incomes dwindled significantly in the last five years, and one-half, that their financial situation deteriorated considerably. Seventy-three percent of the respondents stated that their troubles and worries were greater than five years before this (1979–84). The answers pertaining to health were alarming: 44 percent of the respondents mentioned the deterioration of their health among the major changes in recent years. This opinion should not be treated as a manifestation of a proneness to complain, which is ascribed to the Poles by some

[1] A. Sarapata, *Portrety biurokracji*. Warszawa, 1990.

researchers, but as information about objective facts, such as malnutrition, the highly unsatisfactory condition of health care, shortages of medicines, hospital beds, medical instruments, even disposable syringes, bedpans, not to mention the shortage of physicians, nurses, and other medical personnel, the continuing degradation of the natural environment, a sense of insecurity, fatigue, nervous strain, and lack of better prospects for the future.

The results of national representative studies carried out in 1984 (a sample of 2,184 people) tell us that Polish society commonly experienced many privations of various kinds. The answers to the categorized question containing a list of eighteen sources of dissatisfaction took the form of macro-conditions: the situation abroad, 19 percent, and the situation at home, 92 percent. These were followed by insufficient incomes (85 percent), unsatisfactory financial status (82 percent), living conditions causing nervous strain (72 percent), an insufficient sense of security about the future (68 percent), lack of leisure time (61 percent), lack of entertainment (57 percent), bad housing conditions (47 percent), a monotonous life, lack of sufficient education, poor health (40 percent), lack of happiness of one's children (28 percent), lack of a happy family life (20 percent).[2]

The list of eighteen elements presented to the respondents for appraisal in 1984 does not cover all major objects of desire. For instance, it includes neither such an important element as the condition of the natural environment and such values as freedom and justice.

The lack of rest, also commonly reported by the respondents, has an exceptionally dramatic meaning. It points to the accumulation of hardships in everyday life, queues in shops, shortages of goods, hard working conditions, helplessness, powerlessness, and lack of better prospects for the future.

The high percentage of the respondents who mentioned in their desires "more time for entertainment" is mainly due not to any exorbitant expectations but to the permanent monotony of life. The respondents are exhibiting a reaction to the fact that when it comes to entertainment, the country looks like a desert, towns and villages are gloomy, and social bonds have been weakened or broken, among other things as a result of the rush for money and the high cost of social events. This is also a reaction to fatigue, the lack of a sense in life, and helplessness.

The lack of satisfactory housing conditions is felt by 47 percent of the respondents, that is, by almost every second respondent. The lack of a good, interesting job, by 37 percent, which means every third respondent. Nearly one-half of the respondents (44 percent), mentioned the lack of a better education, and 40 percent, the lack of good health. The lack of a happy family life is felt by every fifth respondent. Family life and friends are the only more common sources of satisfaction with life.

[2] *Ibid.*

The results presented prove that Poles commonly experience deprivation in the basic spheres of life.

As has been said, the question about the sources of dissatisfaction did not refer to other spheres that are essential or even very essential for the respondents. Many contemporary Poles are embittered about time irretrievably lost and the wasted years of their life. Many of them do not see opportunities for themselves. Very many live with the sense of having been wronged.

Most respondents who declared a lack of some factor conducive to satisfaction with life hoped that it would disappear in the future, except for insufficient education and poor health. But relatively high percentages of them showed a pessimistic view and did not treat the present privations as temporary. Out of all respondents, 26 percent did not expect a better situation at home, 32 percent did not expect a better financial situation, and 16 percent did not expect better housing conditions.

The general assessment of the degree of one's satisfaction with life is linked in varying degrees with its various sources. The strongest influence is exerted by financial status, income, the family, nervous strain, a monotonous life, a sense of security about the future, one's job, and housing conditions, in that order.

More than one-half of the respondents were critical of the food supply and the standard of services. The supply of industrial goods was negatively assessed by 83 percent of the respondents. About one-third of the respondents negatively assessed the standards of health care, the infrastructure, including the number of day-care centers and kindergartens and local and intertown public transportation. Critical opinions were voiced on housing construction (70 percent of the respondents), repairs of houses (81 percent), supplies of building materials (89 percent). Critical opinions on the supply of agricultural machines were voiced by 87 percent of farmers, on the supply of various industrial articles (scythes, pitchforks, chains), by 61 percent, and on the supply of fodder, by 55 percent. The opinion that "the inhabitants find it difficult to work jointly for the good of their locality" was declared by 64 percent of the respondents, that "people in our locality are concerned solely about their own interest," by 65 percent, and that "in our locality there are few genuine social workers," by 67 percent. Readiness to change their place of residence was declared by 29 percent of the respondents.

The results reveal a considerable disintegration of numerous local communities, vast privatization of individual goals, and lack of commitment to and identification with one's place of residence. When combined with the commonly criticized infrastructure, the unfavorable description of one's place of residence yields a strongly negative picture.

On the eleven-level scale of happiness/satisfaction with life (from 10 – the best life, to 0 – the worst life), the mean for the totality of the respondents is

4.78 and thus below the mean level of the scale. The levels from 0 to 3 were mentioned by 21 percent of the respondents, from 4 to 6, by 55 percent, from 7 to 10, by 14 percent. The mean values of satisfaction with life for the five selected socio-occupational categories are as follows:

farmers – 5.00;
unskilled workers – 4.40;
skilled workers – 4.67;
white-collar workers without higher education – 4.88; and
white-collar workers with higher education – 4.96.

Skilled and unskilled workers are below the mean for the totality of the respondents, while white-collar workers and farmers are above that mean.

The average evaluations of personal life, happiness, the situation in the locality in which one lives, and the situation of the country for all respondents were, on the eleven-level scale, as follows:

personal life – 4.8;
situation in the locality – 5.1;
situation of the country – 3.7.

This means that the best evaluation, but only at the average level, was that of the locality in which one lives, that of the situation of the respondent was slightly worse, and that of the situation in the country was the worst.

The assessment of one's own situation is largely linked to that of the situation in the country. Thus, it is not the case as it has been suggested by people in power and some researchers, that the state is growing poorer and poorer but people are getting rich or that the crisis strikes the state but does not affect the inhabitants. The lot of many people is believed to be closely linked to the fortunes of the country. But in the opinion of the respondents, the situation in the country deteriorated between 1979 and 1984 much more than their own situations:

Average Assessment of the Situation

	In the Country	Of the Respondents
1979	5.8	5.3
1984	3.7	4.8

Who Is To Be Blamed?

The above results, which point to a dramatic degradation of the country and the fall of the already not good situation of individual respondents, lead one to pose the following questions: What have been the causes of that degradation? What accounts for the fact that the country is in crisis? What hampers the development of the country? What accounts for the fact that the situation of the majority of the inhabitants continues to be difficult, and that of many just tragic? What share in their own lot and the misfortune of their country is ascribed by people to themselves and what to external factors? What are the attitudes of a society in crisis toward those who are primarily blamed for that crisis?

By addressing these questions to the respondents and asking them to select the four principal obstacles from the list of thirteen, we obtained the social evaluation of the importance of the selected factors. They enable us to become acquainted with public opinion on "the guilt of society," "the guilt of the authorities," and the role of some single causes.

The division of the factors under consideration into two groups is, of course, conventional and imprecise, and it may prove misleading. On the one hand, some of society's feelings of guilt must to a large extent be ascribed to the authorities, e.g., a lack of discipline and respect for the authorities, passivity and indifference on the part of the inhabitants, and laziness are logical and inevitable consequences of the fact that society is disorganized, reified (by public administration), and frustrated. On the other hand, society is to a large extent the coauthor of the sins of public administration, because people working in that administration are members of that society, whose attitudes/approval, criticism, courage, etc., influence the style of the functioning of public administration.

Out of the thirteen obstacles listed in the questionnaire, six can be ascribed to society: laziness, production of substandard goods, alcoholism, lack of discipline and respect for the authorities, passivity and indifference, and lack of courage in voicing one's own opinions. Seven of them can be ascribed to public administration and the authorities: faulty organization of the economy, lack of the influence of ordinary people on the decisions of the authorities, cronyism and cliques, corruption and bribery, abuse of power, restricted field of activity for enterprising, creative, and ingenious people, and thwarting of criticism. But in this connection the influence of society on public administration and vice versa must be borne in mind. Each of the obstacles signifies grave social dysfunctions that disturb the normal life of society, dysfunctions that are extremely difficult to eliminate. These obstacles, which can ultimately be reduced to demotivation and demoralization, offer a pertinent characteristic of Polish society and Polish bureaucracy.

Unskilled workers and farmers universally mentioned social vices: alcoholism, laziness, production of substandard goods, and lack of discipline and respect for the authorities. Two-thirds of them mentioned the first two vices as the most important obstacles and much less frequently referred to the vices of the authorities: faulty organization of the economy, lack of the influence of ordinary people on the decisions of the authorities, thwarting of criticism, and the restricted field of activity for enterprising, creative, and ingenious people. Skilled workers and white-collar workers held society and the authorities responsible in more or less the same degree, using the classification of obstacles adopted here. White-collar workers with higher education much more often saw those obstacles in the faulty organization of the economy (61 percent), a lack of the influence of ordinary people on the decisions of the authorities, (42 percent) and the restriction of the field of activity for enterprising, creative, and ingenious people (33 percent). They thus mainly blamed the authorities, ascribing a much lesser role to alcoholism and laziness.

The Lazy Poles

The stereotype spread by managers, people in power, and a large part of society states that Poles do not value work, that they are to blame for their attitudes toward work.

The studies show that work occupies a high place in the Poles' hierarchy of values, that not so much they as the conditions of work caused by the economic system, wrong decisions of political and administrative decision makers, and managers who lack proper intellectual, organizational, and moral qualifications are responsible for their improper attitude toward work.

It is not the intention here to deny that a considerable number of Poles are oriented toward moonlighting and leisure and that many treat work lightly, but these attitudes are not dominant. Over the course of forty years, the authorities did much to deprive people of their enterprise, willingness to work, ingenuity, and above all sense of responsibility. They caused people to unlearn how to work well. Of course, not all the blame is to be placed upon the system and the authorities; many people see in them the justification of their laziness, alcoholism, etc. Society at large is also to blame.

The studies carried out in 1984 confirmed many findings of previous research. For instance, it was found that the attitude of the overwhelming majority of employees toward work was in general favorable, but it happened to be unfavorable in specific cases because of the conditions under which they had to work. In other words, existing conditions deprive employees of their willingness to work. Working conditions and the general situation account for considerable conflicts of interest between employees and managers, the "góra" (people in power). There is insufficient concern for proper remuneration – one could hardly speak about systems of motivation – for the physical conditions of work, and for the social condition of the employees. All this intensifies employees' demands concerning the level of salaries and wages and their just distribution. The disregard of the employees' aspirations to participate in management and the faulty work of the managers intensify the demands of the employees in the sphere of their supervision of the functioning of their respective workplaces. The incompetence and arrogance of the bosses cause the employees to lack confidence in them and cause them justly to demand that their dignity be respected. The decisions and exhortations of the bosses are not supported by the employees, who witness everyday waste and mismanagement and find it impossible to make sensible and constructive use of their forces and skills.

Unfavorable working conditions, including the faulty system of motivation and bad living conditions in general, account for the universal decrease of the importance attached to work and of the willingness to work. The opinion that "in our country little can be achieved by work" is fully accepted by 29 percent of the respondents and partly accepted by 41 percent. The statement that "I am losing faith in the possibility that one can achieve something by work" is fully accepted by 23 percent of the respondents and partly accepted by 36 percent. Between 1978–79 and 1984, a decrease of the willingness to work was declared by 24 percent of skilled workers, 27 percent of unskilled workers, 25 percent of farmers, 30 percent of white-collar workers without higher education, and 42 percent of white-collar workers with higher education. One-half of the respondents voiced the opinion that it did not pay to save money for one's old age.

Personal aspirations of many respondents, amounting to a large part of society, find no opportunities for being materialized. In workplaces, only one-fourth of employees may openly tell managers what they think; the rest are either afraid of speaking (about 27 percent) or declare that the situation varies from case to case. Less than every fifth employee is of the opinion that criticizing the management is effective; the rest claim that criticism is ineffective (some 30 percent) or of little effect.

The satisfaction of the most important occupational aspirations – a quiet and secure future (owing to one's work), large incomes, respect, full use of one's abilities and qualifications, full use of one's ingenuity and enterprise – does not even reach the satisfactory level or exceeds it only slightly. Deprivations in the sphere of elementary needs are glaring, especially in the case of unskilled workers.

The strategic role of socialized enterprises in socialist society makes it imperative to inspect more closely the industrial bureaucracy and above all the top managers of enterprises.

Industrial Bureaucracy

The comments that follow, largely applicable to the state administration as well, seem useful both for a fuller picture of the conditioning of the attitudes of the inhabitants and employees toward bureaucracy and for a sketchy description of the second constituent of the relationship between society and the bureaucracy. We shall be interested mainly in factors that influence the quality and efficiency of the principal heroes of the industrial bureaucracy.

Let us list the most important and specific factors influencing the behavior of socialist top managers.

Individual Professionalism of Top Managers

Strictly speaking, the occupation of manager is not a profession in Poland, and that in spite of a number of symptoms of professionalization.

The slow process of the professionalization of the occupation of manager – largely due to a strong resistance that is ideological and political in nature (the fear of the emergence of a managerial elite) – means very serious losses for society: managers learned their role on the errors they committed, many of them did not, and still do not, have sufficient qualifications, the lack of a professional organization of managers was detrimental to society, etc. The slow process of professionalization at the same time forced managers to engage in individual professionalization, which was toilsome, ineffective, and costly from the public point of view.

Nomenklatura

Appointments to managerial posts were mainly based on political criteria, with the political authorities – the so-called nomenklatura – having a decisive say. Very many specified posts were to be filled by people who had the explicit approval of the Polish United Workers Party – until recently, virtually all top managers were members of that party.

The characteristic feature of the nomenklatura was not confined to the fact that appointments to managerial posts, and many other posts as well, depended on the candidate's possession of a party card and not on the market, but also on the specific characteristics of the party card bearer. In the opinion both of society at large, which disapproved of the mechanism of selection to leading posts, and of party circles as well, the candidate had to be passive, mediocre, but faithful (in the Polish original, these three adjectives rhyme: bierny, mierny, ale wierny). The first two features meant that the man in question would not cause trouble for the administrative and political authorities, while the third assured his full subordination, obedience, and functioning in the role of a passive executor of instructions.

The Centralist Model of the Socialist Economy

The centralist model of the economy was marked by the concentration of almost all economic decisions at the central level, by a detailed plan fixed at the top, and by the injunctions passed downward. Under this model, the manager of a given enterprise was greatly restricted by the regulations and directives he received, he had a very small margin of freedom in choosing products to be turned out, in choosing subcontractors, in choosing customers, in fixing prices, in fixing the remuneration of the employees, and in selecting his personnel. His main duties consisted in carrying out 100 percent of the imposed production plan, in urging the personnel to work, in enforcing labor discipline, in enforcing the obedience of the personnel (the de facto prohibition to strike), in thwarting conflicts and dissatisfaction, in bringing up the personnel in the socialist spirit, in concern for socialist property, in a socialist attitude toward work, in socialist labor competition, etc.

Next to the systemic factors listed above, which essentially hinder effective management and the efficient functioning of enterprises, other factors deserve mentioning as well. In studies covering a group of top managers, national representative samples show that more than one-half of the respondents referred to many factors that cause considerable or great problems in the functioning of enterprises or in running them. Those factors mentioned by more than one-half of the respondents include: irregular supplies of raw materials and semi-finished products (84 percent), lack of tools and instruments, excessive numbers of directives, contradictory directives and instructions, and unrealistic directives.

The managers covered by the studies universally complained about the instability of the principles according to which the enterprise was to function and by which the manager was to be guided, about the obscurity and inaccessibility of the evaluations of the manager's work, about which he was not informed, and about the faultiness of the criteria of such evaluations. These three factors signally affected the manager's work, including its ethical aspect.

Ideology

The primacy of politics (ideology) over economics – the total lack of any economic calculations, the apotheosis of socialist property combined with discrimination against the private ownership of means of production, degenerated egalitarianism, recourse to ideological motives, appeals for good work, merely nominal labor competition and other forms of activating employees, combined with economic exploitation and short-sighted thinking – freed managers of responsibility. The signal consequences of the primacy of ideology over economics were the ruin of the national economy, the destruction of natural resources, pollution of the natural environment over vast areas of the country, low living standards of the population, low health standards, and unfavorable phenomena in the sphere of human attitudes.

The Style of Management

The studies showed that many socialist managers adopted the autocratic style of management, which favors the alienation of employees. Contrary to declarations, the democratization of the working milieu encountered serious obstacles in many enterprises, and the self-management of the personnel was frequently merely ornamental.

The considerably limited influence of the manager on the fortunes of his enterprise, his personnel, and his own career, numerous obstacles and inconveniences encountered by him in his work, lack of confidence on the part of his superiors, a sense of loneliness, a sense of insecurity in his job – all this affected his efficiency and his ethics.

A sense of insecurity, fear of losing one's job – much greater and much more common than among managers in most countries in which analogous studies have been carried out – and the strong barriers to self-realization are very important factors determining the manager's style of work and his often unfavorable attitude toward the political and economic bureaucracy.

Bureaucracy

Society's opinion of the functioning of the state administration is highly critical. This criticism is manifested both in answers to general questions pertaining to the functioning of its offices – very good, 3 percent of the respondents; rather good, 45 percent; rather bad, 35 percent; bad, 17 percent – and in those to questions about specific problems. Answers in the negative were given to the following questions: Do people in the local office work quickly and efficiently? (62 percent); Are they patient and well disposed in contacts with the inhabitants? (52 percent); Do they treat all the applicants in the same way? (53 percent). Furthermore, 71 percent of the respondents were of the opinion that there were too many clerks in their local office.

The respondents were equally critical of those in power in the local state administration office. The opinion that the authorities in the local offices were helpless in local matters was voiced by more than one-half of the respondents; that they were not interested in what the inhabitants think and need, by 44 percent; that they did not take the opinion of the inhabitants into account, by 50 percent; that they did not keep their promises, by 59 percent; that they were concerned mainly about their own interests and advantages, by 47 percent; that they enjoyed privileges about which an average inhabitant could only dream, by three-fourth of the respondents; that they hampered the enterprise of the inhabitants and did not support individual farmers, by one-fourth; that they did not support craftsmen and small producers, by one-third; and that they persecuted and made life difficult for those who have opinions different from the official ones, by more than one-fourth.

Opinions on the state administration and attitudes toward it, e.g., respect for and confidence in clerks and officials, are based, as follows from an analysis of collected empirical data, on the satisfaction of the needs of the inhabitants and on satisfactory standards of service. As is self-evident, the higher the satisfaction and the level of service, the more favorable the opinions. The prestige of, and confidence in, the office head and his subordinates is based on the quality of their work. The data show that a good office is one in which people work efficiently and quickly, are patient and kind to the applicants, and care about the opinions of the inhabitants. Those officials and clerks enjoy the respect and confidence of the inhabitants who are interested in the problems of the latter and take their opinions into consideration.

Let it be added at this point that in the report "Poles '84," we find that to the open question about the causes of the crisis in Poland, 81 percent of the respondents mentioned "dishonesty and theft committed by those in power."

The classification of the respondents by their attitudes toward local authorities shows that the latter are universally negatively assessed. Decidedly favorable attitudes were represented by 2 percent of the respondents; moderately favorable ones, by 28 percent; moderately unfavorable ones, by 43 percent; and decidedly unfavorable ones, by 27 percent.

The low level of the satisfaction of the inhabitants' expectations accounts for the fact that very many people have little respect for and no confidence in the occupational and moral qualifications of the employees in public administration. This applies to rank-and-file clerks and chief officers in the provinces, cabinet ministers, and deputies to the Diet. Confidence in cabinet ministers was voiced by 50 percent of the respondents, who answered "yes" and "rather yes"; lack of confidence, by 30 percent, answering "no" and "rather no"; the remaining 20 percent stated that "it is hard to say." Further, 31 percent of the respondents who were employees of socialized factories had no confidence in top managers.

The attitudes of respect for and confidence in cabinet ministers and chief officers in the provinces are strongly linked to the respondents' assessment of the situation at home. An unfavorable assessment of that situation is accompanied by the universal lack of confidence in those whom society holds primarily responsible for the existing state of affairs.

A lack of confidence by a great part of society in officers and their staffs accounts, among other things, for the fact that the institution of appeals and complaints is regarded as ineffective at best. To the question whether it is worthwhile making appeals and lodging complaints if one has been wronged or finds it difficult to have one's case settled, 17 percent of the respondents replied that it was not worthwhile because this would yield no result, and 12 percent that it was not worthwhile because one might get oneself into trouble; 53 percent of the replies were in the affirmative, and 18 percent of the replies were "it is hard to say."

A consciousness of the country's being in a deep crisis, a sense of helplessness, and a lack of confidence in public administration accounted for the fact that 45 percent of the respondents did not hope that their own situation would improve in the next five years, i.e., in 1984–88, while the overwhelming majority of them were pessimistic about the future of the country. The average on the eleven-level scale of prosperity, from 0 to 10, was 5.8 in 1979, 3.7 in 1984, and 4.8 in 1988.

The concern of the state for the interests of ordinary people was believed to be small or very small by 45 percent of the respondents and as considerable or great by only 8 percent. The most critical opinions came from unskilled workers, 57 percent of whom stated that the concern of the state for their interests was small or very small.

The general dissatisfaction with the situation of the country and of individual respondents; the general belief that public administration is not interested in the needs and problems of the inhabitants; lack of confidence in office heads, chief officers of the provinces, cabinet ministers, judges, deputies to the Diet, and councilors; low respect for secretaries of local PUWP organizations; the belief that appeals and complaints are ineffective; the belief that inhabitants have no influence on the election of good councilors, and the fictitious character of such elections; essential discrepancies between the real participation of inhabitants and employees in the management of their localities and workplaces, respectively, and the demands for influence in these matters; lack of belief in the sense of work and in privations for the benefit of the country; a high level of alienation and a low level of optimism – all these are indicators of the specific political culture in Poland in the 1980s, which is marked, among other things, by a disregard for the separation of executive, legislative, and judicial powers recommended by Montesquieu, the prohibition to form associations, a low level of democratism, and few opportunities for voicing opinions.

The respondents were of the opinion that inhabitants and councilors have least to say in matters concerning their respective localities; they claimed that it is the higher administrative authorities and the local PUWP organizations that have the greatest say; and they demanded that the inhabitants and the councilors have the greatest influence on what is taking place in their places of residence.

The Last Years (1985–1988)

Three things can be forecast from the diagnosis based on studies conducted in 1983–84. First, that the bureaucracy's attitude toward society will continue, and that the bureaucracy will continue to use the methods and tricks by which it tries to subordinate society. Second, that society will refuse to tolerate the existing situation and the authorities responsible for it. And, third, that the bureaucracy will in various ways defend its position.

The first of these is manifest in, among other things, the perseverance of arbitrariness, the elimination of criticism and social supervision, the appearance of reforms, and empty phraseology.

The proclamation of new slogans, announcements of programs intended to improve the situation in the country, and programs (1985–88) that are vague and general in character and are being implemented slowly do not result in any marked change in society's attitude toward the authorities, nor do they encourage people to work more and support the authorities. The Poles, on many occasions disappointed by promises that were not kept, by flawed programs, erroneous philosophies, irresponsible decisions of political and economic authorities, and also by the burden of debts they had not themselves incurred but that will for many years to come fetter their progress to prosperity, are afraid of further disappointments and are mistrustful of the authorities. The overwhelming majority of Polish people neither expect the authorities to act as a tender father nor do they accord them that role. They have lost their confidence in the authorities, hence they do not want gestures, gifts, acts of good will, or subsidies. They demand democratization, socialization of the state, and supervision over the government and all other authorities.

Systematic surveys of the Center for the Study of Social Opinion in 1985–88 revealed the decline of public confidence in sociopolitical institutions and organizations, confidence measured by answers to questions about whether the activities of these institutions and organizations serve society well and are in accordance with its interests and about the deteriorating image of key political figures representing the system and the authorities.

The percentage of those who voiced the opinion that the activities of the government, and the cabinet in particular, are in agreement with public interest dropped from 71 in December 1985 to 34 in August 1988; the analogous figures were 76 and 45 for the Council of State, 79 and 61 for the Diet, and 53 and 27 for the PUWP. The percentage of those respondents who think that the activities of these institutions are at variance with public interest rose as follows during two and a half years: from 31 to 51 in the case of the government and the cabinet, from 9 to 30 for the Council of State, from 9 to 23 for the Diet, and from 28 to 52 for the PUWP. In August 1988, a far greater number of people said that it is the PUWP that is to serve society and not vice versa. The decline of confidence in the government reflected the growing disapproval of its activities and the criticism of its incompetence, megalomania, and arrogance. People more and more often emphasized a lack of good prospects for both individuals and the country as a whole; people more and more often spoke about being tired of the stupidity of the authorities. More and more people, especially young people, spoke about emigrating and in fact have left the country.

People in power claim that the dissatisfaction of society is due to the fact that the Polish state assumed too many duties, which it is unable to discharge. The justification that the state did so in order to be "good" to its citizens seems grotesque. The bureaucracy took possession of vast areas of public life in order to dominate them, to control them, and to derive profits from them. It deprived people of their property, of the opportunity for free action, enterprise, responsibility, and the right to make choices. And it is not inclined to abandon its position of authority, its privileged and undeserved financial benefits, the exceptionally profitable function of the monopolistic distributors of rare goods: commodities, raw materials, permits, etc. This is tellingly confirmed in recent year, when society is with difficulty winning back small margins of freedom of action. We still, and perhaps even more often, observe barriers to the development of agriculture, crafts, and free enterprise and witness pathological fiscalism. Various regulations still deprive enterprises of freedom of action.

As has been said earlier, the opinions of the public were very critical of the state administration in the years 1985–88. Such dramatic facts as economic regression, the collapse of the market of consumer goods, the unsatisfactory pace of democratization, growing ecological dangers, deteriorating health standards, deteriorating standards in the educational system, the decreasing value of work, the excessive repressions provided for in penal law, and emigration agitate people and, in their opinion, prove the incompetence, sluggishness, and arrogance of the authorities. Public criticism does not influence the bureaucracy, which is not inclined to modify its functioning. It engages in purely illusory operations, slowly and very reluctantly abandons small privileges, and defends its jobs and positions.

The second tendency, the inclination of those in power to defend themselves and their positions, manifests itself in the slogan calling for accepting the past. Such formulations as "We shall not waste our time on settling accounts" and "There is no point in recalling the past, the past is the past" do not appeal to present-day Poles. They antagonize the public, as did the declarations of the government spokesmen, and do not help to increase public confidence in the authorities.

The demand that personnel at the ministerial level be exchanged is vehemently opposed by representatives of the highest level of the state administration, who claim that it is not admissible to replace the personnel. To substantiate their position, which is a highly illustrative contribution to the self-portrait of the highest level of state administration, they adduce the following arguments: (1) the picturesque argument of "crossing the river": "We are in the process of carrying out a great reform: one does not change horses in the middle of the river"; (2) the argument of regrouping: "This is not the time for personal experiments: regrouping is intended to make the optimum use of the skills and abilities of the entire leading team without changing it" – A.S. In current opinion, this argument is termed a "merry-go-round" and is provided with the comment: shuffling the cards does not increase the number of aces in the pack; (3) the argument that administrative personnel are not interested in their armchairs, implying that they are very good but would defend their positions; (4) the argument of a new philosophy: the personnel are good and should not be touched: the only correct solution consists in a change of philosophy; and (5) the argument of a change of mentality: the personnel are excellent, only their mentality must be changed.

Other methods of leaving important and urgent problems unsolved are disregarded here. One such long-standing one is to declare that appropriate regulations are being prepared or have been issued. The authorities often say that "nothing can be decreed, everything is a process, we have to wait." This method, also used in making decisions, while often correct, frequently means delaying things and postponing the decision *ad calendars graecas* until the authorities gain in strength and then the matter can be dropped or other important problems emerge.

The last months of 1988 have brought a new tide of critical opinions formulated by eminent experts, strikes, and something extraordinary in socialist countries: the vote of no confidence in the cabinet, which was followed by the equally extraordinary resignation of the latter.

Society, Bureaucracy, and Social Change

In the Second World War, Poland was the first country to fall victim to aggression. Her losses in terms of human life and national property were the heaviest. Her fight was the longest; she was always a dedicated member of the victorious alliance, and her soldiers fought in all the war's theaters. In 1945, Poland was theoretically one of the victors. Theory, however, had little in common with practice. In practice, as her allies looked on in tacit consent, there was imposed on Poland an alien system of government, without precedent in Polish tradition and unaccepted by the nation, together with an alien economy, an alien law, and an alien philosophy of social relations. The legal Polish government, recognized by the nation and leading the struggle of all Poles throughout the war, was condemned, and those who remained faithful to it were subjected to the most ruthless persecution. Many were murdered, thousands vanished somewhere in Russia's east and north. Similar repression befell soldiers of the underground army fighting the Nazis. It is only now that we are discovering their bones in unmarked graves scattered in forests.

These atrocities were followed by the persecution of all those who dared think independently. All the solemn pledges that were made in Yalta about free elections in Poland were broken.

This was the second great national catastrophe following the one of 1939. When other nations were joyously celebrating victory, Poland was again sinking into mourning.

These excerpts from the speech delivered by Lech Wałęsa, leader of Solidarity, to the American Congress[3] are quoted here for several reasons.

First, because they are (as is the whole speech) an excellent synthesis of the experience and feelings of Polish society. Their content, pertaining mainly to political issues, which are disregarded in this essay, essentially completes the list of the major causes of a lack of confidence by the overwhelming majority of society in the Polish United Workers' Party and the state administration.

Second, the facts mentioned in the speech pertain to problems that will dominate the lives of Poles in the coming months and years. The thoughts and attention of many Poles will be focused neither on the present nor on the future nor on the national economy but on the tragic facts of the recent past. The Polish officers murdered at Katyń, the graves of Poles murdered by the security service that have already been found and those that are still undiscovered, the Home Army persecuted by Bierut and his successors, deportations to the Soviet Union, expulsions from the motherland, various wrongs, and the distorted history of their country can only now be discussed freely.

The abolition of the totalitarian authority will make the overwhelming majority of society enthusiastic and proud and will also be a source of lasting confidence in the new government, for all the mistakes which that government, consisting largely of nonprofessionals, will probably commit.

Society, after its experience with the socialist economic and political system, will turn toward the market and privatization and against state monopolies. Until now it had its enterprise fettered, but now it will vigorously engage in economic and other activity. Yet in this process, it will face serious obstacles due both to the economic crisis and to the obsolete regulations and provisions of the law, which effectively hamper development. To this we have to add the acquired incompetence of the state administration and the intensive maneuvers of the opponents of the new system, mainly the former numerous nomenklatura occupying high posts in public administration and in management.

In the current discussion on how the present situation could be improved and on the methods of overcoming the crisis, a special role is assigned to the state administration. Most consider bureaucracy antipathetic to social change. They argue that bureaucrats are security minded, prefer to obey rules faithfully, and do not like to take risks. Some people are of the opinion that the state administration must be made much more efficient, others think that

[3] Address to a joint session of the U.S. Congress on November 15, 1989.

it is not reformable and that the ways of improving the situation of the country are to be sought elsewhere.

In his report "From Diagnoses to Action,"[4] Professor Jan Szczepański, after formulating sharp critical remarks addressed to the state administration, stated:

> I think that remaking the state administration, which has become bureaucratized, is an illusion. One can only restrict its prerogatives and reduce the number of those employed in it. Its prerogatives could be passed on to civic organizations, to self-governing institutions consisting of private persons, and to voluntary organizations of various kinds. State administration by nature does not know how and cannot release social forces. The only thing it can do is to supervise the enterprise and actions of the country's inhabitants and to adjust them to the provisions of the law. This is to say that it can become a factor that bridles social forces and restricts their use for overcoming the crisis.

The demands that the prerogatives of the state administration should be limited, that public supervision of the state administration itself among other things should be increased, that ordinary people should be politically emancipated, that the role of the local government and employee self-management should be radically increased, and that the formation and development of social organizations should be promoted find full confirmation in the data gathered. These demands are the principal suggestions of a practical character. Bureaucracy seems to be essential to social change and might be essential, but it has to be sufficiently developed, financed, and supervised by society.

Both society and the state and industrial administration will have to learn what they could not have learned under the socialist system and what is indispensable for overcoming the crisis and bringing about the desired social change: democracy, cooperation, responsibility, and honest work.

[4] J. Szczepański, "Od diagnoz do działania," *Rada Narodowa*, special issue of July 3, 1987, containing the report to the chairman of the Council of State on the third meeting of the Consultative Council.

ATTITUDES ON EVERYDAY LIFE IN THE EMERGING POSTSOCIALIST SOCIETY

Piotr Łukasiewicz
Andrzej Siciński

During over forty-five years of "real socialism," a particular syndrome of attitudes on daily life and popular thinking of Poles has formed. In the first phase of the current transition, the impact of this heritage was easily perceptible. On the other hand, since the middle of 1989 we have witnessed how the new institutions and rules of a political and economic life enhance the new attitudes and thinking at the everyday level. What are the practical consequences of a collision between the old habits of mind and heart and the requirements of the new order?

Poland is no longer a "socialist" country. But what it is and particularly what it will be is difficult to say. A capitalist country? – but with what type of capitalism? A mixture of socialist and capitalist mechanisms, institutions, and attitudes? – but could such a hybrid function effectively over the long term? Almost everybody currently accepts the idea that Poland urgently needs democracy and a market economy. But how should these concepts be understood?

We have formulated these questions with the aim of stressing the fact that we intend to discuss here attitudes and orientations of a society that lives and acts in a revolutionary (or, more strictly, "evolutional revolutionary") period, at a time when many remnants of old ideologies and convictions still exist, but also some new ways of thinking and feeling appear. In such a transitionary situation, any analysis of social expectations and aspirations, which sometimes lag behind but sometimes forego "objective" changes, must have a highly hypothetical character.[1]

Remnants of "Socialist" Attitudes

It is true that a large number of Poles benefited directly from the communist system, e.g., party activists, members of the security forces, part of the administration and managers of state owned industry, etc. However, from 1945 to 1989, the majority of Polish society has seen the system as imposed by foreign forces and as a threat to national identity and tradition. But this majority also had to live with this system for forty-five years and to look for various ways of adapting to it.

It should be explicitly stated that we are talking here about a *passive* resistance of the Polish population, a resistance aiming mainly at the preservation of national cultural identity. Only a very small minority (mainly from the intelligentsia) was involved during this time in an *active* resistance. Since the late 1970s, this resistance was clearly visible, e.g., during the first visit of Pope John Paul II in Poland in 1979, then again in 1980–81. When the two forms of resistance, active and passive, merged, what resulted was the emergence of the anticommunist labor union Solidarity, having nearly ten million members.

In such a situation, one might expect that Polish society, with its first opportunity to shake off the communist grip, would immediately reject all communist institutions and, first and foremost, the communist ideology and the communist way of thinking. Now, a year after the taking over of the government by Solidarity representatives, it is clear that such a conviction was an illusion. It is difficult for us to realize to what extent our habits and customs, our thinking and feeling, our imagination and aspirations, and our whole perception of the world is still distorted by the communist system and Weltanschauung.

Let us point out here some examples of this sort of "ballast."

First (but not necessarily most important), it is a popular conviction that an "*ideological unity*" of Polish society is both a fact and an important value. One of the most visible symbols of that unity is the Catholic religion and the Catholic church. Theoretically, most Polish people are for democracy, but democracy is understood as a full consensus in public life (the old Polish tradition of "liberum veto") rather than as an interplay and competition of

---

[1] Some elements of the sociological analysis of a "breakdown of the existing system" were discussed in A. Siciński, "Two Sociologies: Of Times of Stability and of Times of Crisis," *The Polish Sociological Bulletin*, 1981, no. 3–4: and in P. Łukasiewicz and A. Siciński, "Stabilization, Crisis, Normalization and Life styles," *Sisyphus. Sociological Studies*. Vol. 5 (Warsaw, 1989).

various groups, viewpoints, and ideas. The effects of such an attitude have been clearly visible recently. The majority of Polish society has not approved of recent disputes between two mainstreams, both pretending to represent the Solidarity movement and legacy. Moreover, people have not understood the differences between these orientations, not to mention that they have not been interested in the programs of numerous, but very small, parties. Also the young generation, which was not involved in the events of 1980–81, seems not to be interested in "battles among the combatants." That was one of the reasons for the success of a dark horse, Stan Tymiński, in the first round of the Polish presidential elections in November 1990.

Second, a primitive *egalitarianism*, often expressed by the saying "We all have the same stomachs," should be mentioned.

This conviction is closely related to the third, usually called a *"claiming attitude,"* i.e., the expectation and demand that a caring state is obliged to satisfy all the needs of its citizens.

Polish people would like to have immediately what is obviously impossible: an efficient market economy improving their standard of living on the one hand, and egalitarianism and "socialist" social security on the other. The government led by Tadeusz Mazowiecki was not able to perform such a miracle in fifteen months (since taking over in August 1989). Thus, the first noncommunist prime minister in the previously socialist countries was the main loser in the presidential elections.

The fourth issue is related to the particular role of the *workplace* (usually in a state-owned enterprise or in the administration). Home, on the one hand, and the workplace – but not the local community or association – on the other, are perceived as the most important centers of organization of daily life. However, this does not necessarily mean that the work process is of tremendous importance to the people; social contacts ("privatized" to the extreme) are important, as are facilities (privileges) connected with the job.[2]

The fifth attitude that should be mentioned here is a kind of *apathy* of Polish society, apathy that has become particularly strong since the imposition of martial law in Poland on December 13, 1981, i.e., since the great aspirations and energy of the society were blocked by force. Lack of hope and interest connected with the future combined with a concentration on present problems and difficulties are characteristic for the majority of the population. Older people often see some hope only in the distant future of their children;[3] younger people are often interested only in emigrating.

Finally, we would like to mention the feeling of generalized *mistrust* prevailing within large segments of Polish society – mistrust of the au-

---

[2] See A. Rychard, "Zdrowie w perspektywie instytucji," (Paper presented at the conference "Człowiek Środowisko Zdrowie," Jabłonna, Poland, November 1984).

[3] On temporal orientations of Poles, see E. Tarkowska, *Czas w życiu Polaków* (forthcoming).

thorities, of the elite of various kinds, and of the media. It has developed on a foundation of long-lasting frustration and false promises offered by the communist system (the results of the November 1990 presidential elections proved that this mistrust is deeply rooted).

We do not intend to estimate the range, in terms of statistics, of the above-mentioned attitudes and convictions. We simply think that they are significant in the life of present-day Poland and that they form a part of the "social personality" of the Poles. We also believe that they do not meet the requirements of a market economy and of a pluralistic, democratic order, which the Poles intend to build.

The communist period resulted not only in the appearance of some "socialist" attitudes but also in the disappearance of some traditional ones, or in their transformation.

Two problems seem to be particularly important here. First, there is a kind of "privatization" of people's orientations, which has had various manifestations. One of these is a tendency to restrain the scope of social bonds. Home and family orientation is still very vivid, and sometimes also bonds between friends; bonds connected with the "second economy" are often important as well. But rather exceptional are closer bonds on the basis of an association or on a political basis. In fact, contemporary Polish society is lacking any developed social "*mezzo-structures.*" Such structures (between an individual and family level on the one hand and a national level on the other) were strongly repressed by the communist regime. At the same time, because of the lack of a middle class, there was no natural basis for such structures. In any case, the development of a "civil society," one of the main conditions of a democratic system, still seems a difficult task.

Privatization is also visible in the realm of *morality*: people are expected to observe some moral rules in their everyday private contacts, in relation to private property, etc., but not so much in public life, the workplace, or in relation to public (state) property. For years and decades, public life was seen as a domain of "their," not of "our," activity, and state property was treated as nobody's property.

In fact the problem is more general: we may say not only that attitudes toward property are ambivalent but that general esteem for the law, for any rules in public life, is rather low. How can one build democracy having such orientations?

The second problem is a *decline in aspirations* – particularly educational and cultural aspirations – observed in the last decade. Such aspirations were traditionally developed and propagated by the Polish intelligentsia, but their popularity in other strata as well was often seen as a specific feature of Polish society. In the long term, the decline in aspirations may be harmful *from the point of view of the Polish national identity*.

At the present time, the attitudes and orientations of Polish society present a syncretic combination of elements having different genealogies and originating in different periods of Polish contemporary history. Sometimes these elements coexist "peacefully," without creating any cognitive dissonance, but sometimes they come into collision. It should be stressed, however, that there are some important differences of attitudes and orientations of different segments of the population.

First, there are differences between *generations* – a new phenomenon in postwar Poland, where, at least until the end of the 1970s, we observed a lack of any principal disagreement, not to mention a gap, between generations. Older generations stress the role of tradition, of traditional institutions (e.g., the home), of patriotic motivations, as well as the role of Gemeinschaft-type solidarity. Young people usually have much more individualistic orientations and are interested rather in their own opportunities and their own private aspirations (one of the effects of such attitudes is an interest in emigration to the United States or to Western Europe).

Another significant difference exists between the *political elites* and the "masses," amounting, in fact, to a "cultural gap." The majority of Polish society is interested mainly in its present, everyday problems. Political elites are no less interested in the present questions but quite often discuss and interpret them from the viewpoint of the past: of historical tradition and historical experiences. The masses are neither interested in political programs proposed by elites nor do they understand them clearly. On the other hand neither the political elites nor the broad public have any more or less clear visions of the future. A deficiency of long-term thinking is, we believe, a serious problem of contemporary Polish society. In this respect we do not have in mind plans or blueprints for the future but some general ideas concerning what is desirable and what is possible in this future.

The New Order and the Old Clichés

The historical formation of real socialism has generated a specific syndrome of perception and interpretation of the domestic social order. This syndrome manifested itself at the level of a common, colloquial discourse. It related to the rules on which the regime was established (in particular, persons, events, institutions, and symbols that were either politically significant or "permeated" with politics) and to conditions of daily life (the standard of living) that existed under this regime. This syndrome of, so to speak, popular public wisdom and the "folkspeak" of socialism were quite durable, to the extent that the specific sociopolitical identity of the postwar system was durable, because these phenomena resulted immediately from the very substance of this system – its inefficiency and the imposed restrictions.

Generally speaking, this "private" public opinion was expressing the generalized critical feelings and attitudes toward the surrounding sociopolitical reality. They sometimes took on a conventional form, as in popular sayings, jokes, rumors, and ritual complaints. The meanings and submeanings of these kinds of popular messages – which put together made up a specific folklore of the era of socialism – were widely comprehensible and used.

The ancien régime initially found itself in a crisis of creeping stagnation, and then it collapsed. Along with these processes, the "objective" conditions, which had constantly determined more or less the same attitudes toward the regime, should pass away. In particular, one may say that the division between "us" and "them" should vanish – in real terms, as political differentiations take another course, and in symbolical terms, as some former, stereotypical objects of social refutation ("the regime," "the Russkiis," "the partyiniks") melt away or loose their previous identity.

The popular political discourse also fulfilled some adjustment functions, giving relief to accumulating frustrations and negative emotions and making it possible to bear what was hardly bearable. In the face of political domination, the domination of propaganda, and the domination of hardships of daily life, which were so vexing under communism, they offered a possibility of symbolic compensation all the more so since the possibility of such an "easy resistance" was widely and constantly accessible.

It is hard to say to what extent this sort of consciousness may be continued in the newly emerging order in Poland. But we would like to point out here at least two examples of such a tendency.

In the above-mentioned popular folkloristic messages, carrying common convictions and images, the figure of the "enemy" was sketched very clearly. One may call him a "generalized red" or "generalized commie," who showed up under various embodiments (in political jokes, it was mostly the first secretary of the Communist Party; in rumors, it was members of the nomenklatura accused of corruption and taking advantage of privileges; in popular sayings, the "red" was held responsible for the miserable shape of the country: "Because here everything is upside down"). In all these cases, one can see an inclination to identify those who held responsibility for the unacceptable state of the country, and furthermore, to evade the feeling of one's own responsibility for this state.

After June 1989, the immediate responsibility for the country was taken over by the social and political forces accepted in "almost fully" democratic elections. Also, the meaning of the responsibility of all citizens for their country is being now restored. In this context, one should pay attention to the voices demanding a "final reckoning" with the communists and all the alleged remnants of the ancien régime, which were heard after the stabilization of Mazowiecki's government. Since much is still left to be desired in present-day Poland, people may easily return to the same convenient pattern of blaming a scapegoat, which makes it possible to evade a feeling of responsibility. Also, Mazowiecki's defeat in the presidential elections of November 1990 showed that his ruling camp had been considered as the new establishment that could be blamed for the desperate economic situation.

Our second example is similar. Just at the time when Mazowiecki's reforms were most intensified, one might hear from the "man in the street" in Poland that "Nothing has changed." We may find here an image of the world that is simplistic to the extreme and an authoritativeness that is so typical of common-sense judgments. Whatever the social basis for such a statement, it is worthwhile to consider its meaning. The formula is reminiscent of a sententious saying that had earlier summed up the Communist regime: "We were better off before the war." In psychological terms, the conviction that no serious changes had been undertaken seemed (or seem) to be justified: people who had looked for changes for such a long time wanted to "sense" them, to experience their effects. If this is not the case, the changes that are in progress but do not meet the people's high expectations are regarded as a withdrawal. Moreover, if the process of reform is extended in time, the frame of reference (and of comparison) moves forward as well: it is not an ancien régime any longer but, for instance, the situation from two months before. The slogan about acceleration, under which Lech Wałęsa ran for president, proved that it was not communism but the Mazowiecki's period that can be defined as the "ancien régime."

The opinion that "Nothing has changed" expresses a radical, general disapproval not so much of some single facts as of the *global* situation in the country. For the time being, when there are still good reasons for social dissatisfaction – although they are entirely different than previously – reaching out for the old clichés of common sense explanations of the world may turn out to be the easiest thing to do, since these explanations are tested as the means of expressing and discharging the mood of criticism. To use them automatically for defining a transformed reality may result in the popular ways of perceiving social issues and phenomena not being renovated; on the contrary, they will stick to traditional (in the negative sense of the term) schemes, to which the new reality will be adjusted "by force." As an example, we may point out the term "new nomenklatura," which the new authorities are sometimes called. Using such a term no doubt fulfills some critical functions, but its descriptive value is misleading. This example shows that the popular consciousness, having developed around the division between "them" and "us," looks in a sense for some new divisions around which it might develop anew.

As we have noted, some messages circulating in the nonformalized circuit of social communication made a kind of "folklore" of socialism. In many such cases, a traditional, plebeian culture, one permeated by mass society, although not rural, mixed with the political content. Both circuits overlapped: folk production, which was always rooted in the sphere of personal interactions, colloquial language, and popular categories of perceiving the world; and politically marked texts with a critical edge, which were pushed into such an underground circuit because of censorship rulings. The political jokes were a typical example of a mixture of the contents taken from both these currents: a satire of customs and obscene satire was combined with ridiculing official figures and propaganda manipulations; and rumors, in which a curiosity of the private life of "high society" was combined with political animosity against the ruling elite.

Which elements of this colorful popular discourse will survive? The production and circulation of the folkloristic texts is, in relative terms, a universal phenomenon. On the other hand, the habit of nonprofessional, private politicizing grew up on grounds that were inherent in a specific historical sociopolitical system and that have already faded away (or are fading away). According to our observations, far from being systematic, the circulation of strictly political jokes stopped along with the political transformation of 1986–89, and so has the circulation of the rumors that fulfilled a substitutive *informational* function, e.g., as an echo of foreign radio stations. However, one can hear some new rumors (their range is hard to estimate) related to representatives of the present authorities. It is hard to assess whether they are a sublimation, or rather, vulgarization, of critical attitudes based on political grounds being manifested through old, tried-and-true channels, despite the fact that new channels have been opened; or "folk news," by nature leveled at any establishment and providing a rationale for eternal man in the street mistrust toward the bigwigs. The presidential campaign of 1990 proved that some rumors relating to the candidates – their private lives, their well being, their biography and genealogy – were even more trusted than reliable media reports and played an important role in shaping candidates' images.

In a world of unfriendly institutions and unaccepted ideology, on which the stability of the communist regime was founded, these kinds of popular messages made it possible to preserve and manifest one's own identity, be it social or national. They did not undermine the regime directly, but in a way they helped to maintain the collective morale of the community living under this regime. In a sense, these were pathological phenomena, but since the life of society was not quite "normal," one may take them as a manifestation of psychosocial self-defense against the imposed restrictive system. Will they vanish now, when the life of society is striving for "normality," or will they become a dysfunctional factor of this process?

The inherited patterns of the popular perception of the social world and public life do not fit the rules of the "new thinking," which are (or should be) in favor of the construction of a new political, social, and economic order.

They previously helped us keep the unaccepted reality at a distance, but they have subsequently moved us into a sphere of some lack of responsibility for the reality per se (and for the words that define this reality). Patterns of this sort may also implicitly stimulate and justify a turning back from present-day reality.

We do not suppose that these habits may lead to any collective actions, which in turn might disturb the processes of transformation, but to some extent they may affect the atmosphere in which these processes will take place. They may affect the atmosphere of susceptibility or unsusceptibility to the arguments explaining the regularities and requirements of the transformation. Thus, they may become an element of the *culture of public life* and the culture of *thinking about public issues* in a society that is looking for its new identity. And the course and results of the presidential elections showed that in fact they did.

Emerging Attitudes

Until now, we have been discussing some psychosocial consequences of forty-five years of communism. But the period of its collapse, which started at the end of the 1970s, culminated in 1989, and is still continuing, also brought new attitudes and orientations. Some of these can, in our opinion, be functional in terms of building a new political and economic order in Poland, but some are obviously dysfunctional.

First we would like to mention a kind of shift of Polish thinking from "romanticism" to "positivism."[4] This shift was manifested in the actions of Solidarity in 1980–81, which sometimes have been called a "self-restricting revolution." Also, the years following the strangling of Solidarity (December 13, 1981) were marked by "positivistic" attitudes (e.g., efforts aimed at building a "civil society," developing underground publishing houses, etc.) rather than by "romantic" manifestations. Finally, the Roundtable (talks between the opposition and party-government representatives in the spring of 1989) and – despite individual strikes and protests – the patience with which people endured their dramatic economic situation in 1989–90 were also to a certain extent the result of pragmatic ("positivistic") thinking.

The next, quite new, phenomenon is the fact that people more often than previously decide to take at least part of their troubles into *their own hands*. One of the most interesting examples was the rapid development of an

---

[4] The problem of "romantic" and "positivist" orientations in Polish thinking is discussed in G. Houle, P. Łukasiewicz, and A. Siciński, "*Social and National Consciousness Transformations in Dependent Societies,*" in R. Breton, G. Houle, G. Caldwell, E. Mokrzycki, and E. Wnuk-Lipiński, eds., *National Survival in Dependent Societies. Social Change in Canada and Poland.* Ottawa: Carleton University Press, 1990.

ecological movement in the 1980s, indicating that people started to understand that not so much the paternalistic state as they themselves had to have
an influence on their everyday lives – that they had to make use of existing
legal possibilities to try to create new possibilities for shaping their lives.
However, the local elections in May 1990 – for the first time after World War
II the free elections of a real self-government – showed that these new
orientations have not yet spread, as evidenced by a very low turnout for these
elections.

The new resourcefulness has some negative manifestations as well. For
instance, in the sphere of the economy, people still resort to smuggling, illegal
business, and other short-term undertakings rather than to long-term and
legal investments. This is obviously also a consequence of experiences
connected with real socialism.

When we mentioned the new but dysfunctional attitudes, we had in mind,
above all, two additional problems. One is a tendency toward strong
nationalistic feelings and attitudes. It is still not widespread, but it spoils the
image of Polish society. Such a tendency can disturb the process of building
a democratic system.

Another negative, and much more visible, process is a *brutalization* of
everyday life, brutalization of behavior and of language. Again, it spoils the
self-image of the nation, which not only for years and decades but for
centuries aspired to the role of a bearer of high culture. It also makes it more
difficult to build a "civil society."

Closing Remarks: From Abnormality to Normality

The transition that Poland is presently undergoing is described in many
ways, depending on how one defines the starting and the terminal point of
this process. Thus, it is said that Poland is on the road from socialism to
capitalism, from a closed to an open society, from totalitarianism to
democracy.

But it seems that the most common desire of the man in the street is that
Poland move from a state of abnormality to *normality*. Over the course of the
last forty-five years or so, Poles have had a strong feeling that the system in
and with which they have had to live was not quite normal. In the first place,
the communist system failed in meeting the people's needs – not extravagant
ones, but those that are considered reasonable and fair in twentieth-century
Europe. Poles had a sense of belonging to a certain civilizational circle, and
accordingly they demanded that some elementary goods and services be
provided by the socioeconomic system. Geosocial, so to speak, comparisons
(i.e., not only with the richest countries but also with those that had in the
past started from approximately the same level of development) and

sociochronological comparisons (i.e., with the standards of "our times") proved that we "could do better." Hence the popular image of the existing socioeconomic system was that of a "spoiler system":[5] the one in which everything turns to evil.

At the macrosocial level, serious discontinuities and incongruencies were easily visible in Poland between the values and beliefs, including religious, of society and official ideology; between the perceived reality and its promoted propagandistic presentation; and between private life and public life. We may also mention the repetitive economic crises and political upheavals tracing a cyclical, and not linear, development. One of the principal rules on which the former "abnormal" order was founded was the *rule of substitution.* The natural mechanisms and relationships of "normal" society were either suppressed or imitated by makeshift institutions. These deformations were partially compensated by some spontaneous processes in those spheres of life that stayed out of state control, e.g., the moonlighting economy or informal social communication.

At the microsocial level, evidence of "abnormality" was even more striking: in the roles of a customer, a petitioner, and an employee, each citizen had all too many opportunities to witness the violation not only of economic and technical rationality but simply of the requirements of elementary common sense.[6]

It seems, therefore, that the vision of normality – epitomized by the one golden rule: "Things are what they are and what they should be" and nothing else – may have a strong appeal among Poles. But the hope for a normal society also holds some menace. Simply speaking, the concept of normality may be taken over (and abused) by various political and ideological camps that will aim at identifying their specific programs and ideological concepts with the concept of "normal" society, established on a seemingly "natural" order.

The popular image of a normal society is defined in negative terms: it is a society that is free of all the mischievous shortcomings of the communist regime. But paradoxically we may also lose some social values on the way to "normality" or some elements of social relationships that were, so to speak, "positive" in terms of sociological considerations. Let us mention just three examples.

1. A by-product of attempts to escape "the system" strengthened some social spaces, which functioned as asylums of sorts or parallel social institutions. Home was one of these – home understood in the first place as a set of social roles and values as well as the bonds linking a family-and-friend group.

---

[5] J.T. Gross, *Revolution from Abroad.* Princeton: Princeton University Press, 1988.

[6] On the concept of a feeling of "normality," see P. Łukasiewicz, "Daily Life, the Social System and the Feeling of Normality," *The Polish Sociological Bulletin,* 1987, no. 2.

2. The second example concerns the ethos of the intelligentsia, which is fading away presently with a decreasing interest in university-level education and a decline of the prestige of intellectuals. One could say that we are witnessing a rotation of ethoses: some are vanishing (the ethos of the nomenklatura and the ethos of political opposition), while others emerge (the ethos of the managerial and business groups).

3. The third phenomenon we would like to mention is a monetarization (or fiscalization) of social consciousness (M. Marody).[7] Money becomes a universal mean for mediating social relations, interpersonal ones as well. On the one hand, this process destroys semi-legal, corruptive ties and leads to a sane economic life; on the other, it may affect the informal ties that made the microsocial tissue so vivid.

So perhaps, having our long-desired normal society already established, we will periodically long for a few things from the "dark age" of communism.

Methodological Postscript

We feel that it is necessary to add some explanations concerning both the empirical basis of our chapter and the way of presenting our conclusions.

The chapter is based, first, on our own systematic, but rather "qualitative," studies of styles of life, alternative ways of life, and some social movements in Poland. Such studies have been carried out since the end of the 1970s.[8] We were also interested in the results of public opinion polls by various agencies. But on the other hand, we have drawn some conclusions from an analysis of such nontypical materials as jokes and rumors passed around in Poland in recent years.[9]

Our interpretation of various facts was also based on analyses and comments we had found in the Polish press. Finally, an important basis for our findings was provided by our own, rather active, observation of the private life and participation in the public life of Polish society.

Basing ourselves on such different, mostly qualitative, data, we were not able to present any specific figures or percentages in our chapter. We tried, rather, to characterize some prevailing phenomena and trends. So when we write, for instance, about the "apathy of Polish society," this does not mean that each Pole is apathetic; or, when we talk about the "shift of Polish thinking from 'romanticism' to 'positivism'," it should not be interpreted that there are no individuals or groups that are still quite close to the 'romantic' tradition.

[7] M. Marody, "Awans i krach," *Polityka*, April 30, 1988.

[8] See *Style życia w miastach polskich (u progu kryzysu)*, A. Siciński, ed., Warszawa 1988.

[9] See also P. Łukasiewicz, *Porządek społeczny w potocznych wyobrażeniach i przekazach, (spojrzenie na społeczeństwo polskie)*, Warszawa: IFiS PAN, 1991.

PUBLIC OPINION, VALUES AND ECONOMIC REFORM

Krzysztof Nowak

In the initial period after the imposition of martial law, the stability of the system was maintained by direct force. As time passed and with the diminishing capacity of the underground Solidarity to organize open protests, the importance of force declined and the role of political factors increased. This by no means meant the "restoration of credibility" of the official structures of the communist state or building a system for representing the interests of various social groups but a sort of unwritten contract in which society – more precisely, certain groups – would give up political aspirations in exchange for social security.[1] Certain economic interests – even if they were not articulated in the political system – were satisfied by the post-December order, which has a preservative effect on the entire political system. What were these interests and what was the mechanism of their stabilizing influence?

Jadwiga Staniszkis has called the rise of Solidarity and its actions before and after the imposition of martial law a "nontransformative rebellion."[2] This meant that the "rebellion," that is, the withdrawal of political obedience on the part of workers (wage earners or the entire society), did not result in a change of the basic elements of the political and economic communist order (following Marx, Staniszkis attributes basic importance here to the question of property rights). On the contrary, some of the features of the way in which demands and interests were articulated contributed to the stabilization of this

[1] M. Marody, "Sens zbiorowy a stabilność i zmiana ładu społecznego," in M. Marody and S. Sułek, eds., *Rzeczywistość polska a sposoby radzenia sobie z nią*, Warszawa: Instytut Socjologii Uniwersytetu Warszawskiego, 1987.

[2] J. Staniszkis, "Bunt nietransformacyjny czyli o kilku paradoksach artykulacji politycznej w Polsce," in W. Morawski, ed., *Gospodarka i społeczeństwo. Wartości i interesy zakładów przemysłowych*, Warszawa: Instytut Socjologii Uniwersytetu Warszawskiego, 1986.

system. The author points out the dominant role of moral motives in political thinking, the concentration on expression of identity instead of the articulation of interests connected with position in the class system (the independence of political views from factors determining this position), or the demands for the redistribution of incomes, which strengthens the role of the state in the economy. To put it briefly, according to Staniszkis, the situation of the suppressed political conflict after December 1981 promoted a "we–they" division in the public mind, a vision based on moral and political criteria, but it made difficult – even impossible – a picture of the world and collective actions that could lead to a program of political and economic reform, including property rights. Dislike for the market economy – according to Staniszkis – thus united the authorities and society (or at least a considerable part of it), helping to block the program of reforms and stabilizing the system of communist domination over society. The findings of numerous studies confirm such a thesis.

In one of the surveys of the Center for the Study of Public Opinion (October 1985), the question was asked, "What can really help improve the economic situation?" The most frequently chosen answers (five were chosen from among nineteen) were the following: "prevent waste," "reduce the indebtedness of the country," "stop the rise of prices," "increase the profitability of exports," "improve the supply of the market," and "attain food self sufficiency." "Only a dozen or so percent (12–16) of the respondents," writes the author of this report, "selected 'increasing the role of the market in the economy' and 'giving private enterprises freedom of action' as important for the economy."[3] The author interprets these findings as evidence that the vox populi agrees with the policy of the authorities in economic matters: "If we compare the wishes of most citizens (if only those mentioned above) suggesting what to do with what we heard and read on this subject in the utterances of politicians, then one can see that both sides are in agreement on this question."

In other studies from this same period, respondents were asked to choose between two opposite economic models: in the first, the state centrally manages all economic matters; in the second, the authorities do not occupy themselves with running the economy at all. It turned out that 63 percent of those polled regarded the first variant as more advantageous, 20 percent opted for the second variant, and 17 percent had no opinion. Even more important are other findings concerning the protective function of the state: "Once again the respondents were presented two variants. In the first, the citizen as producer works hard with the thought that thanks to this the state is growing in wealth and that it will care for him and his material situation. In the second, the citizen works primarily with the thought of providing for his

[3] S. Kwiatkowski, "Opinie o gospodarce," *Polityka*, December 12–27, 1985.

own material security, without expecting help from the state. ...The subjects were asked which model enables the state to achieve better economic results. A clear majority (62 percent of the responses) opted for the model of the welfare state, while 29 percent were in favor of the second variant. ...A similar way of thinking, which gives priority to the 'social safety net' is evident in answers to the question on the best way to raise the incomes of the population. Forty-four percent of the respondents suggested a raise for those earning the least and those with the smallest pensions; 29 percent for those working the best, the most efficient workers." In summing up, the author writes that "for Polish society, questions of social and material security are of fundamental importance. Public opinion would be willing to accept mechanisms for wage differentials, but not at the risk of losing social security."[4]

A mechanism that ensures security on a minimum level is rationing. In surveys of opinions on this subject, a large number of respondents were in favor of punishing those who violate this principle, and it was generally found that rationing – though regarded as a necessary evil – was supported by society.[5]

The above picture of public opinion and people's reactions to the crisis becomes even more complicated when we take into consideration the political options linked with various economic views. In the previously cited surveys, the respondents were asked about the reasons for the rise of prices, a phenomenon that is perhaps the most important for common opinions about the economic and political system. The author writes that there were four different ways of thinking about the reasons for inflation;

– seeing the causes in the poor organization of work, wastefulness, and unconscientiousness;
– stressing international determinants and arbitrary price setting by the private sector. Such thinking was especially typical for those who were convinced that the economic situation was tolerable and that the policy of the government for overcoming the crisis was effective;
– the political determinants of inflation (military outlays, neglect on the part of the government of the living conditions of society, and excessive prices for agricultural products were most often mentioned by people who evaluated the economic situation as not very good, the policy of the government as not necessarily guaranteeing the overcoming of the crisis, and the stabilization of prices as something remote;
– internal economic determinants (the necessity for equalizing wages,

---

[4] B. Dr., "Z badań OBOP. Świadomość ekonomiczna Polaków," Życie Warszawy, September 9, 1985.
[5] R. Sobiech, "Reglamentacja w świetle badań opinii publicznej," and J. Kurczewski, M. Fuszara, and I. Jakubowska, "Reglamentacja, poczucie sprawiedliwości i pomoc wzajemna," in J. Kurczewski, ed., Umowa o kartki, Warszawa: Instytut Profilaktyki Społecznej i Resocjalizacji Uniwersytetu Warszawskiego, 1985.

increasing social benefits, investments, outlays for the modernization of industry). People thinking in this way had a favorable opinion of the economic policy of the government and the chances for the stabilization of prices.[6]

The above remarks show that in the middle of the eighties there was a strong need for the protective action of the state and disapproval for economic actions on its part that would increase the economic risk borne by the population. There was also convergence between attitudes of hostility toward the political system and the perception of the causes of the economic crisis in the political situation.

At first glance, the attitude of workers toward the idea of a proefficiency reform in the economy is puzzling, for obviously sooner or later everyone would benefit from greater economic efficiency, and, on the other hand, the situation in the plants – poor organization of work, waste, no connection between the quality of work and remuneration – had always been a source of frustration for the workers. This picture becomes clearer, however, when we take into consideration the specific features of the socialist workplace as a social system. The socialist plant is not only a productive unit but also an institution that has protective and control tasks in relation to the workers; and it is this "second life" of the plant that allows workers to satisfy many needs they would be unable to satisfy elsewhere. For example, in periods of difficulty in shopping for food and other basic commodities, when many goods were rationed, places of work assumed the function of distributing goods. With the overlapping of criteria typical for the socialist economy, in its role the plant was simultaneously a trading unit organizing the supply and sale of goods and an organ of the administration making decisions on giving the right to purchase these goods to particular persons or groups. E. and Z. Rykowski's study of the system of organizing access to various goods in one of the large Warsaw plants in the first half of the eighties revealed a complicated and formalized structure of privileges determining the possibility of purchasing many goods – from jam and bread, which were available to everybody in kiosks on the plant grounds, to automobiles and bicycles, whose purchase required meeting many conditions, having a long seniority on the job, and gaining the approval of many plant organizations and institutions.[7]

In addition to the function of the supplier of scarce goods, plants also acted as the organizer of employee holidays thanks to having their own vacation resorts or having access to the nationwide network of employee vacation resorts; the organizer of recreation during time off from work, distributing tickets for shows or organizing excursions; and even the

---

[6] Kwiatkowski, "Opinie o gospodarce," *op. cit.*

[7] Z. Rykowski, "Rozdzielnictwo artykułów spożywczych i przemysłowych na terenie zakładu pracy: studium przypadku," in J. Kurczewski, *Umowa o kartki.*

organizer of housing services thanks to company apartments, housing construction, or putting pressure on the public administration responsible for the allocation of apartments.

The performance of such functions was obviously possible only thanks to the absence of a market, to shortages of goods, and to the artificial lowering of prices for scarce goods, that is, in a situation of economic planning that was in a state of crisis. The possibility of performing them – and thus in some sense the protective role of the plant in relation to the workers – was the other side of the role of the plant. For as the location of an industrial conflict that could easily become a political conflict, the plant also simultaneously performed a repressive and control function. Obviously the possibility of distributing scarce goods promoted this function by opening up the way for manipulation, making the workers economically dependent, and fostering corrupt practices.

The "official" benefits for the worker from employment in a state-owned plant – wages, sharing in group consumption and privileges connected with easier access to scarce goods – were only part of what he could gain. The second, no less valuable, part were benefits from the informal – and illegal – privatization of plant assets. Describing the social situation of state-owned plants in the seventies, T. Żukowski writes,

> The informal mutual exchange of goods and services also extended to workers' relation with their superiors. We see this from the high evaluations of immediate superiors by their subordinates, in spite of the overall dissatisfaction with the organization and conditions of work, the tolerance by overseers and foremen of violations of work discipline, bungled work, and the drinking of alcohol by workers. In exchange for this, the workers carried out a minimum of tasks, were ready to pitch in when work piled up, were loyal. ...Various informal ties also appeared among workers. Researchers have recorded solidarity in controlling the pace of work by working groups, organizing private jobs on company time. ... Evidence of the large role of various forms of group ties can be the fact that the climate of interpersonal relations in the plant were quite 'warm,' 'homey,' and people were rather satisfied with their jobs and attached great importance to relations with colleagues, in spite of the negative evaluation of work safety, its organization, and wages.[8]

The well-organized social system of the socialist plant, which performed distributive, control, integrative, and only in last place productive functions, broke down with the appearance of the open political conflict in 1980–81. At first this conflict flared up in the plants, from where it quickly shifted to the

---

[8] T. Płukowski, "Fabryki, urzędy i ich ewolucja. Rozważania o ładzie społeczno-gospodarczym w polskich zakładach przemysłowych," in W. Morawski and W. Kozek, eds., *Załamanie porządku etatystycznego*, Warszawa: Instytut Socjologii Uniwersytetu Warszawskiego, 1988, p. 160.

upper levels of the political system. What remained in the plants of this conflict concerned "supplementing plant rules of the game with democratic procedures and institutions, strengthening the position of the crews, which had the de facto right to veto management decisions, and making the distribution of goods and services more egalitarian and open."[9] At the same time, the managing directors of enterprises had to become politicians who knew how to mediate conflicts and maintain social peace in the plants.

After the imposition of martial law, most plants were militarized, which meant an increase in the repressive and control function and also a worsening of relations between workers and superintendents and managers. However, as resistance weakened and the conflict grew less intense, the "spirit of solidarity" returned to the plants. T. Żukowski writes, "Actions were noted to defuse tensions, and managements made efforts to gain the loyalty of workers. Managers tried to keep workers in the plant by fighting with higher levels of management for higher wages, supplying workers with scarce consumer goods, tolerating poor quality and slow pace of work, creating a 'homey' atmosphere."[10]

Superiors, who aimed at political stability and a smoothly running production line, as well as workers created informal in-groups. They exchanged services among themselves on a large scale, thereby indirectly privatizing plant assets. There was a plethora of "in-group" forms, which was accompanied by a specific subculture and a "homey" atmosphere to which the drinking of alcohol greatly contributed. The reality of the plan was shaped by various kinds of more or less informal services and "in-groups" springing up in a cozy, homelike climate.[11]

These processes transformed the factory into a "protective" institution approved by most of the crew, a place in which work was disagreeable (because of low wages and poor working conditions and organization) but where many things could be "taken care of" and one could feel rather well.

Apart from the period of the open conflict in 1980–81 and the sharp but suppressed conflict in the first period after the imposition of martial law, integrative-protective functions dominated in the socialist enterprise. This obviously took place at the cost of efficiency in its main function – production. Workers were aware that the market reform of the economy would divest them of the benefits coming from the integrative protective function of the enterprise. Such a reform would make it impossible for them to enjoy the fruits of the "informal privatization of assets,"[12] while these losses would not

---

[9] *Ibid.*, p. 166.

[10] *Ibid.*, pp. 178–81.

[11] *Ibid.*

[12] I. Białecki, "Poczucie uzależnienia i struktura społeczna," in P. Kuczyński, ed., *U progu zmian. Szkice socjologiczne o polskim społeczeństwie lat osiemdziesiątych*, Warszawa: Instytut Socjologii Uniwersytetu Warszawskiego, 1990, pp. 90–91.

be compensated by the positive effects of greater efficiency. The workers lacked confidence in a double sense: first, they lacked confidence in the success of such an undertaking in the plants they knew from their own experience (and very likely did not believe in the success of the Polish economy as a whole); and second, they lacked political confidence – i.e., the workers regarded themselves as a politically underprivileged class with no political representation and facing a hostile system and its party-state bureaucracy alone. So in view of the lack of political protection, they could expect to be burdened with excessive costs of the economic changes.

Thus the specific feature of the socialist enterprise, which consisted in the performance of diverse social, economic, and political functions, survived the sweeping changes of 1980–81 and the first years of martial law. This feature had a stabilizing effect on the economic and political system, though this stabilization of the "official" system – to use A. Rychard's expression – took place thanks to departures from its rules, that is, thanks to the functioning of the "unofficial" system.[13]

The need for the plant to perform a protective function obviously also applied in large measure to its "official" rules. Though demands were addressed to the plant and its management, the real addressee was the state, whose interests the plant represented. K. Kosela demonstrated this in his analysis of the expectations of workers in relation to the protective enterprise:

> The list of goods and services that the plant ought to guarantee the workers (according to their expectations) shows an acceptance of the principle of guardianship. This acceptance extends to health, education, and even social life. This means that society accepted the guardianship of the state. As empirical studies show, people hold out their hand to the plant, believing that they will receive things from the owner of these plants. ...The diverse demands addressed to the employer leads us to surmise that the reason for such extensive claims is the strong need to satisfy important wants. On the other hand, the similarity of answers in categories of respondents made up in various ways is evidence of the universality of catalysts fueling the revindicative attitude. Nearly everyone demands almost the same protectiveness. When the stake is survival, the possibility of making independent choices becomes a luxury.[14]

Thus in the years after the imposition of martial law, political stability and the absence of political and economic reforms were the result largely of an economic situation in which the effects of the economic crisis increased the

---

[13] A. Rychard, "Władza i gospodarka – trzy perspektywy teoretczne," in W. Morawski, ed., *Demokracja i gospodarka*, Warszawa: Instytut Socjologii Uniwersytetu Warszawskiego, 1983, pp. 37–38.
[14] K. Kosela, "Specjalność zakładu pracy opiekuńczego," in Morawski and Kozek, *Załamanie, op. cit.*, pp. 309–10.

need for the protective functions of the state, and the representative of the state – the enterprise – was able to respond to this need while simultaneously using these possibilities to make its employees dependent.

The shift of the conflict beyond the plant was also very important. This process consisted in the disintegration of the structure of action of the social movement. The political conflict, whose stake was reform of the political system and modification of the structure based on domination, became symbolic and turned into a struggle to preserve identity and express moral arguments, while the industrial conflict between employees and employers yielded to informal institutionalization.[15] The instruments of this institutionalization were informal agreements between various social forces in the plant, and a certain role was also played by the "new" trade unions – even though they were unpopular among most employees – and workers' councils.

The question of workers' councils deserves some comment. These bodies acquired political importance in 1981 when the dilemmas connected with the evolution of Solidarity involved the social movement in a conflict concerning control of the economy. Solidarity was a trade union, and a solution in which the workers – organized on the Yugoslav pattern in a workers' self management body – would become the collective owners of the plants (or at least would have the function of owners) was one of the possible forms of collective action in the conflict over the economy.[16] After the imposition of martial law, the workers' councils were the only organization uncompromised by collaboration with the martial law authorities, which cannot be said of the "new" trade unions, and simultaneously were a forum of mediation and a channel for the articulation of workers' interests in the plant. It is hardly surprising that they were reactivated or established in most plants. In 1985, workers' councils existed in 70 percent of the state-owned enterprises, that is, in 80 percent of the plants with the right to create such institutions (some types of plants did not have this right). Workers' councils were active in plants employing 5.5 million workers, while 1.3 million worked in plants without a workers' council even though these plants had the right to form one.[17] The extensiveness of the workers' self-management movement among crews did not mean, however, that workers' councils played a big role everywhere. The author of a study conducted in December 1983 on a representative sample of employees of large Warsaw plants stated that "the workers' council as an institution articulating and representing the interests

[15] K. Nowak, "Działania społeczne i problem prawomocności. Trzy modele kryzysu legitymizacyjnego," in A. Rychard and A. Sułek, ed., Legitymacja. Klasyczne teorie i polskie doświadczenia, Warszawa: Polskie Towarzystwo Socjologiczne and Uniwersytet Warszawski, 1988.

[16] A. Touraine, F. Dubet, M. Wieviorka, and J. Strzelecki, Solidarité. Analyse d'un mouvement social. Pologne 1980–1981, Paris: Fayard, 1982.

[17] P. Kuczyński, "Ruch samorządów pracowniczych między walką a grą z systemem," in Morawski and Kozek, Zalamanie, op. cit., p. 313.

of employees does not function in the consciousness of the crews."[18] More than 50 percent of the respondents answered that there is no workers' council in their plant or that they do not know if there is one, in spite of the fact that there was one everywhere, and 68 percent of respondents (if they were party members) to 88 percent of respondents (if they were nonparty members) were unable to say what the workers' council did. From the fact that more respondents were able to identify persons in the workers' council than to say what the workers' council does the author concluded that this institution was a facade.[19] Even if such a conclusion is regarded as too sweeping, the findings do show that the workers' council was not an institution in which the workers place much hope. One can cite still other findings, this time not quantitative ones, from studies on various forms of workers' self-management. The goal of these studies was to find out how self-management institutions articulate interests, whether they bring them into the decision making system, and how they promote resourcefulness and self-help. On the basis of materials gathered in many plants, the author states:

> After 1982 the activities of workers' councils are characterized by a continual decline of interest on the part of the crews, diminishing attendance at sessions of the council and meetings of delegates, concentration chiefly on wage issues (and in some councils on social matters), handing over the initiative in plant matters to the management. ...The administration of the plant exerts an ever greater influence on the activities of the council, which manifests itself in passing on the council ready solutions for acceptance. ...The workers' council is a place in which the interests of various units of the plant administration collide (this rarely concerns the interest of individual groups of workers).[20]

Later studies (from 1987) enable us to put forward the thesis that in about 10 percent of the enterprises, "the interest of the crew is combined with its readiness to participate actively in the work of the council,"[21] while "one can speak of a few hundred enterprises nationally in which the workers' councils remain independent of the other power centers in the enterprise."[22] In the other enterprises, the workers' councils were either passive or remained under the full control of other forces. W. Morawski writes that "this most often takes the form of action in the narrow circle of the so-called 'plant

[18] M. Jarosz, *Samorząd przedsiębiorstw w oczach zakładu*, Lublin: Polskie Towarzystwo Ekonomiczne i Politechnika Lubelska, 1984, p. 10.

[19] *Ibid.*, p. 14.

[20] J. Hrynkiewicz et al., "Instytucje samorządu społecznego – raport z badań w województwie płockim" (Unpublished paper), pp. 27–28.

[21] M. Federowicz, "Fenomen samorządu pracowniczego – społeczne zasoby zmian," in Kuczyński, *U progu zmian, op. cit.*, p. 164.

[22] *Ibid.*, p. 159.

collective,' which is made up of the managing director, the first secretary of the party organization, the head of the trade union, and the head of the workers' council. This is an informal body but – as one can gather from studies in 334 enterprises (1985) – of decisive importance in about 85 percent of the enterprises."[23]

So what were the workers' councils in Polish enterprises in the middle of the eighties? The above data show that in most cases they were part of the institutional system politically subordinate to the higher authorities, though they functioned according to their own logic – representing and mediating various interests – and were only partially formalized. A small number of them, which can be estimated at about 10 percent, had some autonomy in relation to the other forces representing worker interests. P. Kuczyński has described them with the term "borrowed identity"[24]: "The self-management movement is a certain continuation of 'Solidarity' in so far as there is no change in the overall conditions (the power system, property rights, management) in which they have to work." This author states that the real stake of the struggle of the self-management movement as a social movement is the "fight for the market" as an institution guaranteeing stable rules of the games. If this were really so, the workers' councils – at least in a certain area – could become a factor of political and economic changes, for the fight for the market in conditions of a state economy and the communist political order requires a fight for structural changes in the entire system. For many reasons, however, the thesis on the "fight for the market" of the self-management movement was more a postulate than a description of reality. Even the workers' councils that had a "borrowed identity" and continued certain traditions and directions of action of Solidarity – as was the rule in those plants where Solidarity was strong and its structures had not been broken up during martial law[25] – had to perform various and mutually contradictory roles. The main contradiction was between the role of "functional owner" of the plant appointing and controlling management and role of representative of employee interests vis-à-vis management, that is, the role of trade unions. The workers' councils – continuators of Solidarity primarily in that they retained autonomy and independence – leaned strongly toward the latter role, and this was expected of them by the crews.

The above points confirm the thesis on the "nontransformative" nature of collective actions in the eighties. Neither the underground Solidarity, which was fighting for the right to legal existence, nor the legally operating workers' councils – its continuators in a very narrow area – could draw up a program of market oriented economic reforms owing to their origin as representatives

[23] W. Morawski, "Samorząd pracowniczy: wizja i realia," in Morawski, *Gospodarka i społeczeństwo, op. cit.,* p. 419.

[24] Kuczyński, "Ruch samorządów pracowniczych," *op. cit.* p. 318.

[25] *Ibid.,* p. 319.

of workers' interests. Nor was public opinion supportive of such a course. This picture changes somewhat, however, when we look at it from the perspective of the dynamics of the attitudes and opinions of society.

When we observe the changes of opinions on the political situation – as an imprecise measure of political confidence or satisfaction – we notice that these opinions had a tendency to improve. Between December 1984 and December 1985, the percentage of persons evaluating the political situation as bad fell from 25 percent to 15 percent.[26] On the other hand, in the same period the percentage of persons evaluating their material conditions as bad increased from 18 percent to 25 percent, while those evaluating the economic situation of the country as bad rose from 38 percent to 46 percent. This shows that the economic problem was becoming the most important problem for society. At the same time, changes took place in opinions on market solutions in the economy.

"There is a widely held opinion," writes L. Kolarska, "that Polish society is egalitarian and will not accept market reform that would widen economic differences."[27] In fact, numerous studies have shown high levels of egalitarianism. The author notes, however, that egalitarianism cannot be understood simplistically as the postulate of equality of economic position. Toward the end of the seventies, egalitarian postulates expressed a protest against unjust criteria of distribution. Thus they had as much economic as political meaning. A closer analysis of these postulates shows that they concern equality of opportunity and not equality of rewards. Both the existing system and the one preferred by the workers are nonegalitarian, but the criteria of unequal remuneration are different in the two cases. In the second case, they assume equality of opportunity in the sense that they make earnings independent of political criteria.

Kolarska notes that egalitarian attitudes became less intense between 1980 and 1981, which is confirmed by the thesis that the language of egalitarianism served to express political views hostile to the official system. Since the freedom to express political opinions increased considerably in 1981 in comparison with 1980, there was no need to express them in egalitarian slogans. The trend that had started in 1980–81 continued, however. A comparison of research findings from 1980, 1981, and 1984 indicates a further decline in indicators of egalitarianism. To the question on whether a legal upper limit ought to be set on wages, 90 percent of the respondents answered positively in 1980; in 1981, 78 percent; in 1984, 56 percent; while the postulate of wide differentiation of wages depending on qualifications was supported by 54, 62, and 81 percent of the respondents, respectively.[28]

[26] S. Kwiatkowski, "Nieco więcej nadziei," *Polityka*, January 18, 1986.
[27] L. Kolarska, "Niereformowalna władza czy społeczeństwo?" in Morawski and Kozek, *Zalamanie, op. cit.*, p. 224.
[28] *Ibid.*, p. 228.

These facts suggest that we take a different look at the results of previous studies showing disapproval for market solutions in the economy. It turns out that the principles of efficiency and differentiation of incomes depending on the amount and quality of work were becoming ever more widely accepted by the society, but this increase in their acceptance was accompanied by continued approval for the protective obligations of the state toward the citizens and the plant toward the workers. Yet the economic system that emerges from these data is a hybrid of two systems: the efficiency and justice (in the sense that it combines remuneration with productivity and quality of work) of a market economy; and the social security, protectiveness, and lack of a risk of a socialist economy.

In the middle of the seventies, a change began to appear in how society reacted to the prolonged economic crisis. At first the shortages of even basic commodities, the disorganization of the market, and the disintegration of the infrastructure of everyday life increased the necessity for the plant and the state to perform protective functions, but in the middle of the eighties the belief became ever more widespread that the socialist economy is unable to overcome the crisis and insure the society decent living conditions. The attractiveness of work in the state sector also diminished. "The flight from the state sector," writes Kolarska, "is not of great significance on the scale of the economy as a whole. But it does call forth a strong response, since it acts on the principle of imitation and creates alternative models of behavior. ...Employees transferring to the private sector lose various social benefits, but they agree to this loss in exchange for higher wages, better organization of work, and greater independence in the private sector."[29]

In the study "Poles '84," the supporters of egalitarian and permanent employment solutions were primarily unskilled workers and in part farmers, while the supporters of nonegalitarian and market solutions were persons working for themselves, specialists, and technicians. "Skilled workers," writes Kolarska, "though it is hard to include them among the firm minded supporters of the nonegalitarian order, are closer in their views to the group of specialists and technicians thanks to unskilled workers, while in 1980 and 1981 both of these groups were the mainstay of egalitarian views. The changes in thinking that have taken place since 1980 affected skilled workers the most strongly of all socio-occupational groups."[30]

When on April 26, 1988, the steel workers' strike in Nowa Huta ushered in a new stage of political changes in Poland, the question of structural reforms in the economy was not among the strikers' postulates. Among the seven postulates announced on the first day of the strike, six concerned wage hikes, the indexation of wages to offset inflation, extra pay for work in arduous

[29] *Ibid.*, p. 233.
[30] *Ibid.*, p. 235.

conditions, and sick benefits. In the seventh postulate the steel workers demanded that the plant leaders of Solidarity who had been sacked during martial law be given back their jobs. On May 2, one week after Nowa Huta, the Gdańsk shipyard went on strike. Though they were similar to those of Nowa Huta, the Gdańsk postulates went much further. Only their order was different. The first postulate concerned wage hikes, the second, the legalization of Solidarity. Other demands included freeing political prisoners, reinstating workers who had been sacked, and safety for the strikers. So in both cases, economic questions in the strike postulates appeared only as demands for higher wages.

In light of the above remarks and what we know about the strikes of the seventies and eighties, this is hardly surprising. At the moment of a strike, the most immediate interests of those who undertake collective action are put first. The strikers come forward first and foremost as wage earners, and their interests connected with this role are expressed primarily in the form of wage demands. The more difficult it is to mobilize workers for a strike, the weaker its organization and the less integrated the actions; and simultaneously, the greater the fear and atomization of the group, the closer to bread-and-butter issues and more dispersed are the postulates. In certain conditions, the evolution of collective actions can lead to a generalization and expansion of the demands to embrace structural changes. For example, in the case described, the shift in focus from economic revindication to political demands took place when Lech Wałęsa, the head of Solidarity, assumed leadership of the Gdańsk strike. In this way the collective actor changed his identity. Workers demanding higher wages became citizens demanding political freedoms, but they simultaneously remained in the role of workers by this time demanding trade-union freedoms. In order to demand a structural market reform in the economy, however, the workers had to agree to give up the satisfaction of their job related interest in the short run and step forward in the role of collective owner of the means of production. Obviously, they then would find themselves in conflict with themselves as employees simultaneously aspiring to the role of owners.

The problem, which J. Staniszkis has called the "nontransformative nature of the rebellion," was that the question of property rights was unsolvable within the system of articulation of the interests of various social groups as it had taken shape as a result of the rise of Solidarity and its subsequent evolution. According to this author, no change of the political system of domination of communist power over society is possible as long as the economic foundations of this power remain intact. This power rests on state ownership of the means of production and control over this property by a monopolistic party. The system of ownership in turn cannot be toppled by a rebellion of the "working class," for in a certain sense the latter would have to act against itself: it would have to strive for the abolishment of state ownership, which is inefficient in the long run but provides jobs, security, and informal benefits. In the final analysis, the "nontransformative" nature of the rebellion is a question of the configuration of the political forces preserving the communist system of domination. The paradox is that this configuration is the product of the communist revolution, which abolished the class of owners of the means of production and created – in a poorly industrialized Poland – a strong working class concentrated in large industrial plants, especially of heavy industry. The latter circumstance is of some importance. In accordance with Stalinist economic theory, the primacy of heavy industry is also preserved by this configuration of political forces, for the interests of the workers of this industry converge with the interests of the party nomenklatura ruling over this industry in such a way that both sides work to preserve an inefficient and outdated economic structure: the former, so as not to lose power and its privileges; the latter, so as not to lose their jobs.

So in spite of the fact that the collective actions of workers ushered in political changes – trade union freedoms in 1980, more effective channels of political representation, and limiting the domination of the Communist Party over society – it did not result in a permanent change in ownership. Thus economic reform, which is inconceivable without a change of ownership, remained outside the goals of the social movement of Solidarity, the only independent political force in late-communist Poland of the eighties. Unexpectedly, the first step toward ownership changes was taken by the adversary of the movement: plant managements and the local state-party administration.

Control over state property – theoretically, the common property of the entire society – is dispersed. Investments, distribution, and redistribution are controlled by central organs of the administration, which in turn are under the control of the polymorphous party. These organs also run individual enterprises; for example, they have a lot to say about filling top managerial positions. Local authorities of the ruling party also have an influence on these appointments through the nomenklatura system – a procedure of approving candidates for top positions by party committees at various levels. In spite of this double subordination at the enterprise level, there is a certain autonomy of organizational interests. The enterprise managements contend both with higher levels and with their own crews. The fight with the central economic administration is over the resources that the latter allocates: raw materials, energy, money for wages and investments, tax breaks, etc. Due to the fact that the central administration is unable to exercise detailed control over the enterprise, the latter has an informational advantage. This advantage evens out the chances of the enterprise in the fight for resources with the central administration. Thanks to being able to carry on this fight, the enterprise can retain some autonomy. The socialist manager is an entrepreneur of a special kind, who simultaneously is involved in an economic and a political contest. This manager has a rather broad range of political power, from which come certain economic privileges, but he has no ownership rights over the assets he manages.

In December 1988, the Sejm passed a much more liberal law on the creation of private industrial, trading, and service companies. The aim of the law was to stimulate the economy through the development of the private sector and open a crack in the door for foreign capital. Two months later, the Sejm passed another law allowing state enterprises to sell or lease their assets to other economic units, including private persons and companies of private persons. Both laws created the legal possibilities for the emergence of a new phenomenon in the socialist economy – the state-private sector.

"Favorable conditions for setting up companies resulted in a rapid growth in their number," we read in a report of the Chief Board of Supervision of November 1989. "At the end of June 1989, 2,139 companies were registered in the state sector, and of this number 1,302 had been set up in 1989. In the private sector, 5,839 companies were registered, which is a fourteenfold increase in comparison with the previous year."[31] The setting up of private state companies operating on the point of contact of the private and state sectors served mainly to avoid the regulations pegging down the state enterprise, e.g., caps on price increases or taxes on higher wages. Much more important, however, was the second aim – to privatize state property by handing it over to those who in the past had only managed it:

> The managers of enterprises entered into companies with their own capital or became members of the boards of companies whose partners are the enterprises they manage. ...The managers of enterprises who are simultaneously members of the boards of companies, especially when there are ties between them, fall into a conflict of interests. Controls have found that as a rule in such situations there is a tendency to favor the company at the cost of the state enterprise. In order to increase the profits of private persons, it is a common practice to underestimate the contribution of the state enterprise to the company. ...Irregularities in fixing the value of such assets were found in two-thirds of the cases audited.[32]

From the above document we give one example illustrating the strategy used by the managers of state enterprises to take over these assets:

> In an enterprise that in 1989 sold its product to thirteen trading companies, the assistant managing director was responsible for establishing contacts with these companies and for setting up several of

[31] *Informacja o wynikach kontroli powiązań przedsiębiorstw państwowych ze spółkami prawa handlowego*, Warszawa: Najwyższa Izba Kontroli, 1989, p. 3.

[32] *Ibid.*, pp. 6–7.

them. Together with his wife and daughter, he had shares in eight of the eleven companies audited. In four of them, his wife had a management position, and he himself was employed in one of them. Other shareholders included persons in executive positions in the local economic administration and political organizations.[33]

Here one might ask why such practices, which in most countries would result in penal proceedings and a court sentence, were tolerated in Polish law? In a situation of political stability, there was no need to expand control and actually take over assets as one's own property. Political power ensured privileges, while there was less responsibility than when one was a full fledged owner. In 1988, after the strikes in Kraków and Gdańsk, the political situation changed, however. More strikes were expected, and the disintegration of the communist system of domination became every more visible. The passage of a law making possible the covert and gradual privatization of part of the state assets by members of the political and economic establishment (privatization that in fact was a subvention, because property was acquired at artificially low prices) opened up the possibility for a new survival strategy of this establishment.

In a situation of conflict coming out into the open, the strategy of defending the group economic and political interests of the communist authorities quite likely would have led to an escalation of violence and another state of martial law. The experience of the eighties laid bare the ineffectiveness of this strategy in the long run and its catastrophic effects: the civilizational regression of the country and the impossibility of recreating the political foundations of domination. In 1988, a repetition of the scenario of martial law, which had already failed once, was unthinkable as a reaction to the reviving capacity of the society to act.

The notion of "enfranchisement of the nomenklatura" (i.e., giving them subventions) preceded the Round Table, which prepared the withdrawal of the establishment to "positions chosen in advance." In this way, the loss or limitation of privileges from the possession of political power could be partially offset by the privileges of ownership. In this sense, one can say that setting in motion the process of taking over property prepared the way for the handing over of power by the communists. A class of owners began to emerge from the communist establishment.

Enfranchisement – and especially self-enfranchisement – of the nomenklatura was a short-lived episode. Since these processes took place in a gray legal area, we lack data on their magnitude. There is no doubt, however, that opening up the way to private business reduced the attractiveness of the martial-law scenario for defending the interests of the communist authorities and was an alternative that was not available in 1981.

---

[33] *Ibid.*, pp. 19–20.

During the deliberations of the Round Table, at which a new political contract was concluded that included the relegalization of Solidarity and the limitation of the power of the Communist Party, the main postulate of Solidarity – apart from political ones – was the demand for the indexation of wages to offset the shrinkage of workers' wages caused by inflation. Meanwhile, the economy continued to disintegrate.

In 1989, industrial output was 3.4 percent lower than in the previous year, and this decline continued. In November and December of that year, it had already fallen to 10 percent below the industrial production of those same months in 1988. The purchase of agricultural products from farmers was 12.7 percent lower for all of 1989 and showed a sharply declining trend, with a decline of purchases in each successive month. Supplies to the market worsened; in particular, the sales of foodstuffs declined. "Social anxiety resulted in the buying up of commodities," writes the author of a study of the economic situation of the country in 1989. "This generated anticipatory demand caused by fears of higher prices, which in turn resulted in the running down of stocks."[34] Inflation heated up. At the beginning of the year, it was running at 10 percent a month, and toward the end of the year, it had accelerated to about 55 percent a month.

In October 1989, the government announced its plan for a radical market reform in the economy: the removal of food subsidies, liberalization of trade, bringing about the exchangeability of the zloty, and in the longer run, a sweeping restructuring and privatization of the economy. Owing to the high rate of inflation, the most important short-run goal of the plan was to achieve financial stability. It was obvious that radical measures to reduce inflation would bring about a recession, a fall in the standard of living of the society, and unemployment, which in postwar Poland was something unknown.

The program of economic reform was drawn up by the government that had emerged from the first free elections (in spite of certain restrictions placed on the voting process by the contract negotiated at the Round Table). Thus the reform was launched "from the top" and, in the bargain, with no organized political forces that would identify their own group interests with its success. The most important political force, which was the base of Solidarity and the prop of the new government, were the workers. In the short term, they would gain little from the reform but would lose much. Already in the first months of the reform, real wages fell by more than a dozen percent, and the first pockets of unemployment appeared. Along with this there was a reduction in the social-welfare functions of the state and the enterprise and an increase in requirements and risk. And a new class of

[34] P. Wyczański, *Wstępna ocena sytuacji gospodarczej Polski w 1989 roku*, Warszawa: Studia i materiały Ośrodka Prac Społeczno-Zawodowych KKW NSZZ "Solidarność", 1990, p. 98.

owners, which would be the first beneficiary of a market economy, did not exist as an organized political force. Farmers achieved a relatively high degree of political organization, but for them a program of market reform is the most dangerous, for the introduction of market mechanisms and putting the Polish economy face to face with the competitive challenge of the Western economies would lay bare the great inefficiency of Polish agriculture (which is due to its archaic structure). The average farm in Poland has about five hectares, and about 40 percent of the population lives in the countryside. Hence there is a pressing need for the modernization of agriculture, with all its social and economic consequences: the elimination of many farms, the necessity of population shifts, and changes of occupation and the traditional lifestyle of a large part of the rural population. Farmers therefore fear radical market reform, because changes threaten their existence as a class, which not only has specific interests but also its own culture and lifestyle. So on the face of it, economic reform was being implemented in a political vacuum, without the support of important political forces. Those forces that would be capable of articulating their interests on the reform stand to lose in the short run, while those that could identify with the reform are too weak to drum up meaningful support for it. In spite of this, however, there was almost universal approval of the reform program, in which no secret has been made of the probable costs, the necessity for sacrifices, and the riskiness of the entire unprecedented undertaking.

What were the sources of this support for the program of radical market reform? Three factors seem to have been responsible for this support. The most important was the high level of support for and confidence in the new government. In January 1990, when the reform program was being launched and brought in its wake big jumps in prices, an economic recession, and the threat of unemployment, the Center for the Study of Public Opinion conducted a poll on the popularity of the new leaders. To the question "Does the activity of this person serve the interest of society well" 90 percent of the respondents gave positive answers in the cases of Prime Minister Mazowiecki and Lech Wałęsa, and about 60 percent gave positive answers in the case of the author of the program, Leszek Balcerowicz, minister of finances and deputy prime minister.[35] Political support for the new government and the politicians identified with the new economic order was an indispensable condition for the success of the economic program, the more so since its first effects meant a fall in the feeling of economic security and a decline in the standard of living. The positive effects of the reform in an across the board rise in the standard of living were further down the road and required effort and patience. A very high degree of political confidence is required to offer the entire society a deal in which the payoff is in the indefinite future.

[35] *Raporty CBOS*, Warszawa 1990.

In the first six months of the economic reform, this confidence tended to decline. In July, approval for Prime Minister Mazowiecki fell to 76 percent, for Lech Wałęsa to 62 percent, for Deputy Prime Minister Balcerowicz to 45 percent. This meant that, on account of the growing weariness and impatience of society, the credit that had been granted to the government to carry out the reform was gradually being depleted. Simultaneously, a rearrangement of the political scene was under way, with the emergence of new ideological trends, political parties, and orientations from the Solidarity movement. These orientations expressed their more or less favorable attitude toward the economic program, which meant that instead of having the nebulous "support of society," it was becoming the object of normal political dispute, horse-trading, and political negotiations.

The second factor generating comprehensive support for the economic reform program was the catastrophic economic situation inherited from the ancien régime. On the one hand, this situation created a feeling of hopelessness, but on the other, a conviction that only a sweeping and really radical reform could change things. The necessity for such a change, which was partially articulated and partially subconscious, was the third factor spawning support for the idea of a "leap into a market economy," which the government offered to society at the end of 1989. Only a really radical program and a complete break with the past could blunt the not fully articulated feeling that nothing in the Polish economy can be changed.

Market reform in the economy was launched not because there were concrete political forces that saw in it a chance to realize their group interests but because there was a universal need in society for a profound change, a sentiment that the present situation must not continue and that a rapid, even if risky and costly, movement forward was necessary. The strategy of implementing the reform "from the top," in some measure contrary to everyone's immediate interests though in everyone's interests in the long run – under the condition that it was successful, of course – was accepted because it was proposed by a popular government. To some degree this was "carried forward" popularity, resulting from the fact that the government was a political continuation of the Solidarity social movement.

PUBLIC OPINION
IN POLAND'S TRANSITION
TO MARKET DEMOCRACY

David S. Mason

Public Opinion in Poland in the 1980s

Public opinion research in Poland has changed dramatically in the last ten years in terms of its methodology, scope, and role in political change. During the "first" Solidarity era (1980–81), the genie of public opinion was let out of the bottle, and even martial law could not entirely put it back. Public opinion polling in the 1980s became more sophisticated and more common and began to tackle increasingly sensitive political issues. Public opinion came to play a role in the political process and to give the Polish population a sense of its own purpose and values. It also revealed the depth of antipathy to the communist regime and leadership and in doing so further eroded the already fragile legitimacy of the regime. When in the late 1980s the regime realized it could not succeed at winning back the allegiance, or at least acquiescence, of the Polish population, it agreed to negotiate with the opposition. The result was the emergence of the first noncommunist regime in Eastern Europe.

The Emergence of Public Opinion

In a classic study of public opinion in the United States, V.O. Key contended that "all governments ...must concern themselves with public opinion. They do not maintain their authority by brute force alone; they must seek willing acceptance and conformity from most of their citizens."[1] Public opinion in

[1] V. O. Key, *Public Opinion and American Democracy*, New York: Knopf, 1961, p. 4.

democracies, therefore, often acts as a negative factor; it sets the boundaries for political action but does not necessarily assure that action will be taken by decision makers. In the state socialist societies of Eastern Europe, however, even this boundary-setting function was often absent. The regimes may not have relied only on brute force, but they also paid scant attention to the voice of public opinion. Rather, public opinion became part of the process of political socialization. It was used to *shape* public attitudes, or to demonstrate popular conformity with official regime norms, rather than as a mechanism of determining how to respond to such attitudes.

In some countries, and in some periods of unusual openness (such as Czechoslovakia's Prague Spring), pressure from social scientists or the regime's needs to broaden the base of legitimacy led to an expanded role for public opinion research. But the impact of public opinion on policy was always limited by the absence of independent interest groups and competitive parties that would aggregate and process alternative demands and pressure the authorities to act on them.[2]

Public opinion research was always more developed in Poland than in the other countries of Eastern Europe, due partly to the rich sociological tradition in the country and partly to the relatively open atmosphere in Poland, especially in the academy. In Poland, too, the openness of public opinion research coincided with the openness of the political system. The "thaw" after the death of Stalin, for example, led to the formation of a number of new sociological research centers. But this renaissance of public opinion research began to fade in the early 1960s, just as Gomułka's reform program did. With the advent of the new Gierek leadership at the end of 1970, there were renewed hopes for political change, and Stefan Nowak, the dean of public opinion researchers in Poland, appealed for a revitalization of public opinion research in an article that appeared in the party's monthly theoretical journal.[3] But Nowak's advice was largely ignored. Increasingly interesting research was in fact being conducted, some of it demonstrating a public opinion that was increasingly at odds with the demands and expectations of the authorities. But by the end of the 1970s, as the director of the official public opinion center OBOP (Ośrodek Badania Opinii Publicznej) put it, most of the more revealing surveys ended up "on the shelf, forgotten."[4]

After the strikes of the summer of 1980 and the formation of Solidarity, the whole of Polish society became more open, pluralistic, and critical. This was also true of academic researchers, and during 1980 and 1981 public

[2] Z. Gitelman, "Public opinion in communist political systems," in W. D. Connor and Z. Gitelman, eds., *Public Opinion in European Socialist Systems*, New York: Praeger, 1977, p. 32.

[3] S. Nowak, "Społeczna przydatność badań postaw i opinii," *Nowe Drogi*, 1971, no. 9.

[4] A. Kania, in an interview with *Życie Warszawy*, August 1, 1981.

opinion research was more openly pursued, discussed, and published, and was conducted by a greater variety of institutions than ever before. The openness of survey research in Poland during this period was unprecedented for any communist country, as even Solidarity formed its own public opinion research centers. In fact, Solidarity became the necessary vehicle for public opinion to have influence in Poland. As Zvi Gitelman and others had pointed out, in order for public opinion to have an impact, there need to be autonomous groups to aggregate and process societal demands into a program that can serve as an alternative to those in power. Solidarity performed this function, which contributed to the power and influence of both Solidarity, the medium, and public opinion, the message.[5]

During 1981, public opinion research also became a weapon in the country's political battle. It was the implicit recognition of the power of public opinion, in fact, that led Solidarity to create its own public opinion research centers and to issue its own reports, sometimes based on the same questionnaire items used by government research centers. By the end of the year, both the regime and Solidarity were able to use public opinion surveys to bolster their positions. Solidarity could point to the continued strong support for the union and for its most important demands. The regime, on the other hand, could point to the population's declining support for Solidarity, its willingness to assign Solidarity part of the blame for the country's continuing crisis, and the significant degree of support for more "law and order" in society.

In the early months of martial law, public opinion research was much more circumscribed and the results were not always made public. As before 1980, the regime could once again control all aspects of public opinion research and use the data, sometimes selectively, to bolster its own position. But in several respects the situation after December was not the same as before August. Public opinion had been unleashed in 1981, and the regime would have to deal with it. At first it tried to control it by establishing yet another public opinion research center, the Center for Research on Societal Opinion (CBOS – Centrum Badania Opinii Społecznej) under the direction of Colonel Dr. Stanisław Kwiatkowski, and by squelching some of the more independent centers of public opinion research.

The Jaruzelski regime, however, seemed to recognize the force of public opinion, and Jaruzelski himself asserted in a Sejm speech in 1982 that the authorities must become accustomed to the systematic use of public opinion research. Similarly, Col. Kwiatkowski stressed the importance of providing the public with "knowledge about itself" and admitted that public opinion was not well reflected in "individual talks and people's pronouncements at

<hr />

[5] For a discussion of the role of public opinion in Poland, see D. S. Mason, *Public Opinion and Political Change in Poland, 1980–1982*. Cambridge: Cambridge University Press, 1985, especially chapters 1 and 9.

public meetings."[6] The authorities were viewing public opinion in a different way than before 1980: it was providing both the authorities and the public with knowledge about popular attitudes. In the absence of genuine representative political institutions, public opinion became a surrogate for democracy.

During the 1980s, the Jaruzelski regime tried all sorts of measures to elicit popular participation and acquiescence, short of allowing the reemergence of Solidarity. The government created new "mass" organizations (such as PRON – Patriotyczny Ruch Obrony Narodowej), formed governmental advisory councils, sent more bills through the Sejm, allowed multicandidate elections, and held a number of referenda. Like pubic opinion research, however, these formulas were empty without the activating presence of autonomous representative institutions and political parties and could only be temporary expedients.

Because of the open political environment of 1980–81 and the revelations of public opinion, everyone now *knew* what Poles thought and, in particular, the extent of disaffection with the ruling Polish United Worker's Party. The fragile legitimacy of the Jaruzelski regime could be held together by compulsion for only so long. The advent of the Gorbachev leadership in Moscow in 1985 and the declining willingness of the Kremlin to support the hardliners in Eastern Europe increasingly left Warsaw with only one option: to deal with Solidarity. The renewed workers' strikes in the summer of 1988 forced the issue, led to the Roundtable negotiations, the elections, and the formation of the first noncommunist government in Eastern Europe.

The increasingly more open political atmosphere in Poland has allowed more open discussion of the role, methodology, and influence of public opinion. It has also led to a reconsideration of sampling techniques, questionnaire design, reliability, and validity, all issues that continue to confront public opinion researchers in the United States as well. The democratization of the political system has also raised some new concerns about the results of public opinion surveys; in particular, the extent to which the beliefs, values, and attitudes of Polish citizens are conducive to a political and economic environment that will require participation, tolerance, compromise, competition, and patience. The reforms of the new Mazowiecki government also entailed a reduced commitment to policies promoted by the previous communist regime, including social welfare, full employment, and a relatively egalitarian structure of personal incomes. Popular acceptance of the new policies and political orientations are crucial to the success of the postcommunist regime. Public opinion surveys can help to reveal the extent of such commitment.

---

[6] S. Kwiatkowski in an interview in *Słowo Polskie* (Wrocław), January 4, 1983, p. 4.

Critiques of Public Opinion Methodology

Serious criticisms of the reliability of Polish public opinion surveys began to surface even before the momentous changes of 1989. Criticisms were raised about the methodological problems of surveys, especially in authoritarian societies, and about the political manipulation of surveys. An article by Krystyna Lutyńska of the Academy of Sciences in 1987, for example, while focused on the issue of refusal rates in Polish surveys, went much beyond this issue in questioning the reliability of surveys conducted in Poland.[7]

The issue of refusal rates itself is serious enough, in that a large percentage of nonresponses in a survey can distort the sample and therefore seriously affect the representativeness of the survey. Nonresponse rates are routinely recorded and reported in scientific surveys in Western countries. Until 1982, according to Lutyńska, refusal rates were rarely even recorded in Poland, and though this has been required in most surveys since then, many still do not do so. Where records were kept, refusal rates in the 1960s and 1970s appeared to be relatively low, ranging from about 2 percent to 12 percent (U.S. surveys generally experience refusal rates of between 10 percent and 30 percent). After the implementation of martial law, however, refusal rates soared, sometimes to 50 percent, though these rates were still often not reported with the results. For surveys conducted in 1982–85, the most important variable in response rates was sponsorship of the survey. Refusal rates for surveys conducted by official survey centers (e.g., OBP [Ośrodek Badań Prasoznawczych] in Kraków and CBOS and OBOP in Warsaw) ranged from 16 percent to 50 percent; while those for surveys conducted by academic institutions were only 3–14 percent. Obviously many people were refusing to participate in official surveys, out of either aversion or fear.

Lutyńska was skeptical, however, of the validity of the results even for those who did respond. She contended that people who agree to be interviewed (at least in this post-martial-law period) do so for one of four reasons: fear of refusal, good manners, a sense of civic duty, or "to have their say and to tell the truth regardless of the consequences."[8] She argued that only those in the last category are likely to give honest answers to sensitive political questions. The others are likely to give answers that they believe are officially acceptable or expected of them by the interviewer.

Of course, interviewer effects are also a problem in the United States, and there have been numerous studies of the impact of age, sex, race, appearance, and institutional affiliation on the response rate and honesty of responses. Lutyńska's assessment may be overly pessimistic, but it does raise the

---

[7] K. Lutyńska, "Questionnaire Studies in Poland in the 1980s," *Polish Sociological Bulletin*, 1987, no. 3, pp. 43–54.

[8] *Ibid.*, p. 52

question of the validity of public opinion surveys conducted, first of all, in extraordinary conditions (e.g., martial law), and secondly, by an institution that is perceived as responsible to the political authorities.

A similar kind of criticism was raised by a Warsaw University sociologist, Antoni Sułek, who compared the responses to similar questions posed by CBOS, an official public opinion research center, and by the Academy of Sciences and Warsaw University in their series of "Polacy" surveys.[9] Antoni Sułek found considerable differences in the survey results, for example in confidence in public institutions; the CBOS surveys showed higher confidence in the party and lower confidence in Solidarity than did the *Polacy'88* national survey. The *ranking* of the fifteen institutions, however, was almost exactly the same. (This author found the same patterns in surveys conducted by the government and Solidarity in 1981.)[10] Sułek attributes the differences not to deliberate distortion but to bias in the way questions were designed, the nonrepresentativeness of samples, and the intimidation effect of CBOS interviewers, almost all of whom were from either the army propaganda apparatus or the state bureaucracy.

Criticism of official surveys became even more blunt and hard hitting after Solidarity's astonishing sweep of the parliamentary elections in June 1989. Numerous articles chastised Kwiatkowski's CBOS for underestimating Solidarity's support in pre-election surveys and even for deliberately distorting the results to influence voters. Maciej Kozłowski, writing in the independent Catholic weekly *Tygodnik Powszechny*, said of CBOS:

> For years we have lived in an artificial world in which the ruling party apparently enjoyed mass support, with the opposition having only a very narrow margin. Such a picture of Poland was presented to us by Colonel Kwiatkowski only a few months ago, and even after the August 1988 strikes he assessed support for Solidarity at only 18.9 percent.[11]

Others complained that CBOS's surveys had made the authorities overly confident, self-satisfied, and isolated from society's real feelings. Kwiatkowski responded by arguing that the polls only measure attitudes and affiliations at a particular point in time, and that people may well have changed their minds as the elections approached. There is probably some truth to both the criticisms and the defense. Even many nonofficial surveys showed relatively low levels of support for Solidarity in the year before the election. The overwhelming support for Solidarity in the elections was due *in part*, at

---

[9] A. Sułek, "O rzetelności i nierzetelności badań sondażowych w Polsce," *Kultura i Społeczeństwo* vol. 33, no. 1 (January-March 1989), pp. 23–49.

[10] See Mason, *Public Opinion and Political Change, op. cit.* p. 118.

[11] *Tygodnik Powszechny*, June 18, 1989; cited in Radio Free Europe Research, Polish Situation Report (hereafter RFER, PSR), no. 12, July 28, 1989.

least, to a vote *against* the party. After forty years of rule by a single party, this was the first opportunity for Poles to "throw the rascals out" (to use a phrase from the American political lexicon). The election's plebiscitarian character led Wałęsa to admit that people had cast votes as a way of "getting even" with the communists rather than as a deliberate choice between political and economic platforms.

This more open discussion of the reliability and validity of surveys is a most healthy phenomenon, however, and will lead to increasing refinement of Polish survey methods. The more open political climate, on the other hand, is likely to have a mixed impact on public opinion research. On the one hand, it will allow inquiry into more sensitive political issues, the proliferation of independent public opinion research centers, and a greater willingness of respondents to answer sensitive political questions. At the same time, the emergence of independent interest groups and political parties will allow public opinion to be translated into political muscle. On the other hand, with the emergence of a more open and competitive political atmosphere, public opinion surveys will no longer have to act as a surrogate for genuine political participation and representation. This may well remove public opinion somewhat from the political arena, allowing it to develop along more scientific lines.

The Lessons of Public Opinion for Poland's Future

The Shallow Impact of Political Socialization

The most astounding feature of the 1989 changes in Poland (and Eastern Europe) was their thoroughness and rapidity. First in Poland, but later in elections in Hungary, East Germany, and Czechoslovakia, the communists were overwhelmingly defeated, despite their advantages of incumbency and their last minute efforts to change their images, policies, and even names. The scope of this popular hostility is especially surprising given the forty years of political socialization pursued so deliberately by the communist regime.

Even before 1980, however, it was apparent that the ideological principles of Marxism-Leninism had little acceptance in Poland. In 1958, only 13 percent of Warsaw students identified themselves as Marxists; twenty years later, still only 18 percent.[12] Despite the rejection of Marxism, though, most Poles before 1980 seemed to accept the general commitment to *socialism*, even if they felt the regime had not lived up to those ideals. Stefan Nowak reported widespread social acceptance of the nationalization of industry, agrarian reform, economic planning, and the transformation of the prewar

[12] A. Jasińska-Kania, "National Identity and Images of World Society: The Polish Case," *International Social Science Journal* 34 (1982), pp. 93–112.

class structure.[13] Poles also evidenced a strong egalitarianism, particularly regarding incomes.

With the crushing of Solidarity in 1981 and the continued deterioration of the economy in the 1980s, even this limited commitment to socialism began to wither away. This was recognized and admitted even by the regime. At a 1983 party conference on ideological problems, one eminent ideologist bemoaned an "ideological crisis" manifested in "the undermining of the faith of a large part of the Polish society in the value of socialist ideals and socialism itself."[14] Official publications complained of the lack of commitment from young people, especially given the resources lavished on their political education: "What has happened to the hundreds of millions of zlotys that were spent on seminars, camps, conferences, competitions, meetings, and all of the other forms of political training? All that money seems to have been completely wasted."[15]

Support for Marxism, particularly among young people, had practically disappeared by the mid-1980s. A survey of Gdańsk high school students in 1984 found only 2 percent declaring themselves Marxists; and support was not much higher among university students.[16] The shift in attitudes was not restricted to young people. In a cross-national survey conducted in Eastern and Western Europe in early 1990, only West Germans (81 percent) reacted more negatively to the term "communism" than did the Poles (80 percent). And of all the countries, the Poles had by far the *most* positive response to "capitalism." Indeed, East Europeans in general responded more favorably toward capitalism than did respondents in the capitalist countries![17] The Polish attitudes toward capitalism and communism are a culmination of a trend that began in 1980, with increasingly large numbers of people favoring a market-oriented approach to the economic system and a shift in emphasis from favoring equality toward favoring freedom. These tendencies will be discussed further below.

State socialist societies are sometimes referred to in the West as "mobilized" societies, in that the regimes in those countries attempt to foster high degrees of political awareness and political participation, albeit controlled participation. Thus in Poland as in other East European states, there were numerous mass-membership organizations, such as the party itself, but also youth organizations and other special-interest groups. Furthermore, formal participation in the political process, both in terms of voting and in

[13] S. Nowak, "Values and Attitudes of the Polish People," *Scientific American* 245 (1981), pp. 245ff.

[14] *Nowe Drogi*, October 1983.

[15] *Sztandar Młodych*, November 18, 1983.

[16] *Polityka*, August 11, 1984.

[17] A. Riding, "Survey Finds 2 in 3 Poles Opposed to German Unity," *The New York Times*, February 20, 1990.

the number of people who serve in elected office, was very high compared to pluralist societies.

Despite the regime's efforts at political mobilization, however, such participation by Poles has been ritualistic, at best. Poles neither participated much in politics nor even evinced much interest in politics, and this abstention from political activity increased during the 1980s. Even in "normal" times, a surprisingly large number of Poles were not aware of even major political issues and events. Surveys done in the mid-1970s showed that less than 20 percent of the residents of six cities could name the president, the first party secretary, or a single representative in their electoral district.[18] An official poll in 1985 found that only 15–17 percent of adult citizens were "interested in politics," and about half of those were party members.[19] This lack of political interest and involvement turned into a major embarrassment for the regime in a November 1987 referendum on the economic reforms. Too few people voted to enable the government to win the required majority of all *eligible* voters. The government proceeded with the reforms anyway.

This political disinterest continued even through the remarkable events of 1988 and 1989. In August 1988, during the second wave of strikes which forced the government into talks with Solidarity, as many as 44 percent of people admitted to being unaware of this decision; a third of the respondents admitted to apathetic attitudes toward political developments and to not paying any attention to them.[20] And during the Roundtable talks, despite extensive media coverage, most Poles had little knowledge of the participants. Even supposedly well known opposition figures like Jacek Kuroń (62 percent) and Adam Michnik (49 percent) were recognized by less than two-thirds of the respondents. Future Prime Minister Mazowiecki was known by only 20.9 percent of the respondents.[21]

There are many ways to explain this political apathy and erosion of acceptance for the regime's norms. The most straightforward, perhaps, is simply the frustration and disgust that most Poles felt at the regime's martial-law crackdown on Solidarity. For many people, this was the last straw and proved that the regime was incapable of reforming itself; fewer and fewer people believed in "state-controlled democratization of the state."[22] There was also increasing recognition and rejection of the privileges and

[18] K. Jasiewicz and A. Jasińska, "Problem zaspokajania potrzeb i funkcjonowania władz lokalnych w percepcji mieszkańców," in J. Wiatr, ed., *Władza lokalna a zaspokajanie potrzeb*, Warszawa: Polska Akademia Nauk, Instytut Filozofii i Socjologii, 1981.

[19] S. Kwiatkowski, "Polling Center Looks at Support for Opposition," *Polityka*, February 1, 1986; translated in Joint Publications Research Service, *East Europe Report*, May 16, 1986.

[20] S. Kwiatkowski, *Polityka*, 1988.

[21] S. Kwiatkowski, "Dowcip Bratkowskiego," *Polityka*, January 7, 1989.

[22] S. Magala, "Local Truth in Global Setup (Poland's Shifts 1982–1987). Unpublished manuscript, 1988.

corruption associated with the political leadership. But there are longer-term, more fundamental, reasons as well. Lena Kolarska-Bobińska, a sociologist at the Academy of Sciences, argues that in the 1970s people came to depend on the state as a provider of basic economic, social, and educational needs. By the 1980s, as the economy continued to deteriorate, many perceived the state as failing at this function and gave up on it, often trying to fulfill these needs outside the public sector, either legally (the private market) or illegally (the black market).[23]

The Decline of Political Legitimacy

No political regime, democratic or authoritarian, can last long without a political socialization process that breeds at least some support for the government's basic values and institutions. In Poland, as we have seen, the political socialization process seems to have broken down altogether, particularly after the declaration of martial law at the end of 1981. This led to a further erosion of the already debased legitimacy of the communist regime. In Poland, as in the rest of Eastern Europe, political legitimacy had increasingly come to rest on the satisfaction of basic economic and social needs. There was a kind of "social contract"[24] or "social accord"[25] in which the populace left politics to the politicians and in return the state provided economic growth and social services and did not demand much in the way of commitment or effort from the population. Indeed, some surveys suggested that Poles accepted this as the proper, even desirable, function of the state.

Though the population may not have expected much from the regime in terms of political rights, it did hold sizeable expectations in the economic and social realm. As Stefan Nowak put it in 1981, most Poles held the state responsible for "the equalization of life opportunities, for the development of the potential of all citizens, as well as for the satisfaction of their basic needs."[26] In addition, in the 1960s and early 1970s, there was a high degree of social mobility (both real and perceived) in the country that allowed a sense of constant improvement. With the slowdown in social mobility in the 1970s and then the slowdown in the economy itself, the government became increasingly unable to deliver on its part of the "compact." By 1980, polls showed that Poland had *three times* as many dissatisfied people as there were, on average, in eight Western nations. Ironically, Poles had especially bad

[23] Lena Kolarska-Bobińska, "Poland Under Crisis: Unreformable Society or Establishment?" In Roger Clarke, ed., *Poland: Economy in the 1980s* (Essex: Longman, 1989), pp. 131–32.

[24] P. Hauslohner, "Gorbachev's Social Contract," *Soviet Economy* 3, no. 1 (1987), pp. 54–89; J. Bielasiak, "Reform and the Working Class in Communist States: A New 'Social Contract'?" (Paper presented at the American Political Science Association, September 1988, Washington, DC).

[25] Kolarska-Bobińska, "Poland Under Crisis," *op. cit.*, p. 126.

[26] Nowak, "Values and Attitudes," *op. cit.*

ratings for social services (which is supposed to be the strength of socialist societies), such as medical care, housing, the environment, and egalitarian policies.[27] An analysis of the "Polacy" surveys in the mid-1980s concluded that only about a quarter of the population could be counted as "pro" regime.[28]

In capitalist democracies, the government is not always held responsible for economic slowdowns, which are often seen as an inevitable consequence of the market. In state socialist societies, however, since the government controls the economy, the government gets the blame when the economy falters.[29] As long as the economy was improving, legitimacy was preserved. With the collapse of the economy, even this source of legitimacy disappeared. The Jaruzelski regime searched desperately for alternative sources of legitimacy, for example in appeals to Poland's national traditions[30] and by seeking support from the Soviet Union. But with the accession of Mikhail Gorbachev to the Soviet leadership in 1985, even this external legitimation began to dry up. The Polish communist party regime was doomed.

The declining faith in the system was reflected in more concrete ways in diminished trust in official institutions and public figures, in increasingly outspoken resentment about privileges and corruption, and in increasing support for a more pluralistic political environment. The most obvious aspect of this was in declining confidence in institutions. When the government, and then Solidarity, first began publishing such polls on trust in institutions in 1981, these consistently showed that the *unofficial* institutions, especially the Church and Solidarity, were much more highly rated than official ones. The Polish United Workers' Party (PZPR) always fared badly in such polls, usually ending up in last place. In the 1980s, however, the levels of trust in virtually *all* institutions, official and unofficial, steadily declined, though the relative rankings remained about the same. While the party continued to fare poorly (with only about a quarter expressing trust in the *Polacy '88* survey), the regime's newly created institutional structures did not do much better: the Patriotic Movement for National Rebirth (PRON) had the confidence of only 40 percent in the 1988 survey, and the new trade unions, of only 34 percent.[31] Confidence in the party was even lower among urban workers. A December 1988 survey of 1,200 persons in seven industrial

[27] R. Inglehart and R. Siemieńska, "Changing Values and Political Dissatisfaction in Poland and the West," *Government and Opposition*, vol. 23 (Autumn 1988), pp. 440–457.

[28] K. Jasiewicz, "Kultura polityczna Polaków: Między jednością a podziałem" *Aneks*, no. 48 (1988), p. 70.

[29] See E. Gucwa-Leśny, "Attitudes Toward Egalitarian Policy – Implications for the Economic Reform," in D. Kemme, ed., *Economic Reform in Poland* (JAI Press, forthcoming).

[30] S. Burant, "Official Political Culture in the Peoples' Republic of Poland" (Paper presented to the American Association for the Advancement of Slavic Studies, Boston, November 1987).

[31] W. Adamski and K. Jasiewicz, "Dynamika postaw kontestacyjnych," in W. Adamski et al., *Polacy '88: Dynamika konfliktu a szanse reform*, Warszawa 1989, pp 232–33.

enterprises in Warsaw showed only 6.8 percent expressing trust in the PZPR
– probably less than the total number of party *members* in those enterprises!
These results and others led the authors of this Warsaw study to conclude
that "the political system is questioned or even rejected at all its levels: at the
level of the main organs of the state, at the level of industrial organizations in
which the respondents work, and at the level of individual behavior."[32]

This lack of trust in the party and the party's sharply decreasing legitimacy
led Poles increasingly to question the necessity of maintaining the party's
"leading role" in society. The *Polacy '81* survey showed that over half of the
sample were in favor of a system *without* such a role for the party, and
follow-up *Polacy* surveys in the 1980s showed similar results.[33] The *Polacy
'88* poll, conducted at the end of 1987 and the beginning of 1988, revealed
only about a third of the respondents favoring maintaining the power of the
party. Another third was in favor of reducing the power of the party, and the
remaining third were undecided or uninterested.[34]

Curiously, though, this antipathy toward the party did not, through much
of the 1980s, translate into a desire fundamentally to transform the system.
Even during 1981, according to the *Polacy '81* survey, only a quarter of the
respondents favored constituting new political parties, apart from the PZPR
and its satellite parties, the Social Democratic Party, and the United Peasant
Party. There was also little support for the proposition that Solidarity should
create a political party to operate alongside the union. Only 20 percent of the
overall sample and 23 percent of Solidarity members favored this idea.[35]
During the mid-1980s, similarly, most people seemed to be more interested in
improving the economic situation rather than fundamental political change.
When asked in CBOS polls about what was the main thing that needed to be
done to improve the country's situation, the largest numbers of people
mentioned "inducing people to work better" (50–60 percent in various polls)
or to "reform the economy" (40–57 percent). Many fewer suggested "changing
the government" (5–17 percent) or "changing the political system" (5–15
percent).[36] This "apolitical" response was probably due to the resignation and
apathy that characterized Polish society after the imposition of martial law.

In the latter half of the 1980s, however, this attitude began to change, and
Poles came increasingly to favor democratizing and pluralizing changes in
the political system. A survey conducted by the Academy of Sciences in 1985

[32] B. Cichomski and W. Morawski, "The Perception of Justice in Poland" (Paper presented at
the International Studies Association, London, March 1989).

[33] Jasiewicz, "Kultura polityczna," *op. cit.,* pp. 75–76.

[34] A. Rychard, "Ład polityczny: Centralizm i pluralizm w opinii Polaków," in *Polacy'88, op.
cit.,* p. 281.

[35] W Adamski, et al., *Polacy'81. Postrzeganie kryzysu i konfliktu,* Warszawa: Polska
Akademia Nauk, Instytut Filozofii i Socjologii, 1982, pp. 207ff.

[36] Reported by S. Kwiatkowski in *Przegląd Tygodniowy,* September 7, 1985; cited in James
McGregor, "Economic Reform and Polish Public Opinion," *Soviet Studies* 41, no. 2 (April
1989), p. 221.

found overwhelming support for "respecting freedom and the political rights of the citizen" (90.5 percent) and for "participation by citizens in the making of basic state decisions" (82 percent).[37] This began to be translated into more concrete demands as well. In this same sample, 65 percent agreed that elections must involve "competition of various political parties." By 1988, support for a similar proposition, that "citizens should be able to choose between candidates of various political views," was even stronger, supported by over 72 percent. In the 1984 *Polacy* survey, the sample was about evenly divided on whether opposition groups should be legalized. By 1988, many more Poles favored a legal opposition (47.3 percent) than opposed it (26.1 percent).[38]

As Krzysztof Jasiewicz points out, a whole series of surveys during the 1980s points to a "slow but steady shift in societal preferences from 'equality' ...to 'freedom' – an acceptance of various forms of economic, social, and political activity and the differing consequences of that activity."[39] A similar conclusion could be drawn from the survey of workers in Warsaw enterprises. When asked in which type of society they would prefer to live, the most frequent response was "a free society" (36.5 percent) and a "rich society" (21.1 percent). The responses for the kind of society promoted by the communist regime were much lower: for a "just" society, 20 percent; for one "based on friendship and solidarity," 12 percent; for one that "provides personal safety," 8 percent; and for one "with a good welfare system," only 3 percent.[40]

There are two sides to this movement: one *away* from equality; and the second *toward* freedom. As to the former, Poles exhibit a dramatic move away from egalitarianism during the 1980s. One sees this most clearly in the *Polacy* surveys, where from 1980 to 1988 there is a dramatic decline in those "decisively" favoring limiting the highest earnings (from 70.6 percent to 27.5 percent) and in those strongly favoring a policy of full employment (50.6 percent to 25.3 percent) and a sharp increase in those favoring high differentiation in wages based on qualifications (from 25.8 percent to 40.4 percent). There is also an increase from 1984 to 1988 in those favoring expanded possibilities for the private sector, from 59.5 percent to 73 percent.[41] Ewa Gucwa-Leśny refers to this as a shift "from supporting the

[37] S. Gebethner and A. Uhlig, "Rozumienie demokracji oraz wymiary jej postrzegania w opiniach i poglądach obywateli," in S. Gebethner, ed., *Demokracja i wybory: Raport z badań 'Opinie Polaków – Jesień'85,'* Warszawa 1988, p. 139.

[38] Rychard, "Ład Polityczny," *op. cit.,* pp. 276–84.

[39] Jasiewicz, "Dynamika przemian postaw politycznych w latach osiemdziesiątych" (Unpublished manuscript, 1989).

[40] Cichomski and Morawski, "The Perception of Justice in Poland," *op. cit.*

[41] L. Kolarska-Bobińska, "Poczucie niesprawiedliwości, konfliktu i preferowany ład w gospodarce," in *Polacy '88, op. cit.,* p. 115–16.

equity in poverty policy toward one of supporting a just inequality based on the clear criteria connected with the efficiency of work."[42] These changes in popular consciousness are reflected in the policies and stances of Solidarity, which became increasingly less egalitarian by the time of the Roundtable talks in 1989.

This increasing commitment to the principles of democracy was connected with a revival in support for and confidence in Solidarity. In the early 1980s, Solidarity, like all institutions, suffered a sharp drop in popular confidence from over 90 percent support in 1981 to only 11–13 percent in 1984 and 1985. But by 1988, this started to pick up, with the *Polacy '88* survey showing confidence in Solidarity up to 25 percent.[43] Solidarity's approval rating increased sharply over the next year, to 75 percent in March of 1989.[44] In the same period, the perception of Solidarity as an institution beneficial to society grew from 18.2 percent to 67.2 percent.[45]

There seem to be numerous reasons for the turnaround in Polish public opinion the late 1980s. First of all, the period of frustration and apathy caused by the martial-law crackdown had begun to mellow a bit, as Poles, especially younger ones, increasingly came back into the political arena. Many of the strike leaders in 1988, for example, were different and younger than those who had led the strikes in 1980. Secondly, there was increasing popular frustration and disillusionment with the reforms efforts of General Jaruzelski and his government. The "Second Stage" of the economic reform was continuously revised and delayed, and meanwhile the Polish economy, and Poles' standards of living, continued to decline. While Poles had seemingly put their hopes in a nonpolitical approach to change, this no longer seemed to work. This leads to the third point, which is an increasing awareness that serious economic changes were not possible without accompanying changes in the political realm. Fourth, despite the lack of real success with the market-oriented economic reforms, the population came increasingly to accept the regime's own *rhetoric* in support of the market in the economy and democratization in the polity. Finally, there is the impact of Gorbachev. At an increasing pace, especially from 1987, the Gorbachev leadership began to introduce reforms in the Soviet Union, some of which were ahead of change in Central Europe. Increasingly, too, Moscow began to back away from the principles of the Brezhnev Doctrine, to pressure the East European leaders to push ahead with their own reforms, and to promise noninterference in the internal affairs of those countries. This had the effect of reducing the element of fear of change in Poland and of undercutting the strength of the conservatives in the leadership who resisted change. It greatly widened the "limits of the possible" in Poland.

[42] Gucwa-Leśny, "Attitudes Toward Egalitarian Policy," *op. cit.*

[43] Jasiewicz, "Dynamika przemian," *op. cit.*

[44] J. Głuszczyński, "Nowy wizerunek," *Polityka*, April 1, 1989.

[45] *Polityka*, March 4, 1989, p. 5.

The Obstacles to Democratization and Stability

The changes in public opinion in the late 1980s in Poland were part of a thoroughgoing rejection of the existing system of "real socialism." The elections of June 1989 gave the population the opportunity, for the first time, to demonstrate this in a legal and irrefutable fashion. The combination of attitudinal change and structural change (with the formation of a noncommunist government) marked a *revolutionary* transformation in Poland: the old system, its values, policies, and institutions, was swept away. This provided a kind of clean slate on which the new Mazowiecki government could write its economic and political revolution.

There is, however, a darker underside to these changes. The old system having been swept away, a new system needs to be put in place. This requires the rebuilding not only of the political and economic structure but also of the structure of values, attitudes, and patterns of behavior. In normal circumstances, in any society, these are passed down from one generation to the next, at least partly through the process of political socialization. As we have seen, however, this process had already broken down even before 1989, and it may take a while before a new process takes its place. This entails, among other changes, the restructuring of the educational system, the rewriting of textbooks, and a new role for the mass medial.

Thus, as in any revolutionary situation, the necessary changes are complex, deep, and wide, and they will not be accomplished within just a few months or years. Just looking at the political system, for example, students of the process of democratization suggest that it takes *twelve years* or more for authoritarian states to make the transition to a "consolidated" democracy.[46] The transitions from state socialist to market economy and from "subject" to "participant" political cultures may take even longer. In the meantime, the fledgling democratic government in Poland, lacking the stability and legitimacy that is purchased by time, will have many challenges and obstacles to overcome.

Among these problems are some aspects of the existing Polish political culture that may not be favorable to the years of patience, tolerance, and compromise necessary for the consolidation of democracy and the market. These phenomena include a continuing sense of cynicism, pessimism, and apathy, a remaining commitment by many to egalitarianism and socialism, and a relatively weak sense of, and experience with, democracy.

We have discussed above the long-term and increasing sense of apathy and frustration that characterized Polish society in the 1980s. The events of 1989 and 1990 temporarily reversed this trend, but despite the formation of a Solidarity-led government in the fall of 1989, there remains a surprisingly

---

[46] P. Schmitter, "The Consolidation of Democracy in Southern Europe"(Unpublished paper, Stanford University, 1989).

high degree of apathy and pessimism. The signature of the Roundtable Agreements in April 1989 occasioned little celebration or popular fanfare, and the streets of Warsaw on the following day were surprisingly normal. Polls in March 1989 showed only about 30 percent of the population willing to join Solidarity and 47 percent saying they had no such intention.[47] When Solidarity was finally legalized after the Roundtable Agreements, only about 2.2 million people joined the union by the summer, far short of the 9.5 million members in 1981. In the June 1989 elections, turnout was far lower than expected. Both sides had thought 80 percent would participate, but only about 62 percent did so. The runoff elections two weeks later attracted less than 15 percent of the electorate.[48] In the first completely open and contested elections – for local government councils in May 1990 – only 42 percent of eligible voters participated. This was not the same fervor and activism seen in 1980–81.

This continued political apathy and lack of participation was due in part to the continuing frustration and pessimism regarding the economy. Negative evaluations of the economy and pessimism regarding its future had grown sharply during the 1980s, becoming almost universal by the end of the decade. This trend, too, seems to have been reversed, at least temporarily, with the election of a Solidarity government. Initially, people overwhelmingly supported the new Mazowiecki government and expected it to improve the economy. But in a December 1989 poll, only about a quarter of the respondents expressed hopes for improvements, with 30 percent having more fears than hope for the future, and 29 percent expecting Poland to sink further into chaos and crisis. Almost 60 percent of the respondents expressed a willingness to take a job in the West.[49] During the first half of 1990, monthly public opinion polls showed a steady decline in pubic confidence for *all* political leaders and institutions.[50] These were not hopeful signs and indicate how thin was the reservoir of support for the new government. Further economic difficulties were likely to lead to a revival of pessimism, apathy, and withdrawal.

This political apathy, which is due in part to the many years of suffering authoritarianism, is linked to a relatively weak sense of democracy, also due in part to the lack of experience with democratic processes and institutions. The 1985 study on popular understandings of democracy found much higher levels of support for civil rights and even equal access to material goods than for institutional and procedural aspects of democracy such as a multiparty system, contested elections, and a critical opposition. On this last issue, only

[47] Głuszczyński, "Nowy wizerunek," *op. cit.*

[48] *Polityka*, October 14, 1989, p. 2.

[49] S. Nowicki, *Polityka*, December 23–30, 1989, p. 7.

[50] *Rzeczpospolita*, July 25, 1990, and *Polityka*, June 30, 1990.

36 percent "decisively" agreed that the Sejm should have a "legal opposition criticizing the government." Overall, the authors of this study found that only about 55 percent of the sample had a "decisively pluralistic orientation."[51] The flip side of this weak commitment to democracy is a disconcertingly strong degree of support for "law and order" in Poland. The *Polacy '88* survey, for example, found almost 78 percent of the sample agreeing that Poland needed a "strong leader who would bring order to the country."[52] In fact, more respondents agreed with this statement than with the proposition that voters should be able to choose among candidates of various political views (73 percent).[53] These data led Krzysztof Jasiewicz to characterize the Polish political culture as "sharply polarized" between "two contradictory syndromes of values: authoritarian populist and democratic-liberal."[54] Of course, these surveys were conducted before the 1989 revolution, but it remains to be seen if these syndromes have significantly changed since then.

Another potential challenge to the Mazowiecki government, though this more in terms of economic policy than politics, is the continuing strong strand of egalitarianism in Polish society. Numerous studies, including some alluded to above, point out the sharp decline in egalitarian attitudes among Poles. Furthermore, some have contended that the egalitarianism of the 1980s was primarily *political* in character, a reaction to the corruption and privileges of the political elite.[55] Other studies, both national and local, have pointed to the increasing acceptance of the market and especially of inequalities in wages and incomes.[56]

However, the other side of this issue is that the *majority* of Poles still (at least as of 1988) support some key egalitarian principles, especially regarding wages, incomes, and prices. The *Polacy '88* survey showed that 57 percent supported limiting the highest wages and 60 percent favoring a policy of full employment. These figures were far below what they had been in the early 1980s, but they were still high enough to suggest some opposition to the "shock" of the market introduced in January 1990. On the other hand, there is strong popular support for other important aspects of the reforms, including private ownership of property.[57]

---

[51] Gebethner and Uhlig, "Rozumienie demokracji", *op. cit.*, pp. 139–40; also see Jane Curry, "The Psychological Barriers to Reform in Poland," *Eastern European Politics and Societies*, vol. 2, no. 3 (Fall 1988), p. 495.

[52] Similarly high levels of support for law and order in 1989 are reported in Krzysztof Jasiewicz's contribution to this volume.

[53] Rychard, "Ład polityczny," *op. cit.*, p. 284.

[54] Jasiewicz, "Kultura polityczna," *op. cit.*, p. 95.

[55] Kolarska-Bobińska, "Poland Under Crisis," *op. cit.*, pp. 133–34.

[56] For example, Cichomski and Morawski, "The Perceptions of Justice," *op. cit.*

[57] A national survey in 1989 found 60 percent accepting private ownership of property. Witold Morawski, "Reform Models and Systemic Change"(Paper presented at the IV World Congress for Soviet and East European Studies, Harrogate, England, July 1990).

Commitment to the market is stronger in some sectors of society than in others: as might be expected, unskilled manual workers, clerical workers, and (to a lesser extent) farmers remain fairly egalitarian. Indeed, Poland's official trade-union (OPZZ – Ogólnopolskie Porozumienie Związków Zawodowych) leadership tried to capitalize on this sentiment at the time of the January price increases: "We cannot agree to the policy of free prices and frozen incomes for working people," Miodowicz declared, "that would lead to further impoverishment of a considerable part of society."[58] Perhaps the key question here is the following: If Polish egalitarianism *was* primarily directed against those in power, and those in power are increasingly being replaced, will Poles return to the more traditional economic egalitarianism of the 1960s and 1970s, which would stymie the market reforms, or will they be brought over to the economic inegalitarianism of the market? Again, time will tell.

Conclusions: Polish Political Culture in Comparative Perspective

The previous pages may have painted an overly pessimistic view of Poland's chances for the consolidation of democracy and the transition to the market. It has been customary for both Polish and Western social scientists to point to data on Polish public opinion and call attention to the high degree of cynicism and apathy, the continuing strands of authoritarianism, and the conflicting attitudes held by the same people. In the past, it may have been appropriate to view Poland in isolation from Western countries, partly because the system was so different and therefore the political context of public opinion was so different from the West, and partly because the nature of survey research in Poland made it difficult to compare to surveys in the West. But as Poland moves more toward the West, these differences diminish and it becomes more important to place Poland in a Western context. It becomes more appropriate, and more relevant, to compare the political culture of Poland with that of Western countries: to compare, for example, the social conditions for acceptance of the market and democratic institutions. Such a comparison would shed further light on the potential for Poland's successful transit.

Such comparisons are beyond the scope of this essay, but a few examples may illustrate the point. In the section above, we addressed some of the obstacles to change in Poland, including the widespread sense of apathy and pessimism, the low degree of political participation, and the continuing support for both egalitarianism and the market. But there are similar phenomena in Western democracies. Political apathy and low levels of participation, for example, are a continuing source of concern in the United

---

[58] *The New York Times*, January 3, 1990.

States. Only about one-half of Americans vote in presidential elections, and only about a third cast ballots for the highest state offices (such as governor) or in Congressional midterm elections when the presidency is not at stake. Less than 10 percent of Americans are active enough politically to attend party meetings or work in political campaigns. Americans are also abysmally ignorant about their political system: only about 40 percent can name their two U.S. senators, and less than a third know that the term of a U.S. House member is two years.[59] By these standards, Polish political awareness and participation is quite high.

Similarly, we discussed above the cynicism and pessimism that is characteristic of the Polish political culture and raised the question of whether this would eventually be directed at the non-communist government as well. It may well happen, but Western democracies are also characterized by high degrees of cynicism and mistrust. In the United States, for example, only 39 percent believe that government is run for the benefit of all, while 55 percent believe that government is run pretty much for a few big interests. A majority of Americans feel that the government wastes a lot of money and that you cannot trust the government to do right most of the time.[60] Despite all this, most Americans express feelings of pride in the country and the system of government.

We also saw above that Poles have been highly concerned about what they perceive as excessive privileges and corruption within the political elite but also about the degree of inequality within society generally. Here, too, though, Polish sensitivities are not out of line with those in other societies. In the United States, over 40 percent of the population thinks that "quite a few people running the government are a little crooked." In Inglehart and Siemieńska's comparison of Poland with Western countries, they found that while 72 percent of Poles thought (in 1980) that some groups had unduly privileged positions in society, this figure was lower than in any Western societies in the study.[61] Another comparison of three socialist and seven capitalist countries found that popular perceptions of inequalities were relatively high in Poland, but at levels similar to those in France and Yugoslavia.[62] And while it seemed paradoxical that Poles would favor both a more market-oriented economy and a commitment to full employment policies, the same is true in the United States, where 81 percent favor guaranteed jobs so that people could earn a decent income.[63]

---

[59] American public opinion data drawn from P. Johnson et al., *American Government: People, Institutions, and Policies*, 2nd ed. (Boston: Houghton Mifflin, 1990), pp. 193ff.

[60] *Ibid.*, p. 221.

[61] Inglehart and Siemieńska, "Changing Values..." *op. cit.*, p. 450.

[62] Cichomski and Morawski "The perception of Justice in Poland," *op. cit.*

[63] R. Lane, "Market Justice, Political Justice," *American Political Science Review*, no. 2 (June 1986), p. 392.

In the end, the key task for the new government in Poland is to convince the population, either by rhetoric or action, that the new order is a just one, both legitimate and fair. In the past, justice had been promised, and to some extent delivered, by the polity, and people came to expect justice from the regime. When these expectations were shattered in the 1980s, people lost both confidence and hope. With the transition to a market economy, the government no longer will satisfy all the demands for justice – now the market will share some of that burden. In the United States, as Robert Lane has pointed out in his article, "Market Justice, Political Justice," people see the market as just but have low expectations of political justice. Most people believe that in both market and polity people are animated by self interest: "In the market, however, self-interest is thought to be both fruitful for the common good and policed by competition, while in the polity self-interest is seen as neither fruitful nor properly constrained."[64] Since in the United States expectations for the political system are not high, the widespread apathy, cynicism, and distrust is not particularly threatening to the system.

In some ways, Poland is in an advantageous situation in that expectations have not traditionally been very high, and the Mazowiecki government has tried to keep expectations under control with constant reminders of the difficult days ahead. Most of the warnings by Mazowiecki and his government, however, have been about the state of the economy. It may also be necessary to temper expectations for democracy. A democratic government will not cure all of Poland's problems, just as it has not cured all of the problems in North America or Western Europe. Furthermore, democracy is not a fact but a process. It requires continuous work and adjustment. Poland still has a long way to go in creating both a new government and a new economy, but it has begun, and Poles now have the chance to build the kind of society *they* want.

---

[64] *Ibid.*, p. 392.

Part 3

From Control to Pluralism

PARTICIPATION AND INTERESTS
DILEMMAS OF THE EMERGING
SOCIAL AND POLITICAL STRUCTURE
IN POLAND

Andrzej Rychard

The Problem of Structures: Two Hypotheses

It is possible to analyze the problem of the social and political structures in Poland in terms of two contradictory hypotheses. Both concern the emergence of these structures and the relations between them.

According to the first hypothesis, the political breakthrough in Poland was possible due to the social activity and popular support for the changes. The alliance between workers and the intelligentsia, which started in 1980, has lasted for ten years and made possible both the summer of 1980 and the collapse of communism ten years later. According to this concept, the most important division in society was a dichotomous one: the power elite and its supporters on one side, and the whole "class of employees" on the other. According to J. Kurczewski (1982), this group could be called the "new middle class." Although it is perhaps not a "class" in the strict sense of the word, its members revealed many common features. The "new middle class," consisting of the most skilled and frustrated parts of this "employee class," was the most active element of society. Now, after the formal collapse of communism, institutional and political structures are the major obstacle to further changes because they block already existing social activity. Society wants to participate, but there are no mechanisms enabling it to do so. According to Kurczewski's hypothesis, transformation is promoted by the social forces dynamizing the structure, and the constraints are caused by the lack of adequate political and institutional mechanisms enabling this social dynamic to be activated.

The second hypothesis is the opposite: There is no social force in Poland now that can implement democracy. Democratic order is not supported by the middle class, which can emerge as a promotor (and to some extent the result) of a free market economy. The reason is simply that this class has not yet emerged (H. Domański, 1990). This view was expressed most clearly by Z. Bauman: "In today's Poland, political democracy is ahead of the society that this democracy is to serve" (1990, p. 37). New institutions of democracy and a free market cannot be activated because of a lack of the social forces that could do this. There are neither real economic nor political interests: the structure of Polish society is, as a result of communism, "prepolitical" and "preeconomic" (see J. Staniszkis, 1990). According to this hypothesis – in contrast to the former one – the reasons for the blockages in political and economic participation are not institutional but social: the chances for transformation are located in the institutional structures, and the constraints, in the social structure.

Both of these hypotheses were presented here in the form of their "ideal type," although many of their elements can be found in the literature. The dispute between these two positions is to some extent the continuation of an old, not only Polish, dispute: Are communist societies "Sovietized" or not? The period of postcommunism, which we are now entering, can enable us to answer this question and let us know whether all of communism really collapsed or whether something was left in the social structures and patterns of behavior.

This essay supports the idea that both of these hypotheses are true, because each deals with a different period of Polish history. The first hypothesis (society as the main actor of change and institutions as the constraint) can explain coping with communism and the massive rejection of it. The second hypothesis (stressing the lack of institutionalized social forces supporting democracy) can be used to explain the constraints to the transition from the first phase of postcommunism to the second phase.

But some elements of the first hypothesis are also true during this transition. Not only are social forces supporting democracy not very well developed but also the institutions of democracy are weak. What is more important, the weakness of these institutions constrains the emergence of "prodemocratic" social forces and as a result makes the transition more difficult – the transition from mass, popular support based on a value system to selective support based on interests. We are most likely approaching this transition period. The results of the 1990 presidential elections were the critical point that showed the exhaustion of mass, popular support based on the rejection of communism as a unifying force. The problem is, however, that the exhaustion of this type of support has not yet paved the way for the emergence of a new support system based on interest.

The "old" social forces, which were sufficient during the destruction of communism, will not be sufficient during the creation of a new order. This is why the second hypothesis can now be true: new social forces have not yet emerged. The so-called "new middle class" (i.e., the alliance between skilled workers and the intelligentsia), which destroyed communism, is different from a real new middle class, which is now needed but lacking.

The remainder of this essay is devoted to a description and explanation of these two stages of postcommunism on the level of institutional and social structures. Due to the fact that the subject of this analysis is an ongoing process, the main aim here is more to address questions and pose hypotheses than to answer these questions and test the hypotheses. For this reason, the format of this essay is one in which many questions are still open.

Institutional Structures and Social Divisions:
The Dynamic of the Transformation

The institutional nature of· the ongoing transformation is still not clear and not well defined. It is waiting for its own paradigm that would describe and explain it. Is it a change of the system, of the deepest rules at its core, or is it only a change of elites and persons ruling this system? Is it spontaneous or controlled (or even manipulated)? Is it transformation toward a new system or toward the restoration of capitalism? These are some of the questions that are still not definitively answered.

For many students of the Polish situation, it is becoming increasingly clear that it is something in between: a change of the system and a change of persons, both spontaneous and controlled. This is the reason why such concepts as T. Garton Ash's "revolution," combining different sources of changes, are gaining popularity. This transformation actually consists of various elements.

The history of the changes in Poland did not start in 1989 with Solidarity's electoral success. It started in the very beginning of the communist system. The legacy of these changes is also present now and *determines the types of participation during the first phase of postcommunism.* We can divide the sources of the ongoing transformation into three groups.

First, these were all attempts at changes *within the system.* These were official, communist-led reforms, which always collapsed because of their inconsistency. It was impossible to build a market economy within the framework of "real existing socialism," especially with the dominant role of the Communist Party, which was trying (unsuccessfully but continuously) to control the economy. Although we have moved far from the "reform" today, some of the reform legacies are still present. These include: the general direction of change (toward a market), some personal continuities (the reformers are implementing the transformation), and the philosophy of change (from above, according to the elaborated "project," rather than spontaneously). Some of these legacies can be regarded as constraints to the ongoing transformation.

None of the reforms succeeded during the communist era. Disappointed with these attempts, society stepped *outside the system*, and this was the second source of changes. Informal strategies, going abroad, "dissident" activities – all these phenomena represented attempts to create an independent system, outside the official one. Although the core of the system still remained generally the same, some of these changes located on the peripheries of the system were also modifying it. This was the case with private businesses that began "outside" the official system and then became part of the official ideology. There were disputes about whether some forms of activity "outside the system" promoted or acted as obstacles to the transformation. This was especially true of many informal activities that were ways for society to cope with the system. People adapted to formal requirements by modifying them, sometimes in illegal ways. These mechanisms definitely contributed to the erosion of the communist system. But at least part survived the collapse of communism. The phenomena of corruption, avoiding formal rules, etc., are still vivid. They can also create constraints to transformation. As a result, it is not only the simple legacies of communism that are constraining; some ways of coping with communism are constraining as well.

The time of a *change in the system* finally came, that is, the time of the political breakthrough,[1] which was possible due to the mass rejection of communism and the peaceful way in which this rejection manifested itself. Both of these features also resulted in some peculiarities of the first stage of postcommunism.

The type of popular support given to the first noncommunist government was a consequence of the mass rejection of communism. The rejection of the old order was a more important integrating factor than a vision of the future. For this reason, workers, who contributed the most to the collapse of communism, were one of the most important social forces. But both these factors can also create some constraints. Support based on the moral rejection of the old order and the dominant role of workers often employed in completely inefficient enterprises produce many tensions in the transformation to a market economy.

The peaceful character of the changes also paved the way for some criticism: there are those who believe that the evolutionary nature of the

---

[1] The distinction between changes within the system and changes of the system is presented in the literature (Boskoff, 1976, p. 345). A. Kamiński (1988) makes a distinction between reform (which is implemented within the system's identity) and revolution (which changes this identity). The concept of reform as a change that is radical but still fits the rules of the system's identity is accepted by Polish scholars (T. Kowalik, 1988; Balcerowicz, 1985). In this three element typology, I use some distinctions presented in the concept of the "fourfold" system (Rychard, 1987).

changes helped the old "nomenklatura" social actors to survive, especially on the level of local power.

The current transformation in Poland may be seen to combine all three sources of changes: *within the system (reforms), outside the system (informal strategies), and of the system (the political breakthrough)*. This mixture is a characteristic feature of the first stage of postcommunism. The social logic of this stage consists in the fact that *each of the three sources of the changes also creates its own constraints to them*.

There are many legacies of the old attempt at changes in the process that is taking place and also many legacies of constraints to the changes. There is thus reason to oppose the idea of a "thick line" between the past and the present. This idea, formulated by the government of T. Mazowiecki, was understandable as a sociotechnical device: do not think about responsibility for the past, let us think about the future. But this is not a satisfactory scientific device. Past and present are connected by many thin lines and not distinguished by one thick line. The legacy of the past is the legacy of former changes and also the legacy of former constraints to these changes. Sometimes it is difficult to distinguish between these two type of legacies. For example, some elements of the "reform paradigm" can now be regarded as a constraint to the transformation that is taking place.

We really do not know how important the lack of a clear social definition of changes is for society. We know, however, that this is a problem for scientists. They are still looking for a theoretical paradigm to describe and explain the changes. But what about society? On the one hand, Polish society is quite well adjusted to a system of unclear, inconsistent identity, as was the case with Polish communism. On the other hand, the lack of a common "social definition of the situation" can create some stress on the level of the societal value system if we still believe that values are important in directing people's behavior.

This unclear period, however, has its own logic and dynamic. The logic consists in the combination of the three sources of change described above, which determine the type of social participation. During this period, there is a *consistency among the philosophy of the economic program, the institutional structure, and the social structure*. This consistency is now exhausted, accounting for the transition to the second stage of postcommunism, which we are now approaching. This is what is meant by the dynamic of this period.

In order to illustrate this thesis, the logic of the first stage of postcommunism will be described in terms of the philosophy of the economic program, in terms of the institutional structures, and in terms of the type of social involvement corresponding to them (participation). The consistency among these three factors was the main source of the success of the first stage (overcoming hyperinflation and introducing the first steps of privatization).

The philosophy of the economic program consisted in implementing change in a way that was "negative and from above." This was especially the case with the economic program. Hyperinflation was to be overcome and demand was to be decreased through central decisions, through the implementation of the "reform project."

This method of implementation has some important consequences resulting in the type of *social support and social participation*. Such a program requires passive tolerance rather than active support. Social support based on moral values, not on interests, also fits this model of change. People supported the economic program because it was "our" government, even if this program was harmful. Finally, the support was more emotional than rational. According to some data, this was the nature of popular support in Poland during the first stage of postcommunism, which was to some extent the first stage of the economic program. It was mainly emotional: 56.3 percent supported privatization and only 10 percent understood it (data from CBOS [Centrum Badań Opinii Społecznej]), *Gazeta Wyborcza*, March 21, 1990). Support was based on moral grounds: according to the sociological research, the economic program was perceived to be more helpful for the national economy than for individual interests. The passive character of the support was also reflected in the results of the CBOS studies: there was no correlation between trust in Solidarity institutions and readiness to join them. People supported but did not participate. This type of support was in keeping with the logic of the implementation of the program, which to some extent corresponded to the "reform paradigm."

Due to the massive political support, open rejection of the program was less probable than the informal ways in which some groups and enterprises were trying to avoid or modify it (Kolarska-Bobińska and Rychard, 1990). Thus the mode of participation combined passive support and some informal strategies of modifying the program. This mixture represented to some extent the legacies of the "reform paradigm" (changes within the system) and the legacies of informal adaptative strategies (changes outside the system).

This type of support was also consistent with *structural, mainly political, conditions*. Solidarity was still acting as a unified force and internal divisions were not institutionalized. The Solidarity government enjoyed popular support, but this support was not organized. There were no political parties that could create the institutional base for active support. During this stage, workers were still one of the important social actors: their tolerance made the first stage of the economic program possible. But this was only tolerance that was expected of them.

The consistency among the program, the support, and the structures was sufficient until the middle of 1990. It worked, enabling the main economic goals to be achieved. But this consistency began to disappear and finally vanished, which was reflected in the results of the 1990 presidential election.

The "old" social forces, which destroyed communism, experienced a deep crisis of identity. The rejection of communism was the goal that unified the alliance between the workers and the intelligentsia more than the vision of a free market economy and political democracy, which can disintegrate this alliance. In that sense we can say that *during the first phase of postcommunism, there was a social base for transformation, and the erosion of this base is paving the way for the second phase, in which new social forces are needed.*

There were several reasons for the exhaustion of the logic of the "first phase." The most important seems to be the fact that "moral-based" support was decreasing while "interest-based" support had not yet emerged. According to the data, support for the prime minister, although still high, was continuously decreasing: from 93.1 percent in November 1989 to 64.3 percent in July 1990 (CBOS reports). On the other hand, support for the Balcerowicz Plan – which to some extent may represent "interest based" support – being always significantly smaller, was decreasing even faster.

The philosophy of the second stage of the economic program (privatization) requires a completely different type of social participation and involvement. Not passive tolerance but active participation is needed, "participation from below" that could create the new social forces supporting the market. This is in contradiction to the philosophy of the first stage and does not fit with the logic of it.

In this situation, a new political orientation emerged that purported to express the need for an acceleration of changes, the need for transformation to activate society and fulfill its interests. This is the program of the Center Alliance. As a reaction to it, the Civic Movement–Democratic Action (Ruch Obywatelski–Akcja Demokratyczna – ROAD) emerged, representing the evolutionary philosophy of changing the government. Solidarity was no longer the only force on the political scene. The nature of the division between these two orientations reflects the changes in the social composition of the forces participating in the Polish political arena.

At first glance, the division between these two orientations reflects more the division inside the political elite itself than the heterogeneity of the social interests. From this point of view, this is a very peculiar form of pluralism: pluralism from above that has no continuation on the level of mass society. This is the effect of the peculiar character of social participation. As mentioned above, this was "passive" participation based on values and not on interests. This moral, value-loaded support (which can be called nonparticipative support) is now coming to an end, but interest-based support has still not emerged. At first glance, this division is not clear to society and is associated more with personal differences than with differences between the programs. On the other hand, there are many social groups that do not have their own representation. This peculiar pluralism *may cause a situation in which we will have in Poland representation without interests on the one hand and interests without representation on the other.* At the moment, this type of division, which is limited only to the elites, can cause the abuse of the label "populism." In a situation in which the main division refers to the elites and it is more important for each side to define itself in relation to the other side and not in relation to the society, everything that is "below" seems to represent the "populist" orientation. Society is to some extent treated as an object and not as a subject of the political process.

The peculiarities in the representation of interests results from the weakness of the interests themselves. From this point of view, the peculiarities of the social divisions in Poland now confirm the hypothesis on the weakness of the social structure presented in the first part of this essay. The structural conditions for the emergence of these interests are still not fulfilled. The changes in the patterns of ownership in the economy seem here to be the most important precondition. As a result, the mass, "moral-based" support of the whole "class of employees" is now decreasing, but the interest-based support is not yet emerging.

It was mentioned above that this division does not reflect social interests. But this is only a first impression. This division also represents an important, deep division inside Polish society. Unfortunately, the institutionalization of this division does not bring us closer to the emergence of new social forces that can create a free market economy and political democracy. *In fact, this institutionalization draws us back, to the "premodern" shape of the social structure.*

Not all of Poland is the Poland of educated, skilled intellectuals and professionals. There is also the Poland of unskilled workers, of the rest of the "average" citizenry. Sometimes even the concept of "two Polands" (that of Wałęsa and that of Mazowiecki) is used (see Pacewicz, 1990). During the first stage of postcommunism, these "average" groups did not gain much. It is quite possible that after the rejection of communism on the level of the elites, the time of its "popular" rejection has come. These types of aspirations are sometimes expressed in Polish political disputes.

The presidential elections of 1990 showed even more divisions. The phenomenon of S. Tymiński emerged, representing the "third Poland" – neither Wałęsa's nor Mazowiecki's, as commentators have pointed out. The results of the election simply illustrate the exhaustion of the first phase of postcommunism. There were of course many reasons for the defeat of T. Mazowiecki, but one of the most important was structural: it was the result of the dynamic of a process in which moral-based support was already not sufficient. The nature of the split between Wałęsa and Mazowiecki was also an important factor: many people simply did not understand this split or did not accept it because, as was mentioned above, it was unclear. As a result, by supporting Tymiński people could vote against both of them. Moreover, Mazowiecki's presidential campaign was very weak, based mainly on his achievements as prime minister without any genuine "presidential issues." All these factors support the hypothesis that the results of the election reflect the dynamic of the transition from the first phase of postcommunism to the second phase.

The most important problem is that divisions that emerged before and during the election are not functional for the creation of a new order: they can cause – perhaps unavoidable – constraints to it. The uniqueness of Solidarity was that it united the "two Polands" and enabled them to cooperate. Now this unity is coming to an end; the political and economic beliefs of the representatives of these two orientations were closer to each other while they were fighting with communism than they are now. A new orientation, which does not identify itself with Solidarity, also emerged (the electorate of Tymiński). It is very difficult to analyze these orientations in terms of their social composition: they are not real social groups up to now, although we can say that the majority of the Tymiński electorate consists of young workers from small towns for whom Solidarity is not a part of their individual experience. But there are also workers among Wałęsa's supporters.

These divisions reflect various hopes and frustrations. For example, workers who supported Wałęsa probably expected that after his victory their situation would improve. But if he implements a real privatization program, these hopes may turn into a deep frustration.

The only clear result of the existing division is that it destroyed the unity of Solidarity, which was already very fragile. The problem is that this disintegration and these types of divisions do not seem to lead to the creation of a real middle class; rather, they can restore the old, "communist," divisions.

Social Structure: The Emergence of New Divisions or the Victory from Beyond the Grave of the Old Concept?

The official vision of the "socialist social structure" was constructed on the "two-plus-one" principle well known in Poland. According to this concept, the social structure in Poland consisted of two classes (workers and peasants) and one "stratum" (the intelligentsia). This concept was present in many scientific works, and it was to some extent based on the Marxist criterion of the ownership of the means of production. However, sociologists tried to prove that this concept is not very useful in explaining what really takes place in society, especially during periods of conflict. No important social conflict could be analyzed within the framework of this concept due to its inadequacy. A dichotomous structure reflecting the division between "us" and "them" better fitted the reality. Position in the power structure and in the system of dependencies created by this structure is the most important factor determining the interests of a given group and the location of this group in the social structure (see for example Adamski et al., 1982; Kennedy and Białecki, 1989).

The divisions that emerged in the postcommunist period inside and outside Solidarity are different. The dichotomous picture (which was never, as a matter of fact, as simple as pure dichotomy) does not fit the reality well. There are some elements of this type of division in the social consciousness – especially when people talk about the "new nomenklatura" – but there are also new, important dimensions of social differentiation.

To some extent, the difference between the Center Alliance and ROAD reflects the division between *workers* and the *intelligentsia,* with some oversimplification of course. *Peasants* are also trying to create their own political representation. Thus one may ask whether the "Marxist" class concept ("two-plus-one") did not begin to work better after the collapse of the system that was based on Marxist ideology. This would be one of many Polish paradoxes. It is too early to answer this question due to the fact that these divisions within the elites have very weak continuation in the "lower" classes. It may be that only part of these divisions reflects real interests, those of workers, or at least of some workers. But it is most probable that these political orientations will have to transform themselves in order to survive and find their real social bases.

Both groups – workers and the intelligentsia – were supposed to have been the main pillars of socialism, and they both, acting in alliance, destroyed this socialism. Now the end of this alliance has come. But will these groups survive as the most important actors on the social scene? Most likely not. Their interests will, of course, survive, and there is a real need to find the representations of these interests. But on the other hand, the role of both groups – the intelligentsia in its traditional form and "industrial workers" – will probably decrease as the privatization program is developed. New actors are needed, and they may emerge during the privatization process. But this will be a long and painful road. Workers are still one of the largest groups in Poland, and their proportion is much higher than in Western countries. Their decreasing role can create many tensions in the system.

In order to illustrate the possible frustration, let us refer to some empirical data. In a Polish-French comparative study on the actors of modernization conducted in the spring of 1989, during the beginning of the collapse of communism, it was found that Polish workers perceive themselves as the main actors of change more often than other groups and more often than French workers. The hierarchy of the evaluation of "people like me," which can be regarded as an indicator of "self-legitimation," was as follows: Polish workers were the highest, Polish managers were lower, after them were French managers, and the lowest self-evaluation was revealed by French workers.[2] In Poland, self-legitimation is the opposite of the formal hierarchy,

---

[2] The respondents were the employees of three French and six Polish enterprises. The research was done in the spring of 1989. The respondents were presented a list of several occupational categories in the enterprise and asked whether each of these categories should stay as it is, should transform itself, or should not be present in the enterprise. On the basis of these questions,

and in France it corresponds to it. In the opinion of Polish workers, the higher a given group is located in the formal structure of the enterprise, the lower legitimation it has. The opposite is the case in France: the higher the level evaluated, the more legitimacy is ascribed to it (Rychard, 1990).

The structure of the actors of change and the structure of perceived legitimation in the opinion of Polish workers are more functional for the rejection of communism than for the creation of a new system. It is impossible to create a new economic order while ignoring the formal hierarchy that is a universal phenomenon in modern societies. The main challenge of the Polish situation now seems to be the creation of such legitimized actors of change who will also be located on a higher level of the hierarchy and not opposed to it. This type of consciousness is not likely to vanish completely when old "nomenklatura" managers disappear. Some element of the "overevaluation" of Polish workers is probably rather stable and can produce real tensions in the system.

One of the reasons why the hypothesis on the lack of new actors for change in the social structure now seems to be true is the type of integration in Polish society. This is also the obstacle to the emergence of a real new middle class. A few years ago, Stefan Nowak posed the thesis that Poles are integrated on two extreme levels: on the level of national and religious symbols, and on the level of microstructures. The communication between these two levels is very weak (Nowak, 1979, p. 160). The world of institutions, placed between these two extreme levels, is perceived as alien. According to Nowak, only through informalities was it possible to adjust to this hostile world. According to the concept of Elżbieta and Jacek Tarkowski (1990), there is a struggle on the level of microstructures among the small groups that are integrated internally but aggressive to each other.

Nowak's and E.J. Tarkowski's concepts show the society as a series of competing small groups that sometimes refer to such values as "nation" or "church" and are surrounded by hostile institutions that become domesticated only when corrupted. How does this correspond to the image of a society in which the leading role is played by a movement called Solidarity? Polish solidarity (as a feature of the structure and not as a movement) is mainly the solidarity against something rather than for something. Many students of the Polish situation have noticed the prevailing role of protest in social integration. It is also solidarity on the two extreme levels: macro and micro. The "mezzo" level – that of institutions and organizations, of social groups – is very weak. This means that the possible interests can emerge only on the micro level, the macro level is dominated by moral values, and there

the index of "self-legitimation" was constructed. The research was part of a collaborative study on modernization done by Polish and French scholars. The authors of this part of the research were E. Wnuk-Lipiński, A. Rychard, L. Kolarska-Bobińska, and M. Federowicz (Polish Academy of Sciences, Warsaw, Poland) and R. Sainsaulieu and N. Mauchamp (Centre Nationale de la Recherche Scientifique, Paris, France).

are no "mezzo" interests as the instruments of integration (Rychard, 1987, p. 100). This composition of social integration was sufficient to destroy communism, but it is not enough to create a new order.

The dynamic of the transformation, some of whose elements have been described here, has its own logic. After the exhaustion of the first phase in which the most important role was played by the social forces that destroyed communism (workers, the intelligentsia, or the whole class of "employees"), the time of the disintegration of these forces has come. As was inevitable, the new "structuring" of society is meeting many constraints. The new divisions contributed to the erosion of the Solidarity value system, to the erosion of the worker–intelligentsia alliance based on common *values*, but did not result in the emergence of divisions based on *interests*. There are many economic claims, especially in the working-class groups. These can produce many tensions and frustrations in society, but these claims and group interests are "defensive" ones and cannot be a substitute for the "creative" interests of a new middle class, which has still not yet emerged.

Would it be possible to replace the divisions described above by their opposite, *based on differences of interests but still referring to the common Solidarity value system?* Searching for a positive answer to this question may be one of the most important challenges facing today's Poland.

The most important factor constraining the emergence of real interest-based divisions is still the legacy of communism. This legacy consists not only in institutions, which can be destroyed, but also in the ways of coping with communism: through corruption, revolts, and other mechanisms. Some of these, and some of the social forces activating them, can create constraints to the future transformation.

References

Adamski, W., et al. 1982. *Polacy'81. Postrzeganie kryzysu i konfliktu*. Warszawa: Instytut Filozofii i Socjologii PAN.

Balcerowicz, L. 1985. "O źródłach trawałości systemu nakazowo-rozdzielczego." Mimeographed manuscript. Warszawa.

Boskoff, A. 1976. "Functional Analysis as a Source of a Theory: Repertory and Research Tasks in the Study of Social Change." In *Social Change*. G.K. Zollschman and W. Hirsch, eds. New York: A Halsted Press Book.

Bauman, Z. 1990. "Kilka wybranych problemów: uwagi obserwatora z zewnątrz." In *Studia nad ładem społecznym (Zeszyt 2)*, W. Nieciuński and T. Żukowski, eds. Warszawa: Uniwersytet Warszawski.

Domański, H. 1990. "W oczekiwaniu klasy średniej." In *Więź*, July–August, Warszawa.

Kamiński, A. 1988. "Granice reformowalności." In *Res Publica*, no. 7, Warszawa.

Kennedy, M. D. and I. Białecki. 1989. "Power and the logic of distribution in Poland." In *Eastern European Politics and Society* 4, no. 2.

Kolarska-Bobińska, L. and A. Rychard. 1990. *Między buntem a tolerancją.* Expertise for Civic Parliamentary Club. Report. Warszawa.

Kowalik, T. 1988. *On the Crucial Reform of Real Socialism.* Working paper No. 122. Vienna Institute for Comparative Economic Studies, Vienna.

Kurczewski, J. 1982. "The Old System and the Revolution." In *Sisyphus. Sociological Studies,* vol. 3, Warszawa.

Nowak, S. 1979. "System wartości społeczeństwa polskiego." In *Studia Socjologiczne,* no. 4, Warszawa.

Pacewicz, P. 1990. "Reforma czy rewolucja." In *Gazeta Wyborcza,* September 11, Warszawa.

Rychard, A. 1987. "Konflikt i przystosowanie: dwie koncepcje ładu społecznego w Polsce." In *Rzeczywistość polska i sposoby radzenia sobie z nią,* M. Marody and A. Sułek, eds. Warszawa: Uniwersytet Warszawski.

—— 1990. "Les acteurs du changement et de la stabilité dans les entreprises." In *Modernisation des entreprises en France et en Pologne dans les années 1980.* Paris: CNRS IRESCO.

Staniszkis, J. 1990. "Ontologia realnego socjalizmu (Ontology of Real Socialism)." In *Krytyka,* Warszawa.

Tarkowska E. and J. Tarkowski. 1990. "Are the Poles amoral familists? On social disintegration in Poland of the 1980s." Mimeographed manuscript.

POLISH ELECTIONS OF 1990
BEYOND
THE *"POSPOLITE RUSZENIE"*

Krzysztof Jasiewicz

"Solidarity brought communism in Poland to its end. But with the end of communism comes the end of Solidarity." This bitter message came from Zbyszek Bujak, the legendary leader of Solidarity, the fugitive who for five years, escaping captivity, led the underground movement through its most difficult period: the times of martial law and subsequent "normalization." He spoke these words in July 1990, at the Fourth World Congress of Soviet and East European Studies in Harrogate, England. At the congress, scholars from the East and the West assembled to share their astonishment with what has been so senselessly called "The Autumn of Nations."

Autumn means decline, decay, fall. But this was the fall of communism, not of a nation! For the nations of Eastern Europe, it is their new beginning, their spring – like the original Spring of Nations, that of 1848. So was it really the spring of nations and only happened to occur in the fall? It certainly was, but ... spring also means joy, and in Eastern Europe, "the party is over," but the joy is over as well.

New beginnings too often mean new troubles, or the old troubles multiplied several times. Ethnic strife, inflation, unemployment, and on top of all this now the oil crisis. But Bujak's bitterness comes, one may suppose, not from the mere recognition of all these problems. He knows, as do most politically aware Poles, that our task must be to create a new economy and a new society – in a perhaps friendly but not quite cooperative international environment. But he – we – could have hoped that to build a new, democratic political system would be the easiest of all our efforts.

From its very beginning in 1980, Solidarity has struggled for democracy, using democratic means. Even if there has been an authoritarian component

– in personalities of some leaders or, understandably, in actions of clandestine units – the people of Solidarity remained fundamentally democratic. And not only they, but their "fellow travelers" as well. This was proven in the June 1989 elections, when the people of Poland voted the communists out of government. A year ago, the threat to this young Polish democracy seemed to come from the remnants of the ancien régime: the postcommunist president (Gen. Jaruzelski), the "old coalition" 65 percent majority in the Sejm, the communist-controlled army and secret police, the omnipotent nomenklatura. But after his presidency, Jaruzelski did not make a single step to slow down the process of reforms and finally decided to give up his office; the old coalition fell apart, with the formerly puppet Peasant and Democratic parties forming a new coalition with Solidarity; the Communist Party promptly dissolved itself, while the secret police was dismantled by the Mazowiecki government; the army eagerly depoliticized itself; and maybe only the nomenklatura holds some of its old positions, on lower and medium levels.

One could have hoped that the victory over the ancien régime would mean a smooth transition to a well-functioning democracy and a democratic political culture. One could have predicted, however, that different opinions, plans, and programs for a free Poland would emerge from the victorious camp. This was unavoidable; but should this differentiation, or, to put it bluntly, the deep split within Solidarity, come before the establishment of a truly democratic political system? Should it precede fully free parliamentary elections? Should it come during a very deep economic crisis, when the Balcerowicz Plan is only beginning to work? Such doubts may be said to lie at the bottom of Bujak's statement about the end of Solidarity.

Is Bujak right? Is it really the end of Solidarity? It is not the intention to answer any questions of this sort in this essay. Instead, the connections between the actions of political leaders and the attitudes of the people will be shown. In particular, we are interested here in describing in political and sociological terms the potential electorate of the most prominent leaders and orientations emerging from the movement of Solidarity. Also, more and less likely scenarios of political developments will be examined in the context of popular political attitudes.

Political Differentiations

Norman Davies, the British historian, in his excellent book *Heart of Europe. A Short History of Poland*, wrote:

> For the first thing which Poles have to realize in recent years is that the agents of their oppression today are not weird-looking foreigners wearing a pickelhelm or a Tartar cap. The oppressors are Poles like

themselves, instantly recognizable by their dress, their manner, and their jargon, but men and women in the main part from their own towns and villages, from their own families. The line which divides the oppressor from the oppressed runs through the blood and bone of Polish society, and often enough, in the event of divided loyalties, through the heart and soul of an individual person. One of the principal products of a generation of Communism is this division between the "power" (władza) and "society" (społeczeństwo), between the bosses and the people, between "them" and "us."[1]

This quotation comes from a chapter entitled "Two Nations." It was a strong statement. However, in the mid-1980s, when Davies's book was first published, this opinion was shared not only by many scholars (one notable example, the late Polish historian Tadeusz Łepkowski),[2] but also, more importantly, by the majority of Poland's populace. Were they right? Was the mental and emotional gap between the people and a handful of oppressors really so deep? Careful analysis of various survey data gathered in Poland throughout the 1980s indicates that the reality was much more complex.

Lack of space prevents even a partial presentation here of such data,[3] but one could draw from them the conclusion that a dichotomized vision of two – and only two – "nations," two classes with distinct systems of values, attitudes, and political views, could hardly be sustained. Rather, there was a differentiation of those values, views, and attitudes in a linear manner. Moreover, one can find various dimensions to that differentiation – and there was a significant differentiation, with both ends of the political continuum spread, literally, poles apart. At those ends one could find coherent syndromes of political thought: populist-authoritarian (those supporting the communist regime, "the oppressors") and liberal-democratic (the opponents of the regime). One should stress, however, that individuals with consistent political profiles inside each of those two groups were in a minority, and each respective group may be perceived as broad and loose political alliances. So, among supporters of the communist rule were not only authoritarian populists but also quite liberal-minded people who believed, for instance, that geopolitical reality prevented Poland from attaining any other form of government. On the other hand, among those who opposed the established political order were not only convinced liberal democrats but also

---

[1] N. Davies, *Heart of Europe. A Short History of Poland*, Oxford: Oxford University Press, 1984, p. 45.

[2] See T. Łepkowski, *Uparte trwanie polskości*, London and Warszawa: Aneks, 1989.

[3] They are, however, available from several sources (in Polish and in English). See in particular W. Adamski, K. Jasiewicz, and A. Rychard, eds. *Polacy'84. Dynamika konfliktu i konsensusu*, Warszawa: IFiS PAN, 1986; *Polacy'88. Dynamika konfliktu a szanse reform*, Warszawa: IFiS PAN, 1989; *Sisyphus. Sociological Studies*, vol. 5; K. Jasiewicz, "Kultura polityczna Polaków," *Aneks*, no. 48.

individuals who sought authoritarian solutions and supported populist slogans while at the same time rejecting the communist version of authoritarianism because of, say, its Soviet provenance.

Between those two extremes there was an even less coherent "centrist" group, one that should not be perceived as a genuine political center. A true center would consist of persons and groups who consciously express cautious and moderate views, who are inclined to search for a common language with extreme groups, and who would be perceived by other groups as the center. Instead, the "centrists" of the mid-1980s were persons with not fully crystallized views, inclined in certain matters to decide in favor of one side and in other matters in favor of the opposing side, avoiding – at least when surveyed – a firm stand in support of anything or anyone. On the sidelines there was also a sizable group, the "silent minority" – persons who were either too apathetic to hold any political views or may have preferred to avoid an expression of their views in front of the interviewer.

In general, this was a picture of a society in which many persons seemed to accept the established political order in their daily lives, while their values came out in favor of far-reaching changes in the model of public life. The views and attitudes of the people were not dichotomized but rather polarized, with the axis of this polarization drawn by two contradictory syndromes of political thought: liberal-democratic and populistic-authoritarian.

Such a picture of the political differentiation of Polish society in the mid-1980s reflects the general political situation of those days ("normalization," the weakening of Solidarity's underground, crippling economic reforms), but it indicates that there was also a potential for change. And that change, a rapid one, indeed came. First, two waves of massive strikes in industrial centers (the spring and summer of 1988); then, the painful, but successful, process of negotiation between the communist power elite and the leaders of the opposition (the Round Table); finally, the elections of June 1989 – the first elections ever in which a ruling Communist Party was defeated. The suddenness of this process is well illustrated in Table 1, in which the coefficients of confidence in selected political personalities and institutions are presented. (Such a coefficient may vary from -1 to +1. For details, see the *Polacy '88* report).

Table 1
Confidence in Political Personalities and Institutions

Person/Institution	1984	1985	1987	Spring 1988	Spring 1989	Autumn 1989	Summer 1990
W. Jaruzelski	.21	.51	.39	.39	−.01	.25	−.09
L. Wałęsa	.04	−.03	−.09	−.01	.68	.67	.49
M. Rakowski	−.27	−.07	−.28	−.28	−.03	−.64	–
T. Mazowiecki	–	–	–	–	–	.78	.64

Church	.65	.72	.65	.74	.66	.58	.59
Sejm	.31	.49	.45	.37	.13	.58	.45
Army	.39	.46	.42	.44	.19	.16	.41
Government	.17	.39	.26	.26	-.12	.61	.47
PUWP	-.08	.12	-.08	-.17	-.48	-.76	–
OPZZ	-.19	.22	-.02	.00	-.20	-.29	-.26
Solidarity	-.52	-.55	-.23	-.46	.58	.61	.45

Source: The *Polacy '84* and *Polacy '88* reports, and unpublished data from the author's 1989 and 1990 surveys. PUWP stands for the Polish United Workers Party, and OPZZ for Ogólnopolskie Porozumienie Związków Zawodowych, procommunist trade unions.

All of a sudden, sometime in 1988, many Poles gained (or regained) confidence in Wałęsa and Solidarity, while withdrawing or suspending such confidence in Jaruzelski, Rakowski, and the institutions of the ancien régime (note a very stable level of confidence in the Church). This meant, first, the creation of a real political center (those willing to support a compromise between the communists and Solidarity), and, ultimately, Solidarity's landslide electoral victory of June 4, 1989. The majority of voters – the notorious rebels back to back with the hamletizing conformists – when forced to make the dichotomous choice between the ruling coalition or the opposition, dared to vote for the Solidarity candidates.

Throughout the 1980s, seeing no alternative to the established political order, many people fell into apathy or acted in the most opportunistic way. In 1988, when a real alternative emerged, the same people turned against the communist system – the system that they had never perceived as their own.

Parliamentary and Municipal Elections

It is time to explain the mysterious Polish expression in this essay's title. The use of this term in English is justified: one can find in *Webster's Third New International Dictionary* the following entry: *pospolite* [pol. *pospolite (ruszenie)* general levy, fr. *pospolite* (neutr. from *pospolity* general) + *ruszenie* movement, levy] a former Polish militia in Poland called out in case of invasion.

In pre-nineteenth century Poland there was no regular army, and *pospolite ruszenie* played the role of armed forces composed of all citizens (noblemen) to defend the Commonwealth against the enemy. Such a *pospolite ruszenie* won the parlimentary elections of June 1989. People of various political self-identifications: rightists, centrists, and leftists; cosmopolitans, nationalists, and chauvinists; liberals and populists; democrats and republicans; monarchists and anarchists; and those with no political identification whatsoever, all were united in one conviction – no more rule of the PUWP. And so they voted for the Civic Committee Solidarity candidates. To be precise: those voting for Solidarity were not the majority of the electorate but only a plurality. Almost 40 percent of eligible voters stayed home (a silent minority?); almost 20 percent voted against Solidarity and for the "ruling coalition" candidates. To be even more precise: the majority of voters had no idea of the actual consequences of their vote. On the day of the elections, they did not dare to think that the PUWP could be voted out of the government. The communists and their allies had been guaranteed 65 percent of the seats in the Sejm, and – it seemed – the office of the president. But although Jaruzelski was elected (by only one vote in the National Assembly), the communists were not able to form a government, and as of August 1989 the Polish government was led by Tadeusz Mazowiecki – the first noncommunist prime minister in Eastern Europe in forty years.

The *pospolite ruszenie* won the battle – but was it able to run a war? For some time the answer to this question might have seemed positive. The Mazowiecki government was welcomed enthusiastically; there was a widespread feeling that the state and its institutions (see the rapid rise of confidence in the Sejm, the government, and the army – Table 1) were being revindicated by the people. Resistance, particularly by the old secret police and nomenklatura cliques on lower and middle levels, kept the *pospolite ruszenie* together and led it to another battle – the municipal elections of May 27, 1990. And the *pospolite ruszenie* won again.

It is not easy to analyze the results of these elections, due to the complexity of the electoral law (the "first-past-the-post" system in single-seat districts in rural areas; proportional representation in multiseat districts in urban areas), and also due to the vagueness of the political arena. A party system has not yet emerged from the swarm of groupings, cliques, and ambitious individuals; many such groupings formed ad hoc coalitions, hoping in this way to increase their odds; and many of those groupings and coalitions used misleading names rather than proper guidelines for the electorate (one could find former communists running as a Democratic Civic Committee or a Coalition for Free Enterprise!). Nevertheless, it is clear that the Civic Committees Solidarity won: they collected 38 percent of the seats in single-seat and 74 percent in multiseat districts. In single-seat districts, 43 percent of the seats were won by independent candidates, most, one way or the other, coming out of the Solidarity movement. Detailed results are presented in Table 2.

Table 2
Results of Municipal Election of May 27, 1990

| | Percent of seats won in | | |
Organization/Coalition	single-seat	multiseat	total
PSL (Polish Peasant Party)	6.26	.73	5.76
Tenants' committees	.96	2.09	1.06
Civic Committees Solidarity	38.22	74.03	41.47

Solidarity of private farmers	3.57	0.22	3.25
Independent candidates	43.20	2.19	39.52
Solidarity (the trade union)	1.20	3.98	1.45

Source: Unpublished data provided by the Election Commissioner-General's Computer Service; organizations and coalitions that won less than 1 percent of total of seats omitted.

But this was apparently the last victory of the *pospolite ruszenie*. (In this context one should also notice a turnout of 42.13 percent – 20 percent less than on June 4, 1989.) For the last time, united by the common understanding of who was the enemy, the majority of politically aware Poles came out to vote. But in these elections, under the cover of unity, already there simmered future splits and divisions. In several areas they even emerged to the surface. Most noteworthy is the case of the city of Łódź where two civic committees, the Provincial Civic Committee (*Wojewódzki Komitet Obywatelski* – WKO) and the Civic Alliance (*Łódzkie Porozumienie Obywatelskie* – ŁPO) fought mercilessly against each other. Both groups sprang from the Solidarity movement; inside each are very prominent members of the old opposition. It would be difficult to say how they differ from each other as far as their programs (particularly in municipal policies) are concerned. But apart from personal animosities, there is also an ideological dimension to this split. The ŁPO accuses its foes of being "leftists," "pinkies"; the WKO answers with labels of "nationalists"[4] and "populists." In May in Łódź the ŁPO won: out of 80 seats they collected 50, while the WKO attained 24, and the postcommunist *Socjaldemokracja Rzeczypospolitej Polskiej* (SdRP) only 6.

Dimensions of the Political Spectrum

Are the results of the municipal elections in Łódź prophecy for Poland? Is the political future of Poland to be decided by the traditional competition of the Left and the Right? Can both orientations be properly defined in the old, nineteenth-century terms: the Left as cosmopolitan, egalitarian, democratic, and the Right as nationalistic and authoritarian? Is there now in Poland any Left, or Right, or Center at all? It seems there is a lot of confusion. Take the Mazowiecki government: it is a typical centrist, coalition government, composed of various moderate centrist groupings. This government conducts a rightist, neoliberal economic policy and is accused by its opponents of being leftist. ...Before the presidential elections, two major political movements (parties?) emerged out of Solidarity: the Center Alliance (*Porozumienie Centrum* – PC) and the Civic Movement-Democratic Action (known as

---

[4] This word has in Polish, unlike in English, quite a strong negative connotation, although not as strong as chauvinism.

ROAD – *Ruch Obywatelski – Akcja Demokratyczna*). PC labels ROAD as leftist but itself prefers to be identified as the Center rather than as the Right. ROAD tries to escape an undesired label, saying that they are not to the left of the center, but west of the Center Alliance. One can easily notice that PC and ROAD duplicate on a national level what has been going on in Łódź for some time. And again their respective programs do not differ much. Differences lie in the personalities of the leaders, some general slogans (a very catchy "acceleration" by PC), and labels.

How does this confusing picture of political elites look when confronted with popular political attitudes? In the mid-1980s, as we have already indicated, only a minority of Poles held really consistent political views. In 1989–90 the situation has not been different. A description of three major dimensions might be helpful in locating individuals and social groups on the political spectrum. They are relatively independent of each other: to know someone's position on one dimension is not necessarily a good predictor of his/her position on another. These dimensions are:

liberalism versus populism;
democracy versus authoritarianism;
"pan-European option" versus national xenophobia.

Let us briefly examine each of these dimensions.

Liberalism versus Populism

Until shortly before the presidential elections, the results of public opinion polls indicated that the neoliberal policy of the Mazowiecki government (the Balcerowicz Plan) enjoyed the support of the majority of Polish society. Also, on the level of general values, people tended to support a market economy, free enterprise, and privatization of the public sector. It remains to be seen to what extent such attitudes are merely the result of disappointment with an ineffective, centrally planned economy and if there is a genuine procapitalist option. One should bear in mind that the majority of Polish society supports a far-reaching state interventionism, particularly in price control (should not be too high) and simultaneously supports wage control (should vary according to merits, but only to a certain ceiling). Politically, it is a traditional choice: freedom or equality. Exposed for so many years to never-fulfilled slogans of equality, people now opt for freedom. But the people are accustomed to the state's (the government's) guaranteeing their jobs and buying their products, which are not competitive on a real market (obviously important to private farmers, but not only farmers). In general, people are accustomed to the state's taking care of the fulfillment of their needs, at least on a minimal level. That is the popular base for populism – a term that in Polish (and East European) circumstances means a movement based on beliefs in equality, direct political action (strikes), strong leadership, and demanding state protection of a given social class (workers, farmers). Populists often question the value of parlimentary democracy and specific legal regulations and in general have no confidence in political and intellectual elites.

With extremes of laissez-faire capitalism and populism, we observe that most of the people express moderate, centrist views, with many giving support to both liberal and populistic slogans. This means that these views are changeable: during the past year we have seen a slow movement in general mood from liberalism to populism. Yet only tiny minorities within Polish society may be described as solid "liberals" or "populists."

Democracy versus Authoritarianism

As already indicated, the Solidarity movement has been fundamentally democratic, sometimes (in 1980–81) becoming almost obsessed with democratic procedures, a threat of "manipulation," and openness of political process. Also on the level of popular attitudes, a majority of Poles opted for political pluralism, free elections, an independent judiciary, and other fundamentals of modern democracy. But at the same time, an overwhelming majority (in a 1989 study, 85 percent) believes that "Poland now needs a strong leader who would enforce order in the country." Moreover, such a belief is not related to sociodemographic features of individuals nor to other views they hold. This, of course, does not mean that Poles are ripe for a dictatorship. One can imagine a strong leader, elected in a democratic way, acting in congruence with the principles of democracy. The problem is, one may suppose, that behind this demand for a strong leader there often lies an assumption that someone else may come and solve all our problems; that we are in fact not responsible for our own fate. In times of crisis and austerity, such beliefs open an avenue for a dictator to step in.

People with coherent authoritarian or democratic beliefs compose tiny minorities; the majority is somewhere in between these extremes, and, as in the case of the liberal-populistic dimension, its attitudes seem to be changeable. This means that one may attempt to manipulate these attitudes; but it also means that people prefer to hold moderate, even if somewhat inconsistent, views and are unlikely to support leaders who are too radical.

Pan-European Option versus Xenophobia

Ethnic questions have been perceived in Poland as very sensitive; they were seldom the object of surveys, and even more rarely were they researched in connection with other political, social, and economic problems. They have become, however, more and more openly disputed and not only in the context of alleged Polish anti-Semitism. Ethnic questions may become a very hot issue in the forthcoming presidential and parliamentary electoral campaigns. It is not a question of ethnic minorities, although there will probably be political groupings casting doubt upon the loyalty of the German minority in Silesia. But much more important will be the question of the international environment: a united Germany; the Soviet-German, or, rather, the Russian-German, "good neighborhood" treaty; open hostility toward Polish tourists in Germany, Czechoslovakia, the Ukraine, and some other countries. There is also the question of foreign investments: some people fear that Poland may become exploited by German (or French, or Jewish) capital. On political extremes, there are individuals and groups on the one hand who maintain that the only way out of the current Polish problems is to go toward a new, united Europe by opening the borders for a flow of people, ideas, and capital (the pan-European option). On the other hand, remnants of *endecja* (prewar national democrats) and other nationalistic groupings hostile to Germans, Soviets, Ukrainians, and to the West as such look for a cosmopolitan (i.e., Jewish) conspiracy within the Polish government. According to the data gathered so far, a majority of Polish people hold views that fall somewhere in between those extremes: while there are some reservations about whether or not international developments will bring favorable changes to Poland, there is no significant hostility toward other nations or national minorities.

Any individual or any political group can be situated somewhere within these three dimensions. But one should remember that these dimensions are fairly independent of one other – to know someone's position on one dimension does not much help us to predict where he/she would be on the other. One should also remember that most people express moderate views: someone may lean toward, say, liberal or populistic slogans, but such a person is very unlikely to become a militant supporter of radical demands. So even if there are in Poland liberals and populists, democrats and supporters of authoritarian rule, "pan-Europeans" and chauvinists, there are not many individuals in each category. Moreover, there are only a few who may be described as "liberal-democratic pan-Europeans" or "xenophobic authoritarian populists." Nevertheless, these labels and stereotypes were, are, and will be used, along with labels of the Left and the Right, in electoral campaigns.

Presidential Elections

The first round of the presidential election – the first presidential election by popular vote in Poland's history – took place on November 25, 1990. Altogether six politicians managed to collect more than 100,000 signatures in support of their candidacy:
– Roman Bartoszcze, the leader of the Polish Peasant Party;

– Włodzimierz Cimoszewicz, the leader of a major postcommunist faction in the Sejm;
– Tadeusz Mazowiecki, since August 1989 the prime minister of the Solidarity-led government;
– Leszek Moczulski, the leader of KPN (*Konfederacja Polski Niepodległej*) – an anticommunist and anti-Soviet political party;
– Stanisław Tymiński, a previously unknown businessman from Toronto, Canada, and Iquitos, Peru, still holding his Polish citizenship;
– Lech Wałęsa, chairman of Solidarity.

The election was preceded by a short, vigorous, and somewhat clumsy campaign. The above-mentioned labels and stereotypes were often used and abused. Not only these labels: Stanisław Tymiński called Mazowiecki "a traitor of the nation," and himself was in turn labeled and libeled in various ways by Mazowiecki's and Wałęsa's supporters. The negative campaigning, used for the first time in Poland on such a massive scale, probably influenced substantially the outcome of the voting. The official results, as published by the State Electoral Commission, are given in Table 3.

Table 3
The Official Results of Presidential Election, Round I (percent)

Roman Bartoszcze	7.2
Włodzimierz Cimoszewicz	9.2
Tadeusz Mazowiecki	18.1
Leszek Moczulski	2.5
Stanisław Tymiński	23.1
Lech Wałęsa	40.0

Source: Wyniki wyborów prezydenta Rzeczypospolitej Polskiej, Warszawa: Państwowa Komisja Wyborcza, 1990.

The turnout was 60.6 percent of eligible voters. The same source gives the results broken down by the place of residence:

Table 4
Results of Presidential Election, Round I, by Place of Residence (percent).

Total	Bartosz-cze	Cimosze-wicz	Mazo-wiecki	Moczulski	Tymiński	Wałęsa
Rural communes 100.0	17.1	7.4	7.4	2.3	24.2	41.7
"Integrated communes" (town – rural area) 100.0	8.9	9.3	15.2	2.6	27.3	36.8
Towns to 10,000 inhabitants 100.0	2.6	9.4	21.8	2.8	26.8	36.7
Towns 10,000–20,000 inhabitants 100.0	3.1	10.8	18.0	2.5	25.3	40.3

Towns 20,000–50,000 inhabitants 100.0	2.1	11.3	20.0	2.5	25.9	38.1
Cities 50,000–100,000 inhabitants 100.0	1.8	11.1	20.5	2.9	26.1	37.6
Cities of more than 100,000 inhabitants 100.0	1.4	9.5	26.6	2.7	19.4	40.4
Warsaw 100.0	1.1	10.0	27.8	1.5	10.7	48.9
Voting abroad 100.0	1.7	3.8	36.6	2.5	10.7	44.9

Source: Wyniki wyborów prezydenta Rzeczypospolitej Polskiej, Warszawa: Państwowa Komisja Wyborcza, 1990.

On election day an exit poll was conducted – a joint effort by the German INFAS and Polish OBOP public opinion polling centers. From this (unpublished) source, the most representative of all available (10,494 respondents), come the following tables:

Table 5
Voting in Presidential Election, Round I, by Gender (percent)

	Bartosz-cze	Cimosze-wicz	Mazo-wiecki	Moczulski	Tymiński	Wałęsa	Total
Men	7.6	7.1	18.6	3.0	23.5	39.8	100.0
Women	5.0	9.7	23.3	2.1	23.1	36.5	100.0

Table 6
Voting in Presidential Election, Round I, by Age (percent)

	Bartosz-cze	Cimosze-wicz	Mazo-wiecki	Moczulski	Tymiński	Wałęsa	Total
18–25 years old	5.9	7.5	20.8	3.2	31.2	31.2	100.0
26–45 years old	6.6	8.7	20.1	2.9	27.0	34.4	100.0
46–60 years old	5.8	8.8	21.9	2.0	16.5	44.8	100.0
61 years old and older	7.5	6.8	21.6	1.7	7.4	54.7	100.0

Table 7
Voting in Presidential Election, Round I, by Education (percent)

	Bartosz-cze	Cimosze-wicz	Mazo-wiecki	Moczulski	Tymiński	Wałęsa	Total
Primary	12.5	5.6	10.5	3.2	20.3	47.6	100.0
Vocational	7.2	6.0	12.2	2.6	31.3	40.5	100.0
Secondary	4.5	9.5	22.7	2.4	24.3	36.4	100.0
College	2.8	12.4	39.7	2.4	13.2	29.4	100.0

To sum up the above tables most concisely, one may note that out of the three top finishers, Mazowiecki did particularly well among urban professionals, Tymiński among young people with vocational education living outside of big cities, while Wałęsa among the less-educated and older voters. Similar conclusions may be drawn from primary results of various pre and postelectoral surveys and studies. The analyses – most of them still under way – focus on the so-called "Tymiński phenomenon." The researchers try to explain how it was possible that a "man from nowhere" gained within a couple of months enough support to collect almost one-fourth of the popular vote and, above all, to eliminate Tadeusz Mazowiecki, the prime minister of the first noncommunist government in Eastern Europe, from the presidential race. Leaving the full presentation of this author's views for another occasion, it need only be mentioned here that the Tymiński phenomenon is not entirely new. Looking on the data aggregated on the voivodship (province) level, one may notice that votes for Tymiński came from the same areas, all of which

– were reluctant to boycott the quasi elections of 1984 and 1985;

– more often voted against the Solidarity candidates in the 1989 Senate elections;

– more often voted for the National List (composed of communist and procommunist candidates) in the 1989 Sejm elections.

Tymiński, who from a certain point on was perceived as the only serious challenger to the Solidarity candidates, Wałęsa and Mazowiecki, obviously collected many anti-Solidarity votes. These often came from milieus traditionally hostile to Solidarity. What is really new (and requires more elaborate analysis) is the overrepresentation in Tymiński's electorate of young manual and nonmanual workers.

A different kind of overrepresentation may be found in Mazowiecki's electorate. The well-educated dwellers of big cities are the core of his supporters. This seems to be a genuine new phenomenon. As indicated earlier, throughout the decade of the 1980s one could not point out the real political cleavages in terms of status groups or classes. Mazowiecki's electorate is very well defined in these terms. No wonder that after his electoral defeat and resignation from the prime ministership, Mazowiecki decided to organize his own political party (Democratic Union, to which ROAD and Forum of the Democratic Right were incorporated as autonomous parts), trying to represent the interests of urban professionals in the coming parliamentary elections.

Wałęsa's electorate, apart from an overrepresentation of the less-educated and older voters, in general reflects the heterogeneity of Polish society. One should stress at this point that the above generalizations oversimplify the reality: in fact, each of these groups (Wałęsa's, Tymiński's, and Mazowiecki's electorates) is heterogenous, both sociologically and politically. Among

Wałęsa's supporters are liberals seeking quicker privatization and populists looking for a more protective state; Tymiński's electorate seems to be the most frustrated of all, but this frustration comes either from the belief that political and economic change is too fast, or that it is proceeding too slowly. The group of Mazowiecki's supporters is composed among others of the veterans of the Solidarity underground and excommunists voting for Mazowiecki to stop Wałęsa.

Limited data available thus far do not allow us to locate electorates of the major candidates on the authoritarianism versus democracy, liberalism versus populism, and pan-European option versus national xenophobia continua. What seems to be certain at this point is the most liberal, democratic, and pan European option profile of Mazowiecki's electorate, as well as a significant level of national xenophobia among the supporters of Stan Tymiński.

In short, a map showing the electorates of all six candidates, located in sociopolitical space, may be drawn in the following way:

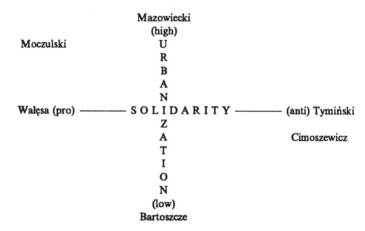

Mazowiecki's defeat and Tymiński's rise from a nobody to a major contender came as a shock. Also, Wałęsa's 40 percent of the popular vote, achieved out of a 60.6 percent turnout, was for many of his supporters, as well as for himself, a most unpleasant surprise. The people of Solidarity, divided into the Mazowiecki and Wałęsa camps, realized suddenly that in a democratic process there is room for outsiders, political gurus, and false prophets; that nobody gets popular support forever and unconditionally; and that the winners of yesterday may become losers tomorrow. No wonder that the *pospolite ruszenie* struck again: in the run-off round Wałęsa collected 74.3 percent of votes, and Tymiński, 25.7 percent with a turnout of 53.4 percent. This means that some 40 percent of Poland's population voted in the run-off for Wałęsa – almost exactly as much as had supported Solidarity's candidates in the 1989 parliamentary elections. The Sejm elected then, with

65 percent of the seats allocated to the communists and their allies, today is an obvious anachronism. The new parliamentary elections will come soon, to reflect a very complex political reality.

Possible Political Scenarios

There will be no *"pospolite ruszenie"* this time. Rather, in the coming parliamentary elections, there will be a battle between the "Mazowiecki *rokosz*" (Democratic Union – UD, composed of ROAD, Forum of the Democratic Right, and other Mazowiecki supporters) and the "Belweder Confederation" (Center Alliance – PC),[5] with some other forces playing a more or less significant role. What is the likely outcome, not so much in terms of who is going to win, but what kind of political system may emerge after all this is over? There are six possible scenarios.

New authoritarianism

As already indicated, there is a widespread desire for strong leadership. The difficult economic situation – in particular, growing unemployment, the dramatically increasing crime rate, low efficiency of new democratic institutions – may open the door for a dictator to step in, a dictator who would promise easy and quick solutions to complex problems. During his campaign Wałęsa kept delivering such promises. But his government is continuing the economic politics of Mazowiecki's cabinet, with Leszek Balcerowicz still acting as the deputy prime minister and minister of finance. On the other hand, it is, indeed, *his* government. The power has obviously shifted from the Council of Ministers to the Belweder (the Polish equivalent of the White House). Wałęsa has concentrated enormous powers in his hands, but he is nevertheless exposed to the control of democratic institutions, such as the parliament and the mass media. Such institutions and the very principles that make them democratic (free elections, opposition in the parliament, freedom of speech, etc.) enjoy the solid support of the majority in Polish society. People who seek a strong leader now may in the future turn against him to protect the fundamentals of democracy.

Neither Wałęsa nor anyone else can promise easy solutions today and fulfill such promises tomorrow. Once imposed, a dictatorship may last long, but its popular base will erode within a very short time.

---

[5] "Confederation" and *"rokosz"* were the names given in pre nineteenth century Poland to various political movements of the gentry. Confederation usually refers to a legitimate, and *rokosz* to an illegitimate movement. It is not, however, the author's intention to indicate who is legitimate here – both parties, by means of their origin, are.

New monocentrism

This means one-party rule – an option that seemed very likely before the split within Solidarity had occurred. But today there are two major parties – political movements – both carrying the Solidarity banner, and several other political groupings, either from the former opposition or from the former regime. A large-margin electoral victory of one party in the parliamentary elections next spring, even if it were to be the president's party, will not eliminate a vocal opposition from the Polish political arena.

Dichotomization

This seems to be happening. At present, the Democratic Union and the Center Alliance are precisely alliances (or movements), not parties, at least in the European sense. They resemble American parties – loose coalitions of various interest groups. If they are able to build up effective electoral machines, they may dominate the political arena for at least the next four years, and then they may reinforce their position by processing through parliament a majority electoral system. Such a system is better understood by the people than a proportional one and, therefore, enjoys popular support.

Trichotomization

This may occur if a strong centrist party emerges. It is unlikely to happen from within the Solidarity movement – the Center Alliance and the Democratic Union consume, it seems, available options. Some see such a future centrist force in the Polish Peasant Party, but except for the critical attitude toward the Mazowiecki government, there are few factors to keep this party together. Peasants, as any other group in Polish society, express a variety of political views. Even more importantly, their interests vary: rich farmers, poor peasants, and agricultural laborers have very little in common. The peasants' presidential candidate, Bartoszcze, failed to win even a plurality of the rural population vote, outscored by Wałęsa and Tymiński. The latter is perceived by many as a likely leader of a third – but certainly not a centrist – party. But his electorate is composed of individuals rather than groupings or movements. Their dissatisfaction and frustration was caused by various factors. They will have many more choices available in the parliamentary elections, and their votes are likely to spread out. If, however, Tymiński or Tymińskiites manage to become a real force in the new parliament, the following scenario will probably occur.

The Grand Coalition

This seemed unlikely until round I of the presidential elections; it occurred in the run-off round and now seems unlikely again – the mutual hostility of ROAD and PC leaders makes them very odd political partners. But if within the Polish political spectrum strong extremes emerge – let us say radical postcommunist populism and radical nationalism with or without Tymiński – ROAD and PC may realize that they have much in common and, instead of looking for support from the extremes, could form a coalition. They may be forced into such a solution if the president comes from one camp and the parliamentary majority from another (a cohabitation model). In any case, such a grand coalition is likely to achieve wide popular support – most people would like to see Solidarity leaders in solidarity with each other.

Fragmentation

The postcommunist majority in the Sejm demands a proportional electoral system, hoping to save their necks in the coming elections. They will probably succeed, supported by some splinter groupings within the OKP (the Solidarity faction in the parliament, Obywatelski Klub Parlamentarny – Civic Parliamentary Committee). In the opinion of many experts, such electoral regulation will ultimately lead to a growing fragmentation in the political arena. With many minor parties represented in parliament, it may become very difficult to form a stable coalition and a strong government. In this context, many recall the 1921–26 period in Polish history (which eventually ended with Piłsudski's military coup). But these fears are based on the assumption that there will be minor parties in the parliament and no major ones. One should remember, however, that both Solidarity presidential candidates together gained almost 60 percent of votes in round I, and post-Solidarity groupings may win even more in the parliamentary elections. If the electoral law sets a minimal level of votes for a party to be represented in the parliament, such a 60 percent of votes may translate into an even larger majority for two major parties. Unless there is a split within any of these parties, fragmentation seems to be quite unlikely.

The future of this young Polish democracy will be decided in the 1990-91 elections. The times of *pospolite ruszenie* are over – no more is there an alien enemy within the borders of the Commonwealth. The old Commonwealth of Two Nations experienced times of glory and times of shame, times of unity and times of anarchy. There is a new beginning now;[6] whether it leads to

---

[6] These words were originally written in early October, and at that time the author had no idea that Wałęsa would name his electoral program *Nowy Początek* – The New Beginning; a phrase, incidentally, sounding quite awkward in Polish, almost like an exact translation of the English idiom.

glory or to shame, to unity or to anarchy, remains to be seen. There are fears arising from the weakness of the economy and the complexity of the international situation. But there are also hopes. One such hope arises from the moderate attitudes of the leading politicians as well as the public. These moderate attitudes do not always come from a conscious choice; they are often inconsistent, incoherent, and filled with contradictions and question marks. But they are moderate: there is no dimension of the public mind in which extremism would prevail.

The author wishes to express his deepest gratitude to Arlene Burraston-White for editing a draft version of this essay.

THE DILEMMA
OF POLITICAL INTERESTS
IN THE POSTCOMMUNIST
TRANSITION

Jack Bielasiak

> Danger and deliverance make their advances together.
>
> Thomas Paine

The transition from a communist to a democratic political order signifies the rediscovery of "normal politics" in the life of Poland. The passage towards a postcommunist system means foremost the formation and legitimation of diverse political interests, and the articulation and representation of these interests in political institutions open to public debate.

This essay will concentrate on issues brought forth from discussions of pluralist democratic theory, namely, on the nature of political interests during the transition period and the opportunities for the resolution of political conflicts among those interests. It is the proposition of this essay that the legacy of real existing socialism and of society's struggle against communism impedes the formation of political interests with sufficient definition and flexibility to engage in pluralist politics.

Pluralist theories of democracy define politics as interactions among a multiplicity of groups formed around diverse, fragmented, and overlapping interests (Dahl, 1956, 1982). Such a structure of interests is essential to form a flexible, nonhierarchical, and competitive political arrangement through which groups are able to bargain over their particular economic, social, or cultural interests. The critical aspect here is the system's ability to process and resolve group conflicts without disturbing the consensus around the appropriate institutional and legal arrangements of the democratic order.

This can be attained only if the system is sufficiently flexible to allow for the rearrangement of the conflicts over time on the basis of changes in the positions of the interest groups or the coalitions formed by these groups (Held, 1987, p. 189).

The identity of interests and the rules of competition are fundamental to the successful integration of the political system. The definition of interest must be sufficiently flexible to engage in negotiations over demands and to allow compromises. The bargaining process must be sufficiently open to allow an uncertain adjudication of interests, i.e., the outcome of the political conflicts cannot be established a priori but must depend on the negotiations. This flexibility in political outcome is a vital defining characteristic of the democratic polity. The existence of group interests must therefore be of such a nature as to facilitate an open process of competitive demands resulting in undetermined political solutions.

The creation of a pluralist system out of the ruins of communism is a complex undertaking. It signifies the recognition of conflicting interests as an essential aspect of politics and the provision of new institutional arrangements enabling the free expression of competing interests. Most important, a democratic order requires compliance on the part of the interest groups to both the institutional arrangements and the outcomes produced within the regulated competition. Under communism, institutional mechanisms could always be by-passed to produce the desired outcomes for strategic groups. In contrast, the democratic polity functions on the basis of certainty in political rules and institutions and uncertainty in political outcomes. The post-communist transition therefore necessitates a change-over from uncertain institutions and certain outcomes toward certain institutions and uncertain outcomes (Bunce, 1990, pp. 400–401; Przeworski, 1988).

In this context, it is vital to distinguish between transition and transformation. While the transition process is specific in terms of what is not wanted, i.e., communism, and what is desired, i.e., democracy and pluralism, there are no clear instruments that assure the movement from communism to democracy. Even in the face of substantial progress toward the new system, there is no guarantee that the ongoing liberalization may not be reversed or that a different, non-democratic outcome may emerge.

The political interests in existence in Poland during the transition period require further development to assure the transformation of the political structure toward a fully functioning pluralist order. The political spectrum of postcommunist Poland is relatively weak in terms of groups that are able to articulate clearly their interests and engage in bargaining over uncertain outcomes. Indeed the ability of diverse social groups to define their particular interests and organize political representation around those interests has been slow in coming. This unclarity about group interests has been enhanced by the propensity to form identities around normative values concerning evaluations of the past, the shape of the current transition, and the political vision of the future.

The identification with such values reflects a visionary version of politics with roots in history, religion, or morality. The holistic nature of such group identity has the consequence of placing the conflict among political entities more in the realm of rigid, exclusionary values than in the more flexible world of interests. Such an approach to politics undermines the process of bargaining and concessions necessary to the pluralist enterprise, for it is more difficult to negotiate over fundamental, exclusive values than over material demands.

The propensity toward the moralistic expression of interests is a legacy of both the communist system and the political struggle against that system. In the conditions of real socialism, the tendency was to deny or sublimate political differences and to proclaim socialism as a unitary social formation aiming at the eradication of political conflicts. Even while reality was far from this vision, the very structure of communist systems deformed the identification and articulation of interests.

A similar outcome, albeit for different reasons, was the consequence of the struggle against the communist regime by Solidarity. The latter emerged as the representative of society against the alien state of communism and as such was infused with an ethos that identified it with normative values – despite the fact that Solidarity was originally a trade union to defend the interests of the workers. The union moved quickly beyond that stage to become a movement of the entire nation against an unwelcome political power. In the renewed conditions of the postcommunist reality, it was difficult for Solidarity to shed that image. As a consensus movement, Solidarity continues to play a significant moral role in the postcommunist transition. Even in the aftermath of Solidarity's split into two competing political entities, the inheritor organizations continue to rely on a moralistic identity and to appeal for popular support.

The particular character of the Polish transition also played a role in rendering the passage into a full democratic system more difficult. The 1989 Round Table was a negotiated settlement between the communist regime and the Solidarity opposition that had as its earmark the assurance of a stable social order. The identification of the initial phase of the transition with this compact was linked to gradual and peaceful political changes. Such an approach tended to preserve a dichotomous image of politics, in the form of Solidarity versus communism, even if one of the sides to the agreement was no longer a viable political force.

One of the basic legacies of real socialism, of society's struggle against communism, and of the negotiated transition was the identification of political groups with normative values that substantiate the prior vision of the moral struggle between proponents and opponents of communism. On the one hand, this vision has continued to be expressed in the symbolism and ethos of Solidarity as the embodiment of the political opposition responsible for the defeat of communism. Solidarity and its derivative political groupings remain the symbols of political independence and the guardians of society as a whole. The Center Alliance and ROAD (Ruch Demokratyczny-Akcja Demokratyczna: Civic Movement-Democratic Action) thus seek to present their political platforms not as the embodiment of particular interests but as the continuation of the moral authority of Solidarity. On the other hand, the ethical struggle between communism and its opponents has been translated into historical terms. On this level, it finds expression in renewed emphasis in the national, community, religious, and traditional values of Poland. The result is an explosion of political parties, organizations, or movements identified with the normative vision of the nation.

The political structure of transitional Poland is divided between the dominant world of the Solidarity and post-Solidarity organizations and the subordinate but numerous "extraparliamentary" parties. Interestingly, however, both substructures rely heavily on a moralistic and symbolic orientation to advance their political fortunes. We turn first to an examination of the conditions responsible for the formation of such a political approach and then to an analysis of the dilemma of political interests during the postcommunist transition.

Interests in Real Socialism

It is now a truism to state that the politization of communism prevented the expression of interests within its system. A defining characteristic of real socialism was the fusion of its political and economic spheres in such a way as to assure the appropriation of all interests by the party-state (Nove, 1980). The political effect was to render all decisions subject to political criteria as defined by the ruling circles. Most important, politics was perceived by the population not as a process of arbitration among different interests but as the imposed outcome of regime preferences (see Marody, 1989).

Various conclusions are drawn from this integration of the economic and political systems. Staniszkis, for example, goes as far as to argue that under the structure prevailing in real socialism, economic interests cannot exist (Staniszkis, 1989). Others, while unwilling to deny the very existence of interests, do not see such interests as the principal mechanisms for the functioning of Polish society under communism. The integration of society is sought through the realm of values, not interests; and for that reason the emergence of an independent society in the 1980s can only take the form of a "moral rebirth" (Narojek, 1989). Still others argue that interests do exist in both the official and unofficial circles, but that these interests do not fulfill "group" functions, that is, they are not involved in the political process (Rychard, 1987, p. 105). Thus, even when interests are recognized, they are viewed as nonfunctional for the politics of real socialism.

The practical repercussion of the fusion phenomenon is to deny the identification of individuals or groups in terms of economic interests or at least to render such identification a minor part of the political undertaking. This view is supported by the empirical findings of the 1980s, which showed that the political orientations of the public were affected mostly by their organizational affiliation rather than by their positions in the social structure or their class identification (Adamski and Jasiewicz, 1989, pp. 250–55; Rychard, 1989, pp. 303–10). What mattered most was not whether someone was a skilled worker or not but whether he or she was a member of the Communist Party, the official trade unions, or opposition groups. In short, individual self-identity was more closely bound with normative values concerning pro or antiregime feelings than with interests derived from class or social positions.

Beyond political identification, the fusion aspect also defined the political process. For despite the fact that the communist system was highly politicized, it was not political. The distinction is vital. Politization meant that ideological and political norms were the decisive elements in formulating decisions and not that a process of decision making was in evidence (Bielasiak and Hicks, 1990). In contrast to normal politics, where the rules of competition are well regulated and the outcomes are open ended, the political process under communism violated rules and preordained outcomes. The paradox of the communist system was that politization existed without politics.

Such a situation had important repercussions for political participation. Citizens did not view the prospect of participation in the political structure as worthwhile. Instead of providing opportunities for "inputs" into policy deliberation, politics was the exclusive province of the authorities. The public was only the recipient of "outputs" already determined by the communist powers (Maj, 1987; Marody, 1989). Politics could be experienced by the public only as "reactions" to decisions already taken, primarily in the form of emotional, moral responses. Thus mass activities such as strikes or demonstrations were defined by participants as redress for the wrongful decisions of the regime, as moral acts against an unjust political order.

The distinction between politics as the manipulative acts of the authorities and as the moral premises of the public meant that politics was associated with the normative world of values and conscience and not with the rational world of interests, bargaining, and compromises (see Marody, 1989, pp. 11–15). Political participation in the official world was formalistic and ritualistic. Political participation in real life was reduced to an emotional stance. In either case, participation was not through a pluralist process of group representation, interest articulation, and conflict resolution. Instead, the legacy of real socialism was the constriction of interests and an identification of the public with the world of values.

The Legacy of Solidarity

The propensity toward moralistic politics was further accentuated by the rise of the opposition to the communist state and the identification of that opposition with the Solidarity movement. In the first place, Solidarity, while born as a trade union to defend the interests of the working class, evolved rapidly into a social movement of diverse social groups. The identity of the movement was formed around normative principles that distinguished Solidarity from the communists. Solidarity was the representative of the "real Poland" and of the collective will of society (Kowalski, 1988). For that very reason it was difficult to question the symbolism and emotional appeal of the movement. This reinforced the tendency to look upon the opposition as a unified movement acting in the best interests of Poland against the usurpation of the nation's true identity by the communist authorities.

Second, the political world of the 1980s was defined in terms of a predominant distinction between society and the regime. Throughout the decade, studies of Polish public opinion found that the dominant division in the perception of Poles was the "we versus they" dichotomy, the "we" representing society, the "they" referring to the communist government (Nowak, 1989; *Polacy* series). In 1988, for example, the primary perception of social conflicts in Polish society was defined by respondents in terms of regime versus society and state versus nation (Adamski and Jasiewicz, 1989, pp. 227–28). Such a view of society reinforced the tendency to treat politics in terms of moral categories. Official institutions or processes were formal and alien to political life. Thus, official elections under the communist regime were viewed predominantly as a meaningless ritual; only the act of nonparticipation in the electoral process took the form of a significant political statement (Marody, 1989).

The third element in shaping the normative world of Solidarity was the strategy pursued by the political opposition in its struggle against communist power (Ash, 1990). The emphasis was on the creation of an alternative to communism in the form of a true civil society. The effective establishment of a civil society depended on social self-organization as a world apart from the official one. The creation of successful alternative organizations depended on the formation of social "solidarities." The movement's strategy, and political success, was defined substantially as the maintenance of cohesion and unified action. Such an approach to the organization and strategy of the opposition was evident throughout its existence, moving from Solidarity itself to spin-off organizations, such as the Citizens' Committee (Komisja Obywatelska – KO) or the Citizens' Parliamentary Club (Obywatelski Klub Parlamentarny – OKP), during the final contest with communism (Domarańczyk, 1990). That does not mean that there were no differences among these organizations, only that there was a strong ethos to present them as unified representatives of the struggle for the real Poland.

Moreover, this vision of the Solidarity camp was bound to the integrative process of the postcommunist society. Citizenship and responsibility meant support for the ideals expressed by the opposition, since it has struggled for and represented the true nation. Such a posture made difficult the assertion of dissent on the Solidarity side, masking instead the heterogeneity of views within the movement. The effect was to delay the open manifestation of differences in the Solidarity camp. In turn, the vision of an integrated movement bound by common values and moral concerns, despite serious policy differences among its leadership, constrained the move to open politics defined by competing political programs.

Solidarity as a "Consensus" Movement

The consequence of all these processes was the reinforcement of Solidarity's identity as a consensus movement during the initial phase of the postcommunist transition (Szwajcer, 1990). This consensus was predicated on the maintenance of the normative values associated with the history of Solidarity. The consensus notion, grouped around the ideas of nation, solidarity, and collective will, assumed the mantle of a symbol, even of a myth. The symbolism was difficult to abandon in favor of a more "political" version characterized by adherence to particular interests and the competitive process. Thus while substantial support was given from the start of the transition to the ideas of pluralism, competition, and democracy, the fact remains that the consensus version was difficult to reconcile with the particularistic and divisive interests of a pluralist structure. Instead, in the visionary world of Solidarity, unity and nation remained universal social goods that helped to define the politics of Poland. From such a perspective, there was only one "true" reality, and there was little tolerance for other points of view that detracted from these values.

Another problem in the delay from value consensus toward the pluralism of interests was the close identification of Solidarity with the stability of the postcommunist order. Solidarity was both the standard-bearer in the struggle against communist power, and the instrument that broke that system through the Round Table negotiations and the June 1989 elections. In a very real sense, then, Solidarity acted as a guarantee of the postcommunist order. The prevailing issue became how to move beyond the transition and create a political system defined by political competition while maintaining the assurance of stability provided by the ethos and consensus of Solidarity.

In essence, this dilemma was the fundamental problem of the transition period: stability versus transformation. Stability concentrated on the consolidation of the political gains attained by the defeat of communism. It relied on the values espoused by the Solidarity-led government to maintain peace and order. To this end, the ethos of solidarity was an essential tool. But such a consolidation of the political situation reinforced the status quo to the detriment of political differentiation.

The further transformation of the system, as opposed to its stabilization, necessitated the activization of new political forces, either within the existing political spectrum or outside of it. Indeed, beginning with the campaign for local elections in the spring of 1990, there were visible pressures in both directions. Within the Solidarity movement, these were generated by a growing crisis concerning the pace of the transition and economic transformation.

Solidarity was faced with a dilemma in regard to the Balcerowicz program (*Program*, 1989). A movement whose organizational strength was tied to the working class was faced by an economic plan that favored rapid privatization and marketization and brought in its wake high prices, unemployment, and a decline in living standards. The Balcerowicz program hit particularly hard at the mainstream of the industrial working class, where most of the support for Solidarity was located. The threat against the workers is one reason why the Solidarity movement has remained organizationally weak. Its membership (some 2.2 million) is substantially lower now than in 1980–81, and its program is not perceived as a positive protection of current workers' interests.

To resolve this relative weakness, the movement must undertake actions that will better represent its natural constituency, the working class. Therein lies the dilemma. For such a step requires the abandonment of the Solidarity ethos as the representative of all of Poland. That image, however, is an important part of the continuing social stability in Poland and of the extensive popular confidence in the Solidarity-formed government (CBOS Report, as cited in *Gazeta Wyborcza*, 17 April 1990). However, this support is based on highly emotional, value-oriented feelings relying on the past struggles of Solidarity with the communist regime rather than on a critical assessment of the specific material interests of the population (Rychard, 1990, pp. 23–24). Thus the Solidarity tradition is important in evoking support for the government as a moral value, but less so as the basis of tying support to the interests of workers or other groups in society.

By the spring of 1990, the forces of Solidarity stood before the choice of retaining the organization's consensus status or of moving toward a more partisan stance. The issue generated considerable tensions within the movement's leadership, revealing major differences in conceptions concerning the postcommunist transformation. The differences were to be found along several dimensions, but the most important appear to lie on the institutional and program levels.

On the organizational side, the conflict centers around the political and trade-union concepts of Solidarity. During the period of real socialism, the distinction was far less significant than during the transition phase. In the fused system of communism, conflicts with management become per force conflicts with the state. In such a situation, Solidarity could simultaneously be an economic and political entity, defending the interests of the workers and representing the nation against the communist regime. In the current conditions, marked by the attempted separation of the economic from the political sector, such a position is much more difficult to maintain. The situation is further complicated by the fact that the government is no longer a communist opponent but consists of Solidarity supporters. Under the circumstances, the movement had to define anew its economic and political roles.

For some, this meant the streamlining of Solidarity's political role to a trade-union position. In practice, this was to lead to the deliberate distancing of the political institutions associated with Solidarity away from its parent organization. The effect was to place the government of Premier Mazowiecki and the parliamentary OKP (Obywatelski Klub Parlamentarny) in the political realm and the trade-union chapters in the economic one. In many ways such a division formalized the already existing pattern, with the intellectual elites formerly within or close to Solidarity having turned to political careers in the government, in parliament, and in political movements. The base of activists in Solidarity remained closer to the unionist perspective. The evolution of Solidarity into these distinct constituencies recreates to some degree the "we" versus "they" division of the previous era, albeit on a different basis. Nonetheless, the image of the politicians and the intellectuals as the "they" responsible for the current economic and social hardships of society is articulated by some proponents of the trade-union stance (note also the statements by Wałęsa at the Solidarity Congress, April 1990, and KO [Komitet Obywatelski] meeting, May 1990).

The second dimension of the differentiation in the Solidarity movement found expression in specific policy outlooks concerning political stability and economic transformation. The origins of the split are located in the political vacuum created by the disintegration of the hybrid power structure established by the Round Table in April 1989. The disappearance of the Communist Party as a viable actor in the politics of the country removed one of the poles in this bipolar political system. Solidarity, as the other pole, remained as the principal agency of political action, still tied to its consensus stance. But under the reshaped circumstances of the postcommunist transition, different concepts soon emerged concerning the political role to be played by the movement and its associated groups.

One formula sought to safeguard the unity of Solidarity by grouping all of the associated organizations in a nonpartisan "civic movement" perpetuating the Solidarity ethos (see Vinton, 1990). The intent was to maintain the collective expression of support for the first noncommunist government in the postwar era. The advocates of this perspective argued against the introduction of political divisions along interest or ideological lines. They specifically rejected a return to either the nostalgia parties of the prewar period or the division of the political spectrum along left versus right, or Christian democratic versus social democratic values (Michnik, 1989; 1990). Instead they sought to sustain the unity of the civic movement as the embodiment of Solidarity's spirit and collective action.

An alternative conception of the postcommunist political landscape argued for more forceful changes across a variety of issues, including the shape of the Solidarity movement. To the Kaczyński brothers and others grouped around this outlook, the attempt to maintain the consensus stance of Solidarity was nothing more than the perpetuation of a particular ideology that had seized the movement and gained dominance over the formal institutions of political power. The criticism was especially directed at the attempt by the "secular left" forces to use the unity and collectivist ethos of Solidarity to perpetuate their political monopoly. Instead the alternative prescription stood behind the slogan of "pluralism" in order to dislodge the secular left from official positions and to diversify the political spectrum of postcommunism.

The Center Alliance was established in May 1990 to force the issue into the open. Identifying itself as a right-center alliance, the movement pressed for a quicker pace of change on the political and economic fronts. Its slogan became "acceleration" of privatization, of open, free elections, and of the selection of Lech Wałęsa as the president of Poland. The advocacy of acceleration was meant foremost to break away from the vestiges of the hybrid political system created by the Round Table agreement as an understanding between the former communist establishment and, in the Center's view, the leftist intelligentsia affiliated with Solidarity (see Vinton, 1990). Indeed the primary task of the new political grouping was to destroy the former compromise, and establish a new political reality.

A reaction to the Center's political stance emerged over the ensuing period to culminate in a rival political movement, the Civic Movement-Democratic Action (ROAD), established in mid-July 1990 (*Gazeta Wyborcza*, July 17, 1990). The motivation for the establishment of ROAD was its leaders' wish to maintain the political stability and democratization process evident since the fall of communism. In many ways, this outlook was a response to the policies of the Center Alliance, which was described as an irresponsible movement appealing to dangerous populist and authoritarian tendencies in Polish society. ROAD thus opposes the "acceleration" demand and is protective of the Mazowiecki government's policies of gradual, tempered change. It is concerned foremost with the assurance of political stability in the country and deplores the introduction of political criteria to purge the system, preferring to judge people according to professional and expertise norms.

Despite the partisan stance assumed by ROAD, its proponents deplore the good old days of solidarity and collective action (Vinton, 1990). Indeed both the Center Alliance and ROAD seek to maintain their ties to the ethos and values of Solidarity, each claiming to be the rightful successor to the Solidarity stance. The attempt to inherit the moral authority of Solidarity is evident in organizational and policy terms. Thus both new formations define themselves not as political parties representing specific group interests or ideological programs but as "civic movements" or "alliances" embracing a coalition of diverse political forces.

The broad nature of representation is a reflection of Solidarity's "social movement" definition, as is the claim to advocate the preferences of society as a whole and not only its particular sectoral or group interests. While this may not be much different from the claims by various political parties in the West to act on behalf of the best interests of society, what is distinctive about ROAD and the Center Alliance, at least until now, is their refusal to define themselves as political parties and provide a clear programmatic self-definition. Both movements prefer to appeal to society as a reflection of Solidarity's legacy, its consensus norm and collective stance. This is because the best political payoff in Poland is still closely tied to the moral authority exercised by the Solidarity movement, even if only in the form of political memory.

This condition is derived from the historical role of Solidarity, which provides the movement and those close to it with substantial political power. In terms of purely practical considerations, association with the image of Solidarity and support of its ethos is a critical factor in the distribution of national power. For that reason few forces associated with Solidarity are willing to overtly advocate the abandonment of the normative vision and symbolism represented by the movement. Rather, they prefer to recast their position in such a way as to lay claim to the moral legacy of Solidarity. In the current conflict there is indeed grave danger of being relegated to the status of political outsiders beyond the mantle of Solidarity's heritage, with all the attendant political costs. For that reason, the prevailing tendency among all points of views derived from the former Solidarity consensus is to seek to remain identified as the true bearers of the Solidarity banner.

Political Fragmentation: Miniparties

While the moral suasion of Solidarity was an initial impediment in the transition to a pluralist democracy, another factor making difficult the aggregation and representation of interests was the appearance of a multitude of political parties, groupings, or movements in the postcommunist political landscape (Friszke, 1990). The two phenomena are not unrelated. The predominance of Solidarity as a political power, enveloped in moral categories, makes it difficult for other political actors to challenge its standing. This is clearly evident in the public opinion polls during the first year of the transition, when Solidarity held a commanding lead in terms of popular support (CBOS Report, as cited in *Gazeta Wyborcza*, May 7, 1990).

There is, however, a critical difference between the two phenomena. While Solidarity represented a conglomeration of views, the new parties reflected the fragmentation of politics in the new era. This is evident in the sheer number of political parties and groups competing for the allegiance of the Polish citizenry. For example, there were over eighty political formations active on the political scene prior to the local elections in May 1990. Most of those are small political entities that number only several hundred members and are likely to play minor roles in the postcommunist system.

Besides their miniparty status, the significant element about the vast majority of the new organizations is the reliance on normative, often exclusionary, values as the basis of their political activism. In that sense, this tier of the political scene is a parallel development to the previously described reality centering around the ethos of Solidarity. The miniparties operate, in general, along a dimension of values, traditions, and norms. They define themselves as the moral guardians of political philosophies, not the proponents of particular interests. Even while some of the groups have an economic basis of political activity, this, too, is couched in terms of a particular vision of the future Polish economy – in the main associated with a liberal, market perspective. In short, the miniparties are the self-identified representatives of the true Poland, the exponents of its real independence, the protectors of its Christian faith, or the advocates of its economic salvation.

Perhaps most significantly, the political contestation within this political rainbow is waged in terms of exclusionary principles, with little room for bargaining and compromises over interests. This situation is fueled by the vacuum existing within the social structure during the period of transition. On the one hand, as we have seen, the system of real socialism precluded individuals and groups from identifying with and articulating private interests outside the realm of values. As a result, there is no tradition of political behavior facilitating the expression of interests and the interplay of group competition. Moreover, the necessary crystallization of the social structure has not yet materialized, so that there are no proper occupational, professional, or sectoral identities able to aggregate as groups. The vacuum in the social structure may be remedied by the economic transformation, which will create the necessary social differentiation to provide for the emergence of social group identity. During the early phase of the transition, however, interest-group activity has been quite weak. Sectoral interests are virtually nonexistent on the political scene, with the exception of the peasant lobby. The stronger presence and identity of workers and intellectuals in the opposition movement's struggle against the communist regime reinforced the propensity of these groups to act in terms of the consensual values grouped around Solidarity. In the case of the peasantry, furthermore, there is the important fact that private ownership defined the agrarian sector for years, since the decollectivization of agriculture in the mid-1950s. This situation enabled a focus on the private interests of the peasantry and thus created the conditions for the emergence of the agrarian sector as the most visible and politically active sectional interest in postcommunist Poland.

This is not to deny that the peasant lobby has been free of internal political differences, as evident by the existence of several agrarian parties. Most interesting is the nature of the divisions among these parties. These are clearly related to normative issues, with relatively little bearing on economic interests. The primary differences center around "ideological" concerns, mainly the relationship to and participation of some peasant groups in the former communist system. The insinuation is that some agrarian leaders and parties betrayed the peasant cause by their alliance with the communist regime, while those who refrained from such compromises preserved the true identity of the Polish peasantry. The norm of tradition and nationalism is thus the defining element in the split. The emphasis on values is also evident in the attempt by all sides in this conflict to tie into the traditions of the Polish peasantry by recapturing the ethos of the country "folk" in its purest moral category. The attempt to reach into the past, along the folk motive, may act as a unifying element within the agrarian movement bringing together the value traditions of the peasantry with the economic interests of the agrarian lobby. Such a marriage of the normative and interest factors was evident in the unification of some elements of the peasant parties in the spring of 1990.

In the main, however, there is little opportunity for the expression and aggregation of economic interests outside the realm of values. Instead, the articulation of political positions is predicated primarily on the advocacy of normative visions. The problem is that such an approach, at least for the time being, finds a hollow echo among the population. On the one hand, this is evident in the proliferation of miniparties without a social base, without mass support, and with enigmatic political programs. Rather, most of the existing political parties are phenomena created from above by individual personalities. The parties' positions are often a reflection of the individual leaders' dynamism or effectiveness in expounding a particular philosophy or vision. They are not, for the most part, parties characterized by successful mobilization and participation of supporters. That development has to await the alignment of political parties as representatives of genuine social forces.

The fragmentation of the political parties, together with the consensus umbrella established over the political scene by the Solidarity forces, has led to a paradoxical result. For one of the most evident features of the contemporary transition period is the coexistence of a high level of support for the political authorities and a low level of actual activation of that support through participation in the political life of the country. This situation is in marked contrast to the reality of 1980, when people were very active in the social movement and had the sense of taking part in great political events. At that time, there was participation without extensive systemic transformation. Today, on the other hand, there is substantial transformation without participation. People remain uninvolved in the political movement of change and prefer to sit out the situation (Staniszkis, 1990). This time, without a visible "revolutionary" impulse, participatory politics is more dependent on intermediary social structures that help to foster the opportunities for an active life in politics. As Stefan Nowak argued some years ago, Polish society tends to be characterized by the weakness of such intermediary institutions, relying instead on identities around primary groups (family, friends) and macro dimensions (religion, nation) (Nowak, 1984; Rychard, 1990). As a result, without the institutional mechanisms needed to help identify and unite intermediate group interests, a blockage of interest identification occurs.

The danger of such a political situation is the fermentation of a growing popular frustration. The incentive for such an attitude is the lack of representative organizations enabling the successful aggregation of economic interests and political choices that translates into active participation and expressive supports. Instead, the lack of an adequate intermediary organization of interests results in the continuing passivity of the public. This state of affairs is precarious for the further development of the pluralist system, since it facilitates the mobilization of the masses on the basis of nondemocratic values. Political forces without the stature of Solidarity or the post-Solidarity movements have a great incentive to mobilize the public. This gap between expressed support and active participation in the postcommunist political order is open to be filled by other claimants for popular support (Rychard, 1990; Staniszkis, 1990). The problem is that many of the mobilization appeals are being made on the basis of values and norms that are inimical to the growth of a democratic, pluralist political culture. Instead, the claims to nationalist or religious purity, to traditional symbols, and to economic righteousness translate often into dogmatic and populist slogans espousing chauvinism, intolerance, and prejudice. Ultimately, such appeals are predicated on the belief that other groups, which do not share the same traditions or values, should be excluded from the political process.

Conclusion

The primary task for the formation of a fully developed pluralist system was to move beyond a political structure embossed in normative visions. The consensus of Solidarity and the fragmentation of the political parties resulted in an emphasis on values that hindered the deployment of pluralist group competition. The recent breakdown of the dominant Solidarity consensus into competing political movements will have the effect of delimiting the appeals of miniparties espousing exclusionary values. The presence of a political choice between the Center Alliance and ROAD is therefore an important step in the movement to a pluralist democracy, although it does not resolve altogether the dilemma of political interests.

The full transformation of the political system toward pluralism is often linked to the formation of a new economic structure. While the fundamental reasoning for privatization and marketization is to establish economic efficiency and rationalization, that idea is also tied to the creation of a social structure that gives birth to private interests. The belief among many policy makers is that only on that basis can groups interact in accordance with the tenets of a fully functioning pluralist structure.

In this perspective, the fundamental problem in the formation of a democratic society is the issue of group identity. The lack of private property and the market has resulted in the lack of an organic social structure built around economic interests. Because of this, there are no proper criteria in the system around which interest groups can be formed. That interest vacuum, the argument states, can only be filled through the building of a market economy, bringing forth the necessary intermediary structures to establish economic interests and form politically engaged groups to advance their material interests. In the meantime, the lack of the proper socioeconomic structure means that interest groups in the pluralist sense cannot be easily activated. Instead, interests and political options remain tied to references grounded in historical traditions, political symbols, or moral postures.

In the end, then, we are faced with the dilemma of a complete transformation of the postcommunist system, which requires not only shedding the economic and social practices of real socialism but also considerable tolerance for the difficulties associated with the process of change into a new reality. After all, the Polish postcommunist system is still in a period of transition. While certain features of that transition were essential for the breakdown of the communist regime, they are not necessarily the best mechanisms for the transformation into a pluralist, democratic polity.

Without doubt the changeover from individual needs into group interests and then into new forms of political articulation is a protracted one. The fundamental task for the new political authorities and Polish society is to avoid the appeals of normative visions and absolute truths and to move ahead to the world of negotiations and compromises. While there is danger in this transitional process, there is also the deliverance from a closed political system into a democratic, pluralist undertaking.

References

Adamski, W., K. Jasiewicz, L. Kolarska-Bobińska, A. Rychard, and Edmund Wnuk-Lipiński. 1989. *Polacy '88: Dynamika konfliktu a szanse reform*. Warszawa: CPBP.

Adamski, W. and A. Rychard. 1989. "Zwolennicy i przeciwnicy reformy gospodarczej w opinii społecznej." In *Polacy'88*, pp. 381–400. See Adamski et al. 1989.

Adamski, W. and K. Jasiewicz. 1989. "Dynamika postaw kontestacyjnych: postrzeganie konfliktów, zaufanie do instytucji i stosunek do pluralizmu w latach 1984 i 1988." In *Polacy '88*, pp. 223–68. See Adamski et al. 1989.

Adamski, W. 1989. "Aspirations-Interests-Conflicts." *Sisyphus. Sociological Studies*, vol. 5, pp. 85–102.

Ash, T. G. 1990. "Eastern Europe: The Year of Truth." *The New York Review of Books* 37: 2, pp. 17–22.

Bielasiak, J. and B. Hicks. 1990. "Solidarity's Self-Organization, the Crisis of Rationality and Legitimacy in Poland," *East European Politics and Societies* 4:3 (Fall), pp. 489–512.

Brus, W. 1983. "Political Pluralism and Markets in Communist Systems." In S. Solomon, ed. *Pluralism in the Soviet Union*. New York: St. Martin's Press, pp. 108–30.

Bunce, V. 1990. "The Struggle for Liberal Democracy in Eastern Europe." *World Policy Journal* 7:3 (Summer), pp. 395–430.

Dahl, R. A. 1956. *A Preface to Democratic Theory*. Chicago: Chicago University Press.

—— 1982. *Dilemmas of Pluralist Democracy*. New Haven: Yale University Press.

Domarańczyk, Z. 1990. *100 dni Mazowieckiego*. Warszawa: Wydawnictwo Andrzej Bonarski.

Friszke, A. 1990. "The Polish Political Scene." *East European Politics and Societies* 4:2 (Spring), pp. 305–41.

Hankiss, E. 1990. "In Search of a Paradigm." *Daedalus* 119:1 (Winter), pp. 183–214.

Held, D. 1987. *Models of Democracy*. Stanford: Stanford University Press.

Judt, T. 1990. "The Rediscovery of Central Europe," *Daedalus* 119:1 (Winter), pp. 23–54.

Kamiński, B and K. Soltan. 1990. "The Trouble with Being First: Transition from Communism in Poland." Paper presented at the 1990 Meeting of the American Political Science Association, San Francisco, August.

Kolarska-Bobińska, L. and A. Rychard. 1983. "Interesy polityczne i ekonomiczne." In W. Morawski, ed. *Demokracja i gospodarka*. Warszawa: Uniwersytet Warszawski, pp. 427–60.

—— 1989. "Polityka i ekonomika w opinii społecznej w latach 1984–1988." In *Polacy'88*, pp. 401–16. See Adamski et al. 1989.

Kowalski, S. 1988. *Solidarność a Polska*. Warszawa: Uniwersytet Warszawski.

Maj, Z. 1987. "Świat polityki w publicznej mentalności." *Biuletyn CBOS* 3:3, pp. 14–70.

Marody, M. 1987. "Sens zbiorowy a stabilność i zmiana ładu społecznego," in M. Marody and A. Sułek, eds. *Rzeczywistość polska a sposoby radzenia sobie z nią*. Warszawa: Uniwersytet Warszawski, pp. 109–36.

—— 1989. "Perception of Politics in Polish Society and Its Consequences for Political Participation." Unpublished manuscript.

Michnik, A. 1989. "A Trade Union is no Longer Enough" *Gazeta Wyborcza*, October 6.8.

—— 1990. "After the Revolution" *The New Republic*, July 2.

Narojek, W. 1989. "The Processes of Group Formation in a Nationalized Society." *Sisyphus. Sociological Studies*, Vol. 5, pp. 67–84.

Nove, A. 1980. "Socialism, Centralized Planning and the One-Party State." In T.H. Rigby, A. Brown, and P. Reddaway, eds. *Authority, Power and Policy in the USSR*. New York: St. Martin's, pp. 77–97.

Nowak, S. 1984. *Społeczeństwo polskie czasu kryzysu*. Warszawa: Instytut Socjologii UW.

—— 1989. "The Attitudes, Values and Aspirations of Polish Society," *Sisyphus. Sociological Studies*, Vol. 5, pp. 133–62.

Osiatyński, W. 1990. "Nie ma szkoły demokracji." *Polityka*, May 5.

Program Gospodarczy. Główne założenia i kierunki. 1989. Warszawa: October.

Przeworski, A. 1988. "Some Problems in the Study of the Transition to Democracy." In G. O'Donnell, P. C. Schmitter, and L. Whitehead, eds. *Transition from Authoritarian Rule: Prospects for Democracy*. Baltimore: Johns Hopkins University Press, pp. 47–63.

Rychard, A. 1987. "Konflikt i przystosowanie: dwie koncepcje ładu społecznego w Polsce." In *Rzeczywistość polska*, pp. 89-108. See Marody 1987.

—— 1987. *Władza i Interesy w Gospodarce*. Warszawa: Uniwersytet Warszawski.

—— 1989. "Wizje przyszłości a szanse reform systemowych w opinii społecznej." In *Polacy'88*, pp. 417–48. See Adamski et al. 1989.

—— 1990. "Szanse i zagrożenia legitymizacji politycznej w Polsce." Unpublished manuscript.

Schoepflin, G. 1990. "The Prospects for Democracy in Central and Eastern Europe." Paper for the Conference on Democratization and Institutional Building in Europe. Warsaw, March 1–3.

Staniszkis, J. 1988. "Gospodarka i polityka w okresie transformacji." In W. Morawski and W. Kozek, eds. *Załamanie porządku etatystycznego*. Warszawa: Uniwersytet Warszawski, pp. 39–88.

—— 1989. *Ontologia socjalizmu*. Warszawa: Wydawnictwo In Plus.

—— 1990. "Sprzeczności okresu przejściowego." *Tygodnik Solidarność* 7, February 16.

Stepan, A. "Paths toward Redemocratization: Theoretical and Comparative Considerations." In *Transitions from Authoritarian Rule*, pp. 64–84. See Przeworski 1988.

Szwajcer, P. 1990. "Paradoks Solidarności." *Po Prostu*, Numer Sygnalny, January.

Urbański, A. 1990. "Przed trzęsieniem ziemi." *Tygodnik Solidarność* 11, March.

Valenzuela, J. S. 1989. "Labor Movements in Transitions to Democracy." *Comparative Politics* 21:4 (July), pp. 445–73.

Vinton, L. 1990. "Solidarity's Rival Offspring: Center Alliance and Democratic Action." *Report on Eastern Europe*, Radio Free Europe, September 21.

PSYCHOLOGICAL DIMENSIONS
OF A SOCIOPOLITICAL CHANGE
THE POLISH CASE

Janusz Reykowski

During 1989 we witnessed a major acceleration of social changes in the countries of the so-called "communist bloc." The turning point in these changes was the collapse of the sociopolitical system that had dominated these countries for over four decades. The timing and the form of the changes were not predicted by anyone. In fact, both politicians and expert sovietologists were taken by surprise.

There have been some attempts at explaining what happened in these countries. These attempts differ with respect to their perspectives. From the perspective of the enemies of the old regimes, their collapse is simply a result of the continuous struggle of societies against an autocratic, inefficient, and corrupted system. Due to the courage and determination of freedom fighters representing the best segments of the respective societies, the totalitarian regimes have been defeated. Once the battle has been won, the main task is to eradicate all remnants of the old system, opening the door to democracy and economic prosperity in the near future.

There is also another view representing the perspective of the supporters of the old regime. According to this view, the changes are the result of the mobilization of reactionary forces that took advantage of mistakes and abuses of ill-chosen party and state leaders. These forces received strong support from big capital, which has vital interests in abolishing the socialistic system.

Both above-mentioned views have something in common: they both conceptualize the changes in ideological and moral terms, and they both remain on a rather superficial level of analysis. Nevertheless, they are quite common among politicians and journalists in different countries. Both positions are ahistorical; they are based upon an assumption that over decades the same forces were fighting for the same issues. And they both rely on some kind of "psychologization" of social phenomena: they imply that the psychological characteristics of the individuals involved (freedom fighters, leaders) can account for what happened.

Social scientists can hardly be satisfied with such "explanations." In fact, to account for the change, one has to consider a number of dimensions of an economical, political, and social nature. But there is also a psychological dimension to the change: sociopolitical attitudes and values of large groups of people, as well as their tendencies toward particular kinds of actions, played an important role in shaping the course of events.

This essay puts forth some hypotheses about psychological factors that played a role in bringing about the social changes in Eastern European countries. This does not mean, however, that psychological characteristics of some individuals who happened to take an active part in the whole process will be considered. Instead, "the states of mind" of larger groups of people will be examined as well as conditions that could possibly affect these states of mind. The analysis will focus on one specific case – the case of Poland. To what extent this analysis can be applied to other countries will remain an open question.

Psychological Prerequisites of the Social Change: The Major Sources of Rejection of the Political System in Poland

The most immediate cause of the collapse of the "communist system" in Poland was the rejection of the system by a large proportion of society, which lent its support to the political movement that challenged the system – Solidarity. At the same time, the social groups and political forces that could be interested in preserving the system were in disarray, their morale was low, their capacity for mobilization almost nonexistent.

The support for Solidarity stemmed from different sources. Three of them seem to be the most significant.

The first was the *political* source: the monocentric, autocratic system was incompatible with democratic principles which were in high esteem among a large proportion of Polish society. Hence, the legitimacy of a government appointed not in accordance with democratic procedures was questioned, and the principle of one-party rule, formulated as the "leading role of the (Communist) Party," evoked fierce opposition. Adherents of the idea of political freedom, firm believers in civil and political rights, rejected a system that did not provide the due guarantee of full participation in political life to citizens. They joined Solidarity – a movement that put the slogans of freedom and democracy on its banners.

Another source of opposition to the system and support for Solidarity was the deep dissatisfaction with socioeconomical conditions that existed in Poland at that time. This can be called the *economic* source. Many people became convinced that the system was an economic failure. Its obvious inefficiencies, periodic crises, the deterioration of everyday living conditions, the lack of prospects for the young generation – all this evoked a feeling of contempt for the regime. At the same time, the Solidarity movement, which originally appeared as a labor union fighting for the betterment of the economical situation of the working class, offered a promising alternative. The alternative was even more attractive since the movement had strong ties to the West, and in Poland the West is a symbol of economic productivity and a prosperous life for everybody.

There was yet another important source of support for the Solidarity movement in Polish society that can be described as a *symbolic* one. In contrast to the communist regime, Solidarity revived some of the important elements of the Polish national tradition: It stressed its affinity with the prewar Polish government (all of whose serious deficiencies were forgotten after several decades), which was tantamount to a reversal of the humiliating experience of the imposition of Soviet rule in Poland at the end of the Second World War. Thus, Solidarity represented the idea of full national sovereignty – independence from the Soviet Union (as opposed to the submission of the communist government to Moscow). And last but not least, it entailed a close relationship with the Catholic church – a great moral authority in Poland.

Thus, the Solidarity movement was in a sense a symbol of democracy, economical prosperity, national sovereignty, the dominance of Catholic values, and a pass to the Western world.

The three above-mentioned sources of popular support for Solidarity – political, economic, and symbolic – can be interpreted as three sets of attitudes widespread in various segments of Polish society. The following questions arise: Where do these attitudes originate? How are they distributed in Polish society?

The Patterns of Sociopolitical Beliefs in Polish Society

The description of the three sources of negative attitudes toward the sociopolitical system in Poland presented above was based primarily upon an analysis of the content of the common complaints and accusations directed against the communist regime. Such complaints and accusations imply that the system was incongruent with some basic normative expectations or, as we prefer to call it, with the sociopolitical mentality of a significant part of Polish society. The term "mentality" is employed here to describe systems of implicit beliefs about social and political life shared by larger groups of people. We assume that an important role in such systems is played by normative beliefs, that is, the beliefs referring to reality as it ought to be; such beliefs seem to be the prerequisites of the judgments about the justice and legitimacy of a given social order as well as about the justice or legitimacy of a particular decision or action. In other words, they can be looked upon as a mechanism generating political attitudes.

We attempted to study patterns of the normative beliefs existing in Polish society. The research program was prepared by the Institute of Psychology of the Polish Academy of Sciences in cooperation with researchers from other institutions.

In the framework of this program, a survey of a representative sample of Polish society was conducted in June 1988 (interviewing about 2,000 subjects). In the discussion of some of the results of the survey, this essay will utilize an analysis of the data that was made by its coauthors, Jadwiga Koralewicz and Marek Ziółkowski (in press).

The main findings that will be used here come from a factor analysis of fifteen scales, measuring, as was assumed, the normative beliefs of our respondents. Varimex rotation provided three factors that describe three different patterns of normative beliefs concerning behavior expected from individuals and characteristics of the society at large.

The first factor (16 percent of variance) describes a pattern constituted of the normative belief that an individual should play an active role in society: he/she should take an enterprising attitude in life and strive for a role of an actor (an independent subject) in the family, in the work place, in society at large.

The second factor (14 percent of variance) is composed of the normative belief that an individual should work hard, have positive attitudes toward other people, and have modest aspirations; harmony in social groups should be his/her main concern.

The third factor (11 percent of variance) mainly contains beliefs of two kinds: that the individual should strive for his/her own advantage, trying to get for him/herself as much as possible; and that authorities (in the state but also in the family) are obliged to care for the well-being of an individual.

We have found that the three above-described factors are associated with different political values and with different attitudes toward political and social reality in Poland. It turned out, first, that approval for democratic values was strongly associated with the first factor ($r = .49$) but not with the remaining two ($r = .06$ and $.08$, respectively). In other words, the belief that the individual should play an active role in society was associated with the preference for democratic order, but there was no such association with the two other patterns of beliefs.

The evaluation of social and political life in Poland was different for different normative beliefs. The opinion that unfair inequalities exist in

Poland was associated with factor one (r = .27) and three (r = .15) while in the case of factor two, the opposite opinion was upheld ("wages in Poland are fair" – r = .29). There was also a positive correlation of factor two with the opinion that Poland is a democratic and law-abiding country (r = .34); the same opinion was negatively correlated with factor one (r = −.31).

The conviction that the crisis has intrinsic sources (that is, the system is a failure) was associated with the first factor (r = .45), while for the remaining two factors, the crisis was explained in terms of extrinsic causes (natural disasters, human failures, etc.). This means that a total rejection of the sociopolitical system in Poland was associated with the first factor but not with the remaining two.

We may conclude that these three factors represent three different sociopolitical normative orientations. In the case of the first factor, we are dealing with normative beliefs focused on political rights: they generate opinions that an individual should have the freedom to pursue his/her goals in life and should have the opportunity to participate in the shaping of the social life of the state, of the work place, and of the family. Using deCharms's concepts, we may say that the individual is seen here rather as an "origin" than as a "pawn" (deCharms, 1968). We may call this the democratic orientation (DO). Obviously, such an orientation is incompatible with a monocentric, autocratic system. No wonder that it was associated with a rejection of the existing system in Poland.

In the case of the second factor, the belief system is based on the principle of modesty – modest demands both in economic and political spheres – for the sake of social harmony. Such beliefs are likely to foster acquiescent attitudes toward the existing political order. We can described it as an orientation on social harmony (SHO).

The third factor describes the set of beliefs focused on social rights and privileges; a social order is evaluated primarily on the basis of its ability to give something – to give in a material, economic sense. We may call this the orientation on social rights (SRO). We may notice that in this case there are no clear indications of the total rejection of the sociopolitical system in Poland. Criteria of evaluation of the system are socioeconomical rather than political. Hence, the economic ineptness of the system must evoke dissatisfaction and criticism.

One point should be stressed here. The three above-described orientations refer to the norms people are allegedly espousing while making judgments about sociopolitical and economic phenomena. This means that we are dealing with criteria of judgments rather than with behavioral tendencies; however, the latter are influenced by the former.

We should bear in mind that the factors are orthogonal; it is possible, therefore, that the same person can manifest different orientations (and not just one); it can lead quite frequently to inconsistency in sociopolitical judgments.

If we now compare our findings with our previous claim about the three different sources of support for opposition against the communist regime in Poland, we notice that there is at least a partial correspondence between these two approaches. There is an apparent resemblance between the "political source" of support and a "democratic orientation" as well as an "economic source" of support and a "social-rights orientation." But we have not found anything similar to the postulated "symbolic source." Instead, we found an orientation that apparently was the basis of the attitude of approval for the regime (SHO).

In fact, this should not be very surprising. First, our initial analysis was concerned with the motives for the rejection of the regime; therefore, there was no reason to mention the attitudes of approval for it. On the other hand, it should be acknowledged that we did not include in our questionnaire items related to the domain earlier described as the "symbolic source," because during the time when the survey was prepared (1987), the topic was politically very sensitive and thus too difficult to deal with in a large-scale project. It may be added that in another part of the project, where small groups of respondents were interviewed intensively and a good rapport could be obtained, we noticed many indices of the role of "symbolic considerations" in making judgments about the system.

Assuming that at least three major normative orientations existed in Polish society (or four, if we accept the notion that there also exists a "symbolic," or "national-rights," orientation), we may wonder how they are distributed in the social structure and how this distribution changed over time.

Forms of Mentality and Social Structure

To answer the question "How are the above-described forms of mentality (orientations) distributed in the society?" Koralewicz and Ziółkowski computed separate mean factor scores for different social categories, such as sex, age, level of education, profession, political affiliation, etc. The results are presented in Table 1 and Figure 1 (p. 230).

We can see, first of all, that there are major differences in orientations related to education: DO is the most probable among higher educational strata while SRO, among the lowest. The relationship is linear: positive in the case of DO and negative in the case of SRO. There is no clear relationship between education and SHO (see Figure 1).[1]

We can also notice that there is a clear-cut relationship between orientation and profession. Democratic Orientation was high among profes-

---

[1] It should be noted that a similar relation has been found between education and modernity as defined by A. Inkeles (Inkeles and Smith, 1974). It seems that education is conducive to major changes in mentality.

sionals, self-employed craftsmen, higher-level managers, and, to a certain degree, among skilled blue-collar workers.[2] On the other hand, Social-Rights Orientation was highest among peasants, unskilled workers, and the unemployed (primarily housewives and retired persons). Social-Harmony Orientation was also high among unskilled workers, among people holding low-skilled white-collar jobs, peasants, and among managers. It was at same time associated with membership in the PUWP (Polish United Workers' Party, the ruling party). The last finding should not be at all surprising if we keep in mind the fact the SHO was associated with support for the existing order.

The main conclusion from this analysis concerns the relationship between education and mentality. We have clear indications that people from the higher educational strata are most likely to espouse a Democratic Orientation while those from the lowest, a Social-Rights Orientation. It should be stressed that the relationship is far from perfect. Apparently, there must be quite a few people from the higher educational levels who do not share democratic beliefs. As a matter of fact, Koralewicz, who conducted a study of authoritarianism in Polish society, described this as "educated-class authoritarianism" (Koralewicz, 1987). She argued that it differs in some respects from the one that is fairly common among the working class.

This authoritarianism can possibly be associated with specific professions – it has been shown that a system of values is influenced to a significant degree by occupation (Kohn, 1969; Słomczyński et al., 1981; Alwin, 1989). Thus, we can expect, e.g., that people functioning within the hierarchical system of a highly centralized state bureaucracy can be less likely to adhere to democratic values. But there are also some personality factors that seem to interfere with the development of a Democratic Orientation (Eysenck and Wilson, 1978; Rokeach, 1960). It can account, at least in part, for authoritarian attitudes among the intelligentsia.

The above-described reservations notwithstanding, we may conclude that dissatisfaction with the regime should be closely associated with the level of education. This conclusion can be supported by other data as well. Jasiewicz and Adamski have shown that approval for the postulate of strengthening the leading role of the party, which amounts to support for the monocentric regime, depends on education. They provided the following figures from their survey conducted in 1988 (approval and partial approval combined):

college education	– 12.2 percent
high school	– 20.9 percent
skilled workers (trade school)	– 31.3 percent
unskilled workers (primary school)	– 45.7 percent

(Jasiewicz and Adamski, 1989).

[2] Note that profession plays a particular role here: self-employed craftsmen have a very high score (in fact, the highest) in factor one, while their level of education is lower than some other groups.

But it should also be remembered that the challenge for the existing regime was coming not only from the "upper" level (higher educated) but from the "lower" level as well. It has already been pointed out that people with SRO belonging primarily to the "lower" groups were deeply dissatisfied with the economic performance of the system. Apparently, it has not met the criteria of justice as conceived in the framework of the Social-Rights Orientation.

Having this in mind we can now look at the whole process from a diachronic perspective.

Diachronic Perspective

The first and rather obvious implication of the reasoning presented above is the proposition that opposition to the system tended to evolve over time. One of the major factors of this evolution were changes in the social structure, especially in scholarship and occupational makeup of Polish society.

It should be borne in mind that in 1945 there were about 80,000 people in Poland with a college education and less than 400,000 with a high school education (the population at that time was 25 million). In the early eighties, the respective figures were 1.5 million and 5.5 million (population about 37 million). If our claim about the relationship between level of education and Democratic Orientation is valid, we should expect that democratic aspirations had a different strength and popularity in various periods of time – in general, one may expect that they grew over time.

There are some empirical findings that seem to support that claim. In the early seventies, S. Nowak found that the concept of a "good social system" contains – for a large proportion of Polish society – concern for social rights. The item "it provides equal chances for everybody" was ranked first (80 percent of choices), and the item "provides good living conditions for all citizens" ranked second (60 percent of choices). Political values (freedom of speech, influence on government) were ranked third and fourth and were mentioned by less than 50 percent of respondents (Nowak, 1976). Fifteen years later the picture changed substantially. In our 1988 study, more than 70 percent of respondents regarded freedom of speech as a necessary characteristic of a good social system.

Of course, there may be various causes for such a change. A likely one could be the heightened political awareness of Polish society resulting from the experience of the early eighties – the rise and fall of the Solidarity movement. But the effect of the Solidarity movement was nevertheless different for different social groups. An example of this difference is an endorsement of the item approving some limitations of free speech. It was approved by 28 percent of respondents from the "primary education" category, by 25 percent of the trade school respondents, by 15 percent of high-school graduates, and by 10 percent of college graduates. We are inclined to conclude that as the proportion of the educated class grows higher, the democratic orientations become more common. This in fact is not an exceptional situation. It has been noticed that economic development entails the emergence of new groups that produce expanded political consciousness. These changes undermine the existing political authority (Hutington, cited in Jenkins, 1981).

While changes in education could contribute to a more or less systematic increase in the proportion of people with a Democratic Orientation and, by the same token, to the increment of dissatisfaction with the monocentric system, there were also changes that had a less systematic effect. People with the Social-Rights Orientation were most likely to alter their attitudes depending upon the economic situation. We can conjecture, therefore, that in some periods of the forty-year history, these people liked the system, while in others, they were deeply disappointed. Such a disappointment was bound to grow substantially over the last decade or more, when the poor economic performance of the system became notorious.

Let us note an important difference in the dynamics of antiregime attitudes originating from two different forms of mentality (two different orientations). While the DO is likely to generate negative attitudes of a "non-reversible" character toward the system, the SRO allows for the reversal of such attitudes if living conditions improve and the system is able to satisfy basic needs. As a matter of fact, this phenomenon could indeed be observed during the eighties. When in the middle of the eighties the economic conditions slightly improved, one could notice an increase in positive attitudes toward the regime among less educated people but not among the intelligentsia.

We do not have much information about changes in attitudes toward the system in people who rejected it on symbolic grounds. Our conjecture is that it is likely to be a fairly stable source of negative evaluations of the system. But even so, such attitudes may change as a function of cues that can make them more or less salient. In other words, the conditions that activate patriotic or religious feeling may intensify these attitudes.

It should be acknowledged that the above description of diachronic change gives only a rough approximation of the whole issue. It does not take into account a number of important factors that are likely to modify the whole process. One such factor is social impact. Attitudes may change more or less rapidly as a result of influence from a powerful source (Latane, 1981). They are also susceptible to changes in mood, which can be not only an individual but also a group phenomenon. Such changes are manifested as the mobilization (or demobilization) of the masses (Jenkins, 1981; Tilly, 1978; Wright, 1981).

All this taken together seems to put into question the widely accepted notion that the entire Polish society (or at least its overwhelming majority) espoused the same sociopolitical values, was inimical toward the system over the entire forty-five year period, and just waited for a convenient opportunity to topple it. The picture in fact seems to be much more complicated.

From Negative Attitudes to Collective Action

Our analysis was based upon the assumption that the major prerequisite of the collapse of the communist regime in Poland was the massive rejection of the system. We have claimed that there were different reasons for such a rejection, and various groups of people differed with respect to their dislike of the system. But such an explanation has some missing links.

In fact, dissatisfaction with a system does not lead inevitably to action aimed at its replacement by another one. It merely creates the potential for such an action – a kind of affective propensity. The transition from the stage at which such affective propensity is aroused to that at which a collective action is undertaken may occur if some specific conditions are met.

On the basis of the general theory of action (Atkinson and Birch, 1978; Schwartz and Howard, 1984), we can mention two such conditions of primary importance. One is the conviction that a collective action is at all possible, i.e., the feeling of hope for success in such an action. Another one is the emergence of a common goal and at least a rudimentary program of attaining it. In the case of larger groups, the formation of a common goal and the construction of a program requires some form of organization and leadership (Jenkins, 1981).

As far as Poland is concerned, the two above-mentioned conditions appeared at the beginning of the last decade. The conditions were not stable, to be sure. We cannot analyze them systematically in the framework of this essay. Instead, let us focus on some major facts.

With regard to the first of the above-mentioned conditions – the hope factor – there is rather popular agreement that its original major source was the pope's visit to Poland in 1979. This was an extraordinary experience for millions of people who gathered in large masses under common banners – for the first time in forty years not provided by the regime. There was an experience of common action: people got together, sang together, prayed together, and got a feeling of the powerful force in collectivity. People were also given the opportunity to conceive of a kind of order that was different from the existing one since to a large degree the gatherings were self-organized. (They were not, as in other instances, provided fully by the state.) In a country whose population is more than 90 percent Catholic, all this had to have a powerful impact on people.

If the pope's visit contributed to the rise of hope – reinforced by the success of strikers in August 1980 – the Solidarity union organized that fall provided purpose, organization, and leadership.

Martial Law, installed in December 1981, changed all this: it took away "the hope" and crushed the organization. It substantially weakened the Solidarity movement. The regime scored a major victory, but, as it later turned out, it was a Pyrrhic victory.[3] Eight years later the peaceful transition of power took place, and the Communist Party which ruled for forty five years was dissolved.

It is not the task of the present author to describe the process of the revival of hope and organization. But it is worthwhile mentioning one more factor that played a significant role in the peaceful transition between communist rule and the Solidarity government.

It should be borne in mind that the changes that affected the whole society affected the ruling party as well. The major one was the change in the criteria of recruiting the political elite. While for several decades the political elite was recruited from the lowest strata of society – from the families of uneducated workers and poor peasants – in the last decade, college-educated people assumed significant positions in the party apparatus, in the state administration, and in business; many of them belonged to the first generation of the intelligentsia. As far as the people from the former group are concerned, their education, outlook, aspirations, and mentality made them suitable as functionaries and supporters of the authoritarian system. But this was not the case with persons belonging to the latter group. Many of them had a much better knowledge and understanding of the contemporary world, they were acutely aware of the gross inefficiencies of the regime, and they longed for a system that would be more rational and more approved by society.

Of course, within the party there was strong opposition to any radical change. The opposition of conservatives (nicknamed "concrete") was in the minority. For example, data from a survey conducted in 1989 within the party indicated that support for the conservative position was declared by less than 30 percent of its membership. Nevertheless, it was a powerful and influential group. It could thwart reforms if not for the fact that its capability for effective political action was considerably reduced. This was due, first of all, to the fact that this group lost support from its staunch allies in the Soviet Union – *perestroika* undermined its strength. And General Jaruzelski by his adroit maneuvering deprived it of its leaders – all the potential leaders of the antireform movement lost their political power during the eighties, and as a result, the reformists in the political elite got the upper hand.

Two important aspects of the mechanisms of change are illustrated here.

One, often overlooked, amounts to the fact that social processes that affect society at large tend to affect the ruling groups as well. This means that ruling groups should not be perceived as monolithic in their opposition toward change. To the contrary, they can generate forces of change within them-

---

[3] The above statement does not mean to suggest that Martial Law was altogether a futile endeavor. There are good reasons to suspect that it saved Poland major bloodshed.

selves (O'Donnell and Schmitter, 1986), although it is rather unlikely that such forces without pressure from below could elicit major modifications of the system. But as could be seen in the Polish case, the forces of reform within the system played a significant role in bringing about its alteration.

The second aspect we may consider here is the role of the previously mentioned factors of "hope" and "organization" but this time in their negative form. It was the erosion of hope and the lack of organization and leadership that prevented the forces inimical to reforms from taking practical action. They left the field without a major battle.

Concluding Remarks

There are some implications of the preceding analysis that should be mentioned here.

We may note, in the first place, that social forces that contributed to the abolishment of the old regime were highly heterogeneous. Only part of the social support that brought Solidarity to power came from groups intrinsically interested in the democratic order. At the same time, a substantial part of its supporters will evaluate the new regime primarily on the basis of its socioeconomic record. And there are also many of those who will closely watch the symbolic issues: for them, one of the important criteria might be the presence (or absence) of the Soviet army on Polish soil.[4] Such a diversity of beliefs and values must, of course, create many conflicts and contradictory expectations. It must also lead inevitably to disenchantment. It is obvious, therefore, that Polish society faces the formidable task of developing a new political and economic organization that will be able to deal effectively with all these contradictions.

If we apply here the concepts of the theory of dynamic systems, we may say that Poland is now in the transition phase. The old pattern of the system, the so-called "attractor" (the state to which all elements of the system tend to converge), broke down; the new pattern (new attractor) has yet to emerge. How might it look?

It seems that there are at least three different possible forms. If the democratic orientation prevails, the country can move toward a democratic order. But there are other possibilities as well. The success of the social-rights orientation may lead to the development of a populist regime, and the success of the symbolic orientation can lead to a situation in which nationalistic sentiments become the major unifying force in the country.[5]

---

[4] The other issue closely related to the symbolic, "national-rights," orientation that surfaced as a problem for Mazowiecki's government concerned the fears of "selling out" Polish property to foreigners that appeared quite widespread in society.

[5] One may also wonder whether the "Social-Harmony Orientation" could act as an "attractor" for a new system. For the time being it seems rather unlikely.

An observation of the Polish political scene clearly indicates that all three kinds of attractors have some chance of realization. Social scientists could have some role in shaping the process if they identified the major factors that influence the pattern of the emerging process and made the public aware of them.

References

Alwin, D. 1989. "Social Stratification, Conditions of Work, and Parental Socialization Values." In N. Eisenberg, J. Reykowski and E. Staub, eds. *Social and moral values*. Hillsdale, NJ: Erlbaum.

Atkinson, J.W., and D. Birch. 1978. *Introduction to Motivation*. New York: D. Van Nostrand.

DeCharms, R. 1968. *Personal Causation*. New York: Academic Press.

Eysenck, H.J. and G.D. Wilson. eds. 1978. *The Psychological Basis of Ideology*. Baltimore: University Park Press.

Inkeles, A., and D.H. Smith. 1974. *Becoming modern*. Cambridge: Harvard University Press.

Jasiewicz, K., and W. Adamski. 1989. "Ewolucja kontestacyjnej świadomości politycznej." In W. Adamski, ed. *Dynamika konfliktu społecznego w Polsce: Polacy 1980-1988*. Poznań: ZMW.

Jenkins, J.C. 1981. "Socio-political movements." In S.L. Long, ed. *The Handbook of Political Behavior*. New York: Plenum Press.

Kohn, M.L. 1969. *Class and Conformity: A Study in Values*. Homewood, IL: The Dorsey Press.

Koralewicz, J. 1987. *Autorytaryzm, lęk, konformizm*. Wrocław: Ossolineum.

Koralewicz, J., and M. Ziółkowski. Forthcoming. *Mentalność Polaków (Sposoby myślenia o polityce, gospodarce i życiu społecznym w końcu lat osiemdziesiątych)*. Poznań: Nakom.

Latane, B. 1981. "The Psychology of Social Impact." *American Psychologist* 36, pp. 343−57.

Nowak, S. 1976. *Ciągłość i zmiana tradycji kulturowej. Raport*. Warszawa: Uniwersytet Warszawski.

O'Donnell, G., and P.C. Schmitter. 1986. "Tentative Conclusions about Uncertain Democracies." In G. O'Donnell, P.C. Schmitter and L. Whitehead, eds. *Transition from Authoritarian Rule: Prospects for Democracy*. Baltimore: Johns Hopkins University Press.

Rokeach, M. 1960. *The Open and Closed Mind*. New York: Basic Books.

Schwartz, S.H. and J.A. Howard. 1984. "Internalized Values as Motivators of Altruism." In E. Staub, D. Bar-Tal, J. Karylowski and J.Reykowski, eds. *Development and Maintenance of Prosocial Behavior*. New York: Plenum Press.

Słomczyński, K.M., J. Miller, and M. Kohn. 1981."Stratification, Work, and Values: A Polish–United States Comparison." *American Sociological Review* 46, pp. 720–44.

Tilly, C. 1978. *From Mobilization to Revolution*. Reading, MA: Addison-Wesley.
Wright, J.D. 1981. "Political Disaffection." In S.L. Long, ed. *The Handbook of Political Behavior*. New York: Plenum Press.

Table 1

Sociopolitical Orientations of People Belonging to Different Social Categories

Means of factor scores

Orientations:	Factor 1 Democratic (DO)	Factor 2 Social Harmony (SHO)	Factor 3 Social Rights (SRO)
EDUCATION			
elementary	−.33	.14	.37
trade school	.00	−.02	.17
secondary	.19	−.06	−.28
junior college	.38	−.08	−.68
college	.41	−.24	−.82
PROFESSION			
managers	.28	.25	−1.12
professionals	.43	−.10	−.78
white-collar workers	.24	−.10	−.22
skilled workers	.06	−.07	.06
unskilled workers	−.36	.16	.23
peasants	−.21	.06	.38
craftsmen	.61	−.50	−.24
military officers	.20	.21	−1.00
SEX			
males	.08	.00	−.11
females	−.08	.00	.10

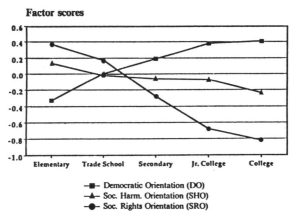

Educational Level and Orientations

Means of factor scores

—■— Democratic Orientation (DO)
—▲— Soc. Harm. Orientation (SHO)
—●— Soc. Rights Orientation (SRO)

POLITICAL INSTITUTIONS IN THE PROCESS OF TRANSITION TO A POSTSOCIALIST FORMATION
POLISH AND COMPARATIVE PERSPECTIVES

Stanisław Gebethner

Since the beginning of 1989 when the Round Table negotiations started in Poland, tremendous and rapid revolutionary changes have taken place in the whole region of Central and Eastern Europe. This process of radical social, political, and institutional changes is still under way. But we can say that the old constitutional, political, social, and economic order known previously as real socialism, or the communist regime, has collapsed. Each country of this region is now struggling to construct its own version of the future. The ultimate goal may be democracy and capitalism, but there is no consensus on how to attain them.

The 1989 peaceful, or revolutionary, radical political changes swept away one ideology in Eastern Europe without replacing it with another that is as clearly defined. Democracy based on free elections, that is, a multiparty system, and a free-market economy may be common and desirable goals, but history (and especially the last forty years), geography, and citizens' awareness (or national psyche) will be influential factors and obstacles in determining how quickly, if at all, they are achieved.

This process of fundamental changes was initiated in Poland and spread over all of Central and Eastern Europe, which had been under Soviet domination for nearly half a century. The postwar European order and the previous military balance of power on this continent is challenged by this same process.

Forty-five years ago, after the Second World War, the new order was established in Europe as a result of an agreement of the Four Great Powers reached at the Yalta and Potsdam conferences.

The Yalta European order was the twentieth century version of the nineteenth-century's Congress of Vienna European order. In effect the main difference lies in the fact that the Yalta European order acknowledged not only the delimitation of spheres of influence and interests between two superpowers: the United States and the USSR. It also accepted a sharp division between Western and Eastern Europe based not only on diversified cultural traditions, but on different socioeconomic and political systems contrasted with each other. At the same time, nations of Eastern Europe were deprived of their right to self-determination and sovereign decisions in shaping their own destiny and especially their own political and constitutional institutions.

For forty-five years Europe maintained peace. It is true that the Yalta European order guaranteed peace, which was understood as the absence of war on our continent. But this peace was achieved at the expense of freedom of the Eastern European nations and their natural right to self-determination.

The difficult peaceful past four decades in Europe were based on a fragile military balance of power. But at the same time, the historical and traditional division between Eastern and Western Europe was deepened. Central and Eastern European countries – Bulgaria, Czechoslovakia, Hungary, Poland, Romania, and East Germany – were subjugated to foreign imperial rule and forced to follow the Soviet economic, constitutional, and political systems. Only Yugoslavia, and then Albania (and to some extent Romania) tried to save their independence. But in fact all these latter three countries also followed the Soviet pattern of an economic system and its political and constitutional system of government. Paradoxically, for a long time the authoritarian (or totalitarian) political systems in Yugoslavia, Albania, and Romania were legitimized by their strong anti-Soviet attitude and opposition to the Kremlin's domination. In fact, the political and economic systems of these three countries were a specific alteration of the Soviet type of regime based on communist ideology.

The Soviet pattern of an economic system was based on a centrally planned economy, the domination of state ownership and the liquidation of private property, and command-administrative management of the national economy with a huge bureaucratic governmental apparatus. This economic system was logically synchronized with a monocentric political system. The core of this system was the monopolistic position of the Communist Party with elimination of political opposition and civic participation in governing on local levels.

The installation of this political system as well as the economic system in Central and Eastern European countries was mainly the result of the communist takeover of power inspired and supported by the Kremlin acting through its political agents and directly aided by the NKVD. However, this historical process of the communist takeover and installation of new regimes was associated with an attractive ideology promising quick economic development, full employment, universal social benefits, and the social promotion of vast deprived strata of the population according to egalitarian ideals.

At the beginning, the effectiveness of new regimes was based on the mixture of economic and social achievements with the terror of secret police eliminating any political opposition.

In the late 1960s and in the 1970s, the centrally planned economic system started to lose its capacity to satisfy growing demands for the further and quicker improvement of the standard of living of the population. The half-hearted economic reforms failed and produced the deterioration of the standard of living accompanied by the devastation of natural resources and the entire ecological environment. The Chernobyl disaster was a tragic symbol of this crucial political issue, strengthening the vast dissatisfaction and frustration of the general public in Central and Eastern European countries.

The economic and social performance of the system lost its ability to legitimize the authoritarian political regimes. The revolutionary source of legitimation vanished earlier. Of course, owing to the character of their installation in the late 1940s, the postwar political regimes in Central and Eastern Europe had never been democratically legitimized through fair and free elections. The acclamatory-type elections with forced (if not falsified) 99 percent turnouts were a superficial legitimation of existing political systems.

At the beginning of the 1980s, the dramatically delegitimized political system in Poland was challenged by a mass civic protest movement with the emergence of Solidarity. This was a strong and widespread revolt against the existing economic and political system. The revolution from below had started. Although it was at that time initiated only in one country, it influenced other Central and Eastern European nations. The virus of the "Polish disease" was attracted by the societies of other countries – the Soviet Union included – although in Poland itself the Solidarity revolt was for a time "neutralized" by martial law. The real conflict, however, was not solved. It was only forced into dormancy for nearly one decade.

The monocentric, authoritarian political system, with the monopolistic position of the Communist Party and huge bureaucratic governmental machine, was unable to solve the economic and social crises with which it was faced.

What are the reasons for the quick and dynamic process of radical political changes in Central and Eastern Europe which we witnessed in 1989 and 1990 – often called the Autumn of Nations? We can focus on the following seven specific premises:

First, a dramatic economic decline caused by an inefficient, centrally planned economy and command management of national industry and agriculture, which produced hardship in daily life and deepened the gap between the socialist bloc and Western countries;

Second, a sharply deteriorating standard of living of the population at large, including a devastation of the ecological environment shortening life expectancy since 1969;

Third, a dramatically growing technological gap between the Western countries and the Soviet-bloc countries;

Fourth, a vanishing legitimation of political systems and the growing aspirations of the general public for liberty and civic rights and free elections;

Fifth, an erosion of the hegemonic position of the communist parties, which were losing the capability both to control the monocentric political system and to direct the national economy (or – as in the cases of Poland and Hungary – to implement economic reforms); they had lost effective influence over public activities of crucial groups of society (and especially the working class);

Sixth, a complete decline of Marxist-Leninist ideology and the total failure – especially within the younger generation – to indoctrinate them with communist ideals and values;

Seven, a change in the Soviet concept of relationships between the Kremlin and the Central and Eastern European countries, i.e., the formal and practical denunciation of the Brezhnev Doctrine.

All these premises were coming to a head in a long process over the course of at least ten or even more years. In 1989, all these factors accumulated in every single country of this region, and the region as a whole ripened to the changes at the same time.

In the past, we had witnessed isolated, premature revolts against the communist regime in 1953 (GDR), 1956 (Poland and Hungary), 1968 (Poland and Czechoslovakia), 1970 (Poland), and 1980–81 (Poland).

A significant characteristic of all these popular revolts, which were often damned as counterrevolutions and were doomed to failure, is that, broadly speaking, they were always revolutions spontaneously bursting out from below. Sometimes they met support from above – they were taken over by a part of the ruling elite of native communist leaders of a given single country – but then they were tamed and eventually betrayed by these leaders (Gomułka in the late 1950s and Gierek in the 1970s in Poland), or the leaders themselves were deposed (Dubček in 1969 in Czechoslovakia) or physically liquidated (Nagy in 1958 in Hungary).

In Poland in 1980–81, the popular spontaneous revolt, being a revolution from below, constituted its own leaders against the will of the ruling communist elite and thus moved out of control of the governing establishment. The old scenario of taking over and taming the popular revolt was inapplicable in this case. It was for this reason that extraordinary measures were eventually undertaken.

Martial law was imposed in Poland on December 13, 1981, to halt the massive popular revolt led by Solidarity. This painful decision may have saved Poland from a civil war or prevented direct Soviet military intervention, which could have seriously challenged the fragile security system in Europe. But at the same time, martial law saved the existing political system, which was the main obstacle to real reforms of the economic system. It is true that under the umbrella of martial law important endeavors to reform the economic system in Poland were made. They were continued after martial law was lifted. These reforms were pointed in the right direction, but they generated as many difficulties as they solved. One result was that a number of state-run enterprises used their independence to exploit their monopoly positions to raise prices but without improving either the quality or the availability of goods. The mood of disillusionment and frustration of the general public emerged with a new force. This dissatisfaction was articulated in two waves of industrial actions that took place in Poland in May and August 1988. Both the ruling elite and the leaders of the opposition gathered around Lech Wałęsa, chairman of delegalized Solidarity, realizing that the way out of the economic, social, and political deadlock lies in an initiation of genuine negotiations between the government and the opposition.

Gorbachev's official visit to Poland in July 1988 and his declaration of the Poles' right to shape their destiny according to their own will and aspirations facilitated General Jaruzelski's undertaking the bold initiative of proclaiming the idea of Round Table talks between the governing Polish United Workers' Party and Solidarity's Civic Committee headed by Lech Wałęsa. This unique – and unprecedented in this region of Europe at that time – adventure took place in February 1989, ended successfully with the conclusion of a significant political agreement securing for the anticommunist opposition a power sharing within the frameworks of the existing political system, and opened the way to participation in semicontested free parliamentary elections.

In the spring of 1989 this great political event in Poland seemed to be an isolated fact limited only to Poland's specific and acute political and economic situation. But once again the Polish experience – this time with the Round Table agreement and its far-reaching consequences – soon sparked all over Central and Eastern Europe and produced the collapse of the socialist authoritarian political system (or the communist regimes) in this region.

What was the real meaning and universal significance of the Polish Round Table? We can point out five substantial distinctive features, which became fairly common for round tables arranged in other countries (with the exception of Romania). Thus in political terms we can say that the essence of a Round Table in the course of events that took place recently in Central and Eastern European means:

(1) a recognition by the ruling communist parties of the existence of a political opposition, i.e., de facto approbation of the fundamental principle of pluralistic democracy preceding constitutional changes;

(2) a resignation of the monopoly of one party being the cornerstone of the previous political system in these countries;

(3) an acceptance of contested – but in fact imperfect – free elections;

(4) a commitment to a peaceful and gradual transition from an autocratic system of government to a democratic one;

(5) bodies that in fact act as constitutional conventions (or constitutional assemblies).

Initially the Polish experience with the Round Table contract seemed to be limited to semifree – or more to the point, semicompetitive – elections and a slow, gradual process of transition from an autocratic to a democratic system of government. However, the results of the parliamentary elections of June 4, 1989, produced a remarkable acceleration of political changes. In practice, the predicted process of gradual transition was overtaken by events.

This unexpected acceleration was caused by the will of the Polish electorate, which expressed overwhelming support for Solidarity Civic Committee candidates nominated to both houses of the bicameral parliament. At the same time, the election results were devastating for the governing Polish United Workers' Party (PUWP). Extremely humiliating was the defeat of the national list of candidates to the Sejm composed of top leaders of the PUWP, including the prime minister at that time, and the two leaders of the then allied parties: the United Peasants' Party (UPP) and the Democratic Party (DP). General W. Jaruzelski was saved only due to the fact that he was not running as a candidate to the Sejm.

The majority of Polish voters rejected the old-guard leadership of the then existing political establishment, although party reformers and architects of the Round Table agreement were nominated on the national list. It is true that some candidates (like Prime Minister M. Rakowski) failed to obtain the 2 percent of votes necessary for the required overall majority. Nevertheless the voters' verdict was clear. The overall majority of valid votes cast were against them. What is significant is the fact that among voters who rejected the national list were not only Solidarity followers but also members of the PUWP. The collapse of the national list articulated the wide popular protest against the ruling establishment.

The electoral defeat of the national list in Poland is extremely meaningful in a historical perspective. It anticipated the downfalls of the top communist leaders of the older generation in other countries.

Some of these, such as I. Pozsgay in Hungary – a devoted reformer who several months previously (in October and November 1989) seemed to be the unchallenged candidate for the post of president of the Republic – were toppled in the 1990 parliamentary elections.

In Czechoslovakia, it was not only the whole old-guard leadership installed by Brezhnev in Prague after the Soviet military intervention in 1968 that was deposed, but also A. Dubček – the communist leader of the Prague

Spring of 1968, symbolizing the concept of "socialism with a human face" – lost in the competition for the constitutionally important post of the president of the Republic to V. Havel, the outstanding spokesman of the long established opposition grouping "Charter 77."

In the GDR, E. Honecker, for nearly twenty years the autocratic Communist Party leader and in fact an executive state president, and his closest aids were ousted from power under the pressure of massive street protest demonstrations and jailed on charges of corruption. His immediate successor, Egon Krenz, was also quickly toppled by the same revolted population demonstrating in the streets of the main cities of East Germany. The postcommunist party of Democratic Socialism called into existence a completely new leadership recruited from the grass roots (with the one exception of a provincial leader, Hans Modrow). They saved – for the time being – their positions in the political life of East Germany thanks to the electoral law enacted in the German Democratic Republic that excluded a personal choice in voting on party lists of candidates.

In Bulgaria the situation was somewhat different. Although T. Zhivkov, the oldest pundit in Eastern Europe, being in power since 1954, was ousted under conditions similar to East Germany and jailed with accusations of abuse of power and corruption. The new political leadership emerged from the younger generation of Communist Party activists with a proreform orientation. Initially they were able to control the situation owing to the weakness of Bulgarian opposition, such as P. Mladenov (president of the republic) and A. Lukanov (prime minister). They even won the first free (but imperfect) elections owing to a favorable electoral system being implemented at that time. However, after elections that were the result of a long-lasting battle, both Mladenov and Lukanov were deposed and replaced by leaders of the opposition defeated in parliamentary elections.

In Romania, N. Ceausescu was overthrown under the dramatic conditions of a framed-up popular uprising and executed after an unfair trial that was outside universally accepted standards of due process of law. This was a typical blood feud of the communist organizers of coups d'etat. So far, it seems that they still control the political system of post-Ceausescu Romania. The situation in Romania is, however, very ambiguous, and it is difficult to predict what will happen in the near future. But the fact is that the old hated political leadership was ousted in a bloody revolution. These circumstances sharply contrasted with the democratic procedure of rejecting ancien-régime top politicians in Poland during the 1989 parliamentary elections.

The Polish Round Table was a revolution from above that satisfied a revolutionary mood articulated from below and channeled the strong feelings of protest of a revolted population into the democratic procedures of parliamentary elections.

The shocking defeat of the national list and the grievous electoral setbacks of the PUWP challenged the fragile Round Table agreement. The very concept of a gradual, evolutionary transition process to the democratic form of a parliamentary type of government was overtaken by events.

The significance of the Polish Round Table agreement lay in the political contract between the "defunct" PUWP, which had ruled Poland for forty-five years virtually as a monopolist (along with the subordinate, allied UPP and DP), and the opposition represented by Solidarity (or strictly speaking, the Civil Committee attached to L. Wałęsa). What the contract in fact said was that the PUWP in coalition with the two other tamed parties was to continue to govern the country, while the independent deputies that would be elected (according to the pre-electoral contract, they could make up no more than 35 percent of seats in the Sejm) would legally take on the functions of a parliamentary opposition. In the second house of parliament, the Senate – elected without any limitations imposed by the pre-electoral contract – the opposition could attain a majority, but then again, the powers of this newly created house were significantly restricted in provisions of the amended constitution. The then ruling PUWP hoped that along with its coalition partners it would gain at least 25 percent of seats in the Senate. As for the Sejm, the expectations were that the candidates supported by the Solidarity Civic Committee would get less than 35 percent of the seats.

The results of the elections on June 4, 1989, completely crossed out these ill-founded calculations, leaving everybody, even the opposition leaders, surprised. All 35 percent of seats in the Sejm allocated to the opposition went to candidates of the Civic Committee, i.e., people who rallied under the Solidarity banner and were blessed by Lech Wałęsa. In the Senate, Civic Committee candidates won 99 percent of seats, while the PUWP and the entire then ruling coalition failed to secure even one seat in the second chamber of parliament. This was a landslide victory for the opposition, namely, for Solidarity, and a devastating defeat for the ruling party and its previous coalition partners.

In effect, the shaky construction of the Round Table agreement was broken down; it failed the test of free elections understood as the expression of the nation's unconstrained will in the fair procedure of universal voting. If the basic goal of the Round Table was to be maintained – i.e., a transition to a pluralistic parliamentary democracy – then it was impossible not to respect the will of the electorate. After some hesitation, Solidarity, as a coalition of oppositional forces, had to take on the burden of responsibility for governing the country. A government dominated by ministers supported by Solidarity, with a non-communist prime minister at its head, was nominated in this part of Europe for the first time since the Second World War.

In other words, in Poland in the summer of 1989, two crucial events of significant consequences for the whole of Central and Eastern Europe took place.

First, for the first time since the Bolshevik Revolution of 1917, a ruling Communist Party conceded defeat in elections and acknowledged in essence the rule of a parliamentary democracy.

Second, for the first time since 1948, the Soviet Union recognized a noncommunist government in the region that was its sphere of domination and interest. This was the practical test of the renunciation of the Brezhnev doctrine earlier declared by Gorbachev during his visit to Poland in 1988.

These two crucial events opened the way for rapid and significant political as well as institutional and constitutional changes in the rest of Central and Eastern Europe.

The very basis of the system of government existing until that time established on the principle of a monopoly of the Communist Party and backed by the Soviet Union was shaken in this region of Europe from the Baltic (including Estonia, Latvia, and Lithuania) to the Balkans (not excluding Albania).

The results of the democratization of the system seem to be more impressive in the political and constitutional dimensions than in the economy and the social domain.

In the constitutional (or rather institutional) dimension, the following important changes that took place in recent months must be mentioned:

(1) the removal from the constitutions of clauses guaranteeing in legal terms the hegemonic position of one party (i.e., the leading and guiding role of the Communist Party), being the formal ratification of the agreements concluded at the round tables;

(2) the proclamation in the constitutions of a multiparty system patterned on a Western-style democracy;

(3) the introduction of new electoral laws based by and large on proportional representation or based on a combination of proportional representation and majority rule;

(4) the deletion from the constitutions of socialist symbols (official names of the state, national emblems or flags);

(5) the changes of constitutional provisions concerning the domination of state ownership;

(6) the introduction of a presidency instead of a formal collegiate head of state;

(7) the dissolution of the old and omnipotent secret police;

(8) the introduction of new institutional guarantees of civil rights;

(9) the reform of local government;

(10) the reinstitution of the concept of an authentic federal system in countries with a formally federal structure.

The Constitution of the Polish Republic in force is still formally dated as the Constitution of July 22, 1952. But the original text of the Constitution of 1952 differs fundamentally from the actual version of the Polish Constitution. This is a result of numerous amendments that were passed not only recently, in 1989 and 1990, but also previously, in the late 1950s, in the 1970s and earlier in the 1980s.

In effect, the present Polish Constitution of 1990 is essentially the opposite of the original Constitution of the Polish People's Republic of July 22, 1952. The constitutional amendments adopted between 1952 and 1980, however, reflected the evolution of the socialist concept of a constitution. Whereas in 1989 and 1990, four important revisions of the Polish Constitution of a fundamental significance took place, which essentially changed the nature of the contemporary Polish Constitution. All reflect the process of profound and rapid acceleration of changes in the political system and their institutional frameworks.

The first of the latest revisions of the Polish Constitution was adopted immediately after the Round Table agreement had been finally concluded. This revision of April 7, 1989, embraced provisions concerning:

(1) the installation of the second chamber of parliament, i.e., the Senate;

(2) the installation of the post of the president of the Republic and the abolition of the Council of State (the collegiate head of state);

(3) the strengthening of guarantees of the independence of the judiciary:

(4) opening the path for free elections.

At the same time, the institution of the Commissioner for Civil Rights (the Polish ombudsman) introduced in 1987 was also anchored in the amended Constitution. The two important institutional issues discussed during the Round Table negotiations, i.e., the reform of the position of the Prokuratura and the reform of local government, were not touched by constitutional amendments adopted at that time.

The second revision of the Constitution voted on December 29, 1989, was the logical consequence of an acceleration of the process of rapid political changes and reforms, which took place both in Poland and in the other countries of this region. In the case of Poland, this was the most important revision of the Constitution.

This wide-ranging revision of the Polish Constitution concerns:

(1) the official name of the Polish state, which was changed from "the Polish People's Republic" to "the Polish Republic";

(2) the Coat of Arms of the Republic, adding to its previous image of a white eagle a gold crown on its head, with reference to the Polish Coat of Arms that existed before 1944;

(3) the deletion of the text of the Preamble to the Constitution, which was unchanged since 1952 and expressed a clear relic of Stalinism and Soviet domination;

(4) the change of the institutional position of the Prokuratura, which is now subordinated to the minister of justice.

Most important, however, was the substantial redrafting of the first two chapters of the Constitution and their replacement by one chapter, entitled "Foundations of the political and economic system."

The contents of this newly adopted first chapter of the Constitution implies a radical – or, let us say, revolutionary – change of the concept of both the political system and the economic system.

First of all, the character of the Polish state has been essentially redefined. Article 1, which previously described the Polish People's Republic as a socialist state is now substituted by new wording. The present Article 1 reads; "The Polish Republic is a democratic legal state [*Rechtsstat*] implementing principles of social justice." This new reading of Article 1 has changed fundamentally the character of the political system, emphasizing a commitment to three significant values: (1) pluralistic Western-style democracy, 2) rule of law, and 3) the social justice of a welfare state.

Second, it is not only the old Article 3 stipulating the hegemonic leading role of one party (PUWP) in the political system that has been deleted from the Constitution, but a new Article 4 has been enacted, which proclaims the foundations for the creation of a multiparty system. This newly adopted Article 4 reads; "1. Political parties associate citizens of the Polish Republic on the basis of their free will and equality in order to influence the making of state policy through democratic methods. 2. The Constitutional Tribunal adjudicates upon the aims and activities of a political party being contradictory with the Constitution." Therefore, there is ample evidence that in the Polish Constitution being revised in 1989, the principles of a liberal multiparty system similar to the Western democratic constitutions (West German, Italian, French, Spanish, or Portuguese) are being accepted. This is a good basis for shaping a new, genuine multiparty system.

Third, in the new wording of Article 2 of the Constitution, the concept of public power being antithetical to the previous Marxist concept of the class nature of the state is expressed. In the Constitution as it was adopted in 1952, Article 1 section 2 stipulated that "In the Polish People's Republic, power belongs to the working people of town and country." Now, after the revision of December 29, 1989, Article 2 section 1 reads, "In the Polish Republic, the supreme power is vested with the Nation." So, it was not only a symbolic change of the official name of the state. The alteration of the name of the Polish state mentioned above thereby reflects a deep change in the very concept of state power owing to abandoning the Marxist-Leninist theory of the class nature of state power.

Fourth, the concept of political representation has also been changed. The Leninist principle of the relationship between a deputy and his constituency assumed a direct responsibility and answerability, including the possibility of the recall of a deputy by his constituency. This principle has now been abandoned and the previous articles proclaiming the possibility of recalling deputies were deleted. So, political representation in Poland is now based on the same doctrine as is accepted in the Western European model of parliamentary democracy.

Fifth, all articles providing for the privileged position of the socialist type of (state or cooperative) ownership, which was treated as the foundation of the socialist economy, were deleted from the text of the Constitution. Instead, constitutional safeguards of the inviolability of all types of ownership were enacted in the new wording of Article 6 and Article 7 of the revised Constitution. Actually, Article 6 reads, "The Polish Republic guarantees freedom of economic activities regardless of the form of ownership; this freedom may be limited only by an act of parliament," whereas Article 7 reads: "The Polish Republic protects ownership and the right to inheritance and guarantees full protection of personal ownership. Expropriation is admissable only for public purposes and for a fair compensation." This new wording of the two articles of the Constitution mentioned above opened the way to a reconstruction of ownership relationships as a basis for establishing the foundations of a capitalist economic system. On this basis laws on privitization and reprivatization were enacted, and the civil code has been amended.

Sixth, the deletion from the Constitution of provisions concerning the principles of a planned economy is in keeping with the above changes. There are now no constitutional enactments that oblige the directing and management of the national economy on the basis of socioeconomic plans voted by the parliament. This constitutional amendment of December 29, 1989, abolished the legal foundations of a centrally planned and command economy. And this amendment has thereby opened the way to a free-market economic system.

The third revision of the Constitution took place on March 8, 1990. It was connected this time with the radical reform of local government.

The whole sixth chapter of the Constitution, formerly entitled "The Local Organs of State Power and Administration," has been replaced by a completely new one entitled "Local Self-Government." The new provisions of this changed Chapter 6 of the Constitution reflect the concept of local government patterned on the Western European model proclaimed in the European Charter of Local Government. Autonomous communes with their freely elected communal assemblies became the core of the new democratic structures of local government. Thereby the last relic of the Leninist concept of democratic centralism was obliterated from the text of the Polish Constitution.

The fourth significant revision of the present Polish Constitution took place on September 27, 1990, and dealt with the election of the president of the Republic.

According to the amendments of April 7, 1989, the institution of the President of the Republic was restored. The post of the president was abolished in 1952 and replaced by the Council of State as a collegiate head of state and as an emanation of the Sejm. At that time the concept of the

Council of State was to a large extent based on the pattern of the Presidium of the Supreme Soviet. In 1989 the Council of State was abolished and the institution of the President of the Polish Republic was installed. Under these circumstances, the restitution of the institution of the President of the Republic could be interpreted as a symbolic tribute to patriotic traditions and a sign of the abolition of a Stalinist legacy. But it was not so. The real premises of the installation of this institution was the idea of laying into the structure of the state's organs a pile that would stabilize the political system as a whole.

In substance, the Round Table agreement meant the abolition of the leading (hegemonic) role of one party and the abandonment of its monopolistic position in the political system. There was a necessity to create some new center of political stability and continuity. In the Polish situation of 1989, the transition to parliamentary democracy was faced with a political infrastructure without an established and stable party system.

Therefore, the constitutional position of the President of the Republic was constructed on a pattern similar by and large to the Finnish or French Fifth Republic model.

According to Article 32 of the Constitution, "The President of the Polish Republic is the supreme representative of the Polish State in internal and external relations" and he "safeguards the observance of the Constitution of the Polish Republic and defends the sovereignty and security of the State, the inviolability and integrity of its territory, as well as the observance of international political and military alliances."

Initially, the president was to be elected for six years by the National Assembly, i.e., a joint session of the Sejm and the Senate, by the overall majority of votes. He could be impeached only by the National Assembly. Now, after the constitutional revision of September 27, 1990, the President of the Republic is elected for five years in direct elections by the whole nation.

The president is vested in constitutional powers to challenge laws passed by parliament by remitting them to the Constitutional Tribunal or by vetoing them. The presidential veto may, however, be overruled by the Sejm voting against it by a majority of two-thirds in the presence of half of the deputies.

The president designates the prime minister and the president of the National Bank, who are finally nominated by the Sejm. The President of the Republic can convene the Council of Ministers and preside over its sitting. He is also the Commander-in-Chief of the Armed Forces and the chairman of the Committee on National Defense. The president can impose both martial law and a state of emergency. He also has the right to dissolve the parliament but only in three cases specified in the Constitution: (1) when the Sejm is unable to nominate the prime minister and his cabinet of ministers in three months, (2) when the Sejm does not approve the budget within a period of three months from its presentation to the parliament, and (3) when the

Sejm votes a law or resolution that would prevent the president from performing his functions (provided in Article 32 of the Constitution) of a guarantor of Poland's international obligations.

It may seem that a powerful president, being more an executive president than a president-arbiter, has been created. But constitutional and political practice of the first fifteen months, when W. Jaruzelski was the president, proved that the first incumbent in this post was rather a neutral president of low profile. It was a specific situational context that determined such a performance of the presidential functions. But Jaruzelski was still playing the role of a guarantor of the peaceful transition to a democracy.

The constitutional – and especially political – position of the President of the Republic changed after the election of Lech Wałęsa to this post by direct universal suffrage. But it is still too early to say what model of the presidency will ultimately emerge.

All four of the latest revisions of the Polish Constitution have fundamentally changed its political and legal meaning, have opened ways to the installation of parliamentary democracy and broad civic participation (especially in local government), and have built up a capitalist economic system in Poland.

The first revision of the Constitution of April 7, 1989, reflects the concept of a gradual and evolutionary transition from an authoritarian political system to a pluralistic democracy. In other words, this revision of the Polish Constitution meant the institutionalization of the Round Table agreements, whereas the second revision of December 29, 1989, and the third revision of March 8, 1990, expressed the will to break away from the legacy of the socialist (i.e., the Marxist-Leninist) regime installed in Poland forty years ago. The very essence of this revision of the Polish Constitution lies in its revealing a deliberate will to safeguard a continuity of the process of adjustment of the constitutional frameworks to the rapid and radical social, political, and economic changes that took place after the June 1989 parliamentary elections.

Constitutional lawyers attach a great significance to the internal systematics of the constitution. Broadly speaking, it reflects the ideological concept of a given constitutional and political system. Thus, it is worthwhile to compare the systematics of the Constitution of the Polish People's Republic as it was adopted originally in 1952 with the systematics of the actual Constitution of the Polish Republic now in force.

In 1952, the systematics of the Constitution of the Polish People's Republic was composed of a Preamble and the following chapters: 1. Political system; 2. Social and economic system; 3. The high organs of state power; 4. The high organs of state administration; 5. The local organs of state power and administration; 6. Courts and prokuratura; 7. Fundamental rights and duties of citizens; 8. Principles of electoral law; 9. Coat of arms, colors, and capital of the Polish People's Republic; and 10. Revision of the Constitution.

The Constitution of the Polish Republic in its reading of 1990 contains the following chapters: 1. Foundations of the political and economic system; 2. The Sejm and the Senate of the Polish Republic; 3. The President of the Polish Republic; 4. The Constitutional Tribunal, the Tribunal of State, the Supreme Chamber of Control, and the Commissioner for Civil Rights; 5. Local self-government; 6. Courts and prokuratura; 7. Fundamental rights and duties of citizens; 8. Principles of electoral law to the Sejm and to the Senate and of the President of the Republic; 9. Coat of arms, colors, anthem, and capital of the Polish Republic; and 10. Revision of the Constitution.

The evolution of the systematics of the Polish Constitution is meaningful, and it corresponds to changes in the political philosophy that underlie the institutional reforms that recently took place in this country. The very wording of the titles of particular chapters (not to mention the content of numerous individual articles) of the Constitution as it was adopted in the Stalinist era in the early 1950s demonstrated the idea of the rejection of the principle of separation of powers characteristic for the Western type of democracy. Instead, the Leninist, or, more to the point, the Stalinist, concept of unique consolidated state power vested in central and local soviets (in the case of Poland this was the Sejm and local people's councils), formally created in plebiscitary elections structured on a basis of democratic centralism, was then accepted in the Constitution of the Polish People's Republic of July 22, 1952.

The Stalinist and Leninist concepts of a unique consolidated state power and of a democratic centralism have now been abandoned. But the classical principle of separation of powers has not thereby been restored. In practice, however, there is a clear division of functions between the legislative (i.e., the Sejm and the Senate) and the executive (the government and administration) bodies with mechanisms of checks and balances. The President of the Republic is constitutionally situated as an arbiter. But now, after his election in direct voting by the whole nation, he is well legitimized in this role, as is the case of France or Finland.

Since 1944, the independent position of courts was reduced by the arbitrary power of political bodies (until 1989, the minister of justice or the Council of State) to dismiss judges. Since 1950, the *prokuratura* was shaped on the Leninist model; in practice it became an instrument of repression in the hands of one ruling party and was infiltrated by the secret police. After the constitutional revisions of 1989, the guarantee of a judge's independence is safeguarded by the constitutional rule of his irremovability and the autonomous and self-governing position of the Council of the Judiciary, which decides on the nomination and promotion of judges. At the same time, the *prokuratura* was returned to its previous functions and has been limited to the role of public prosecutor subordinated to the minister of justice. The safeguards of the rule of law and the protection of citizens' rights and freedoms have been strengthened by the installation of the Administrative Court, the Tribunal of State, the Constitutional Tribunal, and the Commissioner for Civil Rights (ombudsman).

In substance, the present Constitution of the Polish Republic, after the three major revisions adopted in 1989 and 1990 (and including the amendments adopted earlier installing the impeachment procedure and the Constitutional Court), is now an absolutely new Constitution based on philosophical foundations that are diametrically opposed to the ideology of the Constitution of the Polish People's Republic in force until April 1989. Technically this Constitution, however, is still marked as a legacy of the past by its formal origin in 1952 when its initial text was imposed undemocratically, undermining its legitimacy. This legislative technique of introducing successive amendments into the existing old text of this constitutional document expresses a widely shared opinion of the temporary nature of the adopted innovations. In terms of politics this means an enhanced need for an elaboration and adoption of a completely new Constitution. What are the prospects for a new Constitution in Poland?

In the final documents accepted at the Round Table in April 1989, it was declared that the newly elected parliament, i.e., Sejm and Senate, should elaborate further democratic constitutional reforms. After the June 1989 parliamentary elections, the Round Table contract on the gradual, slow, and peaceful transition to a parliamentary democracy and to a multiparty system was relegated to history. One may say that this task of creating an institutionalized framework for a transition to democracy has been substantially fulfilled. The revisions of the Constitution adopted on December 29, 1989, and on March 8, 1990, have not only adjusted the constitutional framework to the rapid process of radical political and economic reforms, but, above all, they opened the way for further democratic institutional and political reforms as well as for free-market-oriented economic reforms.

The political infrastructure – and particularly the party system – is now undergoing a profound realignment. Therefore, large sectors of public opinion – especially articulated by newly created political parties – are raising the reasonable argument that the present parliament does not have a popular mandate to enact the new Constitution. In consequence, it is most likely that the new Constitution will be enacted by the next parliament, constituted after the anticipated parliamentary elections, which will probably take place in the spring of 1991. It is possible that other necessary transitional amendments of the existing Constitution will once again be adopted by the parliament elected in June 1989. These amendments will probably deal with the structure of the bicameral parliament and the relationship between the two houses as well as with the position of the President of the Republic.

Preparatory studies and work on drafts of a future Polish Constitution are under way. Although these studies and preparatory work are fairly advanced, they are still in the initial stage.

It is rather difficult to predict now what the outcome of these studies and preparatory works on a future Polish Constitution will be. It is possible, however, to indicate what could be the main issues that will provoke the hottest debates and most acute controversies. These are:

(1) the position of the President of the Republic and the mode of his election;

(2) the structure of the parliament (and especially the position of the Senate);

(3) the underlying concept of the economic system and the principles of a social policy;

(4) the problem of ownership; and

(5) the fundamental values of the concept of citizens' rights and freedoms.

There are now two separate parliamentary committees working on drafts of a future Constitution of the Polish Republic: one nominated by the Senate, and one by the Sejm.

The Senate Constitutional Committee seems to be more conservative and oriented toward a classic liberal and free-market-economy system of values. On the other hand, the Sejm Constitutional Committee probably represents a more moderate and pragmatic approach to constitutional issues, being more oriented toward a social free-market economic system and a rationalized parliamentary system combined with an active President of the Republic. These differences are not, however, clearly visible to the broad public. The Constitutional Committees of both houses are still working on their proposals, which will probably be presented for open public discussion at the end of 1990.

The most important constitutional change of crucial significance is the deletion of articles declaring the leading position of the ruling Communist Party, which was a cornerstone of the monocentric authoritarian political system. This principle, the very foundation of the whole sociopolitical system of socialism, led to totalitarian deviations. In nearly all the new constitutions of Central and East European countries, the legal principle of one-party monopoly has been dropped.

It is not only that the constitutional clauses sanctioning the monopolistic position of the Communist Party were deleted from basic law; new constitutional provisions proclaiming a multiparty system have been enacted. So the cornerstone of a democratic system of government was formally declared in all of these countries. The realities, however, are more complicated.

After forty years of one-party rule, there is a vacuum in the organized multiparty political infrastructure. Although many new political parties have been created, most of them are in fact nuclei of political groupings at best. It is difficult to treat them as real modern political parties that are well established in society and have clear programs and ideological foundations. This is particularly the case of Poland.

The political parties in the GDR are in an exceptional position owing to the unique situation of the East territory of Germany. In fact, the new party system that emerged during the electoral campaign and has been confirmed in parliamentary and local elections is a copy the West German party system. There are, however, two differences. The postcommunist Party of Democratic Socialism (PDS) has the support of 15 percent of the general electorate. This is better than the support for postcommunist formations in Poland and Hungary. The other specific feature of East Germany is the existence of a civic movement, Bündnis'90, which represents the concept of socialism with a human face.

All in all, one may say that in East Germany the political infrastructure that has emerged after the collapse of the authoritarian communist regime is a clear adaptation of the West German party system to the GDR legacy. This new East German party system was easily constructed with open help from West German political parties and has created a significant basis for the speedy unification of the two German states.

After the parliamentary elections of the spring of 1990, a clearer picture of the party system taking shape in Hungary has appeared.

The leading winner of the last elections was the populist and nationalistic conservative Hungarian Democratic Forum. This party, together with the reborn peasant Party of Smallholders and the Christian Democratic People's Party, obtained 43 percent of votes in the first round of elections. In the runoff second round, the Hungarian Democratic Forum did even better, gaining more seats than the liberal, free-market oriented Free Democrats. Eventually the Democratic Forum, with the backing of the Smallholders and Christian Democrats, got a comfortable parliamentary majority (59 percent of seats at large).

The Free Democrats, obtaining 21.6 percent in the first round, gained, in the runoff, 23.8 percent of parliamentary seats, and constituted the non-socialist opposition together with the Young Democrats (FIDESZ), who obtained 8.96 percent of votes and 5.4 percent of seats.

The Hungarian Socialist Party created by reformers from the former communist Hungarian Socialist Workers' Party lead by I. Pozsgay and R. Nyers obtained 10.72 percent of votes and ended up with 33 seats in the parliament (8.5 percent).

The great losers were the Hungarian Socialist Workers' Party and the Social Democrats. The latter attempted to regain the position of the Social Democratic Party, which twice in the past (in 1949 and in 1956) had been disbanded by the communist authorities.

The final results of the 1990 elections are curiously close to those of 1945, when the Smallholders – then the main party of anticommunist political groupings – got 57 percent of the vote. To a large extent the Democratic Forum, today's Smallholders, and the Christian Democrats all have things in common with the old Smallholders. After the second round, when the electoral procedure was completed, all these new political parties together got 59 percent of seats in the one-chamber Hungarian National Assembly. J. Antall, the leader of the Democratic Forum and now the Hungarian prime minister, takes this to mean that "40 years of dictatorship have not changed the Hungarian people." (*The Economist*, April 14, 1990, p. 59).

In other words, the newly created party system in Hungary is a kind of restored party system – although corrected by the legacy of forty years of Communist Party hegemony in public life – which existed in this country before the communists took power in the late 1940s.

The elections of May 1990 in Romania seem to indicate that in that country a multiparty system with the forceful domination of one postcommunist party will emerge. The National Salvation Front won in these imperfect free and contested presidential and parliamentary elections. The newly elected president, Ion Iliescu, proclaimed his devotion to social-democratic values and ideas and declared the intentions of the National Salvation Front to build in Romania in the forthcoming decade a political and economic system along the lines of the Swedish model, which sounds like the remains of the hectoring Ceausescu style of appealing to the strong nationalistic feelings of ordinary Romanians. So the prospects for a parliamentary democracy and real pluralistic multiparty system looks rather bleak in Romania.

In Czechoslovakia, parliamentary elections took place in June 1990 and were won by civic movements in Czech lands and Moravia (the Civic Forum) and in Slovakia (Public Against Violence). The Communist Party gained about 13 percent of the votes cast, becoming the main opposition party. Most of the parties – among them historical parties like the Social Democrats – were victims of the 4 percent barrier, which kept them out of the Federal Assembly. Since the June 1990 elections, the Civic Forum has split and become a regular political party. It is certain that the new party system in Czechoslovakia is, as in Poland, in the initial stage of its formation.

In Bulgaria, free and contested parliamentary elections also took place in June 1990. The post-communist (and renamed) Bulgarian Socialist Party formally won these elections, gaining the overall majority of seats in the Great National Assembly (the parliament) but obtained only 46 percent of the votes cast. This was one of the reasons for the long-lasting political crisis in the formation of a new government, which was eventually nominated six months after the elections. The future shape of the new party system in Bulgaria is still unclear.

In contrast to the GDR and Hungary, the political infrastructure for building pluralistic democracy in Poland has also not yet established a new party system. The old one ceased to exist in consequence of the June 1989 parliamentary elections.

The PUWP, after four decades of monopolistic rule, disappeared from the political scene in disgrace in January 1990. Its direct successor, the Social-democracy of the Polish Republic (SdPR) is claiming to represent the postcommunist left. Led by the youngest generation (in their thirties) of former PUWP politicians, it is formulating a social-democratic programmatic platform proclaiming a commitment to the ideas of parliamentary democracy. According to the latest opinion poll, the SdPR is supported by about 2 percent of the general public. This party has, however, a tiny representation in the Sejm, because out of 173 ex-PUWP deputies, only 20 declared their adhesion to the SdPR.

A faction of the PUWP composed of forty deputies (mostly running for the Sejm in the 1989 election against the will of the former party apparatchiks) has created a separate Polish Social Democratic Union and constituted its own parliamentary group. This is a parliamentary group that lacks, as yet, any clear constituency among the broad public. Its programmatic platform is, broadly speaking, a socialist one, but more oriented to the center right and trying to absorb the Catholic church teaching on social justice. This party is also trying to emphasize its resolute rupture with the PUWP legacy. Both the SdPR and the Polish Social Democratic Union are perceived by a large part of the general public, however, as post-PUWP political formations.

After the June 1989 elections, the PUWP's two coalition partners, the United Peasant Party and the Democratic Party, are trying to regain their independence and a separate identity and to acquire their own popular credibility. As soon as possible after the parliamentary elections of 1989 they left the coalition in which for the past forty years they were treated by the PUWP as second-hand, subordinate organizations.

The UPP, after a natural rebellion of its rank and file, changed its leadership and came back to the old historical name of the Polish Peasant Party – the party that played a similar role in 1945-47 to the Party of Smallholders in Hungary. New, spontaneously created political groupings, however, are also laying claim to the inheritance of that historical peasant party. The latest attempts at consolidating these diversified groupings seem to be half-hearted so far.

The Democratic Party is in the greatest trouble. In fact, this party has no real constituency. It could be the main victim from among the old parties of the realignment of political forces now under way in Poland.

But the most difficult task is to predict what – and how many political parties – will eventually emerge from the Solidarity movement and the civic committees supported by it and from the opposition acting outside Solidarity. A process of diversification within Solidarity started in the middle of 1990. The new political factions that are emerging from the Solidarity civic movement could be named the post-Solidarity political parties. The very process of political differentiation within Solidarity started both in the Civic Parliamentary Club and outside Parliament.

The Civic Parliamentary Club (Obywatelski Klub Parlamentarny – OKP) was created as a formation in Parliament by the senators and deputies elected in June 1989 under the banner of Solidarity and with the blessing of Lech Wałęsa. From the beginning, however, it was a very heterogeneous coalition of nearly all anti-PUWP oppositional political groupings. It appeared initially as a rainbow coalition of various political trends of the anticommunist opposition and dissidents. The disruption of this profoundly diversified parliamentary formation was inevitable from the beginning. The cracks were becoming more and more visible since the spring of 1990. Differences concerning various aspects of the government program for radical economic reform, which implied some serious belt tightening by a large part of the electorate, gave rise to tensions and social conflicts, which exacerbated these differences even more. After the PUWP disappeared from the political scene and the PUWP's former parliamentary club broke up, the main political adversary ceased to exist, too. The existence of the PUWP as a main political adversary was the chief factor that had kept the Civic Parliamentary Club – all the deputies and senators elected in 1989 – together under the common Solidarity banner. And in 1990 this element was gradually losing its essential significance. The battle against the PUWP as a political foe has since become meaningless.

These divisions within the Solidarity movement at large (and within the Civic Parliamentary Club) became open and visible to the general public when Lech Wałęsa started his campaign for the Presidency of the Republic. They reached their climax in the electoral campaign in which Tadeusz Mazowiecki (then the prime minister) ran against Lech Wałęsa. After the presidential elections, the split between the followers of Lech Wałęsa and those of Tadeusz Mazowiecki became a hard reality of public life in Poland.

Supporters of Mazowiecki left the Civic Parliamentary Club and created a separate parliamentary faction, the Democratic Union. Outside Parliament, the Democratic Union, led by T. Mazowiecki, is a federation of the Civic Movement – Democratic Action (ROAD) and the Forum of the Democratic Right (Forum Demokratycznej Prawicy – FDP). The prospects for this formation are not yet clear. There are deep doctrinal differences between ROAD (with a social-democratic orientation) and the FDP (with a conservatively liberal orientation). It is possible that ROAD will go to the forthcoming parliamentary elections separately, trying to present its social-democratic platform.

In the opposite camp the situation is no clearer.

Not only the partisans of Lech Wałęsa, but also some of Mazowiecki's followers who did not joint the Democratic Union remained in the Civic Parliamentary Club (reduced in number).

Outside Parliament, the balance of forces is more complicated. The Center Alliance, which initiated the idea of Wałęsa's candidacy for the presidency of the Republic earliest, has distanced itself from the newly elected president after his successful election. The Center Alliance leaders are disappointed in the president's policy and in the coalition formula of government proposed by him.

The Center Alliance intends to be a right-wing Christian-democratic party similar to the German CDU or the French Gaullist political formation. But the Center Alliance is also challenged by Christian Democrats, who are consolidating their own separate political party to rival the Center Alliance.

The tiny Congress of Liberal Democrats, which is a party representing the interests of the new class of capitalist entrepreneurs also emerged from the Solidarity movement. The position of this party is strengthened by its participation in the new government, led by a member of this party as the prime minister.

A new socialist-oriented faction, the Alliance "Solidarity of Labor" also appeared within Solidarity.

This family of post-Solidarity political parties also includes the Polish Peasant Party "Solidarity." But the main streams of the fragmented post-Solidarity political groupings are the Wałęsa followers on the one hand, and the Mazowiecki followers on the other hand. In the first round of the presidential elections, both of these candidates together obtained the votes of 34 percent of Poland's general electorate. This means that this segment of the Polish electorate, which voted for Solidarity in the 1989 parliamentary elections, is fairly stable.

A crucial question, however, is whether in the next parliamentary elections such a divided (or even fragmented) political camp of post-Solidarity parties and groupings will be able to repeat this result. It would be rather difficult, because the Solidarity constituency could be further split, if the Solidarity trade unions run separately with their own lists of candidates using the Solidarity banner and symbols. Taking into account the strong antiparty feeling (based on populistic anti-elitist attitudes) that is widely and deeply rooted in the general public, it cannot be excluded that all post-Solidarity political parties will be rejected by the Polish voters. Several sociological surveys are proving that each of these parties would obtain no more than 10 percent of the votes cast.

There are dozens of groupings claiming to be political parties, but they are not political parties in the regular sense of this notion.

In this period following the failure of the old political system of "real socialism," the majority of Poles mistrust any political party. This antiparty feeling is a characteristic feature for all postcommunist societies in Central and Eastern Europe. This phenomenon is clearly proven in many sociological surveys performed in Poland.

The outcomes of three sociological surveys performed in August, November (just before the first round of presidential elections) and December (after the second round of presidential elections), illustrate this significant fact. We asked our respondents: "What political party would you vote for if the elections to the Sejm were held today?"

The answers were as follows (in percent):	August	November	December
Civic Committees "Solidarity"	20.3	15.7	38.7
Polish Peasant Party	8.3	6.0	6.3
Center Alliance	6.0	8.0	–
Democratic Action (ROAD)	5.9	3.9	–
Democratic Union	–	3.8	–
Polish Peasant Party "Solidarity"	3.6	3.4	4.2
Social-democracy	2.0	2.0	1.2
Confederation of Independent Poland	2.8	1.2	2.6
Democratic Party	1.4	0.9	2.1
Christian-National Amalgamation	2.3	0.8	2.3
Polish Green Party	1.0	0.7	2.7
Freedom Party	0.5	0.6	–
Christian Democracy-Labor Party	0.6	0.5	0.9
Forum of the Democratic Right	–	0.5	–
Union of Real Politics	0.9	0.4	0.9
Polish Socialist Party	0.5	0.2	0.9
National Party	0.6	0.2	0.1
Congress of Liberals	0.0	0.1	0.1
Polish Social-democratic Union	0.2	0.0	0.2
For none of the parties	13.8	14.5	6.4
Difficult to answer	28.7	36.5	28.3

Source: National sample surveys of Polish adult population, conducted by the author and K. Jasiewicz.

All three surveys were performed on a representative nation-wide random sample of 1,000–1,300 respondents.

On the basis of results obtained from these surveys, the following general conclusions may be formulated.

Above all, it is evident that antiparty (or at least indifferent) attitudes are very high and growing. In December, half the respondents (51 percent) had no opinion or were not for any political party.

Most popular are the Civic Committees "Solidarity," which are still treated by the general public as a nonparty civic movement. But support for the Civic Committees "Solidarity" is radically decreasing: from nearly 40 percent in August to 15 percent in December.

The support for each individual post-Solidarity political party – the Center Alliance, ROAD, the Democratic Union, and the Polish Peasant Party "Solidarity" – is rather low (below 10 percent). However, the post-Solidarity political parties and the Civic Committees "Solidarity" together obtained 34.9 percent. So, if we compare the results of the 1989 parliamentary elections and the 1990 presidential elections, it is obvious that Solidarity still has the solid and consistent support of one third of the Polish electorate at large.

The other new political parties have rather a very low profile in the public opinion.

The political parties that may be treated as a legacy of the Polish People's Republic, i.e., the Polish Peasant Party and the Social Democracy of the Polish Republic, would be easily eliminated from a future Sejm elected under the electoral law providing a barrier of 5 percent (as it is sometimes proposed).

It must be said that it would be difficult to predict a clear majority in the forthcoming parliamentary elections. It is also very doubtful that these elections will produce a stable and definitive new party system in Poland.

In conclusion it can be said that a new political party system in Poland is still in the process of its creation, and all parties face the same challenge: the widespread mistrust within the general public of any political party. This is probably a specific feature of the Polish transitional period to democracy, which stands in strong contrast to the other countries of this region of Europe.

THE POLITICAL ATTITUDES
OF POLISH SOCIETY IN THE PERIOD
OF SYSTEMIC TRANSITIONS

Mirosława Marody

The basic and fundamental change that took place in the sphere of political attitudes and values in the second half of the eighties was the passage from conditional acceptance to radical rejection of socialism as an ideology defining the shape of the social system. From the perspective of 1990, the amazing thing is not so much the rejection as the fact that it occurred so late even among the youngest generation of Polish people. As late as 1987, 58 percent of respondents gave an affirmative answer to the question put by a CBOS (Centrum Badania Opinii Społecznej) survey to a number of young people: "After the experiences so far, do you believe it is worth continuing to build socialism in our country?" and only 28.8 percent answered in the negative. Two years later, the distribution of answers to the same question was exactly the opposite: 28.8 percent, "yes" and 60.4 percent, "no" (CBOS 1989b). What seems particularly significant is that there was also a radical change in the assessment of the past. In 1987, 69.9 percent of youth still thought that socialism brought the Polish people more benefits, or at least as many benefits as disadvantages, while 23.2 percent were of the opinion that there were more disadvantages than benefits. In April 1989, the first two opinions were accepted by only 39.7 percent of respondents, while the views on the predominance of disadvantages over benefits amounted to 55 percent of the respondents (CBOS 1989b).

What actually happened between the first and the second half of the eighties, what had caused this change? The standard explanation of the rejection of the socialist system pointed at the growing disproportions between human aspirations and the possibilities for their fulfillment within the framework of the existing institutional order. This was certainly a factor playing a substantial role in the process of delegitimation of the socialist system (Tarkowski 1988); nonetheless this explanation seems unsatisfactory, because objectively this disproportion was also occurring in just as high, if not higher, a degree in the first part of the decade, during which we were still noticing a relatively high percentage of persons accepting socialist principles of the organization of social life. The factors responsible for this change should be looked for in another sphere.

Adaptation Processes as a Source of System Delegitimation

After a "decade of success" in the seventies, the steep fall in consumption during 1980–82 was a traumatic experience for Polish society, in particular when the rapidity and depth of changes in life style that followed, as well as the element of surprise they contained, were taken into account. It is true that the stagnation in consumption started earlier,[1] but the ruthless regress of material conditions was a process concentrated in the space of less than two years, and its most visible manifestations appeared within a few months and affected everyone. The shops becoming emptier from one day to the next, and growing queues for the most essential products were forcing restrictions of consumption even on people who were comparatively well-off.

What seems particularly important is that the drop in the levels of material standards was not an ordinary – if one can use such an expression here at all – fall in the level of consumption but was accompanied by the breakdown of social order both on its institutional as well as normative level. The well-known and much-used rules of conduct stopped functioning virtually overnight. If one wished, for instance, to buy cigarettes, one could not simply go to a kiosk because they either were not there, or there was a huge queue, or both. When planning to visit friends, one could not assume that one would be able to use a tram or a bus, for one could not know whether the consecutive wave of strikes has not taken them off the streets. People with whom one had, so it appeared, a congenial relationship were suddenly breaking off all contacts. And so forth, and so on. The impression of chaos, of the dissolution of institutions, of growing social disintegration and feelings of fear, of lack of security, of "how will it all end" – all this led to the fact that the introduction of martial law, although generally condemned, was accepted by many people with some relief as something that was bringing order and stability back to social life. Two years after this took place, 55.7 percent of those surveyed ("definitely yes" and "rather yes") were assessing it as valid

---

[1] J. Sikorska (1987) informs us that during the period 1977–80, the real level of consumption from personal incomes per inhabitant grew by around 10 percent, while in the first half of the seventies, this type of growth was taking place within a year.

(Adamski, Jasiewicz, and Rychard 1986), and the statement that "martial law introduced peace and order" was accepted by 41 percent of respondents (Wnuk-Lipiński 1987).

The conviction that the economic situation was temporary was a commonly shared and most general social experience for at least the first few years after December 1981. It was encouraged by the varied features of the policy of the authorities. The mark of provisionality was carried by martial law itself, which by definition was meant to be a solution of a provisional nature. The legal regulations preceding the economic reform and the economic crisis that reform was meant to overcome were also to be of a limited duration. The life of Polish society at that time was marked by individual actions aimed at protecting previously achieved levels of consumption and by "biding one's time" through the crisis (Milic-Czerniak 1989; Beskid 1989; Sikorska 1987, 1989). A common characteristic of most of these activities was an attempt at going "outside the system," taking advantage of all the devices that would replace or supplement ineffectively functioning state institutions. Two basic patterns of adaptation to the crisis situation were in the foreground. The first might be called *forced traditionalism*. It was an attempt at attaining the aspirations proper to modern societies by means characteristic of traditional ones. It was marked by naturalization of consumption, that is, by a high degree of "self-service" in fulfilling material needs, by the growing importance of small, informal groups – family, friends, social circles, "set-ups" of mutual interconnections – and by transferring developmental aspirations onto children (Marody 1986). The second adaptation pattern was of a clearly innovative character. It consisted of an effort at exploiting the opportunities that the economic reform was opening up for private enterprises. However, these innovative activities had two specific limitations. First, they subordinated almost all individual activities to the pursuit of money to such a degree that one may talk here about a singular "capitalization of social consciousness" (Marody 1988). Second, it was usually limited to "economic utilization," one might say, of the weak points of the institutional system, whose existence in an unchanged shape was the very condition for the effectiveness of this *parasitic innovativeness* (Marody 1987b).

In the eighties, separate elements of both these adaptation patterns were used by the majority of Polish society. However, with the passage of time, for ever larger numbers of people tossing about between "making pickles" and "making money," it was slowly becoming obvious that waiting the crisis out was an unattainable goal. Attempts to escape the system were more amd more often ending with the discovery that the system, to coin an expression, "was running together with me." Money that was made was eaten by inflation, shortages of goods on the market were entangling people in activities that took all their time, the disorganization of the system's institutions was disorganizing family life. What is perhaps just as important, the impossibility of defining future prospects – the choice of this category of answers increased in the CBOS surveys from 28.8 percent in 1987 to 40.6 percent in March 1989 (CBOS 1989a, b) – was causing anxiety and was becoming an additional cause of frustration. The feeling of disproportion between the struggle to protect previously attained standards of living and the resulting effects was becoming the dominating experience, the feeling of moving back in spite of doubling the efforts.

These subjective experiences had their objective causes. The "second society" that had been built during the individual and group processes of adaptation was not creating its own institutions independent of the system. The rationality of individuals was the rationality of a microscale, directed above all at changing individual situations, not at changing the system itself. Improvement in individual well being was taking place not by implementation of new norms of social life but rather through dismantling, breaking down, or at least bypassing the standards operating until then.

This process, whose roots could be sought in much earlier periods but which in the eighties underwent an exceptional acceleration, was accompanied by two phenomena that with the passage of time started to affect the effectiveness of individual adaptive activities. The first can be called, in short, "the cooling down of institutional order" and manifested itself by growing institutional chaos, disorganization of public life, the falling apart of the material infrastructure of society. The second was described by W. Lamentowicz (1988) as "an expansion of factuality" as the main regulator of human activity, which instead of following general norms and rules was becoming ever more often and in an ever more widening scope conditioned by situational factors.

Both these phenomena were expressions of one and the same characteristic of the social reality, namely, the social system's loss of ability to coordinate individual activities on the global level. A full analysis of the mechanisms that resulted in the development of this characteristic goes beyond the scope of this text, but it must be emphasized that among them were not only macroeconomic processes and political decisions but also the above-mentioned individual adaptation activities triggered by these processes and decisions. Taken most generally, it can be said that rationality on the macrolevel was acting in a direction diametrically opposite to rationality on the microlevel (Marody 1987a). With the natural corrective mechanisms blocked, these opposed rationalities furthered the blurring of norms defining ways in which the whole system functioned and in consequence also rules determining people's actions in the whole social space. Social reality was becoming *normatively indeterminant*, which is equivalent to saying that it stopped being the reality of shared meanings and rules of action. Instead of norms and principles valid at all points of the social space, there started to appear local "codes" valid here and now and for only a given group of people engaged in a concrete interaction. Although in the short run and on a local scale they were raising the chances of achieving individual or group aims, in the longer run and on the scale of society as a whole they were making the reproduction of the whole social order impossible, thus leading to the disorganization of the social system on all its levels.

It may be said that the process of decomposition of the social order – which in 1980–82 acquired particularly spectacular form but, it seemed, was stopped with the introduction of martial law, imposing strict and stiff rules of action in all the spheres of social life – in the following years, although less visible, constituted a permanent element of social life. Its objective consequence was a lasting lowering of the material life of society. Much more essential were, however, the effects in the sphere of social consciousness. On the one hand, the advancing impoverishment of society, which, due to an already low level of fulfillment of social needs, was turning into a feeling of civilizational degradation (Marody 1988), could not be justified by any general norms that would give the reason for the necessity of sacrifice. It was so because social order, or rather the *lack* of it, took away from the majority of such norms the power to regulate social behavior. On the other hand, there was an increasing social "visibility" of affluent groups of people, who were thus providing examples of spectacular financial careers based on rules difficult to comprehend by an outside observer, yet unmistakably originating from outside the system. By their very being, they were advocating the acceptance of paradigms of rationality different than those provided by the system.

Referring to somewhat different language, it may be said that if in the first half of the eighties the sociopolitical system existing in Poland was rejected mainly in the symbolic sphere but maintained in day-to-day activities (Marody 1986; Rychard 1987), so in the second half of that period the rejection of the system included the level of individual actions as well. Not only was the legitimacy of the social order questioned, but this order stopped being upheld in everyday individual interactions. In other words, the process of delegitimation of the socialist system spread out not only over the concrete rules of functioning of systemic institutions but also over the most general principles underlying this type of social order.

First, there came an almost total rejection of state monopoly in the economy. This could be seen most clearly in the case of foreign trade and heavy industry, where state monopoly was still accepted in 1983, correspondingly, by 55.7 percent and 76.9 percent of respondents. In 1988, the state monopoly in foreign trade was approved by only 10.8 percent and in heavy industry, by 31.5 percent of respondents. Meaningful shifts also took place in the descriptions of good social order. Taken most generally, there was a movement here from imaginings that corresponded to socialist ideology – emphasizing the equality of chances in social life, egalitarism of incomes, citizens' rights, general fulfillment of material needs – to views accentuating the nonegalitarian division of goods, pluralism of world views, and a poly-centric model of political power (Banaszek 1989). Support for the statement that the state should lower its expenditure for social care for the under-privileged has also increased significantly (Kolarska-Bobińska 1989).

Transition from conditional acceptance to radical rejection of socialism as an ideology defining the form of the social system meant, therefore, the acceptance of a totally new rationality determining profits and losses of individual actions in the social space. This transition did not take place overnight but was a process extended in time, a process whose development was influenced by the growing normative indeterminacy of the social reality, which was the result of adaptation processes and at the same time limited their effectiveness to a significant degree. On the systemic level, this was leading to the breakdown of the socially indispensable minimum of confor-mity and integration, by this very fact preventing the reproduction of the social order. On the individual level, it was taking away from people the minimum knowledge of the rules according to which others were playing, thus preventing the rationalization of individual activities. In both cases it was creating a singular vacuum, which could without difficulty be filled with norms and rules even diametrically opposite to previously existing ones.

The Change of the System Versus the Change of Political Attitudes

The rejection of socialism as an ideology determining the shape of the social system found its political expression during the June 1989 elections, as a result of which power in Poland was taken over by a team of a diametrically different ideological orientation. Put most generally, this orientation can be defined as promarket and prodemocratic, because the changes in the institutional order introduced by Mazowiecki's government are pointing to the establishment of a market economy and a democratic political system. From the beginning these changes have been accompanied by a high level of support for government policies, a high level of trust in the leading figures of public life, and the acceptance of the necessity of large, although limited in time, renouncements in the material sphere.

One would like to say on the basis of these and similar data that Polish society in June 1989 not only rejected the prosocialist orientation but also accepted the prodemocratic orientation and with it, the norms and rules underlying a democratic order. However, the results of sociological surveys throw serious doubts on the matter.

One's attention is first of all turned to the strongly asymmetrical confrontation, reflected in the respondents' replies, of political forces in which Solidarity and people associated with it find no counterbalance in any of the remaining groups or even in their theoretical coalition. In answer to the question posed by CBOS in November 1989, "Which party would you vote for if the elections to the Sejm and the Senate were to be held next Sunday?" 60 percent of respondents mentioned Solidarity, 30 percent gave indecisive answers or acknowledged a lack of readiness to take part in elections, and only 10 percent mentioned some other party or political group (CBOS 1990a).

More detailed analyses of the organizational and electoral support for Solidarity led to two additional conclusions that seem particularly important from our point of view. First, trust in Solidarity meant favor, sympathy, and belief that it would be representing the interests of the whole of society and not a readiness to participate in its activities or even simply to become its member. Second, Solidarity was perceived as an element of a one-party model (the ruling party–satellite parties–extra-systemic opportion from outside the system) rather than a parliamentary model (ruling party–undecided center–opposition parties) (CBOS 1990a).

The fall in potential electoral support for Solidarity by 15 points between November 1989 and February 1990 did not change this picture. Respondents who were withdrawing their support for Solidarity were not transferring it to other parties and political groupings but were increasing the number of people unhappy with the policy of the current government, not finding, however, any alternatives for it in the programs of other parties (CBOS 1990b).

One may therefore say that in spite of substantial institutional changes, the political scene appeared to the respondents in 1990 in a way not very different from the one dominating the social consciousness in earlier periods, let us say, in the seventies. There are still two main actors: on the one hand, the government party (or as one may wish, a social movement), which is the leading force of the nation, the symbol and guarantor of social changes; and on the other, society, which benevolently (at least for a time) watches its doings without itself getting engaged in them. Essentially the only potential form of *political* reaction – because we are not interested here in the psychological reactions, like apathy or withdrawal – to the decisions of the state administration that do not find social acceptance remains the act of social disobedience.

It is quite significant here that the confidence and support for the reforming endeavors of the present government team are based first of all on confidence in the people who are part of it – in particular in Prime Minister Mazowiecki – and not on clearly articulated political interests. The sense of material deprivation or of being threatened by the deterioration of living conditions does not create a foundation for establishing identities of groups aware of the particularity of their social standing. Actual and predicted economic differentiation does not become the source of political differentiation even in the case of a group with so clearly articulated interests as the farmers. Though it is true that the rural population supported Balcerowicz's stabilization program somewhat less (33 percent) than town people (42 percent), no connection was found between the attitudes of farmers to this program and a postulate for greater help from the state, a postulate totally contradictory to the solutions implemented in the institutional sphere (CBOS 1990c). Political choices still have feeble links with group interests, or rather, they express moral rather than political support.

This support, as a matter of fact, limits itself to "holding one's breath," to reducing activities to a simple endurance while awaiting the moment when Vice-Premier Balcerowicz will announce on TV that the transition to a market economy has already taken place and therefore normal functioning might be resumed – the kind of support to which we were more or less accustomed until now, only this time without queues in shops, with plenty of goods, and with efficiently working offices with smiling employees. In the political sphere, this vision is completed by the removal of the former nomenklatura and its replacement by those worthy of people's trust.

The acceptance of surrendering to the consequences of market mechanisms introduced by the government is in this situation more a moral choice than compliance with necessities having a socially obvious character. It is – to use an expression coined by I. Białecki (1990) – a form of "escaping into a collective lot," a reaction to a threat perceived (consciously or not) as external, looking for psychological support in the spirit of community and the sense of social solidarity. This is the result of a confidence that delegates to the authorities full responsibility for the process of reforms and at the same time absolves everyone of the necessity of making personal decisions about his/her future.

At this point a question arises, which most succinctly can be formulated in the following manner: If so much has changed over the last year, then why has everything remained the same? What is most striking in analyzing the political attitudes of 1990 is their quite amazing *structural* similarity to the well-known and often-described attitudes of earlier periods.

Naturally, instead of "communist authorities" we have "Solidarity authorities," but in both cases politics has been perceived as a realm of those actually in power, whose task it is to build a better life *for* society. In both cases the surrender of responsibility for the prosperity of society into the hands of the administrators has led to a situation in which the basic dimension defining political life becomes the dimension of "trust versus lack of trust," and the fundamental category elucidating the political options becomes the category of faith. Finally, in both cases the only solution when faith in the concrete governing team is lost seems to be not the transfer of support to other political groupings but a direct declaration of disobedience against the government by strike actions, protest, manifestations, unrest, etc.

Put in different terms, instead of leading to the revival of political participation, to the pluralism of world views, to making choices among different political programs, the change of the institutional order has resulted in an escape to a collective lot known from the past. Not much has been changed by the fact that this time this lot was not imposed by force but accepted by society having trust in its new administration. One ought to remember that the "escape to a collective lot" contains within itself a risk that must always be taken into account: overnight and often without warning, it may transform itself into "escape *from* the lot" that society with greater or lesser self-sacrifice has so far accepted.

From the Will for Change to Social Change

For all the differences of aims and social support, the transformation of the social system that we have witnessed in Poland since June 1989 has at least one trait in common with the restructuring initiated forty-five years ago by the communists. In both cases we are dealing with an attempt from the top to usher new institutions of public life into a society whose functioning for a long time had been determined by a totally different institutional framework. Thus in both cases the essential problem that the reformers have to face is the fact that everyday individual actions are modeled by habits formed as a result of social experiences totally different from those that should become the content of the new institutions.

The word *habits* is used here in a sense that is closest to the concept of *habitus* as it was defined by Pierre Bourdieu (1977). Most concisely, habitus is the system of unconscious patterns of thoughts, perceptions, and dispositions that mediate between the structures of the external world and practice, or, between the level of systemic characteristics and the level of individual actions. So defined, habitus is a product of the environment and the conditions of life and is formed during the process of socialization. At the systemic level, it accounts for continuity and the proper working of the social world. At the individual level, it constitutes socially formed cognitive and motivational structures.

The important characteristic of habits described in this way is that they are perceived as obvious and natural and in consequence escape critical reflection, directing human activity as if without conscious control. A change in the objective structures that formulated them does not lead to a spontaneous modification of cognitive and motivational patterns, and by sheer force of inertia they may continue to determine individual behavior for a long time.

It seems that the attitudes described under previous headings are examples of such habits. What they have in common is the perception of politics as a sphere unattainable to individual actions, as an area appropriated or dominated by the authorities, whose decisions may only be contested by society but cannot be influenced by it (Marody 1989). The objective characteristics of the communist system, resulting in what W. Narojek called the "nationalization of initiatives for action in collective life," may be charged with responsibility for this way of perceiving politics. Or, the perception of politics as a tool for managing society, which remained at the disposal of the state administration as a source of coercion, which may be resisted but over which people have no influence (Marody 1989), is the direct reflection of forty-five years of the abolition of politics as an autonomous sphere of social life.

The reconstruction of the institutional framework giving autonomy to the political life of societies is in this situation a necessary, but not sufficient, condition. In democratic societies, political life, although performing autonomous functions, is not altogether independent from other aspects of social life. In Poland, if it is to acquire a shape similar to that which we know from observations of Western societies, other conditions have to be met. There has to exist an established social structure allowing individuals to define their interests in social categories by reference to clearly specified criteria of social, and not only individual, differentiation. Formal legal procedures permitting the democratic process of negotiating social interests so defined have to be worked out and accepted. Finally, politics has to be perceived as a tool for establishing aims and ways of social development. However, it seems that none of these conditions is met by Polish society. Furthermore, it may be said that over the long years that adaptation processes have lasted, this society has acquired qualities exactly opposite to the ones mentioned above.

Blurring of the social structure has not, naturally, canceled out social differentiation, but it has managed to direct the attention of individuals above all to the differences between particular social groups and not to what could unite them through common characteristics of their social position. Virtually the only functioning plane of integration was the general social interest put in opposition to the particular interests of the authorities. The division into "us and them" was congenial to the development of a social identity mainly in negative terms, that is, through indicating the differences of interests and not their similarities. It created at the same time an attitude of negative social solidarity, both on a global scale and on the scale of particular social groups. In short, Polish people were finding it easier to integrate and unite against rather than *for* something.

As far as the procedural side of the democratic order is concerned, one should recall here the results of research by A. Jasińska-Kania (1988) confirming the existence of links between the types of standards applied to the assessment of the legitimacy of the political order and the types of moral orientations specified by L. Kohlberg (1981). It is a fact of particular interest to us that judgments assessing the legitimation of political decisions were dependent on the more general structure of moral judgments that influenced the understanding of justice. A fact of fundamental importance in this context is the statement that in Polish society, the dominating type of moral reasoning is the orientation toward consensus and interpersonal harmony (particularly frequent in less-educated groups), while the orientation toward "law and order" is chosen by a surprisingly low percentage of respondents (from 0 percent to 16 percent, most often women with primary education). It is worth remembering here that in accordance with Kohlberg's studies, the orientation toward "law and order" constitutes an orientation dominating the adult population of Americans, and choosing this option should increase with the attainment of higher educational levels.

The consequences resulting from these data for the process of democratization of political life may be summarized by saying that the chances for a quick introduction and acceptance of formal, legal procedures constituting an inseparable element of the democratic order seem to be particularly low in Polish society. The orientation toward persons whose qualifications are assessed in moral terms rather than in terms of their merits continues to be the decisive criterion by which the justness of decisions and actions of a political nature are judged. It is from here that the fundamental role played by the categories of trust and faith when making political choices, as against a much smaller degree of interest in political programs, issues.

As far as the functions of politics in social life are concerned, an attention-drawing fact is that due to the congruency of values defining the directions of social development both in the communist design and in the popular social perception (Marody et al. 1981; Marody 1986; Rychard and Szymanderski 1986; Banaszek 1989), the basic function of politics for Polish society has for many years been the implementation of these very values. In practice, this meant that politics came to be viewed above all as a tool of just distribution of social goods as well as their essential source. Due to the appropriation of politics by the authorities, the average citizen stopped being interested in *how* these goods were to be produced; he was only concerned with how they were to be distributed. This orientation toward the distributive rather than "productive" functions of politics means that social drives in politics will be taking on the character of pressing demands rather than of searching for solutions to urgent social problems.

All these attitudes, habits, and expectations, which developed around the political sphere along with long-term adaptation processes, constitute the essential factors that we have to take into account in considering the chances of constructing a democratic social system in Poland. Their impact on the opportunities created by a new institutional order might lead to effects quite distant from what we are accustomed to associate with democracy.

In Polish society accustomed to solidarism, the currently emerging political divisions are generating a feeling of being threatened rather than hope for political pluralism. Many people are alarmed by internal division in Solidarity and long for unity. Taking into account that the dissolution of the social structure and the lack of identification of a "middle level" are the result of what S. Nowak (1979) described as a "social vacuum," it can be expected that the fundamental category around which this yearning for unity will find its resolution will be the concept of nation, i.e., the democratic institutions of public life might facilitate the development of *nationalism* as one of the fundamental components of political orientations.

The dominance that personal disagreements have at the present time over relatively neglected discussion that could lead to working out concrete programs for finding solutions to urgent social problems also causes a feeling of insecurity among people accustomed to definite "black or white" assessments. Looking for arguments in the sphere of morals rather than merits when determining "who is right" in these disagreements only facilitates the creation of absolute authorities, which in turn might assist in the emergence of *authoritarianism* as one of the fundamental components of political orientations.

Finally, the growing social differentiation – the result of market solutions in a society in which, due to the blurring of the normative sphere, there is a lack of clearly defined rules legitimizing the social standing of individuals (both low and high) – also starts to become a source of social frustrations. In this situation, politics, perceived for years mainly as a sphere of distribution of social resources, can easily be transformed into the tool of equalizing social injustice, thus creating an ambience suitable for the development of *populism* as one of the fundamental components of political orientations.

Obviously, the concrete political orientations that will be developing in the immediate future might be various combinations of the above-mentioned components. It is also clear that the institutional system underlying the democratic political order should not be made responsible for their potential development. Here the causative role will be played, rather, by macroeconomic processes such as, e.g., the growing recession and the unemployment related to it. In this situation, the attitudes and habits that are the result of the adaptation processes to socialism may continue to form people's reactions to social reality, resulting in a particular version of *adaptation to democracy*.

In June 1989, Polish society voting for Solidarity representatives gave unequivocal expression to its will for change. But the pattern of the social order for which it has declared itself is for most people an abstract pattern composed of general values without the backing of individual experiences. In order for the will for change to be able to transform itself into real change, not only the introduction of new institutions but also, and perhaps most of all, the development of new attitudes, habits, and expectations regarding social reality are required, that is, a restructuring of all the elements composing the social habitus. This is a long-term process, and its course will be affected not only by political changes but also by changes in other spheres of social life.

This essay was translated by V. Bibrowski.

References

Adamski, W., Jasiewicz, K., and Rychard, A., eds. 1986. *Polacy'84. Dynamika konfliktu i konsensusu.* Warszawa: IFiS PAN.

Banaszek, H. 1989. "Postawy polityczne młodego pokolenia Polaków w okresie przejścia modernizacyjnego." Unpublished manuscript.

Beskid, L. 1989. "Ekonomiczny i społeczny wymiar przemian warunków życia w latach 1980-1985." In *Warunki i sposoby życia – zachowania przystosowawcze w kryzysie*, L. Beskid, ed. Warszawa: IFiS PAN, pp. 19–58.

Białecki, I. 1990. "Duch wspólnotowy." *Res Publica*, no. 4.

Bourdieu, P. 1977. *Outline of a Theory of Practice.* Cambridge: Cambridge University Press.

CBOS, 1989a. *Jak nam się żyje – oceny warunków życia.*

CBOS, 1989b. *Młodzież'89.*

CBOS, 1990a. *Panorama polityczna w społecznej świadomości.*

CBOS, 1990b. *Spektrum partii politycznych.*

CBOS, 1990c. *Polityka rolna i rynek żywnościowy w opinii społecznej.*

Jasińska-Kania, A. 1988. *Osobowość, orientacje moralne i postawy polityczne.* Warszawa: IS UW.

Kohlberg, L. 1981. *Essays in Moral Development*, vol. 1. San Francisco: Jossey Bass.

Kolarska-Bobińska, L. 1989. "Poczucie niesprawiedliwości, konfliktu i preferowany ład w gospodarce." In *Polacy '88. Dynamika konfliktu a szanse reform.* Warszawa: Uniwersytet Warszawski.

Lamentowicz, W. 1988. "Zimny bałagan czyli kulturowy nieład." *Zarządzanie*, no. 6.

Marody, M. 1986. *Warunki trwania i zmiany ładu społecznego w relacji do stanu świadomości społecznej.* Warszawa: IS UW.

—————. 1987a. "Antynomie podświadomości zbiorowej." *Studia Socjologiczne*, no. 2.

—————. 1987b. "Między współpracą a odrzuceniem." *Polityka*, no. 28.

—————. 1988. "Awans i krach." *Polityka*, no 18.

—————. 1989. "Postrzeganie polityki a partycypacja polityczna społeczeństwa polskiego." *Kultura i Społeczeństwo*, no. 3–4.

Marody, M., Kolbowski, J., Łabanowska, C., Nowak, K., and Tyszkiewicz, A. 1981. *Polacy '81.* Warszawa: IS UW.

Milic-Czerniak, R. 1989. "Adaptacja konsumentów do warunków kryzysu ekonomicznego w pierwszej połowie lat osiemdziesiątych." In *Warunki i sposoby życia – zachowania przystosowawcze w kryzysie*, L. Beskid, ed., pp. 93–156.

Narojek, W. 1985. *Pluralizm polityczny i planowanie, albo: Perspektywy pluralizmu w upaństwowionym społeczeństwie.* Warszawa: IFiS PAN (mimeo).

Nowak S. 1979. "System wartości społeczeństwa polskiego." *Studia Socjologiczne*, no. 4, pp. 155–73.

Rychard, A. 1987. "Konflikt i przystosowanie: dwie koncepcje ładu społecznego w Polsce." In *Rzeczywistość polska i sposoby radzenia sobie z nią*, M. Marody and A. Sułek, eds. Warszawa: IS UW, pp. 89–108.

Rychard, A., and Szymanderski, J. 1986. "Kryzys w perspektywie legitymizacji." In *Polacy '84. Dynamika konfliktu i konsensusu*, W. Adamski, K. Jasiewicz, and A. Rychard, eds. Warszawa: IFiS PAN.

Sikorska, J. 1987. "Wpływ regresu warunków konsumpcji na społeczne zróżnicowanie jej wzorów." In *Warunki i sposób życia społeczeństwa polskiego w sytuacji regresu*. L. Beskid, ed. Warszawa: IFiS PAN, 1987, pp. 83–130.

——————. 1989. "Społeczne zróżnicowanie wzorów konsumpcji w warunkach polskiego wzrostu i kryzysu." In *Warunki i sposób życia – zachowania przystosowawcze w kryzysie*, L. Beskid, ed., pp. 157–94.

Tarkowski, J. 1988. "Sprawność gospodarcza jako substytut legitymizacji w Polsce powojennej." In *Legitymacja. Klasyczne teorie i polskie doświadczenia*, A. Rychard and A. Sułek, eds. Warszawa: PTS UW, pp. 239–68.

Wnuk-Lipiński, E., ed. 1987. *Nierówności i upośledzenia w świadomości społecznej.* Warszawa: IFiS PAN.

Part 4

From One Truth to Many Voices

THE LEGACY OF REAL SOCIALISM, GROUP INTERESTS, AND THE SEARCH FOR A NEW UTOPIA

Edmund Mokrzycki

"We are against the communist ideology and real socialism. Forty-five years of experience is enough." These are the words of Zheliu Zhelev, the leader of the Union of Democratic Forces in Bulgaria,[1] but it may be said, with minimal exaggeration, that they would be echoed by the whole of Eastern Europe. Nevertheless, ideological consciousness in Eastern Europe is not unambiguous: for all the appearances and declarations like the one quoted above, it is marked by an ambivalent attitude toward real socialism and a tendency to think in terms of utopias. This is due to indoctrination and to habits that developed over a half-century, but above all to the structure of real interests in postcommunist society.

The Legacy of Real Socialism

So-called real socialism – that is, the system that took shape in the Soviet Union and in European socialist countries – is a social system in the strong sense of the term; it has its own equilibrium mechanisms, its own dynamics, and the ability to reproduce its constitutive characteristics (which is not to say that it is a viable system). Paradoxically enough, this fundamental attribute of real socialism is evident now, even in a period of profound crisis. It is most visible in those countries in which systemic reforms are most advanced, that is, in Poland and in Hungary.

[1] Quoted in *Gazeta Wyborcza*, June 7, 1990.

This paradox is easy to explain. The incessant resistance offered by societies in East European countries to the totalitarian system imposed from outside was, in accordance with the logic of the totalitarian system, a generalized resistance directed against all aspects of the system. Hence it seemed that in spite of the revolutionary economic and social changes and the pressure intended to consolidate society, the social substance remained essentially unimpaired. It was accordingly universally believed – by both the apparatus of power and the opposition – that as soon as the political system changed (the Communist Party lost power) East European societies would as it were automatically return to their original state. But it was not clear what that would mean in practice: a return to their state preceding World Ware II, or their state preceding World War II but somehow corrected in accordance with the trend of development of other European countries. There was no answer to that question. It was merely taken for granted that once freed from communist control, East European societies would reveal characteristics proper to societies in Western Europe, at least in their nuclear form. It was precisely on that assumption that the Polish reform was based.

The first months of the reform partly confirmed that assumption. For instance, the syndrome of social phenomena connected with the economy of shortages, as described by Kornai, started to vanish rapidly.[2] But at the same time new phenomena appeared, prompting us to take a new look at the effects of "the building of socialism" in Eastern Europe and the prospects for "a return to Europe" by the countries in that region. It seems that we need to reexamine the scope and nature of the social change brought about by four decades of the development of real socialism. This is the key to the question of the character of postcommunist society and its options for development.

These issues can be analyzed at various levels: political relations, personality changes, style of life, social structure, economic conditions, and so forth. In all these spheres we note symptoms indicating that the socialist experiment had a greater impact on the societies of Eastern Europe than was previously recognized.[3] The same applies to the issues of group interests and ideological options with which we are concerned here. Let us see how these matters look in Poland.

Group Interests

Group interests are derivative of the social structure, and the latter reflects the basic mechanisms of social differentiation. It would seem that the main

[2] Cf. J. Kornai, *Economics of Shortage*. Amsterdam: North Holland, 1980.

[3] I have written more on this subject in *Marxism, Sociology and "Real Socialism"*, forthcoming.

elements of the social structure in postcommunist Poland correspond to the elements of the social structure in precommunist Poland and also have their equivalents in the structure of Western communities. If we confine ourselves to class structure, then the post-1945 changes in Poland may be summarized as follows:

1. the elimination of the "exploiting classes" (landlords and the bourgeoisie);

2. the numerical growth of the working class and the intelligentsia (professionals), mainly at the cost of the peasant class;

3. rapidly increased interclass and intraclass mobility combined with a reduction of interclass distances.

In fact, however, the changes were much more fundamental, because the mechanisms of social differentiation changed. The mechanisms determined by property rights and the market were replaced by mechanisms determined by a certain ideological principle of social justice and central planning. The long-term consequence of that change in one of the main mechanisms of the social order must have been, and was, the erosion of the traditional, presocialist, web of the social structure and the emergence of a new, socialist, one. Briefly put, the change in the mechanisms of social differentiation led to a change in the character of the various elements of the social structure and the relations among them. Under real socialism, the worker did not cease to be a worker, but he became a socialist worker: his social status, formerly determined by spontaneous socioeconomic processes, was not only mediated but also determined by the central planner in its fundamental dimensions.

If so, then the socialist (and, obviously, postsocialist) class structure was only seemingly a continuation of the presocialist one. Its basic elements were gradually changing their nature to become, with the lapse of time, something entirely different.[4] These processes can best be observed in the case of Polish peasants.

The peasants have remained individual (private) agricultural producers, but, isolated from the market and absorbed by the centralized socialist economy, they have lost many of their fundamental class attributes connected with economic independence and autonomy. State control of the means of production (in a situation marked by chronic shortages), the state monopoly on purchasing agricultural produce, and the constraints imposed on the ownership of land turned Polish peasants into a social category *sui generis* (in other East European countries, it is still different in view of the

---

[4] W. Wesolowski in his *Does Socialist Stratification Exist?* Colchester, U.K.: The University of Essex, 1988, took up another aspect of this problem. He posed a question about the relation between the theoretical model of socialist stratification and the realities of real socialism. In that context he suggested the answer in the negative to the question posed in the title. I fully agree with that answer and think that it is in harmony with the thesis advanced in the present essay.

collectivization of agriculture). The feature that makes this category differ from both traditional East European peasants and contemporary farmers consists in the fact that its economic relations with the rest of society are mediated by the socialist (now postsocialist) state. This is to say that the scope, manner, and conditions of the exchange of goods between the Polish peasants and the rest of society are determined by the central political authorities to a much greater degree than in any Western country.

This naturally results in the economic incapacitation of the peasants and in making their situation similar to that of the socialist manual workers and other groups of hired labor employed by the state. Much has been written about this, but almost solely in terms of economic exploitation and social deprivation. But the phenomenon has other aspects, which become important now that the system of real socialism has collapsed: the aspect of economic and social privileges.

When speaking about the exploitation of Polish peasants, workers, or university professors, what is meant is the disproportion between their real and hypothetical situation, estimated on the assumption of a different, market-based, system of the exchange of commodities. Privileges mean exactly the same thing.

In the analyses of real socialism carried out so far, the concept of privilege was used for the description of the special treatment of chosen social groups, as a rule linked to the apparatus of power. This is in agreement with the current sense of the term *privilege*, and it is not the intention here to question that way of describing real socialism. But this term may also be used for the comprehension of the very essence of real socialism, and especially of the principles that control the circulation of commodities under that system.

One of the features of socialism – all socialism, real socialism included – is the distribution of privileges in the sense of the term described above. It is irrelevant whether this is done in accordance with the principle "to each according to his merits" and what would constitute such "merit." The essential fact is that privileges are distributed centrally (although not necessarily directly) in accordance with a certain principle of justice, which by its very nature is supposed to correct the "injustices" of the market economy. In practice, after some time the corrective and ideological role of the distribution of privileges is pushed to the background, while its role as an instrument of power, of running the economy, and of relieving social tensions comes to the fore.

In this way the distribution of privileges becomes one of the fundamental economic and social institutions in the country. That institution regulates social and economic behavior, but it also determines the expectations of individuals and social groups, i.e., the system of the distribution of privileges, originally imposed in the name of a certain abstract ideal of social justice, with the lapse of time becomes embedded in the socioeconomic system and society accepts it as its own whether it likes it or not.

Thus under real socialism the distribution of privileges becomes not only a functional but also an axiological equivalent of success in the market economy. This means that the relatively fixed rules of the distribution of privileges enjoy the social sanction of moral rules. Under real socialism the various groups and the various individuals know fairly well what is due to them, accept that as morally just, and are inclined to defend it even if they are hostile to real socialism as such and are in favor of capitalism (a market economy and a parliamentary democracy) not only in the abstract sense but as a model for Poland.

We lack sufficiently reliable data to determine whether we have here to do with a *sui generis* double thinking on a mass scale. But there is no doubt that Poles in 1990 are inclined simultaneously to accept two incompatible social axiologies: that of the market and that of socialist privileges.

Let us go back to the structure of real interests in Polish society. That structure corresponds, of course, to the situation described above. The interests of the various social groups have been linked to the system of central planning, consolidated for decades, and hence to the fixed system of distribution of privileges. Privilege has become an integral element of life in Poland in almost all its aspects. It has become an object of everyday endeavors and long-term plans in life. More important still, privilege has become an integral part of the economic activity of all occupational categories, including the private sector, which was persecuted throughout the period of real socialism.

In order to understand this, one has to realize that the difference between the hypothetical, market-based situation of the Polish "businessman" and his *de facto* situation under real socialism consists not only in what he receives from the state and what the states takes away from him, but also in all his profits and losses resulting from the corrective activity of the state, which – in this case quite radically – modifies the effects of market mechanisms. Briefly speaking, the socialist state in this case not only gives and takes directly but above all radically changes the milieu in which the Polish "businessman" acts.

There is no place here for a description of that milieu. Let us therefore mention only two of its features: the chronic shortage of almost all goods, and a lack of competition (as a result of the restrictions imposed upon the private sector). The former feature guarantees demand for all products and services, virtually regardless of their quality, and the latter averts what is the greatest challenge in the case of the Western businessman. The combined effect of these two factors creates conditions for the functioning of private enterprise that are not encountered in the West. If we take into account other realities of the centralized socialist economy, such as hyperbureaucracy, corruption, and the primacy of politics over economics, then we have to conclude that under real socialism private economic activity is something entirely different from "the same" activity in a market economy. It also requires different skills and dispositions and shapes a different workplace. From our point of view, the most essential aspect of the problem is that private enterprise in Poland in the late 1980s was adjusted to the conditions prevailing in a planned socialist economy, adjusted in the most objective sense of the word. Transforming that enterprise into a market economy, with its competition, the struggle to win customers, the necessity of making innovations, etc. – and that is what the assumptions of the Polish reform imply – does not free this undertaking from the nightmare of socialist limitations, because this is the element in which it is used to functioning. Rather, it means dooming it to functioning under conditions that are alien to its nature. These conditions are felt by the Polish private entrepreneur as a danger. If we are to judge by the official statistical data, that danger is real, especially in the sphere of production and services (where the number of enterprises that are liquidated exceeds that of new ones being formed).

Private farms are in a similar situation. One of the goals of the reform, assumed and often formulated by the government in early 1990, was to activate a positive selection of farms. It was assumed that larger, stronger, more modern, and more productive farms would better adjust themselves to the reform than would the small ones, which use a primitive technology and are marked by low productivity. It has turned out, however, that so far just the reverse has proved true. The error in the assumptions was the underestimation of the connection between more developed farms and their socialist milieu. Unlike the autarkic primitive farms, the more developed and, in particular, specialized ones were adjusted to cheap credits, to centrally fixed and relatively stable prices of supplies and agricultural produce, and above all to an economy marked by chronic shortages, which made the purchase of means of production extremely difficult but guaranteed the easy and centrally organized sale of all products, of virtually any quality and in any amount.

Today there is no doubt that the assumptions of the agrarian policy of the government, built into the plan of the reform, must be corrected. The problem is complicated by the functioning of aggressive postsocialist monopolies in agriculture, mostly operating on a pseudo-cooperative basis. Nevertheless, the trend of the future correction, enforced by peasant strikes, seems fairly clear. The point is not so much to improve the functioning of the market in agriculture as to increase the protection granted by the state to agriculture. The demand of the farmers, which the government will probably have to meet at least to some extent, is for protection on the part of the state to go far beyond the state interventionism in Western countries. The goal of the farmers is essentially state-guaranteed economic profitability of all of agriculture at its present level. This would mean in fact the suspension of the reform with respect to agriculture and the return in that matter to central planning, although carried out by economic methods. If one listens to some active representatives of the farmers ("the job of the farmers is to produce food, the job of the state is to secure means of production for them and the opportunity to sell"), then one can hear the voice of "socialism with a human face" in matters of agrarian policy.

This is hardly surprising. The present level of Polish agriculture precludes its competition with agriculture in Western Europe. Aggressive competition at home might mean the immediate economic ruin of most Polish farms. Hence when the representatives of the government and a large part of public opinion claim that the farmers are demanding privileges, they are right. The point is, however, that this means privileges in the sense adopted at the beginning of the present essay, that is to say, "positive" privileges of being protected from the hardships of market mechanisms. Polish agriculture is simply defending itself against the acceptance of conditions to which it is not adjusted.

Privileges in this same sense are also demanded by industry, especially mining, and other branches of the nationalized economy. It must be borne in mind that the neoliberal reform is aimed most strongly at the direct interests of industrial workers, especially those employed in the giant products of "socialist industrialization," which in many cases are doomed to bankruptcy. Note, by the way, that these are the same workers who formed the core of Solidarity in 1980–81 and who, owing to their successes in the struggle against communism, became in fact the "leading force of the nation," as the communist propaganda had been telling them for decades. The social movement of the workers created by that "force" is the only mass movement in Poland that is functioning on a class basis, is well organized, and is skillfully fighting for its class interests. The reform encounters determined and well-organized resistance whenever it strikes at the economic foundations of these socialist industrial giants.

As seen against this background, the second large group of employees, that is, white-collar workers (including professionals), looks like an amorphous category deprived not only of leaders and organization but also of the skill to articulate its own interests. And yet the interests of this group were linked to the system of real socialism in two ways. First, by the overgrowth of managerial jobs, typical of real socialism, and soft financing in culture, education, science, art, etc. These structural aspects of real socialism resulted in the overgrowth and nonrational distribution of people with the highest qualifications, in the overgrowth of certain institutions, and in a lowering of the demands toward employees.

Second, a large part of the intellectual and artistic elite availed itself of state sponsorship. Whatever might be said about that sponsorship and its functioning (the traditional East European respect for science and art was combined with political manipulation), it was in many cases the base of existence of artists and writers.

The greatest danger of the reform to white-collar workers, professionals, and intellectuals comes from the planned rationalization of organizational structure and the end of soft financing in science, art, and culture. The end of soft financing is dangerous in two ways. First, it will reveal the overgrowth of employment and low qualifications of employees in many institutions in which the intellectual and artistic elite of the country is grouped, and it will also call into question the very sense of the existence of some of these institutions. Second, Poland lacks not only developed institutions and mechanisms of hard financing for science, art, and culture, but it also lacks the tradition to which one might refer.

This brief review of the links of real interests in postsocialist Poland with the system of real socialism hopefully allows us to understand why the Polish reform finds support mainly, as it is said, in "theoretical interests." Attention has already been drawn to the role of "theoretical interests."[5] People underestimate the blocking role of real group and individual interests. The point here is to emphasize two issues. First, real group interests are incompatible with the proreformist "theoretical interest" and are already now dragging various groups of Polish people backward, virtually to antireformist positions. The process will intensify as the reform develops. Second, real group interests have been formed under real socialism and hence are rooted there, and the demands for a correction of the reform have taken, and will take, predominantly that trend toward the restoration of some elements of socialism.

The Search for a New Utopia?

Does the above mean also that the ideological consciousness will develop in this same direction? This seems unlikely, and in fact the chances of such an ironical turn of history are minimal. But the problem is not that simple, and the evolution of the existing situation does not incline one to offer unambiguous answers to the question posed above.

On the one hand, there is no doubt that Poles have a deeply rooted and historically substantiated dislike of communism and all ideologies associated with it, and hence of socialism, too. The attitude toward socialism as a social system has been investigated on many occasions and in various ways. The results, taken together, unambiguously point to the generally negative

[5] Cf., e.g., J. Staniszkis, *Ontologia socjalizmu*. Warszawa: In Plus, 1989.

attitude of the Poles toward that system. As a curiosity rather than a proof,[6] we will present the answers to a question in a survey concerning the opinions of young people.[7] The question pertained to the issue being discussed at this point.

Is it worth while to continue socialism in our country?

	1986	1987	1988	1989
Yes	28.8	59.3	58.0	43.3
No	60.4	25.8	29.8	45.5
Other opinions	8.8	15.2	11.1	9.1

On the other hand, one has to take two factors into account. First, as has been said, the opposition to the imposed "socialist" system has had, and still has, in Poland the nature of a generalized opposition aimed at all aspects of "socialism" and hence also at all that is associated with "socialism." This is not equivalent to a thought-out reaction to the content of socialist ideology in general and to its components in particular. On the contrary, it is a stereotypical reaction to a certain syndrome of ideological clichés. This syndrome is clearly linked to the Leninist interpretation of socialism, but the reactions to that syndrome are not the grounds for the conclusion about the attitude toward the socialist doctrine as such or toward all that combines to form that doctrine. This is confirmed by empirical data. It turns out that the reactions to the various ideas usually associated with socialism depend on the context in which they are presented and, in particular, on whether they are presented to a given respondent in the context of the syndrome of the recently still-valid ideological clichés. More interesting still, the same applies to typically Leninist ideas, such as state ownership of heavy industry and state control of political activity.[8]

Second, the change in the political system has released normal processes of articulating group interests, frozen for half a century. As we have seen, the

---

[6] The results of such surveys must in Poland be treated with extreme caution. I wrote about this in "Polish Sociology of the Eighties: Theoretical Orientations, Methods, Main Research Trends," in R. Scharff, ed., *Sozialwissenschaften in der Volksrepublik Polen.* Erlangen: IGW, 1989.

[7] The data are drawn from surveys of the government sponsored Center for the Study of Social Opinion. I quote J. Głuszczyński's "Młodzież a socjalizm," *Res Litigiosa,* 1989, no. 1, p. 75.

[8] Two series of studies provide quite a lot of interesting data in this respect. One concerns the attitudes of Warsaw university students, started by Stefan Nowak in the 1950s. Partly comparable data were provided by later studies carried out by Nowak himself and his students. The other is the study *Polacy'80,* carried out by the Polish Academy of Sciences and coordinated by Władysław Adamski.

interests of virtually all numerous and important social groups are deeply rooted in Poland in a system that society as a whole is trying determinately to bury in the past. Those common roots of group interests do not in the least favor intergroup harmony. On the contrary: Poland is witnessing the beginning of a vehement struggle for a share in the dwindling national wealth, although this struggle is screened behind the noble phraseology of morality, Christian principles, and the weal of the nation. In practical terms, it is now mainly a struggle for the preservation of all those socialist privileges that can still be preserved or at least that are indispensable for survival. The strikes of the railwaymen in the spring, the pressure exerted by the farmers and supported by strikes and threats of strikes, the warnings addressed by the miners to the government and supported by the announcement of "statutory actions" (which is a euphemism for strikes) all testify both to the determination in the struggle for group interests and to a rapid development of forms of self-organization of the various groups. The endeavor to introduce the Employee Share Ownership Plan (ESOP) in Poland on a mass scale and the announcement of the setting up of a "network" of factories, which is a multilateral agreement of the trade-union organizations of the largest industrial enterprises most threatened by the reform, mark a new and very important stage in the crystallization of group interests and the development of group consciousness.

That group consciousness must sooner or later result in an ideological rationalization of the aspirations and demands voiced by groups. References to Christian ethics and the weal of the nation are possible as long as the government is the only addressee of those demands. But when it comes to a direct clash of group interests – and this is already taking place, as has been proved by social reactions to the strikes of the railwaymen and the peasants and by the polemic over ESOP – a normal ideological struggle will begin. It is hardly imaginable that in a country in which the habits of enjoying the privileges of real socialism clash with aggressive neoliberalism there should be no "discovery" of the leftist argumentation. The phraseology in which that argumentation will be couched is, of course, a secondary matter, dependent on local circumstances.

But let us return to the present day. The ideological landscape of Poland at first glance seems extremely monotonous. Essentially only two points can be distinguished: Polish neoliberalism and the Polish variation of the Christian social doctrine. The former draws one's attention because of its relatively high intellectual level and connections with the Balcerowicz Plan, and the latter, in view of its connections with the Church hierarchy and the *potential* support by the masses of Roman Catholics. There are also interesting ideological groups, which refer to pre-1939 political parties and movements, including the group of socialists and several rightist groups, but the scope of their influence is minimal.

Is then the ideological landscape of Poland essentially empty? This is an erroneous impression, mainly due to the low level of the ideological culture of Polish society. A lack of skills in articulating ideological preferences, quite understandable after fifty years of rule by totalitarian systems, manifests itself in what might be termed ad hoc ideologizing. But it is just that ad hoc ideologizing that reveals the real ideological tendencies of large social groups.

The tendency that is *relatively* clearly marked is the search for a Polish "third road." A "third road" was at one time mentioned by Wałęsa, but it would be erroneous to link the tendency described here with that name or with Solidarity in general. That tendency also has little in common with the political division emerging in the Solidarity elite. That division, by the way, has extremely weak ideological foundations. The "third road" is a tendency emerging from the grass roots, and thus is opposed to the neoliberalism that is accepted, with or without reservations, by all milieus of the new political elite. It is thus a "popular," but markedly urban, tendency characteristic of manual workers, white-collar workers, and a part of the impoverished intelligentsia (the professional milieus). It is a spontaneous endeavor to articulate ideologically the interests of just those groups, which probably sense the greatest danger in the reform.

That sense of danger also largely determines the content of that "ideology." It is vague, but some essential elements can be pinpointed.

1. This syndrome (but not system) of views has state paternalism as its core, in spite of all the experiences to date. Radically anticommunist in its declarations, this paternalism postulates the replacement of "their" government by "our" government, "their" state by "our" state – equally all-embracing and omnipotent. This view contains not only the philosophy of power typical of real socialism but also the philosophy of life shaped by that system. This is the universal feature of real socialism. As is claimed by Dr. Frank Adler of the Berliner Institut für Sozialwissenschaftliche Studien, an average citizen in the German Democratic Republic perceives H. Kohl in the way E. Honecker wanted to be perceived, that is, as a leader and protector who is exacting but also concerned about people (personal communication). It is exactly this style of thinking about the individual and the state (a thinking in which there is virtually no place for society) that is the most important ideological legacy of real socialism. The essential conflict between that philosophy and the philosophy of liberalism, for which all of Eastern Europe allegedly declares itself, has started manifesting itself in Poland.

2. This ideology has its derivative (deserving separate mention) in the principle of socialist meritocracy, which has far-reaching practical consequences. This principle not only postulates "to each according to his merits." More important still, it assumes the existence of an objective measure of merit in a strong sense (not one that is market-based). The basis

of "justice" and social order is seen in a good, objective, "scientific" measurement of merit and in the appropriate remuneration of that merit.

3. It is in this context that one has to interpret the next demand of the "ideology" under consideration, namely, that of the welfare state. It contains, in principle, similar elements to its Western analogue, namely, free health care, free education, "the right to work" (now: the responsibility of the state for unemployment), highly subsidized housing (the right to an apartment at a price "accessible" to an average employee), etc. But the social philosophy of this demand is different. It is treated not so much as the result of a negotiated social contract of fellow citizens as the *natural right* of the citizen, and hence the *natural duty* of the state.

4. The three above elements have their source in real socialism. The next element is linked to the history of Solidarity, in particular, the 1980–81 period: a certain form of employee self-management. Under present Polish conditions, it is manifested in two demands, not always co-occurring. One demands the participation of the staff in the management of the enterprise; the other accords to the totality of the employees imprecise rights to the property of their workplace. The former is clearly receding into the past, while the latter is acquiring an ever-growing importance, which is borne out by the discussion over ESOP. The scope of the influence of these two demands is limited to the milieu of manual workers.[9]

The socialist provenance of the views presented is striking. But this is not the end of the syndrome under consideration. Its remaining elements are associated with entirely different phenomena. They include ideas that are thought to oppose the socialist tradition, such as attachment to religious and national values, which occasionally degenerates into intolerance and xenophobia. On the other hand, absent are such elements fundamental for the socialist world view as faith in progress, typical of the Enlightenment, and the "class" idea of society. At the same time, we note the strongly stressed faith in democracy (firm rejection of Leninist political conceptions) and human rights. Finally, there is a vaguely articulated faith in a market economy.

If the above reconstruction is correct, then it must be said that we are witnessing the birth of a new, postsocialist "popular" utopia. This is not a value judgment, and certainly it is not a negative value judgment. Utopia is an indispensable element of societal life, a way of articulating the problems

---

[9] A. Kowalczuk, W. Pańków, and T. Peszke carried out a survey covering delegates to the second congress of Solidarity: 62.4 percent of the delegates were in favor of the participating of employees in the making of decisions pertaining to their workplace, 49.8 percent postulated the plurality of forms of ownership or large and middle-sized enterprises now owned by the state (which implies the right of the staff to take over the enterprise as their property), and 77.6 percent were for the subsidizing by the state of certain domains of production and services for social reasons.

with which society is grappling. This was also the case of the socialist utopia before it was transformed into its opposite, that is, a plan for arranging the world once and for all.

The emerging postsocialist utopia is a manifestation of the situation of Polish society and its most endangered strata in particular. This endeavor *to live under socialism after it has been abolished* is not a matter of choice but one of necessity. A third road cannot be found – there is no doubt about that after the experience of the last seventy years. In fact, it would not be a *third* road but an odd combination of that to which one had been doomed and which one now finds it difficult to discard, and that which one would like to have for some abstract reasons. But the very process of the search for that third road is extremely important from the societal point of view. First, it indicates that the normal, spontaneous processes of shaping the social order from the grass roots have been stimulated in Poland. Second, it confirms the thesis that the change in the political system prevailing in Eastern Europe is merely the beginning of a systemic change in that area.

TRANSFORMATIONS
OF NORMATIVE FOUNDATIONS
AND EMPIRICAL SOCIOLOGIES
Class, Stratification,
and Democracy in Poland

Michael D. Kennedy

Most will recognize that empirical social research carries certain normative presumptions about real and ideal social orders, even if those foundations are not acknowledged by the researchers themselves. While these evaluative components are often preeminent in the original construction of paradigms that guide empirical research, over time researchers can forget and/or ignore such normative elements. The normative foundations of research paradigms nevertheless continue not only to construct the variety of interpretations offered, but also to determine the range of questions that can be asked in empirical inquiry. Explicit attention to normative presumptions can facilitate reinterpretations of data already collected, but even then the new data analysis remains constrained to operate in the field of questions established by the original paradigm. Part of the sociological project must therefore be, from time to time, to ask whether the "right" questions are being raised.

To inquire into the "right" questions demands that explicit attention be paid to the normative foundations of empirical projects. Nowhere, perhaps, is the salience of assessing the normative foundations for empirical research more important to raise than in contemporary Poland. Of course, this kind of metatheoretical reflection must also be carried out within specific discourses of empirical research already established in order to avoid banishment to a philosophical ghetto. The focus here shall therefore be on that field which is generally considered to be the center of gravity in sociological research: inequality. What is more, attention shall be directed, if not altogether exclusively, to that part of Polish research that has been translated into English. This not only helps narrow the project but also highlights the contributions made by these researchers to the international community. But this focus is not meant to suggest that the principal audience for Polish sociology should be the international community. By contrast, one may hope that by asking the "right" questions, Polish sociologists can contribute to the progressive transformation of their own system in transition, by keeping in plain sight the relationship between inequality and their view of the "good" society.

This essay proposes to examine, first, the normative foundations of some inequality research that has been conducted in Poland, beginning with the series of projects initiated by Szczepański, followed by the Wesołowski series; and then the status attainment-social mobility model, which became one of the dominant approaches to the empirical study of inequality in Poland. That framework for the study of inequality became rather constraining with the advent of Solidarity in 1980–81, at which time the democratic civil society became the new center in Polish sociology. This focus, and especially that of status attainment or social mobility, did not, however, emerge in the context of inequality research. Thus, in the second part of this essay, an alternative line of analysis is suggested, which depends on making a democratic society, rather than either the free individual-open mobility structure or an egalitarian or socialist society, the normative foundation for studying inequality.

Normative Foundations of Polish Research on Inequality

What have been the normative foundations, theoretical frameworks, and research methods used in Polish research on inequality? We can begin to consider how this question has been broached in Poland before the recent period of remarkable transformation with the aid of an authoritative text on inequality research in People's Poland from 1945 to 1975.

Wesołowski and Słomczyński (1977) emphasize the Marxist heritage of Poland's stratification research, noting Poland's prewar legacy in sociology and the special postwar theoretical contributions by S. Ossowski, J. Hochfeld, and J. Szczepański. Empirical sociological research blossomed under the direction of Szczepański, with twenty-eight monographs on the working class and intelligentsia being produced between 1955 and 1965. This is the first period of major empirical research on inequality in postwar Poland.

In Szczepański's general framework, class structure was understood and explained in terms of the relationship between historical foundations enabling continuity and the changes wrought by industrialization and revolutionary transformation. These general themes were taken up by examining how specific groups within each of these larger classes experienced the dramatic changes Poland faced in this period. Inequality was not studied extensively, as class provided the point of departure for examining the consequences, both intended and unintended, for everyday attitudes and behavior of socioeconomic and political changes.

The normative foundations for this research cannot be understood apart from the political context in which they were structured. After the decimation of sociology during Poland's Stalinist years, sociology had to provide a framework that would justify its existence to the political authorities while nonetheless struggling to realize intellectual independence. The problem of "unintended consequences" as an organizing theme could facilitate those dual ambitions.

One of the distinctions of sociology – and actually of the Scottish moralists, including Adam Smith, long before – this problem of "unintended consequences" allows social science to move beyond the politician's or layperson's practical sense and demonstrate the intellectual discipline's distinctive value in understanding everyday life. Because of this distinction, sociology can become extraordinarily useful to the rational administration of social life, helping any society's planners anticipate the problems of social life and restructure their plans accordingly. Wesołowski and Słomczyński (1977, p. 26) emphasize this "practical" side to Szczepański's vision: "Sound and systematic knowledge allowed one to make the most rational decisions. In the socialist system, he [Szczepański] argues, where wide socio-economic planning causes several new phenomena and processes, intended and unintended, this kind of knowledge is essential for the rational leadership of social life." This kind of sociology could be compatible with the party's own self-understanding of its leading role, as sociology could provide its services to any elite, be it technocratic or Marxist, that aspires to direct social processes.

Given the political constraints, where sociology was obliged to demonstrate its utility to the political leadership while nevertheless struggling to defend its intellectual autonomy, the explicit normative foundations for social research into inequality were constrained to work within an elitist model, as the old system was. It had to promise that more accurate empirical information about social processes could serve societal elites in their administration of society. This proposition succinctly describes its explicit normative foundations:

> Normative Foundation No. 1: To the degree that sociology can conduct its research without political interference, it can aid the organizers of social life in the rational administration of society by assessing both the intended and unintended consequences of the authorities' actions, thus enabling construction of the good society.

Above all, then, inequality research was constrained by its identification with the authorities. It accepted the vision of the good society promulgated by those authorities, and it explicitly sought only those features of social life that could be addressed and presumably rectified by those authorities. This practical side of sociology diminished a bit in the second phase of the development of the sociology of inequality.

This second phase was initiated when Włodzimierz Wesołowski began to head the Social Structures Research Group at the Polish Academy of Sciences. It simultaneously became more theoretically sophisticated and more systematic in its research methods. It integrated Max Weber's work into a more broadly developed Marxist tradition that included not only the politically revered but also the theoretically innovative, including Antonio Gramsci.

In the main theoretical work of the period, Wesołowski (1966/1979) argued that in socialist society, the traditional domains establishing inequality, notably property relations, had grown less significant, even while other more "Weberian" concerns, including education, prestige, and authority, had grown in importance. In effect, he argued that the division of labor increasingly determined the distribution of rewards in socialist society, or that individual investments in the occupational structure shaped the material and non-material gratifications for those rewards. This meant, then, that inequality could not be understood exclusively in terms of broad general classes but that empirical research also had to examine socio-occupational categories and occupations themselves.

To the extent that these groupings were understood in terms of hierarchy, their intellectual ancestor was mainly Max Weber; to the extent that these groupings were understood as structuring collectivities without implication of hierarchy, they were understood to be derived more from the Marxist tradition (Wesołowski and Słomczyński, 1977, p.41). Wesołowski was even more clearly working within the Marxist tradition when he argued that the continuing scarcity of goods within socialist societies meant that structurally based contradictory interests would continue, with the possibility that they would also become actual conflicts.

These contradictory interests lead to conflict in capitalist society because they are based on a principle of distribution that is patently unjust: property. In socialism, by contrast, conflict is less likely because its principle of "(i) distribution according to work is recognized by the majority of the population as just; (ii) the long term evolution of society is directed towards the transformation of this principle into an 'even more just' one, namely distribution 'according to need' " (Wesołowski, 1966/1979, p. 124). In this kind of society, therefore, tensions that produce conflict are likely to be minimized to the extent that the principle of "to each according to his work" operates in general and when people are working for society, not the privileged.

Conflict might emerge nonetheless in socialist society, due either to the application of the principle or to its deviation. Class conflict is more likely to occur when the distribution of values in society is cumulative (Wesołowski, 1966/1979, p. 136). In socialist society, income, power, and education are distributed according to autonomous principles, thereby undermining the possibility of values' cumulation into specific groups, Wesołowski (1966/1979, p.137) argues. But the operation of the principle "to each according to his work" might serve to synchronize these values and thus generate conflict.

Conflict could also occur, however, as a result of the decomposition of class attributes when, for instance, the unskilled manual worker earns as much as or more than the more highly educated physician. Wesołowski (1966/1979, pp.118–19) finds that this likely will produce "feelings of social injustice" in the physician, unless a new world view emerges based on the idea that rewards should be differentiated rather than synchronized. It seems that here Wesołowski suggests that the sociologist should investigate the conditions under which such an alternative world view might emerge.

Wesołowski implies that the party should inculcate this world view. But the Communist party's position in these circumstances is problematic, given that its role as the distributor of rewards and moulder of opinions makes it especially obvious as society's "antagonist." Conflict, then, may emerge not as class conflict but as conflict between society and the state to the extent the party remains directly involved in decision making and not merely the guardian of societal institutions and values (Wesołowski, 1966/1979, pp.129–35).

The theoretical and normative implications of this work are considerable and deserve more attention than can be given them here, but its particular concern for justice shall be raised.

Justice is understood both objectively and subjectively. The Marxist emphasis on objective justice, in terms of classlessness, remains prominent in this work, but Wesołowski goes beyond this well-understood normative foundation to emphasize that even with classlessness, certain "perceptions" of injustice may emerge. An uneasy tension between these two notions thus remains. On the one hand, Wesołowski clearly favors the movement toward a society whose distribution is based on need and tolerates the political and ideological domination of a Marxist party to realize it. On the other hand, however, Wesołowski treats conflict as "normal" (in the Durkheimian sense, that is, regular) and implicitly cautions the party to step back from its direct administration of society to avoid the escalation of conflict between it and society. We might summarize the normative foundations of this argument as follows:

> Normative Foundation No. 2: Sociological research can aid the authorities in the construction of socialism by informing their evalua-tion of society's development, but it should help by investigating (a) the degree to which status groups form through the cumulation of valued

goods; and (b) when groups and individuals appreciate this class decomposition rather than oppose it. This research is particularly important as the good society, one of relative consensus and minimal inequality, might not be realized under prevailing modes of socialist construction.

This foundation suggests a tension that was not present in the earlier formulation suggested by Szczepański. This second generation of inequality research does not presume that the authorities can resolve conflicts and feelings of social injustice even if they have adequate information. Instead, it suggests that group conflicts might be inevitable in a socialist society and mitigated only to the extent that the decomposition of class attributes occurs and that decomposition is valued by all groups. It goes further to suggest that not only might the party be unable to resolve these conflicts but, to the degree that it assumes responsibility for them, it will become the object of antagonism.

We can interpret this transformation of normative foundations as a suggestion that justice cannot be reduced to questions of "inequality." Justice in a socialist society must be understood in terms of how its inevitable conflicts over scarce goods are adjudicated and subjectively rendered. Thus, injustice is in part, although not entirely, a matter of subjective perceptions and procedural matters, not only a matter of objective levels of inequality. This then removes injustice from the immediate field of research on inequality.

The normative claims of Marxism about inequality and injustice, that the generation of classlessness resolves problems of injustice, are thus already undermined in Wesołowski's (1966/1979) work, anticipating his later move to Weberian questions of legitimacy, which are more focused on matters of subjective perceptions and procedural matters. But in the process of making inequality less sufficient in moral and social theory, Wesołowski also opens up the study of inequality to a form of stratification research that is both less theoretically ambitious and more empirically driven. With his theoretical argument, Wesołowski provided the intellectual justification for examining inequality in a way more similar to social-stratification research in noncommunist countries. It provided an opening for status-attainment research to enter the Polish intellectual world.

The Normative Foundations of Status Attainment and Social Mobility Research

Blau and Duncan's (1967) status-attainment research is an exemplary model of scientific investigation. Its original paradigm was simple and clear in its concepts and in their operationalizations, as well as in establishing the relationship between variables. In the most rudimentary description, the model argues that the final occupational status of an individual is to some degree dependent on the occupational status of that person's family but may be affected by a variety of factors including, but not limited to, education.

This basic model has been elaborated in a variety of ways. The Wisconsin School, for example, has introduced greater complexity and greater specification by adding a range of factors concerning psychological motivation. The model has also been important in cross-cultural research, clarifying what are the universal and what the peculiarly American features of its approach.

When brought to Eastern Europe, for instance, one of the most important elaborations that had to be made was the distinction between attainment based on structural changes in the economy, called structural mobility, and that based on the openness of the structure itself, called circulation mobility. While this was but an after-the-fact observation in the original Blau and Duncan work that explained the continuing openness of the class structure, structural transformations are a central (Connor, 1979; Pohoski and Mach, 1988), even if not the exclusive, factor (Słomczyński, 1986) in explaining attainment and mobility in socialist systems. Were the normative foundations of the model also changed when brought to Eastern Europe?

The normative foundations and metatheoretical underpinnings of the original status-attainment model in the United States were called into question not long after the model was introduced. Some argued that the approach was "atheoretical," while others argued that it was based on a structural functional model of society. Knottnerus (1987) has recently added that a certain "image of society" was essential to making status-attainment research meaningful. In effect, the image was one of a mass society whose only constraints on occupational mobility derived from two potential sources: (1) a continuing cultural emphasis on ascribed over achieved factors; and (2) an economy sufficiently static that higher-status jobs would not be generated through development. We might add, too, that the society status attainment envisioned was (a) domestic, (b) male, and (c) civil, meaning that it referred only to the nonpolitical and nonfamilial sphere of social life, which had been overwhelmingly male, and was limited only to a single political system. Pohoski and Mach (1988) do provide, however, a valuable comparison between mobility patterns of men and women in 1972 and 1982 in Poland.

Thus, a vision of justice and the good society did indeed reside in the status-attainment model, mainly in terms of assuring the relationship between individual efforts and achievements on the one hand, and occupational status on the other. The notion of the "just" society in status-attainment research was therefore not dependent on "equality," except perhaps in terms of equality of opportunity. But even here, equality of opportunity did not mean the same starting point for everyone; it meant only that achieved factors would be more important in affecting final occupational status than ascribed factors and that structural factors would not pose barriers to these individual efforts. The project was, therefore, never even about equality or inequality. It was about "freedom."

Since the age of Reagan, freedom has been more and more associated in the United States with economic freedom, the opportunity to "get ahead." The antifeudal notion of freedom was also constructed in these terms: a kind of negative liberty which would allow individuals to do whatever they wanted so long as this would not injure others. And of course, as a struggle informed by the position of the bourgeoisie, this was a struggle over freedom of the entrepreneur from the state. It makes sense, then, that this research would have as its sole focus individuals in a domestic civil society.

If we think about the normative implications of status attainment research, this notion of freedom is probably the best contender for claiming foundational status. Of course, we are not here considering the state's constraints on economic freedom, but we are considering constraints similar to those the state imposed on precapitalist society: that certain economic activities were constrained by the station of one's birth. While in feudal society that station might have been rooted in caste or estate, in capitalist society those constraints come from race, gender, or occupational origins.

Such normative foundations for pursuing sociological research have a much less obvious connection to the ruling authorities of capitalist society and therefore realize one important normative foundation of research on inequality: institutional autonomy of the research itself. These status-attainment sociologists were not doing research on any actor's literal behalf. But they were extremely useful in demonstrating that there was a clear connection between one's individual efforts, as in educational attainment, and one's occupational attainment. In this sense, then, the outcomes of status attainment research could be used to demonstrate the openness of the class structure and therefore its justice, so long as economic freedom remained the normative foundation of the ideological structure in which the research was conducted and disseminated. Whatever its ideological use, however, status-attainment research in the United States has been connected to one of the central problems of this culture: just how much individual achievement can affect one's occupational success. The normative foundation for this research might thus be expressed succinctly as follows:

Normative Foundation No. 3: To the extent that individual achievement leads to changes in occupational status, one has the good society.

Working with this normative foundation, Polish sociologists could then engage sociologists from capitalist countries on their very own terms. Polish sociologists could point to the massive amounts of upward social mobility as indication of their society's greater openness and therefore greater justice. In return, sociologists like Connor (1979) argue that this apparent openness was a consequence of industrialization, not anything peculiar to the organization of the economic system or its property relations. Słomczyński (1986) in turn has argued that there was relatively greater circulation mobility in Poland than in the United States in the early 1970s. More recently, however, Pohoski and Mach (1988) found structural transformations to be the central factor explaining mobility in 1972–82.

In any case, this move to status-attainment social mobility research enabled not only direct comparisons of mobility regimes but implicit comparisons of the relative justice of the systems that contained them. Another theme in prestige studies performing similar functions and structuring like debates was the relative position of the blue-collar working class, where in socialist society they enjoyed relatively higher prestige than in capitalist society.

Many of the substantive debates informing these system comparisons then moved forward to determine the methodological artifacts that led the working class to its relatively prestigious position, or the relative impact on structural changes for influencing the true openness of the social structure. But in neither case was the matter turned around. Why should we have such a focus on economic freedom as the measure of a system's social justice? Why should civil society, and not political society, be the object of our inquiry into inequality? And why should the system we consider be only national and not international? Certainly by itself this idea of freedom within domestic civil society is not controversial. It might, however, be considered problematic when it is connected to the kind of culture and society that makes it so central and to the questions that it fails to ask.

The culture, or dominant attitude, that makes status-attainment research fundamental in sociological research is one based on "status seeking." This materialistic mentality was often criticized in the United States for its narrowness, but Blau and Duncan saw something virtuous in this status-seeking disposition. They argued that it was an integral part of the universalism that opened up the class structure to individual achievement rather than inherited ascribed status. Furthermore, this status-seeking mentality was even beneficial to the democratic order, because status differentials came to be understood in this framework as differences in degree rather than as inherent differences of superiority and inferiority. This gave political equality some meaningful referent in the culture of civil society, making variations in status not foundational for questions of democratic governance (Knotterus, 1987).

If status seeking was to be a cultural manifestation of a real social structure rather than a mystification for an unjust order, this mentality had to be a part of a society in which there were few particularities or closed communities based on class or status. The image of "mass society" was thus the macrosociological compliment to this status-seeking mentality. Technological dynamism created the open society that made significant status differentials and turned closed communities into anachronisms. In this mass society, the individual was basically free, as the only constraints on freedom, like the class of one's birth or of one's race, became increasingly irrelevant. Because of unequal access to education, inequalities remained which might themselves have their roots in personalities and cultural legacies, but other than these, there were no real constraints on this individual achievement. Thus, mass society and status-seeking culture are part of the good society, complimentary to and even essential for social justice. Whatever the measure of appeal this argument still holds for society in the United States, it became even more problematic when brought to Communist party-led societies.

Sociologists from these societies could claim that their socialism realized this mass-society condition even better than capitalism. Indeed, the absence from this problematic of political society even made the research paradigm politically feasible for inquiry in socialist societies. To study the partynomial system, as Bauman (1972) called it, in addition to the class system or civil society, might have made inequality research impossible. But aside from this question of political feasibility, does this notion of economic freedom within domestic civil society provide enough normative justification for making the study of status attainment and social mobility so central to the sociological project, especially if it provides some justification for a system that has been so uniformly rejected in the end of the last decade?

There are two plausible answers to this question. First, one could say that while existing socialism has been rejected, the alternative capitalist society to which the Soviet-type system was being compared is not really being embraced in contemporary Poland. Most citizens of the old state socialisms prefer a heavily subsidized welfare state society rather than a cold capitalist one, especially like that in the United States.

While that is a reasonable response, it does seem that even if the general public opinion rejects a harsh market solution to the problem of alternatives, many of Poland's intellectual and now political elites are embracing just such an approach. Indeed, the main lines of discourse depend on a capitalist framework for their resonance: against primitive egalitarianism and learned helplessness, in favor of a much more sharply unequal distribution of rewards and an alternative ethos of self sufficiency. These seem to be part of the essential recipe for a thriving capitalism, at least in ideological terms.

Second, one could argue that those who have conducted social-mobility and status-attainment research were not arguing that this was an essential part of the normative project. And they are undoubtedly right in their personal claims. But at the same time, because they adopted an empirical project developed in the United States that did have a normative foundation elevating economic freedom above other normative claims, these sociologists were, unintentionally if not intentionally, helping to reproduce in Polish sociology the dominant claim that economic freedom within domestic civil society is the social approximation of justice.

On the other hand, of course, we have seen that these very limited normative claims facilitated greater openness of sociological investigation in the socialist countries. In capitalist countries, too, the status-attainment problematic facilitated much research, as the available data and the data that could be collected began to establish more and more the kinds of research that would be conducted. But in this status attainment tradition, the connection to the larger discipline and the bigger questions that motivated it were typically reduced in significance as the increasing sophistication of techniques and the replication of original studies in a wider range of formats became the central preoccupation of the subdiscipline's practitioners. The engagement of these often brilliant sociologists on such questions took them away from the central problems that modern societies must confront, especially when freedom of inquiry and speech came to be supported by the state.

The Normative Shift in Polish Sociology Occasioned by Solidarity's Formation

Even before that freedom was supported by the Polish state, it seemed that Solidarity's example led more and more sociologists to ask questions in the framework of their research that had roots in the normative commitments generated by Solidarity. By this time, the intellectual autonomy of sociological research was more or less taken for granted, but the degree to which questions were asked that were related to matters of broad public significance and political conflict were not all so common. It seems to the outside observer that Solidarity had a great impact on the critical quality of sociological inquiry. In particular, what impact did Solidarity's formation have in studies of inequality?

Two main angles seemed to emerge. On the one hand, sociologists of inequality became more committed to demonstrating the real material deprivations of people (e.g., Lidia Beskid, 1987). On the other hand, we also saw a return to the work of S. Ossowski, who argued that images of class structure were as important to studies of inequality as "actual" patterns. As such, the work of Zaborowski (1986), Słomczyński and Kacprowicz (1986), and the collection edited by Wnuk-Lipiński (1987) suggest a valuable effort to link these subjective and objective dimensions of inequality research, especially in terms that might be linked to questions of just distributions of rewards and images of political domination. In particular, this critical approach to inequality's study began to find in the popular consciousness less the functionalist stratificational images the old sociology emphasized and more an antagonistic view of inequality directed above all against the political authorities (Koralewicz and Mach, 1987, p. 20). Given that the authorities were so important in the society's view of inequality, researchers of inequality were pushed away from such a focus on civil society and its forms of identity to those established in the interaction between state and society. Two chapters from the Wnuk-Lipiński collection illustrate this nicely.

Koralewicz and Wnuk-Lipiński (1987) investigate the deprivation not only in family and collegial relations but also in the public sphere. Not surprisingly, their research on engineers and workers finds that in the first two spheres, needs are relatively satisfied. In the public sphere, however, there is considerable deprivation, which is even greater among workers than engineers. Workers more often than engineers find the possibility of controlling and criticizing the authorities *very* important, for instance. This finding is of considerable significance for challenging the common stereotype that the highly educated are more committed to democratic values than are workers.

Mach (1987) also reworks the stratification literature by challenging the very notion that occupational status is, in fact, so significant. Rather than assuming occupational status fundamental for social self-identification, he asked his respondents to name the group whose life situation is most similar to their own. Although occupational categories finished a respectable fourth with 15 percent of a general Polish sample, being somehow unable to manage was the most common (25.8 percent), the well adjusted second (20.4 percent), and "the ordinary" in third (18 percent) (p. 168). This kind of work was an especially important move even if it was not entirely without precedent. Of course the Ossowski tradition suggests this, but another branch of its ancestry can be found in what Wesołowski (1966/1979) suggested much earlier: that justice has not only an objective but a subjective dimension, especially in terms of class.

These studies tend to move without that status-attainment–social-mobility framework, however, as they consider not only occupational status and the status-seeking mentality but also search for real-world referents of life chances and for broader notions of subjectivity than the status attainment paradigm emphasizes. There were, however, other important efforts that tried to link social-mobility analysis to other major problems of the day, exemplified by the work of Wesołowski and Mach (1986) (see also Mach, 1989).

Wesołowski and Mach (1986) transformed the status-attainment–social-mobility problematic to increase its relevance to a wider variety of sociological questions. Above all, they sought to demonstrate that mobility carries certain "potential functions" for system performance and system reproduction, for economic development, and for the legitimation of the political and social order. In Poland, however, these systemic functions went unfulfilled.

The type of mobility characterizing a socialist regime is dependent on the reigning ideology, they argued. An emphasis on equality of conditions in the

Marxist problematic led to an emphasis on collective mobility wherein differentials among the major classes are reduced. A more meritocratic Marxism led some regime actors to emphasize an individualist qualificational or occupational form of mobility. The extent to which both principles of mobility are linked to one another rationally influences how well mobility contributes to both legitimation and development.

Wesołowski and Mach find that in the first stages of socialist development, the former egalitarian orientation generally predominates, but as problems of economic development and innovation grow more prominent, the meritocratic version becomes more essential. But in the Polish case, collective mobility did not contribute to regime legitimacy, and even individual mobility was not constructed so as to lead to overall economic development. While the ceremonial value of the laboring classes was elevated in the new regime, the "alienating and degrading aspects" of that work did not abate (p. 175) nor did their real political influence increase (p. 176). Individual mobility became nonfunctional, too, because the qualificational-occupational hierarchy in which mobility operates became less significant due to "blockages and disorders in the qualification principle of training, selection, allocation, promotion and remuneration in the economic system" (p. 178).

This line of thinking is important because it rethinks the normative presuppositions of the status-attainment model. Indeed, it extends the model's self-consciousness by noting that not only is an open mobility structure important for realizing freedom from ascriptive discrimination but also that it is essential for a rational social system that apportions talent to the right places, thus enabling continued economic development and legitimation for the political and social order. We might summarize the normative foundations of this reinterpretation of status-attainment–social-mobility research as follows:

> Normative Foundation No. 4: The good society is both efficient and legitimate, which in turn depends on there being a rational link between a meritocratic occupational system and a minimally inegalitarian class system.

Like foundation No. 3, this foundation also takes for granted the autonomy of research, but this is also a reinterpretation of the mobility-attainment problematic designed to make it more relevant to the Polish situation. In some ways, this reinterpretation of the mobility project is a smooth extension from normative foundation No. 2, if we exclude the party allegiance made in that framework. Once again, there is some explicit commitment to minimal class differentiation and to the subjective appreciation of the system, this time expressed through the concern for legitimacy. This project diverges from the old paradigm in two important ways, however. First, there is much less interest in avoiding the "cumulation of valued goods," finding instead a clear cumulation important for the reintroduction of the status-seeking mentality. Second, the interest in subjectivity is expressed in terms of legitimacy rather than in some vision of competing world views. Both are extremely important shifts and mark an explicit turn away from some aspects of the Marxist conception of justice. But in this very shift, a certain contradiction emerges between the first and the second aspects of the paradigmatic transformation.

Power, Legitimacy, and Inequality in Status Attainment

Status-attainment research generally focuses on a civil society effectively devoid of power. The problematic that guides this research finds the only kind of systemic power to be that which limits economic freedom through the elevation of ascripted over achieved characteristics; the only kind of strategic power is that used by the individual to achieve and move up. Power to energize the status-seeking mentality is the only kind of agency theorized in this problematic. Of necessity, scholars from the old socialist countries had to recognize that this civil society was not somehow "natural" but rather was subject to elite policies. Thus, the power to transform mobility regimes is necessarily introduced in the study of status attainment in socialist societies.

Wesołowski and Mach clearly incorporate this recognition into their problematic by noting that the kind of mobility regime and the effectiveness of its operation is a consequence of the elites' policies. Nevertheless, while Wesołowski and Mach thereby introduce power into the problematic, they continue to leave it out of civil society. They restrict the capacity to transform social relations to the elites, be they of revolutionary or technocratic inclination. Wesołowski and Mach explicitly deny the power of the ordinary actor in socialist civil society by noting, for instance, that even after the collective mobility project, "workers do not sense themselves to be either a subject of history or a subject of a political process, in which their interest will, or political action could be, transformed into a state policy" (p. 176). Thus, the system itself denies the transformative subjectivity of class actors. But it does seem to generate an individual subjectivity of considerable measure. Indeed, this individual subjectivity is so great that Wesołowski and Mach consider its operation pathological for the survival of the system.

The individual mobility process has been "gradually deprived of substantive meaning both for the individual and society in Poland," write Wesołowski and Mach (p. 176), with the consequence that qualificational mobility ceased to become a desirable goal of action. Instead, a good family life or interesting private life rather than getting ahead became a central life goal. Several spheres contribute to this deevolution of the status-seeking mentality. The school system encourages obedience rather than talents; the promotional system, although formally based on credentials, ignores real competence in favor of political loyalty; and the remuneration structure does not encourage the individual to plan his or her occupational career strategically. Wesołowski and Mach characterize the Polish crisis by noting that people's activities to survive – cynical obedience, manipulating informal networks to obtain goods, and a move toward private enterprise – have pathological effects for the legitimation and economic development of the system.

In this account of the individual mobility process, Wesołowski and Mach clearly demonstrate the power, or really here the agency, of individual actors. When the status-attainment system is irrational, actors can find other ways of surviving and realizing personal happiness. As Giddens would describe it, actors have the capacity of doing otherwise, thereby demonstrating their agency. But rather than seeing this action as a demonstration of the vitality of subjectivity and the power of individuals, Wesołowski and Mach see it as an example of the pathology of the system. Indeed, given the economic crisis and illegitimacy of the old system, it is not surprising that such subjectivity could be understood as "dysfunctional." But rather than taking this as a point of departure for the critique of the "status-seeking mentality," Wesołowski and Mach use its absence as an indication of the system's pathology.

Thus, one of the essential normative foundations of the original status-attainment model is preserved even in this basic transformation and extension of the project. The principal kind of action that the paradigm recognizes, and now more than ever explicitly values, is that of status seeking. But of course this mentality must operate in a rational system in which status seeking is transformed into a systemic good.

The two system goods that Wesołowski and Mach identify are system effectiveness and system legitimacy. While the former is easily identified with a system based on economic freedom, the latter is far more difficult to assimilate into the status-attainment project, precisely because for legitimacy to avoid its tautological rendition, actors must be sufficiently empowered to *volunteer* their consent to be governed.

Wesołowski and Mach clearly recognize that mobility is but one small part of a system's legitimacy, and that should be noted from the start. They seem to suggest, however, that an effective system with a status-seeking mentality contributes to system legitimacy. Indeed it might, but on the other hand, one might consider that just such a status-seeking mentality undermines the very conditions in which legitimacy might become something other than a tautology.

Peter Blau (1970) called this tautology the paradox of legitimate domination. How can one be sure that it is not fear or coercion but voluntary submission that characterizes obedience? Reinhard Bendix (1962) notes that the idea of legal domination is itself circular, with legal domination being distinguished by the belief that it is legal. Wesołowski (1986) himself considers this matter and agrees with Habermas that a democratic variant based on democratic procedures and democratic values might be the only way to establish this notion of legitimacy in a way that is neither tautological nor paradoxical. In the end, then, Wesołowski finds democracy, both procedural and substantive, to be the best approximation of a legitimate order in which compliance with authority is truly voluntary. The best way to find this, he suggests, is to recognize that "undistorted human communication" might be the best foundation for "testing the truth of society's belief in legitimacy" (p. 49). But how compatible is the problematic of undistorted communication with the problematic of the status-seeking mentality? This will be addressed in the final section of this essay. But first, the arguments of the essay to this point should be summarized, as the section analyzing inequality research in Poland is concluded.

Summary

The problem of inequality has shaped much of sociology's discourse, in both socialist and capitalist countries. In the latter, the normative foundation underlying this research on inequality has varied and has not always been based on the valuation of equality. Indeed, the status-attainment tradition made economic freedom within domestic civil society rather than any version of equality its basic normative guide. In socialist countries, by contrast, sociology's normative foundations were more problematic. Sociology first had to establish the conditions for its intellectually autonomous existence.

To study inequality in this framework would have been impossible, as the communist elites claimed to be engaged in the creation of a fundamentally more just society, especially in regard to material equality. Instead, sociology could reestablish itself only by offering its services to these elites as independent researchers who could help political elites administer society in a rational way, discovering both intended and unintended consequences of policy in various class settings.

Polish sociology's normative foundations seemed to shift as the discipline acquired more autonomy from the authorities. Although the leaders of the discipline implied that sociology could help realize socialism, they no longer refrained from challenging certain basic aspects of Marxist orthodoxy. In particular, it was argued that certain contradictions would remain in socialism and that the party may not be able to resolve them without generating even greater resentment against it. In this shift, the orthodox Marxist association between inequality and justice was undermined, finding that perceptions of injustice may remain even in a classless society.

This intellectual shift facilitated the introduction into Poland of various research projects with a weaker connection to equality as a normative foundation than some varieties of Marxism claimed. Status attainment and social mobility, in particular, developed considerably. But while this research could proceed in gathering data and employing increasingly sophisticated techniques of analyzing the data, it grew further and further away from the normative concerns that generated the research in the United States. Nevertheless, it continued implicitly to reproduce the problem of the good society by asking questions about the measure of economic freedom in various domestic civil societies. In so doing, however, it also remained far away from the normative issues that confronted Polish society.

Polish sociological research shifted its focus after the emergence of Solidarity and the imposition of martial law. Its emphasis on scientific and comparative questions was now supplemented by a concern for social problems, political conflicts, and more peculiarly Polish issues. Inequality research also reflected this shift from scientific to emancipatory normative commitments. Researchers began to emphasize more absolute impoverishment in the system as well as subjective perceptions of inequality and domination. There were also attempts to transform the status-attainment project, to make it more relevant to broader normative issues. In so doing, status seeking became an essential part of the good society, but how that status-seeking mentality relates to the construction of a democratically based legitimacy, the other aspect of the "good society," remains a problem. The second part of this essay will address this issue as it tries to establish democracy, rather than economic freedom or equality per se, as the normative foundation for research on inequality.

Democracy, Inequality, and Justice

The social transformations of Soviet-type societies in 1989 suggest that Wesołowski's emphasis on democracy as a normative foundation is not only intellectually sensible but also politically relevant. As sociologists, we should be historically sensitive to how social transformations can recast our intellectual paradigms. After all, direct observation of the French transformations of 1848–51 led Tocqueville and Marx to some of their most salient analytical points: that undemocratic governments are easy to topple, that class struggle in politics is likely to intensify, and that revolution and reaction tend to produce authoritarian outcomes (Calhoun, 1989). Although a comparison of 1989–90 with 1848–51 would be instructive on analytical grounds, we might also note here as a more relevant point that this nineteenth century shift also established the main schools of subsequent sociological theory on normative grounds, in its social-conservative (Comte), autonomously political-liberal (Tocqueville), and economistic-radical (Marx) guises (Calhoun, 1989). It seems plausible that similar normative differences could emerge from 1989–90, too, as we have conservative advocates of some Party of Order, we have many more liberals in the Tocquevillian tradition, and we even have economistic radicals, except this time the determination of emancipation is that of the free market rather than the socialization of the means of production.

That last exception is fundamentally important to future politics and scholarship. One of the most unfortunate gaps we have seen in the twentieth century is the gap between democrats of socialist and liberal persuasion. In many places, most notably in the third world, democratic socialists have been obliged to ally with revolutionary socialists, while liberal democrats have felt obliged to throw their hat in the ring with authoritarian and dictatorial governments. Instead of the normative splits being over the measure of democracy in the system, the major divergences were over which elites would rule and to what purpose the coercive power of the state might be pushed.

As Communist party-led states fall, or as they become modified and accept the principles of liberal democracy, the traditional oppositions might be recast. Instead of an opposition between socialist and bourgeois politicians and scholars, with the positions of each on democracy being relatively insignificant, the measure of commitment to democracy might become the new line that divides democrats of liberal and socialist stripe from authoritarian advocates of moral and racial purity or of free-market survival. This then becomes the debate between those of authoritarian inclination and those who insist on normative principles that can be found beyond the here and now, who find freedom and democracy an ideal to be sought rather than a tradition to be defended or a luxury that can be put off to some future time. This emphasis on a democratic ideal may become especially important in the conflicts that will inevitably surround the period of post-communist transition.

Several Polish sociologists have noted that systemic transformation in Poland may be obstructed by the distribution of interests generated by the old system (Mokrzycki, 1990; Wesołowski, 1990). In fact, Cichomski (1989) has demonstrated that the workers in December 1988 who had relatively strong feelings about being underpaid, quite apart from their actual material situation, were more confident in the old political economic system and less supportive of market transformations. This could suggest, then, that democratic transition in Poland could well prove difficult if that democracy is to be based on a market system with an empowered civil society rather than a market system imposed by a power elite with a democratic rhetoric.

The heritage of Solidarity can, however, be understood as the struggle of a democratic civil society against a state. The critical sociologies of Poland in the 1980s certainly reflect this conflict between democracy and dictatorship, between civil society and state repression. But the constitution of a democracy where the conflict between civil society and state no longer dominates public discourse demands that an alternative kind of normative foundation rooted in democracy be made explicit. Otherwise, this normative commitment could easily be replaced by other principles that once again subordinate the individual to a system, except this time one that demands some kind of functional rationality or national integration.

Fortunately, at the very time that historical developments have led to the possible recasting of just such intellectual and practical politics, philosophical developments have moved to buttress just such a move. The arguments of Jurgen Habermas and his colleagues that there is a normative foundation that might be introduced making equality an ancillary, even if not a foundational, aspect of justice are convincing. To avoid a long philosophical argument here, we might argue simply that a procedural, rather than substantive, notion of justice is essential for providing this normative foundation for sociology. Democracy, rather than equality or freedom, might reflect this difference. Held (1987) provides a lengthy discussion of different models of democracy, and the following "foundation" is inspired by his discussion as well as that of Dahl (1982).

> Normative Foundation No. 5: Social justice and therefore the good society depend on having an open public space where social problems can be recognized, their origins debated, and their solutions raised and acted upon. This means further that each actor must have access to the public sphere, so that s/he can put forward before the community that grievance which s/he is in a special position to recognize. The public sphere must be so constituted that each problem can be fairly and openly discussed, that no position or argument is repressed without having its fair hearing, and that no position or argument is accepted without being available for critical scrutiny and open criticism. The solutions open public debate obtain must then be implementable and realizable. This means that the public must have an institution of sufficient power and sufficient responsiveness so that its decisions can be enforced. Finally, this instrument of enforcement cannot be so powerful as to be able to override or eliminate the conditions that enable the openness of the public sphere to be reproduced. This, in effect, is the model of a democratized society and a democratized state, connected by an open public sphere.

One can diagram this normative foundation as follows (see p. 302)

Presenting this in diagrammatic fashion, we can more clearly establish empirical problems. Let us consider each briefly, beginning with an identification of each of these concepts:

(1) civil society: the "nonstate" sphere of social activity. This does not traditionally include the family, but under the influence of feminist theory, it can. It also includes voluntary associations like trade unions, privately owned and managed economic enterprises, religious organizations, and so on.

(2) political society: the "representative" sphere of social activity. This includes all those who seek to become, or who are, elected officials whose power is delegated to them by civil society. This therefore includes political parties.

(3) the state: the "administrative-coercive" sphere of social activity. This includes all legitimate uses of violence as well as other exercises of public power whose range is not limited by anything other than the guarantee that the public sphere continues to remain open and influential.

(4) the public sphere: the "informational" sphere of social activity. This includes all media of information but also less formal sites for the actual exchange and debate of viewpoints.

Ideal Democracy

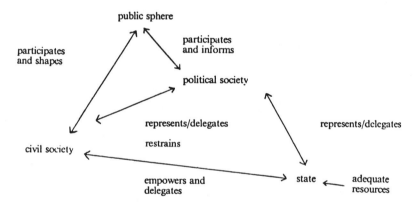

These four basic concepts are connected through various mechanisms. The civil society is the source of all authority for action. It delegates certain responsibilities to political society as its representative. Although political society is obliged to participate regularly in the public sphere in order to inform civil society of its activities, civil society must also have direct access to this public sphere so that the politicians' authority can be challenged not only in the formal electoral arena in which they are elected but also in the matter of specific issues which the public sphere addresses. In particular, this is one place where social movements are important, for they represent a relatively unmediated form of power directly from civil society that can challenge the institutionalized bases of politicians.

The state is delegated power by those representatives of civil society in political society. Because the state is the institution that can affect the policies decided in the public sphere, it must have sufficient resources of both material and moral quality to enable it to act. One of the principal activities of this state is to ensure the conditions that allow for the empowerment of civil society and the equal participatory potential of its actors in the public sphere. In that case, certain rights must be realized, including the guarantee of civil (e.g., freedom of speech) and political (e.g., one person one vote) rights. It must also assure, however, certain economic rights (a minimum standard of living that would allow participation) and social rights (a minimum level of education that would allow participation). Finally, it must also assure reproductive rights, where women would have freedom of choice as to whether to bear or not bear children, in order to assure that public participation not be gendered. The empowerment of civil society thus would not only assure effective public participation but it would also create the conditions to assure that the state's power is also restrained.

Political society need not delegate responsibilities only to the state. It can also delegate responsibilities to civil society. The very idea in the United States, for instance, that utilities should be privately owned is an example of this delegation of what most nations consider a public responsibility to civil society.

Of what use is this ideal model? Although not used explicitly by Polish social scientists, I believe this model can incorporate some of the basic themes of that social science in the 1980s that were explicitly concerned with matters of social justice, even if inequality was not the major theme that they addressed. Instead, it seems that from 1980–81 to the late 1980s at least, the theme of "blocked channels of interest articulation" was the main theme of critical social science.

Poland in 1980–81 and the Normative Foundations of Polish Research

In the first period of Solidarity in 1980–81, the struggle for democracy was based on the democratization of society. In this conflict, the struggle by voluntary associations for independence from the state was the foundation for the establishment of a means of defense for certain civil liberties. Within civil society's associations, too, certain political rights were created, but these rights did not extend to the political society and its state apparatus. Civil society in this period was virtually, in terms of power relations and actual size, coterminous with Solidarity. In this period, too, the state apparatus derived its power from outside the country, its legitimacy resting first and foremost in the eyes of the USSR and its coercive capacity depending on the threat of invasion by that Soviet Union. The public sphere created in this period raised many issues not raised before and through alternative publications issued forth a new openness that postwar Poland had not enjoyed previously.

Civil society was in part empowered by this state, inasmuch as this state provided the minimal economic, social, and reproductive rights that enabled public participation. Solidarity pressed for an extension of these rights, especially on behalf of those least advantaged, including health-care personnel and teachers (see Kennedy, 1991). By virtue of the empowerment by the state, in combination with its new-found autonomy, it could also defend itself from the state. The main barrier to democracy, however, lay in the virtually absent connection between civil society and political society and the sources of the state's resources for its empowerment.

Given this state of affairs, it is not surprising to see in the Polish social scientific discourse of 1980–81 and its aftermath an emphasis on "blocked channels of interest articulation" (e.g., Tarkowski, 1981; Koralewicz, 1987). This blockage occurred before 1980–81 because civil society was not *able* to articulate its interests and in 1980–81 because civil society was not *able* to control political society or the state.

The Democratic Movement, Poland 1980–81*

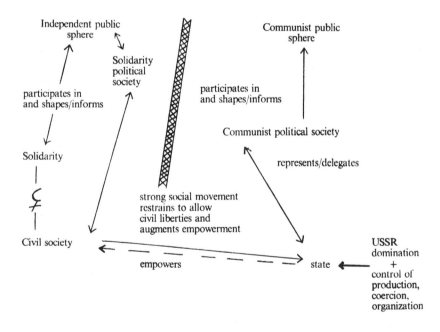

It is important to note, however, that in this version of injustice, inequality has no place. Democracy is the only problem. The only kind of inequality that was represented was that between civil society and the state, with civil society having no power of societal intervention and political society having little dependence on civil society. This is especially obvious in some discussions of legitimacy in Poland, where the contradictions between systemic and social legitimacy were emphasized (Rychard, 1987). By contrast, Wesołowski's (1986) more general discussion of legitimacy suggested the relationship between inequality and legitimacy to be quite problematic. As one point of departure, we might consider not only the general relationship between democracy and inequality but also the relationship of the status-seeking mentality and its associated order with the open public sphere characteristic of a legitimate democratic system.

Poland 1989–90 and Normative Foundations for Empirical Research

The theme of blocked channels of interest articulation can no longer serve as the principal argument of critical social science in Poland. Indeed, inequality might return to a central position as the normative foundation for Polish empirical research. It likely will not return, however, in the Marxist guise, as the tenets of market capitalism and liberal democracy seem to have won the support of all but the most marginalized in Polish society. We might clarify this new research agenda by returning again to the basic model of ideal democracy listed above, but this time with new issues.

Poland 1989–90 and the Democratic State

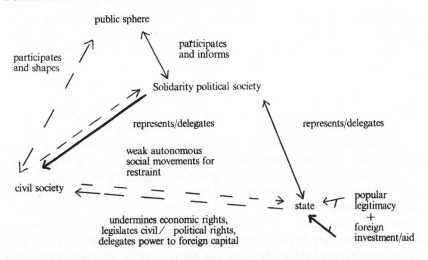

Democratization in the Poland of 1989–90 has been mainly the democratization of political society and of the state and the opening of the public sphere. Open and contested elections for the Senate and for 35 percent of the Sejm in June and the election of Mazowiecki's government in August 1989 suggest that the capacity for political society to represent civil society has increased considerably. The connection between civil society and political society is relatively well made, especially in the direction from political society to civil society.

The struggle for political society to gain control of the state continues, with some considerable progress. The attempt by the Mazowiecki government to appoint a more familiar minister of defense, for instance, suggested a move toward greater control by political society over the state and its apparatuses, even in the coercive arm. The local elections in May 1990 also represented an attempt by political society to gain control over the local state. The vigour of the public sphere impresses the outside observer with its considerably broadened scope and greater access to it by those previously read only in the underground. Indeed, it seems also that the public sphere is much better connected to both civil society and political society, whereas in the past, the underground and official public spheres were connected to civil society and political society, respectively. Although democratization seems to have moved ahead impressively, considerable barriers to democratization appear to remain, especially in the sphere of inequalities.

First, the public sphere and political society, while respectively more open and more formally representative, seem to have become overrepresented by Poland's male intelligentsia. Indeed, the bulk of civil society seems much less politically active than had been expected (Kolarska, 1990; Marody, 1990). Elections to parliament and the mobilization of various information media seem to favor the participation above all by men of the highly educated classes. This may be less problematic for overall democratization if other classes and women are well organized and their interests fairly represented. It does seem that recent debates in Parliament over interest rates for loans to peasants suggest some measure of peasant representation in the Sejm, perhaps even more than for workers. But this measure of representation of other classes and women in a public sphere and political society overwhelmingly dominated by the male intelligentsia deserves empirical research. Here, for instance, beyond the obviously important questions of actual participation by those of different backgrounds, one might analyze the discourse in the Polish media and in the parliament and government itself to see how it frames the matter of various class and gender interests and of inequality itself.

Second, to the degree that a state must depend for resources on sectors that are not from within its constituency, democratization will be frustrated. This is virtually definitional, as the state will be forced to act on behalf of actors who are not within the civil society the state is supposed to represent. This contradiction was most apparent before 1989, when the Polish state was obliged to the Soviet Union's implicit threat of invasion to justify Communist party rule. But this contradiction also exists today, when the Polish state depends on foreign economic resources to complete its economic reform program as much as, if not more than, it depends on domestic popular legitimacy. This means, therefore, that foreign economic dependence and the inequality between domestic civil society and foreign capital will limit the chances of democracy. But this, too, needs empirical research. One might, for instance, consider how the very uneven economic resources of foreign capital and domestic civil society structure governmental support for investment options in Polish society. We might compare investment projects on two scales: their likely contribution to Poland's overall long-term development, and their immediate return to Poland's foreign investors, and compare those projects to similar packages of foreign investment in other countries.

Third, by virtue of this inequality and potential structural contradiction between foreign interests and civil society's perceptions, the state may seek to manipulate civil society rather than empower it. Indeed, it does seem that the kinds of economic reforms the state is obliged to undertake are acting to undermine the social and economic rights the communist state provided. The foremost example of this problem is represented by the problem of strikes. The government argued in its press conference on May 23, 1990, that the wildcat strikes by railway workers on the coast were an illegitimate means of protest in a democratic system, given that workers have other means of pressing their interests. What is even worse, the government argued that their international reputation for business investment was endangered by this action. If the state also becomes too obliged to the Catholic church, especially the sector that wishes to use state power to enforce its particular vision of gender roles and abortion's illegality, the state may also serve to undermine reproductive rights and the capacity of women to participate in the public sphere. In effect, therefore, sociologists might investigate the state's policies toward civil society on questions of the empowerment of citizens to participate in the public sphere.

Fourth, a word of acknowledgment to those who consider democracy utopian, especially in these circumstances. The model that has been used here does not take into account the significance of a stable economy for democracy's development. One might agree with those who argue that economic recovery is a precondition for democracy's survival and that therefore some measure of dependence on foreign capital and repression of domestic rights might be necessary in the short run to assure democracy in the long run. This is an argument that is worth considering seriously, and it can be considered by asking one question: How is this repression of domestic needs in favor of foreign capital, of building better hotels when more apartments are needed, of making sure airports are in good shape before domestic mass transport is reconstructed, handled in the public sphere? Is it being treated and discussed as a consequence of the power relations of the world system, where the power and resources of foreign capital impose certain necessary options on domestic civil society, whose resources are nevertheless delegated to foreign capital with its conditional permission? Or is it being discussed as the return to a natural system of economy? If it is understood in the latter sense, democracy as a fundamental value goes out the window as power relations in the most important dimension of civil society are jettisoned in favor of some natural image of exchange. This is precisely where the question of the "status-seeking mentality" as a pre-eminent orientation to action may become problematic for the realization of democracy in a system.

Blau and Duncan argue that the status-seeking mentality contributes to democracy, especially by undermining the legacies of aristocratic cultures. Wesołowski and Mach argue that it might also help to make (post-?) communist societies more efficient as work and professional competence become something centrally valued. But the inculcation of this mentality into the postcommunist system is not likely to contribute to the realization of democratically founded legitimacy.

The status-seeking mentality removes the actor from the public sphere and moves him to consider only that portion of civil society most closely related to his work and his consumption. What is more, that mentality also moves the actor to an overwhelmingly individual focus, rather than generating the civic consciousness Dahl (1982) finds so essential to the actual functioning of democracy. Instead, what the status-seeking mentality seems to do is to provide the system with an implicit legitimation of some kind of elite domination, except this time of technocracy and foreign capital rather than of technocracy and the Communist party. Whether this leads to an "efficient" system this time may be up for question. It does, however, seem unlikely that it would lead to democracy.

Nevertheless, this, too, is a question for research. Thus, not only might we investigate the differentials among classes or strata in public participation, but we could also tie this to the status-attainment tradition. We might investigate not only the conditions of upward mobility but also how a focus on this mobility influences public participation and the civic consciousness essential for democratic governance. Finally, we might also examine the conditions within classes and strata that increase the capability of individuals to become democratic citizens rather than consider only those conditions that enable individuals to leave their class or stratum.

Inequality research could prove not only interesting but extremely important to constructing democracy in contemporary Poland. But that function might be more likely realized to the extent that a normative foundation of ideal democracy directs its questions. For in that condition, we will ask not only about feelings of deprivation, forms of social self-identification, and conditions of economic freedom, all matters that are traditional questions of inequality research. We will also ask questions that go beyond civil society to political society and beyond the nation-state to the world system. It is in these connections between civil and political society, as well as between national and international systems, that democracy's chances will be discovered.

Conclusions

This essay has been about the relationship between justice and inequality, but not as if these were two objects to be investigated in Polish society. Instead, the "justice" discussed is mainly the normative foundation used by sociological researchers to structure their interpretations and generate their research questions. Inequality, on the other hand, is a broad field of substantive inquiry that has ranged from using class structure as the basic definition of society's makeup to examine how social changes are experienced in different places, to examining how open economic chances are in different societies. In particular, we have asked what normative foundations have underlaid Polish empirical research into inequality.

Although by no means an exhaustive review, this essay has suggested that the explicit link between research on inequality and normative foundations has been reduced with status-attainment research, even while an implicit valuation of economic freedom remains. This research scheme, although facilitating autonomous research with a comparative emphasis, is relatively disengaged from questions of justice beyond this single notion of economic freedom. Indeed, it limits its inquiry almost entirely to the question of inequality within the domestic civil society. The social transformations of 1989, along with the intellectual transformation occasioned by Habermas's theory of communicative action, have introduced a new potential normative foundation that might direct us to a different approach to inequality's study.

If democracy is the normative foundation for inquiry into inequality, we are above all interested not only in who gets what and why or what conditions increase the openness of mobility regimes but also in how unequal distributions of resources affect the capacities of civil societies to govern themselves. This means, therefore, that we must consider the interaction between several spheres and not only limit ourselves to the study of material inequalities within domestic civil society.

First, inequality might be studied in terms of civil society's participation in the public sphere and in political society. Who speaks? Who listens? How is the public sphere constructed? To what degree is it manipulative of civil society, or to what degree is it respondent to civil society's pulse? Who is active in political society, and who is elected? What conditions enable the broadest measure of participation in governance? These, of course, are not novel questions. They are studied in the "style of life" research tradition in Polish sociology. They are studied in political analysis. But these are also important questions of "inequality," especially if democracy is our normative foundation. This might be referred to as the problematic of "inequality between civil and political society."

Second, what is the relationship between civil society and the state? What are the conditions that lead civil society to influence the state directly through social movements, and how does the state undermine or enable these movements? Here, the problematic is one of inequality between civil society and the state, assuming that political society can never represent the interests of civil society perfectly. One should ask, then, what the comparative resources of state and civil society are.

Third, to what extent is political society able to direct the state? Even when there are responsive relations between civil and political society, this by no means guarantees state responsiveness. Actors within the state, usually identified as bureaucrats, have their own resources, which enable them to resist and/or undermine other actors, especially representatives of political society. This was even true in Communist party-led society, as Communist party elites could not direct those who were their vassals given the strategies of passivity those vassals employed (Kennedy and Białecki, 1989).

Fourth, to what extent are the resources that empower the state coterminous with the constituency to which it is formally responsible? In Poland today, as in the past, significant resources for governmental action come from without Poland's borders: from Moscow before, and from foreign capital today. Here, we cannot only attempt to measure the disparity but must also consider the consequences in terms of social action of the relevant disparities. We might even ask, if socialism is not possible in a given country, whether democracy might not be equally impossible.

This essay has only suggested what might be the important questions that should be asked about inequality. By no means should the impression be conveyed that we know what should be asked, for that is more a matter for Poles to decide. But it is hoped that by asking these questions we might learn about some of the work we do not know and perhaps suggest new directions for the work we all have not yet considered.

References

Bauman, Z. 1972. "Officialdom and Class: Bases of Inequality in Socialist Society." In Frank Parkin, ed., *The Social Analysis of Class Structure*. London: Tavistock.

Bendix, R. 1962. *Max Weber: An Intellectual Portrait*. Garden City: Anchor Books.

Beskid, L. ed. 1987. *Warunki i sposób życia społeczeństwa polskiego w sytuacji regresu*. Warszawa: IFiS PAN.

Blau, P. M. 1970. "Critical Remarks on Weber's Theory of Authority." In Dennis Wrong, ed., *Max Weber*. Englewood Cliffs: Prentice Hall.

Blau, P. M., and Otis Dudley Duncan. 1967. *The American Occupational Structure*. New York: Free Press.

Calhoun, C. 1989. "Classical Social Theory and the French Revolution of 1848," *Sociological Theory* 7: 2: 210–25

Cichomski, B. 1989. "Distributive Justice and the Idea of Social Order." Paper presented at the 30th Annual Convention of the International Studies Association.

Connor, W. 1979. *Socialism, Politics, Equality*. New York: Columbia University Press.

Dahl, R. A. 1982. *Dilemmas of Pluralist Democracy*. New Haven: Yale University Press.

Held, D. 1987. *Models of Democracy*. Stanford: Stanford University Press.

Kennedy, M. D. 1991. *Professionals, Power and Solidarity in Poland: A Critical Sociology of Soviet-Type Society*. Cambridge: Cambridge University Press.

Kennedy, M. D., and I. Białecki. 1989. "Power and the Logic of Distribution in Poland." *Eastern European Politics and Societies* 3: 2: 300–328.

Knottnerus, J. D. 1987. "Status Attainment Research and Its Image of Society." *American Sociological Review* 52: 113–21.

Kolarska, L. 1990. "The Changing Face of Civil Society in Eastern Europe." Paper presented at the Polish-American Conference on Socialism and Change: Polish Perspectives.

Koralewicz, J. 1987. "Changes in Polish Social Consciousness during the 1970's and 1980's: Opportunism and Identity. " In J. Koralewicz, I. Białecki, and M. Watson, eds., *Crisis and Transition: Polish Society in the 1980's*. Oxford: Berg.

Koralewicz, J., and B. W. Mach. 1987. "Teoretyczny kontekst projektu badawczego." In E. Wnuk-Lipiński ed., *Nierówności i upośledzenia w świadomości społecznej*. Warszawa: IFiS PAN.

Koralewicz, J., and E. Wnuk-Lipiński. 1987. "Życie rodzinne, towarzyskie i publiczne. Wartości i deprywacje." In E. Wnuk-Lipiński, ed., *Nierówności i upośledzenia w świadomości społecznej*. Warszawa: IFiS PAN.

Mach, B. W. 1987. "Zróżnicowanie autoidentyfikacji społecznych," In E. Wnuk-Lipiński, ed.; *Nierówności i upośledzenia w świadomści społecznej*. Warszawa: IFiS PAN.

————. 1989. *Funkcje i działanie i systemowa koncepcja ruchliwości społecznej*. Warszawa: Państwowe Wydawnictwo Naukowe.

Marody, M. 1990. "Values and Politics." Paper presented at the Polish-American Conference on Socialism and Change: Polish Perspectives.

Mokrzycki, E. 1990. "Varieties of Socialist Utopia." Paper presented at the Polish-American Conference on Socialism and Change: Polish Perspectives.

Pohoski, M. and B. Mach. 1988. "Trends in Social Mobility in Poland: 1972–1982." *Polish Sociological Bulletin* 83: 3: 19–38.

Rychard, A. 1987. "The Legitimation and the Stability of the Social Order in Poland." In J. Koralewicz, I. Bialecki, and M. Watson, eds. *Crisis and Transition: Polish Society in the 1980's*. Oxford: Berg.

Słomczyński, K. M. 1986. "The Attainment of Occupational Status: A Model with Multiple Indicator Constructs." In K. M. Słomczyński and T. Krauze, eds., *Social Stratification in Poland*. Armonk: M. E. Sharpe.

Słomczyński, K. M. and G. Kacprowicz. 1986. "The Subjective Evaluation of Social Status." In K. M. Słomczyński and T. Krauze, eds., *Social Stratification in Poland*. Armonk: M. E. Sharpe.

Tarkowski, J. 1981. "Poland: Patrons and Clients in a Planned Economy." In S.N. Eisenstadt and R. Lemarchand, eds., *Political Clientalism, Patronage and Development*. Beverly Hills: Sage Press.

Wesołowski, W. 1966/1979. G. Kolankiewicz, tr. *Classes, Strata and Power*. London: Routledge and Kegan Paul.

————. 1986. "Weber's Concept of Legitimacy: Limitations and Continuations." Unpublished manuscript. Warszawa: IFiS PAN.

————. 1990. "Transition from Authoritarianism to Democracy: Poland's Case." Paper presented at the Polish-American Conference on Socialism and Change: Polish Perspectives.

Wesołowski, W., and B. W. Mach. 1986. "Unfulfilled Systemic Functions of Social Mobility: Part I, A Theoretical Scheme and Part II, The Polish Case." *International Sociology* 1: 1: 19–35 and 1: 2: 173–87.

Wesołowski, W. and K. M. Słomczyński. 1977. *Investigations on Class Structure and Social Stratification in Poland. 1945–1975*. Warszawa: IFiS PAN.

Wnuk-Lipiński, E., ed., 1987. *Nierówności i upośledzenia w świadomości społecznej.* Warszawa: IFiS PAN.

Zaborowski, W. 1986. "Dichotomous Class Images and Worker Radicalism." In K. M. Słomczyński and T. Krauze, eds., *Social Stratification in Poland*. Armonk: M. E. Sharpe.

Index